China and the World

FOURTH EDITION

China and the World

Chinese Foreign Policy Faces the New Millennium

EDITED BY

Samuel S. Kim

COLUMBIA UNIVERSITY

Westview Press
A Member of Perseus Books, L.L.C.

Dedicated to
Allen S. Whiting:
Chinese foreign policy studies pioneer
great teacher and adviser
warm and loyal friend

Copyright © 1998 by Westview Press, A Member of Perseus Books, L. L. C.

Published in 1998 in the United States of America by Westview Press, 5500 Central Avenue, Boulder, Colorado 80301-2877, and in the United Kingdom by Westview Press, 12 Hid's Copse Road, Cumnor Hill, Oxford OX2 9JJ

Library of Congress Cataloging-in-Publication Data
China and the world : Chinese foreign policy faces the new millennium
    /edited by Samuel S. Kim.—4th ed.
        p.   cm.
    Includes bibliographical references and index.
    ISBN 0-8133-3414-4 (pbk.)
    1. China—Foreign relations—1976–   I. Kim, Samuel S., 1935–   .
DS779.27.C4873   1998
327.51—dc21   98-12270
                                                                                    CIP

The paper used in this publication meets the requirements of the American National Standard for Permanence of Paper for Printed Library Materials Z39.48-1984.

10   9   8   7   6   5   4   3   2   1

Contents

List of Illustrations   vii
List of Acronyms   viii
Preface to the Fourth Edition   xi

Part One
Theory and Practice

1 Chinese Foreign Policy in Theory and Practice,
   Samuel S. Kim   3

2 Structure and Process in the Making of
   Chinese Foreign Policy, *David Bachman*   34

3 International Structures and Chinese Foreign Policy,
   Alastair Iain Johnston   55

Part Two
Interactions

4 Sino-American Relations: Practicing Damage Control,
   Steven I. Levine   91

5 Sino-Russian Relations, *John W. Garver*   114

6 Japan and Europe in Chinese Foreign Relations,
   Donald W. Klein   133

7 China and the Third World: Patterns of Engagement
   and Indifference, *Peter Van Ness*   151

Part Three
Policies and Issues

8 Force and Diplomacy: China Prepares for
   the Twenty-First Century, *Paul H. B. Godwin*   171

9 [In][ter] dependence in China's Post–Cold War
   Foreign Relations, *Thomas W. Robinson*   193

10 Human Rights in Chinese Foreign Relations,
    James D. Seymour   217

11 China and the Multilateral Economic Institutions,
    William R. Feeney   239

12 China's Environmental Diplomacy,
    Elizabeth C. Economy   264

Part Four
Prospects

13 Chinese Foreign Policy: Retrospect and Prospect,
    Allen S. Whiting   287

Bibliography   309
About the Editor and Contributors   339
Index   343

Illustrations

Maps

China and its neighbors   xiv

Figures

3.1   U.S., Russian, and Chinese shares of
world military expenditures   61

3.2   PRC actions directed at the United States:
Cooperative and conflictual percentages   62

5.1   Adjustments in Russo-Chinese Far Eastern land
border under the 1991 treaty   124

Tables

5.1   Composition of Sino-Russian trade, 1996   128

6.1   China's trade with the EEC/EU, 1990–1996   136
6.2   China's trade with Japan, 1990–1996   139

9.1   China's foreign trade dependence, 1978–1996   205
9.2   Trade dependence of China and
selected countries, 1996   206
9.3   Direction of China's foreign trade, 1978–1996   207

11.1   UNDP country program in China, 1979–2000   241
11.2   IMF assistance to China and
key economic indicators, 1981–1996   246
11.3   World Bank annual and cumulative lending
to China, mid-1980 to mid-1996   249
11.4   Summary of total cumulative IBRD loans and
IDA credits to ten largest borrowers, as of mid-1996   250
11.5   IFC commitments to China, mid-1986 to mid-1996   252
11.6   MIGA guarantee contracts with China, mid-1992–1996   254
11.7   ADB annual and cumulative lending to China, 1986–1996   256

Acronyms

ACD	arms control and disarmament
ACDA	Arms Control and Disarmament Agency
ADB	Asian Development Bank
ADF	Asian Development Fund
APEC	Asia-Pacific Economic Cooperation
ARF	ASEAN [Association of Southeast Asian Nations] Regional Forum
ASDF	Air Self-Defense Forces
AShM	antiship missiles
ASW	antisubmarine warfare
AWACS	airborne warning and command system
BIS	Bank for International Settlements
BWC	Biological Weapons Convention
CATIC	China Agribusiness Development Trust and Investment Corporation
CBM	confidence-building measure
CBNT	Comprehensive Ban on Nuclear Testing
CCF	Country Cooperation Framework
CCP	Chinese Communist Party
CD	Conference on Disarmament
CFC	chlorofluorocarbon
CIS	Commonwealth of Independent States
CISS	China Institute for International Strategic Studies
CMC	Central Military Commission
COW	Correlates of War
CPs	country programs
CTBT	Comprehensive Test Ban Treaty
CWC	Chemical Weapons Convention
CWG	China Working Group
DDG	guided-missile destroyers
DMCs	developing member countries
EAEC	East Asian Economic Caucus
EDI	Economic Development Institute
EEC/EU	European Economic Community/European Union
EEZ	Exclusive Economic Zone

EPBs	environmental protection bureaus
FALSG	Foreign Affairs Leading Small Group
FDI	foreign direct investments
FFG	guided-missile frigate
FIAS	Foreign Investment Advisory Service
FPDA	Five-Power Defense Agreement
G-7	Group of Seven
GATT	General Agreement on Tariffs and Trade
GDP	gross domestic product
GNP	gross national product
HDI	human development index
IBRD	International Bank for Reconstruction and Development, World Bank
ICBM	intercontinental ballistic missiles
ICCPR	International Covenant on Civil and Political Rights
ICESCR	International Covenant on Economic, Social and Cultural Rights
ICPs	inter-country programs
IDA	International Development Association
IDF	Indigenous Defense Fighter
IFC	International Finance Corporation
IGOs	intergovernmental organizations
IISS	International Institute for Strategic Studies
IMF	International Monetary Fund
IOs	international organizations
IR	international relations
IRBM	intermediate-range missiles
JSF	Japan Special Fund
KEDS/ PANDA	Kansas Events Data System/Protocol for the Assessment of Nonviolent Direct Action
LDCs	less-developed countries
LRF	Laogai Research Foundation
ME	military expenditures
MEIs	multilateral economic institutions
MFN	most-favored-nation
MIGA	Multilateral Investment Guarantee Agency
MNCs	multinational corporations
MOFA	Ministry of Foreign Affairs
MSDF	Maritime Self-Defense Forces
MTCR	Missile Technology Control Regime
NAM	Non-Aligned Movement
NATO	North Atlantic Treaty Organization
NDPO	National Defense Program Outline

NEPA	National Environmental Protection Agency
NGOs	nongovernmental organizations
NIEO	New International Economic Order
NMD	national defense missile
NPT	Non-Proliferation Treaty
ODA	official development assistance
PLA	People's Liberation Army
PLAAF	People's Liberation Army Air Force
PLAN	PLA Navy
PPP	purchasing power parity
PRC	People's Republic of China
RFE	Russian Far East
RMA	Revolution in Military Affairs
RMB	renminbi
SAM	surface-to-air missiles
SDF	Self-Defense Forces
SLOC	Sea Lanes of Communication
SOCBs	state-owned commercial banks
SOEs	state-owned enterprises
SPC	State Planning Commission
SSBN	nuclear-powered ballistic missile submarine
SSK	kilo-class diesel-electric submarines
SSN	nuclear-powered submarines
SSTC	State Science and Technology Commission
TATF	Technical Assistance Trust Funds Program
TMD	theater missile defense
TNW	theater nuclear weapons
TRA	Taiwan Relations Act
TVEs	town and village enterprises
TWG	Taiwan Working Group
UNCED	United Nations Conference on Environment and Development
UNCHE	United Nations Conference on the Human Environment
UNCLOS	United Nations Convention on the Law of the Sea
UNDP	United Nations Development Program
UK	United Kingdom
USSR	Union of Soviet Socialist Republics
WBG	World Bank Group
WTO	World Trade Organization

Preface to
the Fourth Edition

This collaborative volume presents a major reappraisal of the changing relationship between China and the world in the post–Cold War era. As we approach the new millennium, nothing seems to matter more than an ascendant China and its role or roles in the shaping of the future of the Asia-Pacific and beyond. Indeed, not since the debate in the mid-1960s over containment-with-isolation versus containment-without-isolation has the "rise of China" issue been so controversial as in recent years. For better or worse, this volume has been prepared against the noisy backdrop of the "rise of China" debate in the Asia-Pacific region in general and the United States in particular.

The book poses and addresses several main—and enduring—questions about the major sources, patterns, and consequences of Chinese foreign policy behavior. How constant or changeable is Chinese foreign policy over a period of time, especially in the transition from the Cold War to the post–Cold War era and more recently from the Deng era to the post-Deng era? How wide is the gap between ideals and reality, between policy pronouncements (principles) and policy performance (behavior), and between intent and outcome in Chinese foreign policy? What is the relative weight of domestic (societal) and external (systemic) factors in constraining policy options, and what domestic and international consequences do they entail? How do global systemic structures—economic, military, normative, and behavioral—impact and condition China's national identity and role conception? How are the global structures themselves affected by the rise of China in the post–Cold War world? These questions, which examine in particular the nature, extent, and reciprocal impacts of growing Sino-global linkages and interactions, provide the focus and theme that the present volume seeks to address, with emphasis on the most recent post–Cold War years.

In this fourth edition, the main issues and organizational outlines of the previous editions have been largely retained and expanded. In subjecting this edition to a thorough revision and adding a chapter on China's environmental diplomacy, the contributors and I have given primacy to making it reflect our most recent thinking on China's multidimensional foreign relations in the post–Cold War era. Without prematurely privileging any particular theory or methodology, each contributor has been asked to address some of the essential and enduring questions mentioned above and to do so within the framework of a specific assigned topic. Adopting a variety of theoretical and analytical frames of reference and combining a broad theoretical framework (Part 1) with interaction-specific and issue-specific case studies (Parts 2 and 3), the contributors assess the relative weight of domestic and external factors and the changing domestic and international contexts reflecting and affecting Beijing's policy goals and behaviors in different domains, toward different reference groups, and across time. In doing so, they seek to identify the changes and continuities that have characterized Chinese foreign relations over the years and the reasons why the Chinese behave as they do in the conduct of their international relations.

More than the previous editions, the fourth edition has been subject to substantial rewriting and restructuring to take into account the issues raised by China's increasingly complex and multifarious engagement with the post–Cold War international system. Reference to "China" or to "China's" foreign policy is not meant to connote a single-minded set of decisionmakers in Beijing, much less a single, coherent, and unified China. Indeed, there is now broad scholarly consensus that the Chinese party-state is no longer the almighty Leviathan of yore. The term *China* is used throughout the volume merely for analytical and semantic convenience.

This volume is the continuation, not the culmination, of a collaborative effort that was started two decades ago in the hope of remedying the dialogue of the deaf between China specialists and world politics analysts. From the inception of that effort, it was our intention to combine looking backward with going forward—and to link theory with practice. This book represents a joint venture into the seemingly forbidden territory of interdisciplinary inquiry in the study of Chinese foreign policy. In spite of diverse intellectual backgrounds, methodological inclinations, and theoretical orientations, the contributors are united in the conviction that we can and must study Chinese foreign policy as if international relations really mattered—or, conversely, that we must study international relations as if China really mattered. This volume, the offspring of an invisible college of bridge-builders, has been the work of many. For various reasons, a number of scholars in the field could not contribute to the previous editions, and several contributors to the third edition could not be persuaded to shift gears in the midst of other projects to do the necessary revisions for this volume. I thank Thomas Bernstein, June T. Dreyer, Melvin Gurtov, Harry Harding, James C. Hsiung, Andrew Nathan,

Jonathan Pollack, Robert Sutter—and Davis Bobrow, Steven Chan, Michael Ng-Quinn, Susan Shirk, Bruce Cumings, Chi Su, Denis Fred Simon, Lowell Dittmer, Edward Friedman (previous-edition contributors regrettably absent here)—for their contributions in the various stages of the project. At the same time, four outstanding scholars in the field— Alastair Iain Johnston, John W. Garver, Peter Van Ness, and Elizabeth Economy—have come aboard as new contributors. Laura Parsons of Westview Press has been an invaluable collaborator and invisible contributor to the volume. Special thanks are also due to Carol Jones, Marian Safran, and Elizabeth Lawrence for their efficient steering of the manuscript through the various stages of the production process. The usual disclaimer holds: The editor and contributors alone are responsible for the views and interpretations—and the errors that may persist—in the book.

Throughout the preparation of the first, second, third, and fourth editions, I have received invaluable support from Allen S. Whiting, who, along with contributing the final chapter, has always offered wise counsel. Now that he has attained a stature as a pioneer of the field of Chinese foreign policy studies and reached an age that made recognition of his achievements by friends and colleagues appropriate, the book is dedicated to Professor Whiting with gratitude, respect, admiration, and friendship.

Samuel S. Kim
New York, New York

China and Its Neighbors

PART ONE

Theory and Practice

1

Chinese Foreign Policy
in Theory and Practice

SAMUEL S. KIM

An Ascendant China in a Post–Cold War World

Only several years away from the new millennium, nothing seems to matter more than an ascendant China and its role in the shaping of the future of the Asia-Pacific and beyond. Not since the mid-1960s debate over containment-with-isolation versus containment-without-isolation has the "rise of China" issue been so all-penetrating, all-permeating, all-controversial as in recent years, especially since March 1996, when President Clinton responded to Beijing's missile-firing diplomacy against Taiwan by sending, not one, but two, aircraft carrier battle groups. Such a military confrontation seemed to be just the thing to concentrate the mind or inflame the debate, especially since it was a face-off between two nuclear-weapons states. For good or otherwise, Beijing managed to capture global prime time, with the "rise of China" chorus in the global marketplace turning into the "rise of the China threat" debate in the Asia-Pacific region in general and the United States in particular.

What, then, accounts for the puzzle of an ascendant China and its post–Cold War international démarche in the seemingly benign external security environment? Part of the problem relates to the wrenching national identity difficulties that practically all major powers encounter in trying to adjust to a world in which conflict no longer takes place along an East-West divide. In the absence of the East-West conflict, the relations between the world's lone superpower, with its rooted exceptionalism (America's Manifest Destiny), and the world's most populous country and fastest-growing economy, with its rooted exemptionalism (the Middle Kingdom complex), have become increasingly mired in and symptomatic of highly charged domestic politics in Washington and Beijing. Indeed, the United States has emerged as China's biggest foreign

3

policy challenge, as Levine and Godwin argue in Chapters 4 and 8 respectively, because, on the one hand, the United States, as the only true global power in the post–Cold War world, can do more than any other country to help or hinder China's march to great powerdom. On the other hand, China has emerged as the biggest U.S. foreign policy challenge because by dint of what China *is* and what it *does*, it is inescapably part of both the world-order problem and the world-order solution.

Part of the answer—or part of the problem—has also to do with the profound uncertainties about China's emerging role in world affairs—its future capabilities and intentions and its future foreign policy behavior in the transition from Cold War to post–Cold War regional and global order. The dialectical style of Chinese international conduct and the tendency to try to be all things to all states on all global issues have seemed designed to challenge scholars and policymakers concerned about the shape of things to come in post–Cold War international life. The progressive removal of the Soviet threat from China's security perimeter, extending from Southeast Asia, through South Asia and Central Asia, to Northeast Asia, combined with the growing integration with many international institutions, brought perhaps the most benign external security environment, the deepest peace, and the greatest interdependence that China ever enjoyed in its checkered international life. And yet in recent years Beijing has sometimes acted in a highly provocative manner, as if it were faced with a threat greater than before. Thus China remains the major source of uncertainty in the Asia-Pacific, and the geopolitical and geoeconomic realities of the emerging regional and global order have become substantially muddled, amenable to multiple interpretations and contending prognostications and policy prescriptions.[1]

Indeed, there is an uneasy and shifting balance of competing forces and identities—both conflictive and cooperative—in China's complex, variegated, and omnidirectional foreign policy. On the one hand, Beijing has proceeded with all deliberate speed and determination to beef up its military power projection capabilities, especially air and blue-water naval power, in sync with annual double-digit percentage increases in military spending, while the capabilities and the spending of all other permanent members of the United Nations Security Council have been decreasing. All the same, Beijing has undertaken in the 1990s a sustained technological modernization of the People's Liberation Army (PLA), and Russia has emerged as China's major partner in that military modernization effort. As Garver argues in Chapter 5, this effort constitutes "an extremely important, indeed a truly strategic dimension" of the Sino-Russian partnership, at the same time as Beijing has been somewhat reckless in exporting nuclear technology and materials to countries that deny some of their nuclear facilities to international inspection. Beijing's defense policy has been reoriented from fighting a people's war under modern conditions (against the Soviet Union) to a high-tech strategy of achieving a quick, decisive military victory in a matter of days. This shift to fighting and winning local wars under post–Cold War conditions was also aimed at developing a mobile, rapid-reaction, high-tech military force that is able to fight small "low intensity" border or near-abroad conflicts. In keeping with the shift in general military doctrine, China has, from the late 1980s on, moved from a strategic posture of "minimal deterrence" (requiring a relatively small number of nuclear weapons with no great demands as to accuracy to deter nuclear blackmail) to a strategy of "limited deterrence," requiring a far larger number of increasingly accurate counterforce and countervalue nuclear weapons than China currently deploys. This shift requires greater willingness to consider use of nuclear weapons as part of fighting a war and upgrading, diversifying, and increasing the capabilities and numbers of China's nuclear weapons and delivery systems.[7]

Such developments would not be so alarming, and China would not be seen as Asia's least satisfied revisionist power, according to the realist received wisdom, if the country did not harbor an acute historical grievance and if it did not have so many territorial disputes and irredentist claims on so many of its neighbors, if it did not have a deeply rooted *para bellum* strategic culture, if it did not have a repressive authoritarian regime defying the democratic peace theory, and if it did not embrace hypernationalism as a substitution ideology. Both international history and neorealist structural theory suggest that accommodating an up-and-coming power such as Wilhelmine Germany or post-Meiji Japan has proved to be disruptive. In short, the conflation of China's domestic factors—historical, cultural, political, doctrinal, and behavioral—has led to the "China threat theory" (*Zhongguo weixian lun*).

On the other hand, China's integration into a global network of mutually interactive and beneficial multilateral regimes has continued apace. That integration has had some nontrivial positive or potentially positive spillover effects, such as the emergence of security, economic, human rights, and environmental policy (epistemic) communities within China; the flowering of diverse, if not liberalizing, international and global studies scholarship; and a flurry of white papers on arms control and disarmament, human rights, and environmental protection. Even in the most sensitive domain of arms control and disarmament, China has taken a series of cooperative security steps away from unilateral free-ride or defection strategy in signing on to the Non-Proliferation Treaty (NPT), the Comprehensive Test Ban Treaty (CTBT), the Chemical Weapons Convention (CWC), and the Biological Weapons Convention (BWC). Although not a member, China has also pledged to abide by the norms of the Missile Technology Control Regime (MTCR). Most tellingly, considerable progress has been made in the past three years in Sino-ARF (ASEAN [Association of Southeast Asian Nations] Regional Forum) interaction. As China becomes increasingly engaged with and entrapped by dozens of regional and global multilateral institutions, it becomes more and more difficult for Beijing to free ride, defy, or defect without incurring material and normative costs.

For all the habit-driven trumpery about the Deng Xiaoping theory of building socialism with Chinese characteristics (read: realist theory of building a rich country and a strong army [*fu guo, qiang bing*]), Beijing has been subject to all the external pressures and dynamics of globalization that characterize an increasingly interdependent and interactive world. In a revealing manner, Jiang Zemin in his political report to the Fifteenth Chinese Communist Party (CCP) Congress on September 12, 1997, admitted just as much when he said there is no longer an escape from "the globalization *(quanqiuhua)* of economy, science, and technology" and that there is no choice but to reform, restructure and open up state-owned enterprises (SOEs) to the "survival-of-the-fittest" competition if China is not to forfeit its "global citizenship."[3]

Despite the "rise of China" debate, the question of what really makes a great power in an era of globalization is far from settled. Consider China's actual status as a great power based on the most readily measurable economic numbers. Richard Bernstein and Ross Munro, in *The Coming Conflict with China*, rest their central argument on the assumption that "within a few years, China will be the largest economy in the world, and it is on the way to becoming a formidable military power as well."[4] To be sure, the aggregate economic numbers seem impressive enough. According to the purchasing power parity (PPP) estimates of the World Bank (which are not unproblematic), China, with a 1994 gross domestic product (GDP) just under $3 trillion, has become the second-largest economy in the world, after the United States. It is simultaneously the world's largest recipient of multilateral aid from the World Bank and the Asian Development Bank (ADB) and of bilateral aid from Japan![5] And in 1996 China was the second-largest recipient (after the United States) of foreign direct investment—about $42 billion—accounting for a third of all foreign-investment flow to the developing countries. In mid-1997 its foreign-exchange reserves were $122.8 billion, more than Germany ($78.0 billion). If we accept the projections of a 1995 Rand Corporation study, China's PPP-based GDP will reach $11.3 trillion by the year 2010 (in 1994 PPP dollars) compared to $10.7 trillion for the United States, $4.5 trillion for Japan, $3.7 trillion for India, and $2 trillion for a unified Korea.[6] If we accept the projections of a 1997 World Bank study, China's annual GDP percentage growth for the period 1995–2020 will be in the range of

4.2–6.4 percent. Under a scenario in which savings rate declines from around 40 percent to a still robust 35 percent over the next ten years, GDP growth will be 8.4 percent a year between 1996 and 2000 and will average 6.6 percent over the twenty-five years until 2020, when China's per capita income will approach that of Portugal today but will still be less than half that of the United States.[7] And yet, according to China's plan for long-term targets through the year 2010, the Chinese GDP is projected to reach about 17,000 billion yuan, or about $2 trillion (in 1995 exchange rates), amounting to half of Japan's GDP or one-third of that of the United States.[8]

What is often overlooked in the heated debate is that this remarkable economic growth has been made possible by China's growing engagement with and dependence on the capitalist world economic system. China's expanded involvement in the global political economy translates more easily into greater vulnerability and sensitivity than into greater power. China's external debt stands at about $120 billion and is still growing. Although China has had the fastest-growing economy in the world—its total output quadrupled between 1978 and 1995—its external trade dependence, defined as the sum of imports and exports as a percentage of gross national product (GNP), rose dramatically during the same period, from less than 10 percent to more than 56 percent. Indeed, because of localizing pressures from below and new risks and challenges (e.g., rising unemployment, expanding floating population, growing income inequality, mounting environmental pressures, incomplete market reforms, trade frictions), China will not so easily become the economic superpower that many have predicted. Recent data and estimates show that a larger part of China's burgeoning population is being left behind than was previously estimated, even as the overall economy continues to register impressive growth. More than one-quarter of all Chinese, about 350 million people—rather than the 80 million, or 7 percent of population previously estimated—live below the poverty line, subsisting on less than $1 a day, the international poverty standard.[9] If we factor in mounting environmental pressures and environmental deficit financing (the economic costs of China's air and water pollution alone have been estimated at 3–8 percent of GDP a year, not to mention 289,000 deaths a year that could have been avoided if air pollution alone had been reduced to comply with Chinese government standards[10]), China's impressive growth of 12.15 percent per annum in 1992–1996 drops down to almost zero growth. During the late 1980s, as Economy shows in Chapter 12, China ranked third in total contribution to global climate change and in the mid-1990s ranked second, after the United States; conservative estimates indicate that China will have surpassed the United States as the chief contributor of CO_2 by the year 2020. All the euphoria and grandiose predictions that China would surpass the United States as the largest economy in the world "within a few years" or by the beginning of the next century are now due for a major reassessment.

Despite the claim that the rise of China as a great power has occurred and that the reality of China's great-power status is as certain as anything can be in the transition from a bipolar to a multipolar world, China's actual status as a great power is still indeterminate, if not foreclosed. Most political realist theorists and practitioners readily agree that the concept of power is at the heart of any inquiry, but they seem to agree upon little else and use "power" to mean different things. Although structural realists explain world politics in terms of power or embedded power relations among "great powers," there is no widely accepted formulation of the defining and differentiating characteristics of a great power. This is hardly surprising, as the concept of a great power has always contained interrelated levels of analysis in multiple domains—what such great-power label denotes, where power lies, for what purpose it is wielded, how it can be measured, what domestic and external forces are changing the sources of power and the international hierarchy. In a rapidly changing international environment the very notion of "great power" or "superpower" is subject to continuing redefinition and reassessment. The Soviet Union, a multinational empire that had in the late 1970s arrived at "strategic parity" and appeared on the verge of claiming primacy in the superpower rivalry, suddenly disintegrated. The collapse of the Soviet Union without a fight also shattered the Cold War illusion of a consensus on what constitutes a "superpower," made evident by the rise and fall of the "Japan-As-Number-One" chorus, the sudden "Third Worldization" of the former Soviet Union (South Korea's GNP now surpasses Russia's), and on the part of the United States, a heroic but increasingly ineffective claim of global leadership without bearing the costs and the responsibilities.

In an era of globalization, "power" needs to be conceptualized and operationalized in synthetic terms. The traditional military and strategic concept of power pays too much attention to a state's aggregate material power and too little to the more dynamic and interactive notions of power in various issue-specific domains. Embedded in an interactive and interdependent world are multiple games on multiple chessboards (issue areas) requiring different kinds of power.[11] That is, China cannot be equally "powerful" in all issue areas ("structural power") and in all relationships ("relational power"). Power base and effective control over international outcomes are not the same. Susan Strange, for example, defines "powerful states" as commanding "structural power" not just in a single global structure but in four primary global structures: security, production, finance, and knowledge.[12]

Synthesizing competing realist, liberal interdependence, and postrealist conceptions of power (hard power and soft power), the definition of a great power is as follows: a state that is among the top five in the primary global structures—economic, military, knowledge, and normative—and that, because of massive resource and skill differentials and relative economic self-sufficiency, enjoys relatively low sensitivity, vulnerability, and security interdependence. A great power is a strong state that has the ability to mobilize and translate the country's human and material resources in the service of its worldview and policy objectives. There is also the normative/behavioral requirement of great-power status: A great power is and becomes what a great power does.

By conventional measurements of the rise and fall of great powers (in terms of shifts in the international military and economic power balances), China is a rising great power. Yet it remains an incomplete great power in a rapidly changing world where transnational nonmilitary challenges to and soft sources of power are becoming increasingly important. Thus, China's future as a complete great power remains far from settled. Ultimately, the critical question in assessing China as a great power or its role or roles in the transition from a bipolar to a multipolar world is its behavior. What matters most is not so much the growth of Chinese power but how and for what purposes a rising China will actually wield its putative or actual power in the conduct of its international relations.[13]

Identifying Key Issues

To understand fully how Beijing is responding to the multiple challenges of the post–Cold War era, we need to remember that for all its cultural uniqueness and political self-sufficiency, post-Mao China has been subject to the external pressures and dynamics that are inherent in an increasingly interdependent and interactive world. It seems obvious but somewhat trite to say that the way in which the outside world responds to China is closely keyed to the way in which China itself responds to the outside world. But to what extent and in what specific ways such interaction occurs and what the specific outcomes are is a puzzle calling for plausible hypotheses about causal relationships between these factors (independent variables) and behavior (dependent variable). These hypotheses must be tested as rigorously and verifiably as possible (as Johnston argues in Chapter 3).

As a point of departure, we would do well to reject a dichotomy between empirical analysis and theoretical analysis or theory and science. In the field of Soviet foreign policy studies, for example, many resisted the use of the scientific method because they mistook "the trappings of the physical sciences for the essence of science itself," not realizing that "science is not only quantifiable experimentation in a laboratory, but rather a method of inquiry that can be profitably carried out by a variety of techniques and with varying degrees of precision, as much or as little as the subject matter allows."[14] What Jack Snyder suggests as the triple requirements for the advancement of the study of Soviet foreign policy— richness, rigor, and relevance—seems no less compelling in the advancement of the study of Chinese foreign policy.[15] Empirical richness via case studies, theoretical rigor via hypothesis testing, and policy relevance via the selection of significant issues and problems of common concern to all state actors in world politics should be accepted as complementary rather than conflicting requirements. In short, the ideal theory is supposed to be at one and the same time the most practical theory commanding descriptive, explanatory, predictive, and prescriptive power.

To seek empirical richness, theoretical rigor, and policy relevance, we need to identify several major sets of questions that ought to be on the agenda of Chinese foreign policy studies, such as: (1) How constant or changeable is Chinese foreign policy over a period of time, especially in the transition from the Cold War to a post–Cold War era, and why? (2) How unique and particularistic or general and common is Chinese foreign policy behavior compared with that of other countries, and why? (3) How wide is the gap between ideals and reality, between policy pronouncements (principles) and policy performance (behavior), and between intent and outcome in Chinese foreign policy, and why? (4) What is the relative weight of domestic (societal) and external (systemic) factors in the shaping of Chinese foreign policy, and what domestic and international consequences obtain? (5) How do global systemic structures—economic, military, normative, and behavioral—impact upon and shape China's national role and identity? (6) How are the global structures themselves affected by the rise of China in the post–Cold War world?

Chinese foreign policy today covers a wide and ever-expanding range of domains. For analytical convenience, we may conceptualize the Chinese foreign policy system as a pyramid-shaped structure starting from the most visible and flexible at the top to the most invisible and invariant at the base. This foreign policy structure is composed of four levels of variables: the top level, *policies* (most variable); the second level, *principles* (most vocal); the third level, *the basic line* (*jiben luxian*, reaffirmed or revised every five years at the party congress); and the fourth level, *worldview (shijie guan)* and *national identity* (most constant). All four levels of variables represent inputs to the foreign policy decisionmaking process. And what is the relationship between the levels of variables? Outputs (behaviors) too can be divided into interconnected, interacting, sequential phases of implementation and discrete functional behaviors in issue areas and relational behaviors toward other international actors.

So let us proceed from the premise that what we see and read at one level is not necessarily what we get in Chinese foreign policy as a whole.

To be theoretical, as James Rosenau reminds us, is to avoid taking the fundamentals of foreign policy and international relations for granted, on the one hand, and to be occupied with "puzzles," explaining how diverse sources of behavior might give rise to diverse outcomes, on the other.[16] For analytical purposes, Chinese foreign policy may be defined as an aggregate of purposeful external actions and activities designed to affect the international situation or behavior of other international actors in the pursuit of some values, interests, or goals. A behavior-centered approach is a way of minimizing the vagueness and mystique of "state behavior" by focusing on discrete, observable, empirical units—the foreign policy actions of political leaders in various contexts and issue areas. In international relations, as in law, what really matters for those representing the state, if not for scholars, is manifest behavior of other state actors, not the underlying elite perceptions and motivations. Foreign policy makers seldom have the time or the inclination to probe into the attitudes and motivations that might have brought about such behavior.

Competing Theoretical Approaches

Exploring the causal relationships of independent variables located in the predecisional policy input phase with the dependent variables made manifest in the policy implementation phase clarifies the linked processes that produce foreign policy behavior. For understanding and explaining the sources, patterns, and consequences of state actors' foreign policies and behaviors, international relations (IR) theory offers three basic but sharply contrasting approaches focused on domestic/societal, external/systemic, and domestic/external linkage factors impacting upon and shaping state foreign policy behavior.

Domestic/Societal Factors

The search for domestic factors to explain foreign policy action or change assumes that such policy is an extension of domestic politics. "The foreign policy," as Foreign Minister Qian Qichen publicly proclaimed in 1990, "is the extension of China's domestic policies."[17] Even a cursory review of the literature suggests that the overwhelming majority of Chinese foreign policy specialists focus on a variety of domestic factors in the search for a fitting explanatory model. Not surprisingly, in the related field of Soviet foreign policy there was also growing consensus not only that "domestic sources" had become more important but also that linkages between domestic and foreign policy issues had intensified in the post-Stalin era.[18] A 1982 cross-national study of the foreign policy "restructuring" of Bhutan, Tanzania, Canada, Burma, China, and Chile concluded that domestic factors, defined in terms of the perceptions, values, preferences, and objectives of key decisionmakers, had assumed critical importance in all cases except Canada.[19]

The demise of East-West conflict, combined with the global trend toward democratization, makes it easier for external factors to influence a state's domestic politics even as domestic special-interest groups intervene more aggressively in the shaping of state foreign policy. That the balance between the relative importance of external and domestic factors in shaping foreign policies is moving toward the latter had also been made evident in a flurry of articles and books challenging the structural-realist theory of state behavior in world politics.[20] IR theory too has entered a period of paradigmatic crisis; the discipline finds itself faced with the growing anomalies of structural realism; nevertheless, the primacy of domestic politics has yet to gain acceptance.[21] According to Zeev Maoz, from this unit-level micro perspective, system theories are "useless theoretically," "empirically meaningless," and "normatively objectionable."[22]

Of the domestic factors, historical/cultural approaches are generally resistant to causal linkage with contemporary foreign policy behavior. Although proponents of the historical/cultural legacy approach insist that there is no better way to comprehend and explain the present-day international conduct of the People's Republic than by reference to the tradition of imperial China, this approach, with a few exceptions, suffers from the fallacies of undifferentiation. The various historical and strategic traditions of the pre-1949 period do not all point in the same direction. Moreover, this approach, a theory of continuity rather than of change, tends to ignore one crucial determinant of foreign policy development: experiential and learning effects.

Still, a well-conceived cultural approach to the change/continuity puzzle can open up a potentially promising way of understanding the deeply rooted ideational variables by delineating certain recurring ideas and values that seemed made to order for Chinese leaders to interpret the outside world. Such an approach can even delimit the range of legitimate foreign policy goals and choices rather than establish a one-to-one linkage between the legacies of the past and any specific foreign policy behavior. The feasibility of resolving the richness/rigor dilemma via the feedback between history and theory need not be prematurely ruled out. More rigorous uses of cultural theory are not unrelated to learning theory, as "culture" is now of increasing interest to IR theorists and strategic analysts. By rejecting the a-cultural and a-historical biases of mainstream structural realism, cultural theory seeks to delineate consistent and persistent historical patterns in the way particular state elites think about the outside world.

In the pioneering work, *Cultural Realism*, Alastair I. Johnston utilizes a past-as-prologue backward search to capture China's "strategic culture"

as symbolized and structured in a particular period of Chinese history—
Ming China (1368–1644). Although acknowledging that cultural norms
and behavioral patterns are not the same and the possibility that strategic
culture and strategic policy may be unrelated, with the former confined
to a ritualistic role, Johnston nonetheless posits the concept of "strategic
culture" as a point of departure. Strategic culture is, according to him, an
integrated system of symbols that serves as an overarching conceptual
framework to define enduring strategic preferences by formulating concepts of the role and efficacy of military force in international relations.
Thus, he seeks to establish the historical and cultural baseline for a
macrohistorical inquiry into Chinese thinking on war and peace. This
carefully conceived, historically delimited, and well-documented study
demonstrates that Chinese strategic culture—contrary to the conventional wisdom of uncritically accepting Sun Zi's famous *Art of War* as the
only tradition of Chinese strategic culture—shares many of the same assumptions with what in the West is known as the *para bellum* doctrine; to
wit, warfare is viewed as a relatively constant element in international relations; stakes in conflicts with the adversary are viewed in zero-sum
terms; and pure violence is highly efficacious for dealing with threats
which the enemy is predisposed to make. The Chinese *para bellum* strategic culture also includes two other elements: an explicit doctrine of "absolute flexibility" *(quan bian)* and an explicit sensitivity to relative material capabilities.[23]

Despite historical variations in the external security environment over
the centuries, according to Johnston, China's classical realpolitik strategic
culture persists in Maoist and post-Maoist security thinking and behavior. In short, it is China's rooted *para bellum* strategic culture, not international "anarchy" as in structural-realist theory, that has driven Beijing's
realpolitik in the Maoist and post-Maoist periods.[24]

Closely related to the strategic culture approach is national identity
theory, which explores the interplay between deeply rooted primordial
cultural and ever-changing situational factors. Although the theory pos-
tulates that a national identity, once congealed, may be expected to provide a basis for reasonable expectations concerning state behavior under
various contingencies, or at least to set the outer limits for such behavior,
it does not presuppose specific behavioral choices, modalities, or outcomes of the nation-state identity dynamic. That is because national
identity projection is situation specific. National identity mobilization
and enactment are postulated as subject to leadership styles, particularly
of the "founders," as a crucial intervening variable. Given that type of intervening variables, responses to such situational factors as an identity
threat and/or an identity opportunity may be expected to vary from one
extreme, inertial absorption, to the other extreme, a fundamental trans-

formation of national identity, with a marginal shift in policy options and strategies being the most likely response.[25]

Also related to the historical/cultural approach is the so-called second-image explanation: A state's war-prone behavior depends more on its particular type of national government or social system than on the nature of international society. This explanation, that the international politics of a state have domestic sources, that a state's foreign policy behavior in general and its war-prone behavior in particular depend more on its particular type of national government or social system than on the structure of the international system is IR's new-old debate. Proceeding from sharply divergent premises, Kant, Lenin, and Woodrow Wilson situated the cause of war and the condition for peace in the nature of the social and political systems of the state. Recently, the Kantian second-image theory, or democratic peace theory—that liberal democracies rarely fight against each other—has gained wide, if not paradigmatic, acceptance in IR theory. As Jack Levy writes, "This absence of war between democratic states comes as close as anything we have to an empirical law in international relations."[26] Several important modifications of the democratic peace theory have been advanced by (1) Nils Petter Gleditsch, who argues that nations primarily fight *proximate nations* and that democracies rarely fight one another; (2) Edward Mansfield and Jack Snyder, who argue that partial democracies or democratizing states are more war prone than consolidated and stable democracies; and (3) Henry Farber and Joanne Gowa, who argue that only after 1945 was there a statistically significant correlation between democracy and peace, suggesting that the linked connection may be at most a Cold War phenomenon.[27]

In the post-Mao era the Leninist/Stalinist theory of imperialism and the inevitability theory of war had to be jettisoned as a normative and practical liability that stood in the way of China's integration into the capitalist world system. How else could China cope with Lenin's belief that the slicing of the Chinese melon would be the final drama of "imperialism as the highest stage of capitalism"? Despite all the conceptual and policy changes and shifts in international conduct over the years, the People's Republic of China (PRC) remains an autocratic state that has resorted to the use of military force more often than any other regional or middle-ranking power in the world, validation perhaps of the Kantian democratic peace theory.[28] And yet, there is at best only minimal evidence that Chinese leaders have used military force to promote their domestic political agenda abroad or that the outcome of factional strife has been the key determinant behind China's decisions to go to war. The broader point is that China has yet to resort to military force purely on behalf of the Communist revolutionary cause, nor has China applied the doctrine of "people's war" in any of its armed conflicts from the Korean War to the most recent gunboat diplomacy in the disputed Spratly Islands.

The "strongman" or "Mao in command" model—according to which all important ideological developments, policy shifts, redefinition of the international system, and the "basic line" were authorized, if not personally dictated, by Mao in 1949–1976—has been suggested as a more fitting "domestic" explanation for the redefinition and restructuring of China's foreign policy.[29] Research has yet to find any new evidence to repudiate the "Mao in command" thesis with the possible exception of the Wang Jiaxiang case, which Bachman calls in Chapter 2, "the only known case of a distinct, concrete foreign policy line emerging from within China that was not clearly product of Mao." To the contrary, A. Doak Barnett discovered in his field interviews in Beijing in 1984—including one with then-premier Zhao Ziyang—that "some Chinese who were involved in or close to the process at that time now say that Mao was totally dominant and made almost all of the 'big decisions.'"[30] As Bachman argues, in the post-Mao era Deng as the core of the second-generation leadership was more consultative and consensual than Mao, even though the paramount leader had the last word on important foreign policy decisions until his final years, when he was too incapacitated to intervene. Jiang Zemin as the core of the third-generation leadership is likely to be even more consensually oriented than Deng.

With the growing globalization of the Chinese political economy, the devolution of power at home, and the fragmentation of authority and decisionmaking structures during the post-Mao era, the strongman model becomes increasingly problematic. Indeed, there is now broad scholarly consensus that the Chinese party-state is no longer the almighty Leviathan of yore. Although the structure of the Chinese foreign policy system is still vertically organized, the process at the top continues to be governed by informal politics—the behind-the-scenes process of supplementing or substituting for the formal authoritative decisions concerning power, values, and ideological or policy preferences and commitments. Even though all levels of the foreign policy system have both regular and irregular features, as Michael Swaine argues, the level of influence in the policy process "is often determined primarily by the informal prestige and power of the individual who heads it."[31] As China's interactions with the outside world increase in number and complexity (as both Bachman and Levine argue), it becomes more and more difficult for Beijing to coordinate all the domestic and foreign policy decisions and actions. According to Lewis, Hua, and Xue, the existence of multiple sources of power and influence at the center places the Ministry of Foreign Affairs in the discomforting position of making international pledges and commitments that it has no power or authority to implement at home.[32]

A significant portion of empirical and theoretical literature in comparative foreign policy and international relations in recent years has shown that foreign policy leaders generally engage in "satisficing" behavior rather than "rational" behavior. It has become increasingly evident that the "rational actor" model does not accurately describe and explain how decisions are actually made in a variety of situations. Lieberthal and Oksenberg's recent study of domestic policy making structures and processes takes a fragmented bureaucratic structure approach by combining the "rationality" (policy) and factional "power" models while introducing and emphasizing the bureaucratic structure in which the policy process and elite struggles over power and principle are embedded. What this study reveals is a fragmented bureaucratic structure of authority and a decisionmaking process that is protracted, disjointed, and incremental.[33] Although not focused on foreign policy decision structure and process and hence without clear-cut implications for the foreign policy decisionmaking process, this study nonetheless challenges the rationality policy model implicit in Barnett's study of Chinese foreign policy structure and process, as the "fragmented bureaucratic" model comes close to the "garbage can model," in which the policy outputs (final decisions) depend more on chance conjunctions of factions, interests, issues, and events than on causal logic.[34]

As China's integration with the world economy widens and deepens, different domestic groups and actors with different sets of interests will try hard to "participate" in the making and implementation or nonimplementation of foreign policy goals. As a result, the Chinese foreign policy system will encounter both "software" and "hardware" problems, further accentuating both the word/deed disjuncture and the intent/outcome disjuncture. Despite or perhaps because of the fragmented authoritarian trend, the foreign policy making process is likely to continue to be a central challenge for the core leader as well as a major source of authority and legitimacy. What this means in practice, as Bachman argues in Chapter 2, is that as the rewards of success and the costs of foreign policy failure become more directly linked to the top leader, the center's bureaucratic interests will be overrepresented at the expense of local and provincial interests. The core leader is likely to spend much more of his time on national "security" issues. The driving force for nationalistic behavior is not any sense of a military threat from an external power but the leadership's resolve to project its national identity as an up-and-coming superpower in the Asia-Pacific region, so as to make up for the growing domestic legitimation and security deficits. Thus, the predicted extension of the pluralizing decisional processes of the domestic political economy to the realm of foreign policy is likely to be only temporary, and a pattern somewhat closer to the "Mao in command" model, but without the kind of charisma and dominance of the foreign policy process that Mao had, is likely to reemerge in the coming years—the "Mao in command" model revised and returned, as it were.

External/Systemic Factors

Until recently, the comparative foreign policy literature has been primarily concerned with the linkages between domestic/societal sources and resultant external behavior. As shown above, this domestic (Sinocentric) bias is even more pronounced in the field of Chinese foreign policy studies. Although the breakdown of consensus politics in the United States and China's self-imposed isolationism provided a rationale for the domestic/societal approach in the 1960s,[35] the new realities of the interdependence of economic life in the 1970s and 1980s have highlighted the importance of external/systemic factors. Against this backdrop, various systemic approaches have emerged as alternative models in identifying and explaining what shapes state behavior in international relations.

Practically all systemic/structural approaches proceed from the premise that the foreign policy behavior of states is shaped in varying degrees by external/systemic factors. For space reasons, we need to focus on the most dominant structural-realist theory, as articulated by Kenneth Waltz in *Theory of International Politics*,[36] which is said to have given classical realism the kind of theoretical rigor and parsimony that such traditional realists as Hans Morgenthau and others had long promised but never quite delivered. Indeed, Waltz's structural realism emerged as the *Politics Among Nations* of the 1980s; no other IR theory has commanded as much success—or controversy—as Waltz's work.[37]

Waltz's structural-realist theory is based on three closely interrelated propositions: (1) that the defining feature of the contemporary international system is anarchy (the absence of a world government); (2) that the units making up the system are rational (self-help) sovereign state actors; and (3) that the structure of the system (i.e., the distribution of power) is identified as the independent variable that plays the crucial role of shaping state actors' (balancing) behavior—hence it is also called "balance-of-power theory." As a result, the behavior of states as interacting units and the outcomes of their behavior become both explainable and predictable.[38] By privileging the autonomous nature of a self-help anarchical international system and the systemic constraints that it places on all state behavior, Waltz has elegantly simplified and synthesized classical realism: He has replaced the first image (human nature) with the third image (anarchy) while at the same time ignoring the second image (regime attributes and domestic dynamics). Structural realism departs from classical realism by offering a macrostructural explanation to the micro account of classical realism, which focuses on unit-level analysis and explanation.

And yet, it is both surprising and revealing that the most dominant IR theory has proved to be so wide of the mark, with so little explanatory and predictive power for many of the macrostructural changes in the international system, including the end of the Cold War and the disappearance of bipolarity. The noncatastrophic ending of the Cold War has overturned much of the deeply ingrained realist wisdom about war as the primary means of system transformation as well as about the immutability of the East-West conflict. The failure of structural realism to account for the recent momentous structural changes in world politics has to do with the rigid separation of structures and processes at the systemic level and the equally rigid separation of structures and units (state actors). Structural realism makes no allowance for the possibility that the structure itself might shift or even become transformed through international regimes or through changing identities, norms, and capabilities of units within the system.[39] Waltz also skates over the degree and character of anarchy by treating its relation to order as a dichotomy rather than as a continuum and by ignoring the identities, interests, and norms state actors bring to their interactions and the subsequent impact of these interactions on the nature of "anarchical society" at a given time.[40] The point is that anarchy cannot explain how and why states including China identify friends and foes as they do and the impact of such identifications on their own foreign policy behaviors as well as on anarchical structures. Even in times of stability the international system provides only the context within which a state may act. How each state actually behaves in a given situation depends on a host of other factors, such as its own definition of the international situation (which may not correspond with the reality of the international structure), its perceptions of national interests (which seem to change more rapidly than do shifts in the configuration of power), its negotiating skills and resources, and so on.

As Johnston shows in Chapter 3, major behavioral anomalies of China's alliance/alignment behavior that defy the logic of structural-realist theory are legion. From a neorealist perspective, China should have stayed aligned with the Soviet Union when the United States by any reckoning remained as the dominant hegemonic power (at least until the early 1970s). Yet during the Cold War, Beijing succumbed to wild swings of national identity projection, running through a series of varying roles: self-sacrificing junior partner in the Soviet-led socialist world; self-reliant hermit completely divorced from and fighting both superpowers; the revolutionary vanguard of an alternative United Nations; self-styled Third World champion of a New International Economic Order (NIEO); status quo–maintaining "partner" of NATO and favored recipient of largesse at the World Bank; and now, lone socialist global power in a post-Communist world. China has attained the dubious distinction of being the only country that has participated in both an alliance and a war with both superpowers. Both alliances and both wars proved inconclusive. Tellingly, China's most intensive push for internal balancing to increase relative power was the Great Leap Forward, which was more connected with Mao's status drive than with any major changes in international power structures.[41] Even in the 1990s, as Johnston argues but Garver denies, there has been little internal or external balancing directed at the consolidation of U.S. hegemony. The proximate cause for the precipitous drop in China's overall cooperative behavior occurred immediately in the wake of the June 1989 Tiananmen tragedy, prior to the collapse of the Soviet Union, the end of the Cold War, and the rise of a unipolar world.

The apparent lack of causal linkage between China's security behavior and the changes in international power structure can perhaps be explained by the proposition that post-Tiananmen China is simultaneously a growing and assertive regional power abroad and a weak state at home. The defining feature of a weak state such as China is the high level of *internal* threats to the government's security and legitimacy. External events including the changes in international power structure are seen primarily in terms of how they affect the state's internal stability and legitimacy.[42] The most dangerous "security" threat China faces in the post–Cold War era, as Bachman argues in Chapter 2 (Johnston would probably concur), is internal, not external, and a threat of this kind is not easily analyzed or managed through classical balance of power. Still, the balance-of-power logic of Chinese security behavior should not be prematurely or completely ruled out of court, as Sino-Russian relations have advanced in the 1990s from "constructive partnership" to "strategic partnership." The fifth Jiang-Yeltsin summit in April 1997 produced a lengthy declaration, "On the Multipolarization of the World and the Establishment of a New International Order."[43] Garver sees in the emerging "Russo-Chinese entente . . . the beginning of a new quadrilateral alignment in East Asia in which a 'continental' Russo-Chinese bloc balances a 'maritime' American-Japanese bloc" (see Garver's Chapter 5).

Although structural realists dismiss the role of normative pressure, international norms can be singled out as another set of external systemic factors explaining how and why states behave the way they do. Indeed, from a nonrealist perspective, whether in traditional or contemporary world order studies, international legal or institutional theories, or social constructivist theory, there is no such thing as normless behavior. Human behavior, including the behavior of the state, is conditioned by the continuing interactions between values, norms, and structure of a given society and those of the international system.

International norms are prescriptive or proscriptive statements—principles, standards, rules, customs, or usage—of state behavior appropriate to a particular role or situation, elaborated or codified in accordance with the rules of entry and the rules of play in international institutions or regimes or international lawmaking processes.[44] They vary greatly in scope and degree of precision or effectiveness. International norms may appear in the form of written bilateral and multilateral treaties and conventions, unwritten international customs and usage, hortatory resolutions and declarations of international organizations and conferences, and even unilateral self-restraint. That is, it is interactions among various international actors—states, nongovernmental organizations (NGOs) and international intergovernmental organizations (IGOs)—that provide a theoretical basis and institutional context for understanding how and why one norm rather than another commands a preferred status. Norms that are highly coherent and successful in the evolution of international society and ongoing international contest (negotiation) are more easily accepted and embodied in international law and will be far more resistant to change than those less coherent and less competitive.[45]

China's foreign policy options are delimited not only by international power structures but also by international norms. International norms affect Chinese foreign policy behavior in at least two obvious ways. First, international norms define the terms of the international discourse or negotiations in which states seek to justify their policy or action. In addressing the puzzle of why powerful states obey the seemingly powerless international rules, Thomas Franck suggests the "power of legitimacy" explanation. Legitimacy is defined in terms of the normative potency of a rule or rule-making institution that exerts influence toward compliance even among powerful states largely because its functions accord with generally accepted principles of "right process."[46]

As a country supersensitive to the rise and fall of the mystical but legitimating "Mandate of Heaven," China remains haunted by the decay of its moral regime. The challenge of "remaking" the hard facts of its international behavior to validate its professed self-image leads to a constant reformulation, renumbering, and redramatization of China's basic foreign policy principles. A number of studies have addressed the influence of international norms upon the conduct of Chinese foreign policy during the Maoist era.[47] Yet China's "great legal leap outward" since 1979 has occurred in tandem with a rapid acceptance of international law, which became part of China's effort to catch up with the rest of the world and to seek a stable and predictable external environment.[48]

Second, Chinese foreign policy behavior is affected, in varying degrees, through international socialization and subsequent changes in domestic decisionmaking structures and processes. With China's growing participation in multilateral regimes comes a more solid empirical base for testing various theories—learning theory, epistemic community theory, neoliberal institutional theory, and social constructivist theory—to see how and why old norms compete with new norms in the course of China's social interactions with other actors in various international regimes and how and why some norms are jettisoned, whereas others are reproduced in the input, output, and feedback processes of the Chinese foreign policy system.[49]

As the most-universal international organization, the United Nations exerts diverse and varying degrees of influence on the behavior of its member states. As the most authoritative dispenser of international legitimation, the UN has remained indispensable in the legitimation of newly independent or minted states and in the Chinese quest for absolute legitimation. We may take the evolution of Chinese participatory behavior in the United Nations and its related international institutions as a point of departure for this type of empirical and normative analysis.[50] For Chinese foreign policy behavior, whether or not international norms are at work raises the question whether evidence of normative restraint is tactical adaptation or real "learning." For the latter, there must be evidence that a state clearly eschews behavior that would have been consistent with its interests defined as relative gain.[51]

Of all the international norms, state sovereignty is the most basic and deeply internalized principle of Chinese foreign policy. In the post-Tiananmen period the norm of state sovereignty seems to have returned with renewed vigor to Chinese foreign policy pronouncements. There is little doubt that state sovereignty is the glue holding together the old/new states system in an "anarchical" international society, legitimating certain state behaviors and delegitimating others (e.g., Iraq's invasion of Kuwait). Chinese foreign policy is empowered and constrained at one and the same time by the norm of state sovereignty.

However, the fact that the sovereignty norm commands varying degrees of definitions among sovereignty-bound (state) and sovereignty-free (nonstate) actors in various issue areas of world politics suggests that there are competing international norms that may place contradictory constraints and pressures on state behavior. As Robinson suggests in Chapter 9, there is in Chinese foreign policy thinking and behavior a spectrum of dependence-interdependence-independence across time and across many issues despite China's well-known declaratory emphasis on state sovereignty and independence: "Beijing is simultaneously dependent in certain regards, interdependent in others, and independent in still others." Some Chinese IR scholars have even resurrected the Maoist line espoused in the United Nations in the early 1970s that interdependence in the contemporary world economic system amounted to no more than an asymmetrical interdependence "between a horseman and his mount." In the post–Cold War era, we are told, interdependence in a world without a world government (anarchy) can fuel and accentuate zero-sum power politics by trampling on the sovereignty of weak states; by preventing weak states from controlling their economic, military, and political resources; and by providing more opportunities for some states to interfere in the internal affairs of others.[52]

Yet such anti-interdependence views are increasingly challenged and even replaced by globalization voices within China's IR community.[53] Indeed, offering the mercantilist anti-interdependence argument is increasingly problematic while the restructuring impact of the global political economy is being made evident in many changes that are beyond the immediate control of the state.[54] As we have seen, Jiang's political report to the Fifteenth CCP Congress is noted for his open acknowledgment of globalization as a fact of modern international economic, scientific, and technological life and for detailing China's response to this challenge through state enterprise reform and restructuring. As Robinson argues in Chapter 9, for a variety of reasons the interdependence of the 1970s and 1980s got swept away by the new tides of globalization underscoring "the ease with which societal, ideational, cultural, scientific-technological, educational, and communications ideas and processes cross national boundaries. . . . Globalization is the universalization of interdependence."

Domestic/External Linkage Processes

Most of the theoretical models described above demand an either-or (internal or external) causality choice—either domestic-level factors or the international system is the determinant in framing foreign policy. And yet the most salient impact of globalization dynamics on the state is the intensification of domestic and external linkages. As a result, the conventional realist divide between domestic and external factors is substantially blurred, if not totally erased. With the increasing associated interaction between security and economic policies, the factors that influence Chinese foreign policy behavior no longer fall neatly into the dichotomous categories of domestic/societal and external/systemic variables. Both sets of variables involve structural as well as cognitive elements, and they interact during the decisionmaking process. The domestic/external linkage approach focuses more on the socialization consequences than the initial causes of such interaction, whereas virtually all of the theoretical approaches to the study of Chinese foreign policy have sought to explain state behavior by analyzing the sources of policy rather than its consequences.

In short, globalization dynamics provide a more solid empirical basis for formulating and testing a variety of domestic/external linkage hypotheses for both qualitative and quantitative analyses. Each source, whether domestic or external, should be viewed in a relative and probabilistic rather than an absolute and deterministic manner to delineate the range of permissible and possible foreign policy choices that can be made in a given period. Which factors in the linkage between domestic and external variables are more relevant to decisionmaking is a matter of considerable disagreement among scholars. The global system with its various constraints or opportunities cannot have any significant influence for Chinese foreign policy unless or until it is perceived and acted upon by Chinese foreign policy makers through their own decisionmaking system. Chinese foreign policy is seen here as the outcome of a continuing interplay between decisionmakers' perceptions of needs, interests, and beliefs and their perceptions of and responses to international material and normative pressures. This approach recognizes the restructuring impact of external pressures on foreign policy decisionmaking, but it also stresses the importance of domestic political institutions and policies in the timing and framing of specific responses to such external pressures.

The "second image reversed" thesis offers a promising way of exploring the domestic/external linkage process. As formulated by Peter Gourevitch, the thesis argues that international factors can impact upon and shape the structures and processes of domestic politics: "Instead of being a cause of international politics, domestic structure may be a consequence of it. International systems, too, become causes instead of consequences."[55] For our purpose, the "second image reversed" process can be reformulated as a circular feedback process in which external influences become part of the conceptual, definitional, policymaking, and institution-building processes of Chinese foreign policy.

China's growing integration with the United Nations and all its affiliated multilateral institutions provides a wide range of empirical and behavioral referents for integrating external systemic, domestic, and decisionmaking variables in the study of Chinese foreign policy behavior. The very process of this Sino-UN interaction, whether intended or unintended, greatly widened and deepened the ambit of China's involvement in the UN system, eroding and blurring the boundary between externally conditioned and internally determined policies. Practically all the multilateral economic, science, and technology regimes in the UN system have been reconceptualized as cost-effective sources of bridging China's information, knowledge, capital, and technology gaps in the service of the modernization drive. They have been allowed to enter, some by design and others inadvertently, the castle of Chinese sovereignty as conceptual Trojan horses, influencing the process by which Chinese national interests are redefined and Chinese national priorities are restructured for a better fit with the logic of globalization dynamics.

Epistemic community theory claims that shared understandings about the nature of complex problems more than national power and interests can explain regime formation, maintenance, and transformation.[56] Epistemic communities refer to networks of knowledge-based experts—generally more transnational than national in scope and orientation—who play the "knowledge broker" role of articulating the cause-and-effect relationship of complex problems of common national and global concern, proposing specific policy prescriptions and identifying salient issues and problems for international negotiation. As an epistemic community grows and expands in size and strength, its shared understanding and shared concern become key to its ability to participate in and frame the issues for the international negotiation process.

The UN and all its specialized agencies have served as the major training ground for Chinese diplomats and negotiators abroad and was the chief catalyst for the creation of various epistemic communities within China during the post-Mao era of reform and opening. Participation in the Conference on Disarmament in Geneva (CD) has generated a steady annual increase in the number of Geneva-trained arms control and disarmament (ACD) experts on the Chinese delegation as well as a broader ACD policy community within China. This policy community grew vertically and horizontally in the 1980s and 1990s, with at least 280 specialists having already written articles and essays on ACD issues for leading journals.[57] Thanks to China's participation in the UN-anchored international human rights regime, a human rights policy community and human rights scholarship developed in the 1980s and 1990s.[58] There is a burgeoning environmental policy community in China. As Economy shows in Chapter 12, the interactions—both within the domestic policy community itself and between the Chinese and international policy communities—generated a newly unified and aggressive environmental diplomacy; as a result, an estimated 80 percent of China's environmental protection budget comes from foreign sources.

The question is whether the emergence and growth of epistemic communities in China have effected any fundamental cognitive learning or merely reflect adaptive learning in Chinese foreign policy behavior. There are some promising, if still tentative, changes in the politics of continuing institutional adaptation and agency creation to better prepare China's positions on a great variety of global issues and problems. At a minimum, the growth of epistemic communities seemed to have made it possible for China to participate in multilateral regimes with a greater degree of confidence than before. The somewhat paradoxical consequence has been that the material and normative constraints on Chinese foreign policy behavior have been accentuated, even as China continues to adapt to the pressures generated by these regimes.

There are at least three kinds of changes in post-Mao Chinese foreign policy that have been catalyzed by the expanding interaction between

China and multilateral institutions. First of all, the United Nations and UN-sponsored global conferences have served as the chief catalyst for China's response in the form of a series of white papers. Between 1991 and 1997, China released a series of the white papers on human rights and human rights–related subjects—most notably "Human Rights in China" (1991), "Progress of Human Rights in China" (1995), and "Progress in China's Human Rights Cause in 1996" (1997)—all prompted by a felt need for alternative theories and formulations to cope with the clear and continuing challenge at home and abroad. That China was willing to make such a response rather than walk out of the human rights regime is an acknowledgment—however reluctant—that human rights are a valid subject of international dialogue. Faced with the global complaint about the lack of transparency in military/security policy, China even produced its first-ever ACD white paper, "China's Arms Control and Disarmament" in November 1995, which only makes more transparent China's already stated "principled stand." Most tellingly, China's "Agenda 21" was presented as Beijing's specific response to the global clarion call issued by the 1992 United Nations Conference on Environment and Development (UNCED): "Our government has drawn up 'China Agenda 21—A White Paper on China's Population, Environment, and Development in the 21st Century,' in accordance with the requirements outlined in the document of the 1992 UN Conference on Environment and Development, and in light of China's reality. This document will play an important guiding role in our country's formulation of long-term and mid-term national economic and social development plans."[59]

Second, the process of participation in the UN lawmaking process is inevitably linked to China's international legal behavior and its legislative politics at home. As post-Mao China joined more and more international institutions, conventions, and regimes in the UN system, the logic of a "great legal leap outward" became increasingly self-evident and self-fulfilling. In the course of its participation in the making of the United Nations Convention on the Law of the Sea (UNCLOS), for instance, China gradually accepted the principles of *jus cogens* and of the common heritage of humankind, broadening its conception of the sources of international law and relaxing its conception of absolute sovereignty. The post-Mao period witnessed a flurry of environmental legislative activities enacting a series of specific environmental laws and regulations on water pollution and marine resources; the preservation of land, grasslands, and fisheries; mineral, water, and soil conservation; and wildlife protection. Even in the area of human rights, the National People's Congress enacted in 1994–1995 a new Prison Law, the Labour Law, the PRC Law on Judges, the PRC Law on Procurators, People's Police Law, the State Compensation Law, and the Administrative Punishment Law.

Third, in terms of substantive policy or behavioral change, there are some nontrivial positive or potentially positive socialization effects. In the most sensitive area of ACD and cooperative multilateral security dialogue, two notable changes have occurred in recent years: China's signing on to the CTBT in 1996 and China's rising comfort level in Sino-ARF interaction in 1994–1997. Indeed, there has occurred a kind of politics of mutual adjustment and legitimation in a feedback or mutually constitutive relationship between the initial ARF structure at time t, change in Chinese comfort levels within this structure at $t + 1$, and institutional change in the ARF at $t + 2$: The changing level of Chinese comfort through Sino-ARF interaction entails a gradual shift in China's regional security thinking and behavior from a clear preference for no regional multilateral security dialogue, let alone institutionalization, to a preference for a moderate level of institutionalization.[60] As Feeney shows in Chapter 11, the multilateral economic institutions (MEIs) have performed various socialization functions such as (1) sensitizing Chinese policymakers to the psychological, methodological, and policy requisites to successful economic development; (2) tilting Chinese economic policy in the direction of continuing reform while acculturating and socializing an entire younger generation of Chinese technocrats in the techniques of economic growth; and (3) enmeshing China more firmly in the international community and thus raising the stakes against ill-advised adventurism. Despite China's often combative negotiating posture, as Economy argues in Chapter 12, international environmental actors have had a significant influence in shaping its domestic institution building at home and environmental diplomacy abroad. She also argues that the strategy of divide and conquer is not sustainable in the long run, as convergence of domestic and external environmental factors is inevitable.

Still, all the policy shifts and changes in the post-Mao era can be better seen as adaptive/instrumental learning rather than cognitive/normative learning at the basic level of worldview and national identity. In attempting to reconcile the seemingly irreconcilable—unilateral realpolitik security interests versus "idealpolitik" concerns for its international reputation—Beijing projects its "principled stand" on a range of global issues, asking others to follow what it says, not what it actually does. The apparent absence of cognitive/normative learning at this time does not necessarily mean that China's realpolitik views are immutably predetermined or that changes conducive to cooperative common security are totally lacking or cannot occur in the future. The adaptive-cognitive learning distinction, therefore, may be better seen as a continuum rather than a dichotomy. Once entrapped in the political processes of the UN regimes, there is no easy exit—to wit, Chinese adaptive realpolitik, once constrained and more deeply enmeshed, inevitably calls for the readjustment or restructuring of certain policies, principles, and institutions of Chinese foreign policy.

The UN's impact on China's compliance behavior is modest but not trivial. China's growing participation does not ipso facto translate into its greater commitment to multilateral cooperative security, just as a growing commitment to UN-sponsored treaties does not ipso facto translate into greater compliance. As Abram Chayes and Antonia Chayes argue, however, the free-ride or noncompliance problem has been greatly exaggerated, based on the misconceived "enforcement model" of compliance—sanctions with teeth. Compliance at the international level is not a simple on-off or either-or phenomenon. Instead, what is required to maintain compliance with treaty obligations and regime norms at an acceptable level is an iterative process of discourse—called the "managerial model" of compliance— among the parties involved. In this discourse process, not only national positions but also conceptions of national interest evolve and change. Such an iterative process of discourse and learning, combined with general international reputation—membership in good standing in the international organizations and regimes—generates the major pressure for compliance with treaty obligations and regime norms.[61] Assessed in terms of the managerial model, with the iterative process relying primarily on a cooperative discourse approach instead of a coercive sanctions one, China's compliance behavior seems more manageable than generally assumed.

Whither Chinese Foreign Policy?

Predicting the future of international relations has always been hazardous and never more so than at the end of the twentieth century, when the international system itself is undergoing a most profound and long-term transformation. Recent momentous global changes are unprecedented in their nature, scope, and rapidity. To a significant degree, as Robert Jervis argues, the flow of world politics too has become contingent or path-dependent, since certain unexpected events can easily force world politics along quite different trajectories. Hence, past generalizations can no longer provide a sure guide for the future, and the future of world politics will not necessarily resemble the past if the generalizations themselves are no longer valid.[62]

The difficulties of predicting the future shape of world politics are directly connected to the challenge of predicting the future of Chinese foreign policy, since any country's foreign policy will be significantly affected by the structures of world politics that prevail in any point in time. More specifically, the future of world politics, whether completely dominated by state actors (realism), by a multiplicity of diverse actors (pluralism), by a single, integrated global system (globalism), or by sovereignty-bound and sovereignty-free actors in a multicentric two-worlds system (bifurcationist model), will greatly influence the possible scenarios for the future of Chinese foreign relations. Each of these competing theoretical perspectives starts from different sets of premises and offers different sets of opportunities and constraints with different degrees of pressure upon China for change and continuity.

Viewed in this light, the historically derived correlation between system transition and war causation may no longer apply not only because of the many differences between a rising China and the rise of Wilhelmine Germany and that of post-Meiji imperial Japan but also because world history may well be in a different normative product cycle in the post–Cold War era. Harold James establishes a connection between the checkered history of German nationalism and the German national-identity dynamic on the one hand, and the normative state of international politics on the other. German nationalism quickly withered away after World War II, whereas previous defeats (in 1806 and 1918) had only fueled more aggressive nationalism. The explanation lies in the changing international norms that molded German national role expectations.[63]

Moreover, there is no good reason to assume that the history of imperialism would repeat itself in the coming years. The ascendant-China thesis comes at a time when the coherence of the Chinese state is rapidly deteriorating. The domestic social, political, demographic, and environmental problems encountered by Beijing in its march to great powerdom are legion. Ironically, the West has begun to sing the "rise of China" chorus at a time when Chinese leaders, bereft of their vaunted geopolitical swing value, are shifting from the pretense of being a global power to actually becoming the dominant regional military power in Asia, trailing and mirroring the Asianization of the Asia-Pacific. From Beijing's post–Cold War perspective, Asia is the center of Chinese power and influence, the nucleus of ever-expanding circles radiating outward in all directions. Today, China relies on Asia, we are told, for its status and role as "a special power in the world."[64]

In the turbulent post–Cold War world, in which contradictory forces—globalism, regionalism, statism, and local ethnonationalism—are vying for primacy, all states are subject to the relentless twin pressures of global integration from above and substate fragmentation from below. One of the central challenges confronting post-Deng leadership is how to manage the tensions between localism, nationalism, East Asian regionalism, and globalism.

It is to be hoped that the concepts, methods, and theories for describing, explaining, and projecting Chinese international conduct outlined in this chapter will provide a reliable base for the study of Chinese foreign policy in the post–Cold War era.

Notes

1. See Aaron L. Friedberg, "Ripe for Rivalry: Prospects for Peace in a Multipolar Asia," *International Security* 18:3 (Winter 1993/94): 5–33; Richard K. Betts, "Wealth, Power, and Instability: East Asia and the United States After the Cold War," *International Security* 18:3 (Winter 1993/94): 34–77.

2. Alastair Iain Johnston, "Prospects for Chinese Nuclear Force Modernization: Limited Deterrence Versus Multilateral Arms Control," *China Quarterly*, no. 146 (June 1996): 548–76; and idem, "China's New 'Old' Thinking," *International Security* 20:3 (Winter 1995/96): 5–42.

3. For Jiang Zemin's political report to the Fifteenth CCP Congress, see FBIS-CHI-97-255 (September 12, 1997) (Internet version). Without specifically using the term *global citizenship (qiuji)*, Jiang's political report brings the central point of the intense but short-lived debate (1988) on "global citizenship" back in—that in an era of globalization, China can choose not to emancipate its political economy thinking and fall behind in the technological race, forfeiting its "global citizenship" in the process, or it can more fully integrate itself into and make more creative use of the world market, whereby it will leap into the front ranks of world power. That is, state enterprise reform is justified as a way of responding to the pressures of globalization from above and without. See Lu Yi et al., eds., *Qiuji: Yige shijiexing de xuangze* [Global citizenship: A worldwide choice] (Shanghai: Baijia chubanshe, 1989).

4. Richard Bernstein and Ross H. Munro, *The Coming Conflict with China* (New York: Knopf, 1997), p. 4.

5. *Economist* (London), January 27, 1996, 102; World Bank, *World Development Report, 1996* (New York: Oxford University Press, 1996), p. 188.

6. Charles Wolf, Jr., et al., *Long-Term Economic and Military Trends, 1994–2015: The United States and Asia* (Santa Monica, Calif.: Rand Corporation, 1995).

7. World Bank, *China 2020: Development Challenges in the New Century* (Washington, D.C.: World Bank, 1997), pp. 20–21.

8. FBIS-CHI-97-244 (September 1, 1997) (Internet version).

9. See World Bank, "Poverty in China: What Do the Numbers Say" (Washington, D.C.: World Bank, 1996).

10. World Bank, *China 2020*, p. 71.

11. David A. Baldwin, "Power Analysis and World Politics: New Trends Versus Old Tendencies," *World Politics* 31 (January 1979): 161–94.

12. Susan Strange, "Territory, State, Authority and Economy: A New Realist Ontology of Global Political Economy," in *The New Realism: Perspectives on Multilateralism and World Order*, ed. Robert W. Cox (Tokyo: United Nations University Press, 1997), pp. 3–19.

13. For an assessment of China as a great power along this line, see Samuel S. Kim, "China as a Great Power," *Current History* 96:611 (September 1990): 246–251.

14. Jack Snyder, "Richness, Rigor, and Relevance in the Study of Soviet Foreign Policy," *International Security* 9:3 (Winter 1984/85): 90.

15. Snyder, "Richness, Rigor, and Relevance." For a similar line of reasoning for single-country developmental foreign policy theory, see James Rosenau, "Toward Single-Country Theories of Foreign Policy: The Case of the USSR," in *New*

Directions in the Study of Foreign Policy, ed. Charles Hermann, Charles W. Kegley, and James Rosenau (Winchester, Mass.: Allen & Unwin, 1987), pp. 53–74, idem, "China in a Bifurcated World: Competing Theoretical Perspectives," in *Chinese Foreign Policy: Theory and Practice*, ed. Thomas W. Robinson and David Shambaugh (New York: Oxford University Press, 1994), pp. 524–51.

16. Rosenau, "China in a Bifurcated World."

17. "Qian Qichen on the World Situation," *Beijing Review* 33:3 (January 15–21, 1990): 16.

18. See Seweryn Bialer, ed., *The Domestic Context of Soviet Foreign Policy* (Boulder, Colo.: Westview Press, 1981).

19. K. J. Holsti et al., *Why Nations Realign: Foreign Policy Restructuring in the Postwar World* (London: Allen & Unwin, 1982), p. 208.

20. Bruce Bueno de Mesquita and David Lalman, *War and Reason: Domestic and International Imperatives* (New Haven, Conn.: Yale University Press, 1992); Alastair I. Johnston, *Cultural Realism: Strategic Culture and Grand Strategy in Chinese History* (Princeton: Princeton University Press, 1995); Richard Rosecrance and Arthur A. Stein, eds., *The Domestic Bases of Grand Strategy* (Ithaca, N.Y.: Cornell University Press, 1993); and Jack Snyder, *Myths of Empire: Domestic Politics and International Ambition* (Ithaca, N.Y.: Cornell University Press, 1991).

21. Ethan B. Kapstein, "Is Realism Dead? The Domestic Sources of International Politics," *International Organization* 49:4 (Fall 1995): 751–774.

22. Zeev Maoz, *National Choices and International Processes* (Cambridge: Cambridge University Press, 1990), p. 548.

23. Johnston, *Cultural Realism*; see also idem, "Thinking About Strategic Culture," *International Security* 19:4 (Spring 1995): 32–64.

24. Alastair I. Johnston, "Cultural Realism and Strategy in Maoist China," in *The Culture of National Security: Norms and Identity in World Politics*, ed. Peter J. Katzenstein (New York: Columbia University Press, 1996), pp. 216–269; and idem, "China's New 'Old Thinking,'" *International Security* 20:3 (Winter 1995/96): 5–42.

25. For elaboration of such a synthetic national identity theory, see Lowell Dittmer and Samuel S. Kim, "In Search of a Theory of National Identity," in *China's Quest for National Identity*, ed. Lowell Dittmer and Samuel Kim (Ithaca, N.Y.: Cornell University Press, 1993), chap. 1, pp. 1–31.

26. Jack S. Levy, "The Causes of War: A Review of Theories and Evidence," in *Behavior, Society, and Nuclear War*, vol. 1, ed. Philip E. Tetlock et al. (New York: Oxford University Press, 1989), p. 270. See also Michael Doyle, "Liberalism and World Politics," *American Political Science Review* 80 (1986): 1151–1169; Zeev Maoz and Nasrin Abdolali, "Regime Types and International Conflict," *Journal of Conflict Resolution* 33 (1989): 3–35; Carol R. Ember, Melvin Ember, and Bruce Russett, "Peace Between Participatory Polities: A Cross-Cultural Test of the 'Democracies Rarely Fight Each Other' Hypothesis," *World Politics* 44:4 (July 1992): 573–599; Bruce Russett, *Grasping the Democratic Peace: Principles for a Post–Cold War World* (Princeton: Princeton University Press, 1993); David A. Lake, "Powerful Pacifists: Democratic States and War," *American Political Science Review* 86:1 (March 1992): 24–37; and James Lee Ray, *Democracy and International Conflict* (Columbia: University of South Carolina Press, 1995).

27. Nils Petter Gleditsch, "Geography, Democracy, and Peace," *International Interactions* 20:4 (1995): 297–323; Edward D. Mansfield and Jack Snyder, "Democratization and the Danger of War," *International Security* 20:1 (Summer 1995): 5–38; and Henry S. Farber and Joanne Gowa, "Politics and Peace," *International Security* 20:2 (Fall 1995): 123–146.

28. See Michael Brecher, Jonathan Wilkenfeld, and Sheila Moser, *Crises in the Twentieth Century,* Vol. 2, *Handbook of Foreign Policy Crises* (Oxford: Pergamon Press, 1988), pp. 2, 51, 160–164.

29. For the Mao-domination thesis, see Holsti et al., *Why Nations Realign,* pp. 204, 208–209; John Gittings, *The World and China, 1922–1972* (New York: Harper & Row, 1974); Samuel S. Kim, *The Maoist Image of World Order* (Princeton: Center of International Studies, Princeton University, 1977); Michel Oksenberg, "Mao's Policy Commitments, 1921–1976," *Problems of Communism* 25 (November-December 1976): 1–26.

30. A. Doak Barnett, *The Making of Foreign Policy in China* (Boulder, Colo.: Westview Press, 1985), pp. 7–8.

31. Michael D. Swaine, *The Role of the Chinese Military in National Security Policymaking* (Santa Monica, Calif.: Rand Corporation, 1996), p. 73.

32. See John W. Lewis, Hua Di, and Xue Litai, "Beijing's Defense Establishment: Solving the Arms-Export Enigma," *International Security* 15:4 (Spring 1991). 87–109.

33. Kenneth Lieberthal and Michel Oksenberg, *Policy Making in China: Leaders, Structures, and Processes* (Princeton: Princeton University Press, 1988).

34. For a pioneering work on the "garbage can model," see J. G. March, *Decisions and Organizations* (Oxford: Basil Blackwell, 1988).

35. For an early elaboration of this point as the operational premise of a major interdisciplinary study of the domestic sources of foreign policy, see Rosenau's introduction in *Domestic Sources of Foreign Policy,* ed. James N. Rosenau (New York: Free Press, 1967), pp. 1–10.

36. Kenneth N. Waltz, *Theory of International Politics* (Reading, Mass.: Addison-Wesley, 1979).

37. According to Onuf and Johnson, more than 350 scholarly articles in the field of international relations cited Waltz's *Theory of International Politics* in the period 1983–1992, as counted in the *Social Science Citation Index.* See Nicholas G. Onuf and Thomas J. Johnson, "Peace in the Liberal World: Does Democracy Matter?" in *Controversies in International Relations Theory: Realism and the Neoliberal Challenge,* ed. Charles W. Kegley, Jr. (New York: St. Martin's Press, 1995), p. 180.

38. Waltz, *Theory of International Politics,* pp. 79–96.

39. See Joseph S. Nye, "Neorealism and Neoliberalism," *World Politics* 40:2 (January 1988): 235–251, James Rosenau, *Turbulence in World Politics: A Theory of Change and Continuity* (Princeton: Princeton University Press, 1990); and Alexander Wendt, "Collective Identity Formation and the International State," *American Political Science Review* 88:2 (June 1994): 384–396.

40. Wendt, "Collective Identity Formation and the International State," p. 388. See also Alexander Wendt, "Anarchy Is What States Make of It: The Social Construction of State Politics," *International Organization* 46:2 (1992): 391–425; and John Vasquez, "World Politics Theory," in *Encyclopedia of Government and Politics,*

ed. Mary Hawkesworth and Maurice Kogan, vol. 2 (London: Routledge, 1992), p. 854.

41. See Thomas J. Christensen, *Useful Adversaries: Grand Strategy, Domestic Mobilization, and Sino-American Conflict, 1947–1958* (Princeton: Princeton University Press, 1996).

42. See Samuel S. Kim, "China's Pacific Policy: Reconciling the Irreconcilable," *International Journal* 50:3 (Summer 1995): 461–487. For discussion on the security problematic of weak states, see Barry Buzan, *People, States and Fear,* 2nd ed.) (Boulder, Colo.: Lynne Rienner Publishers, 1991), pp. 96–107.

43. *Beijing Review* 40 (May 12–18, 1997): 7–8.

44. Abram Chayes and Antonia Handler Chayes, *The New Sovereignty: Compliance with International Regulatory Agreements* (Cambridge, Mass.: Harvard University Press, 1995), p. 113; and Friedrich V. Kratochwil, *Rules, Norms, and Decisions: On the Conditions of Practical and Legal Reasoning in International Relations and Domestic Affairs* (New York: Cambridge University Press, 1989), pp. 10–11.

45. See Ann Florini, "The Evolution of International Norms," *International Studies Quarterly* 40:3 (September 1996): 363–389; and Chayes and Chayes, *The New Sovereignty.*

46. Thomas M. Franck, *The Power of Legitimacy Among Nations* (New York: Oxford University Press, 1990).

47. See James C. Hsiung, *Law and Policy in China's Foreign Relations: A Study of Attitudes and Practice* (New York: Columbia University Press, 1972); Jerome Alan Cohen and Hungdah Chiu, *People's China and International Law: A Documentary Study,* 2 vols. (Princeton: Princeton University Press, 1974); and Samuel S. Kim, "The People's Republic of China and the Charter-Based International Legal Order," *American Journal of International Law* 62 (April 1978): 317–349.

48. Hungdah Chiu, "Chinese Attitudes Toward International Law in the Post-Mao Era, 1978–1987," *International Lawyer* 21:4 (Fall 1987): 1127–1166; Samuel S. Kim, "The Development of International Law in Post-Mao China: Change and Continuity," *Journal of Chinese Law* 1:2 (Fall 1987): 117–160; idem, "Reviving International Law in China's Foreign Relations," in *Chinese Defense and Foreign Policy,* ed. June T. Dreyer (New York: Paragon House, 1989), pp. 87–131; and John R. Oldham, ed., *China's Legal Development* (Armonk, N.Y.: M. E. Sharpe, 1986); Byron N. Tzou, *China and International Law: The Boundary Disputes* (New York: Praeger, 1990).

49. James Davis and Andrew Cortell, "How Do International Institutions Matter? The Domestic Impact of International Rules and Norms," *International Studies Quarterly* 40:4 (December 1996).

50. For studies assessing the functional spillovers and feedbacks of China's growing enmeshment with global IGOs, see Harold K. Jacobson and Michel Oksenberg, *China's Participation in the IMF, the World Bank, and GATT* (Ann Arbor: University of Michigan Press, 1990); Samuel S. Kim, "China's International Organizational Behaviour," in *Chinese Foreign Policy: Theory and Practice,* ed. Robinson and Shambaugh, pp. 407–440; Michel Oksenberg and Elizabeth Economy, eds., *China Joins the World: Progress and Prospects* (New York: Council on Foreign Relations Press, forthcoming).

51. For an empirical and normative analysis of China's arms control and disarmament policy that applies and tests learning theory, see Alastair Iain Johnston,

"Learning Versus Adaptation: Explaining Change in Chinese Arms Control Policy in the 1980s and 1990s," *China Journal*, no. 35 (January 1996): 36–43.

52. See Gu Yan, "Duli zizhu shi Mao Zedong waijiao sixiang de linghun" [Maintaining independence is the spirit of Mao Zedong's foreign policy thinking], *Shijie jingji yu zhengzhi* [World economics and politics], no. 2 (1994): 30–33; and Zhao Huaipu and Lu Yang, "Quanli zhengzhi yu xianghu yicun" [Power politics and interdependence], *Shijie jingji yu zhangzhi*, no. 7 (1993): 36–41.

53. See for instance, Wang Yizhou, *Dangdai guoji zhengzhi xilun* [Analysis of contemporary international politics] (Shanghai: Shanghai renmin chubanshe, 1995); Ma Shaolei et al., *Guoji guanxi xinlun* [New theories of international relations] (Shanghai: Shehui kexue chubanshe, 1994); and Cai Tuo, *Dangdai quanqiu wenti* [Contemporary global problems] (Tianjin: Tianjin renmin chubanshe, 1994).

54. Thomas G. Moore, "China as a Latecomer: Toward a Global Logic of the Open Door," *Journal of Contemporary China* 5:12 (July 1996): 187–208.

55. Peter Gourevitch, "The Second Image Reversed: The International Sources of Domestic Politics," *International Organization* 32:4 (Autumn 1978): 882.

56. For a fuller discussion of the concept of epistemic communities, see the special issue on this topic, "Knowledge, Power, and International Policy Coordination," *International Organization* 46:1 (Winter 1992); and Karen T. Liftin, *Ozone Discourses: Science and Politics in Global Environmental Cooperation* (New York: Columbia University Press, 1994).

57. For the development of China's arms control policy community in the 1980s, see Johnston, "Learning Versus Adaptation," pp. 36–43. For a list of some prominent experts in China's ACD policy community, see Michael Swaine's chapter essay in *China Joins the World*, ed. Oksenberg and Economy.

58. For further analysis, see Samuel S. Kim, "Human Rights in China's International Relations," in Edward Friedman and Barrett McCormick, eds., *What If China Does Not Democratize?* (forthcoming).

59. Foreign Minister Qian Qichen's speech at the forty-ninth plenary session of the General Assembly, delivered on September 28, 1994. For full text, see FBIS-CHI-94-189 (September 29, 1994), pp. 1–5; quote at p. 4. See also UN Doc. A/49/PV.8 (September 28, 1994), p. 11.

60. See Alastair Iain Johnston, "The Myth of the ASEAN Way? Explaining the Evolution of the ASEAN Regional Forum," paper presented at Joint Conference on Security Institutions: Effects and Dynamics, March 17–19, 1997, Free University of Berlin and Center for International Affairs, Harvard University.

61. Chayes and Chayes, *The New Sovereignty*.

62. Robert Jervis, "The Future of World Politics: Will It Resemble the Past?" *International Security* 16:3 (Winter 1991/92): 39–45.

63. Harold James, *A German Identity, 1770–1990* (New York: Routledge, 1989).

64. FBIS-CHI-97-002 (January 2, 1997) (Internet version).

2

Structure and Process in the Making of Chinese Foreign Policy

DAVID BACHMAN

Since the onset of the Deng Xiaoping era in China, knowledge of the policymaking process in the People's Republic of China (PRC) has grown dramatically. Partial access to the archives of the Mao period (and to the archives of the former Soviet Union) has added substantially to our understanding of critical junctures in the making of Chinese foreign policy, such as China's participation in the Korean War and the forging of the Sino-Soviet alliance.[1] Interviews with top leaders and émigré accounts have greatly increased the depth and sophistication of knowledge about the policy process generally and in the realm of China's relations with the external environment specifically.[2]

As with all good research, the growing consensus about, and knowledge of, the policymaking structure raise as many questions as they answer. It seems quite clear that the policymaking process for the Mao period and large parts of the Deng period was vertically organized, especially for foreign policy issues. Mao and Deng were the final arbiters of Chinese foreign policy making. But is it an immutable aspect of the nature of power in China that the top leader always takes foreign policy making as his prerogative, or is it a reflection of the particular authority and power associated with both Mao and Deng?[3] Although we now know a great deal about the structure of the decisionmaking process, does this really tell us much about the resulting foreign policy? Regardless of the decisionmaking structure, Chinese statesmen are basically realist analysts of international affairs, some insightful observers argue.[4] Most of the recent revelations about foreign policy decisionmaking have focused on diplomacy and the role of the Ministry of Foreign Affairs or on particular instances of the use of force. But there is little systematic work done on the integration of diplomatic, military, and foreign trade–related decisionmaking. How are the diverse elements of China's interactions with the outside world integrated into a more or less unified whole? Finally, how do international and domestic influences affect the nature of the decisions reached by the Chinese leadership on international issues? Thus, our knowledge has grown dramatically, but the number of issues resolved by this new information is still relatively small.

In this chapter I will survey the decisionmaking apparatus as it bears on China's international posture and will describe the structure of the system as it has developed over time. I will present five short case studies of important or telling incidents in the history of China's relations with the outside world, drawing some conclusions about the nature of the policymaking process from them. I will conclude with the likely evolution of the foreign policy making process and decision rules in the emerging post-Deng era.

The Elements of China's International Posture

As with all countries, there are multiple dimensions to China's foreign relations. These include the normal forms of diplomatic interactions, national security policy, foreign economic relations, and, more peculiar to the Chinese case, at least until recently, formal relations with other Communist parties and policies toward Hong Kong (and Macao), Taiwan, and Overseas Chinese generally. This list does not exhaust the range of policymakers and actors involved with international developments— many subnational actors are now important in the international economy and the open door policy—and the list excludes, to some extent, actors involved in "twenty-first-century issues," such as environmental problems, illegal emigration, drug trafficking, and criminal organizations.

It is important to realize that, in practice, foreign policy has a narrower focus in China than it does in the United States. In the Chinese context, *waijiao guanxi* (foreign relations) is almost exclusively diplomatic in nature. Military and international economic aspects of foreign relations are not central in accounts of Chinese foreign relations if they are mentioned at all. Instead, what in Chinese is called *waijiao* is best seen as diplomacy—negotiations, affairs of state, and so forth, as executed between China's Ministry of Foreign Affairs and its counterparts in other countries.[5]

The lack of a broad history of China's relations with the world should not be taken to imply that political-military strategies and the use of force have not been central to China's interactions with the outside world. China has used or has threatened to use force extensively since 1949. To give an incomplete listing: China fought in the Korean War from 1950 to 1953; rendered significant aid to the Vietminh in French Indochina in the early 1950s; fought battles with Taiwan's navy in the early 1950s and seized islands controlled by Taiwan in 1955; bombarded the island of Quemoy in 1958; organized support for the Laotian Communist Party in the early 1960s; fought a war with India in 1962; provided military assistance to North Vietnam from 1964 to 1968; fought border skirmishes with the Soviet Union in 1969 and sporadically in the 1970s; seized islands from South Vietnam in 1974; fought a war with unified Vietnam in 1979; and seized more islands and fought skirmishes in the South China Sea in 1988; and tested missiles ten miles off the coast of Taiwan in 1996.[6] Moreover, throughout most of its history, the PRC faced direct challenges to its security from either and, on occasion, both superpowers. Indeed, the international security challenges to China were the core elements of China's foreign affairs until 1989 or so. These challenges reverberated profoundly within China—causing Mao to push for the development of nuclear weapons in 1955 and nuclear-powered submarines in 1958, as well as for a series of nuclear-capable missiles in the 1960s and 1970s.[7]

Again, as with all major states, in China the realm of foreign policy is not limited to diplomacy and national security policy either. International economic relations are a salient element of China's foreign relations, one that is growing in importance as China's relationship with the world deepens. There is a tendency to argue that Mao's China was self-sufficient and that international economic relations were not important to China prior to 1978. This glosses over the Soviet and Eastern European contribution to China's economic development (and defense industrialization) in the 1950s, which continues to have a profound effect on China's political economy to this day, and the subsequent periods when aspects of foreign trade policy were important political issues, and had important economic effects. For example, in the aftermath of the Great Leap Forward famine, Chinese leaders found it necessary to import grain, and they found it expedient to continue to import grain for the remainder of the Mao period. Export production bases were discussed in the early 1960s (and at times in the 1950s) and were a source of inspiration for the Special Economic Zones of the 1980s. In the early 1970s, Chinese leaders examined issues related to joining the World Bank, expanding exports by relying on China's plentiful labor power, and contracting foreign loans. Complete plant imports were seen as a way to jump-start Chinese industrial modernization in the mid-1960s and early 1970s. Even in the nuclear weapons and submarine programs, self-reliance was not total.[8]

Other dimensions of China's foreign relations include its once-extensive foreign aid program, its policies toward ethnic Chinese resident abroad, and its policies toward Hong Kong, Macao, and Taiwan.[9] This list does not exhaust the realms of Chinese contacts and relations with organizations, people, and states external to the PRC. Increasing global interactions are bringing about contacts among groups and organizations that previously had little or no concerns with foreign interactions. China faces emerging world order issues, but as in most major states, "old world order" issues of war, peace, and economic well-being remain at the core of Chinese foreign relations today.

The Making of Chinese Foreign Policy

There is rough agreement among the major analysts about the basic organizations, leaders, and processes involved in the making of Chinese foreign policy.[10] At the center of the decisionmaking system is the "core" of each generation of Chinese Communist Party (CCP) leadership. From the founding of the PRC until his death, Mao Zedong was the undisputed leader of the CCP and the PRC. He had the last word on all issues when he chose to involve himself, and China's position in the world and its security were among his major intellectual and political concerns. After a failed succession by Hua Guofeng, Deng Xiaoping emerged as the core of the second generation of Chinese leaders (Mao's generation was born in the 1890s, Deng's in the first decade of the 1900s). Although Deng was more consultative and consensual than Mao, Deng had the last word on Chinese foreign policy until he was too incapacitated to intervene, perhaps sometime in 1995–1996. Party documents refer to Jiang Zemin as the core of the third generation of CCP leadership. There are good reasons to believe that Jiang's future as Deng's successor is more secure than Hua Guofeng's was as Mao's, but Jiang's authority is clearly less than Deng's was, and his ability to have the last word on foreign policy issues is unknown at this time. He is likely to be even more consensually oriented than Deng.[11]

The core leader has many responsibilities and depends on others to help plan and implement Chinese foreign policy. Zhou Enlai played this planning and implementation role for Mao, Zhao Ziyang largely did it for Deng, and it appears that Li Peng is doing it for Jiang Zemin.[12]

Issues in Chinese politics are usually organized vertically, in what are called *xitong* (systems). The components of *xitong* have changed over time, and in some cases what constitutes a system is context dependent. But the strength of vertical organization of issues at the expense of horizontal contacts has been a major theme of the literature, though some of the vertical elements of the policy process may be breaking down. Except for the key individuals who are often the top "nodes" of the systems, formal horizontal contacts across issue areas are weak. To compensate for this, ideology, control over the personnel system of all Party and state organizations, and the holding of many key concurrent posts by leading individuals (and other mechanisms) have all been used in the past to try to increase coordination horizontally. Obvious coordination mechanisms across the various systems exist in the form of the budget and planning processes (which affect the military and foreign trade systems much more than they do the diplomatic), and politics serves to make connections across areas, but except at the very top of the system, there are few forums in which issues are integrated across systems.[13]

In addition to the more personal supervisory role of the core leader's chief lieutenant in Chinese foreign policy, certain formal organizations exist to plan and direct Chinese foreign policy. The most important is the Foreign Affairs Leading Small Group (FALSG).[14] Established in 1958, the original FALSG was led by Foreign Minister Chen Yi and contained representatives from the major diplomatically oriented ministries and departments. The FALSG disappeared during the Cultural Revolution (most of its members were purged or attacked before or during the late 1960s), and it was not revived until after Deng came to power. At that time, Li Xiannian was head of the group, with Zhao Ziyang as the vice director, and the membership included the top-ranking officials in the foreign relations field. Zhao replaced Li Xiannian sometime in 1984–1985. In 1987, Li Peng became director of the group (as well as premier). The foreign minister, the foreign trade and economic cooperation minister, and the minister of defense were other significant members. The appointment of the minister of defense marked the first time that the People's Liberation Army was formally represented on the FALSG.[15] In late 1996, Jiang Zemin replaced Li Peng as head of the FALSG, but Li was retained, serving as deputy director. This concentrated a remarkable number of foreign affairs–related positions in Jiang's hands. He is the CCP general secretary, the top party position; president of the PRC, a formal, largely ceremonial role; chair of the Central Military Commission of both the CCP and the PRC (China's military commander-in-chief); director of the FALSG; and director of the Taiwan Affairs Leading Small Group.[16]

The FALSG is not a "line" organization and therefore does not occupy a distinct position in the bureaucratic chain of command. Instead it is a staff organization that may provide options, coordinate policies, or otherwise serve the interests of the top leader. As is often said, China is ruled by men, not by laws, so the actual role of the FALSG in practice—its influence over events and policies is far from clear—is undoubtedly affected by how the top leader chooses to interact with it. With Jiang now chairing the organization, it is probably now at its most influential stage.

Basic staff support for the FALSG is provided by the Foreign Affairs Office of the State Council. This body is also known as the Central Foreign Affairs Office of the CCP Central Committee. It has a staff of about twenty. Consequently, much of the real options work for diplomatic relations is undertaken by staff of the Ministry of Foreign Affairs.[17]

But a focus on the FALSG misses key points in the Chinese foreign policy process. It was not until the late 1980s when a member of the military establishment formally served as a member of the FALSG. National security policy was certainly not ignored throughout the history of the PRC. National security policymaking (broadly defined) has been incorporated in the overall policy process by various means: through key individuals, organizations (other than the FALSG) that have incorporated People's Liberation Army (PLA) leaders, vertically organized structures that have run through the formal military chain of command, and the creation of special ad hoc groups.

In the case of the key individual, Zhou Enlai was the key figure who personally sat on all the major bodies in the early 1950s. He was premier, foreign minister, and a member of the CCP's Central Military Commission (CMC) between 1949 and 1954. As premier, he oversaw foreign trade. His role as foreign minister made him responsible for diplomatic work, and as a member of the military commission, he was one of twelve top leaders at the pinnacle of the military high command. But Zhou was dropped from the CMC in September 1954, and thereafter although his relations with the membership of the CMC were extensive, he did not officially have a chair at the CMC table.[18]

Another means by which overall policy, including military policy, was integrated was in the Party Secretariat. The Secretariat had two periods of organizational ascendancy, 1956–1966 and 1980–1987. In the first period, Deng Xiaoping was the CCP's general secretary, and the Secretariat also included leading military figures.[19] Thus, military and foreign affairs leaders were brought together with Party and economic specialists to supervise the implementation of Party policy. But although policy implementation affects subsequent decisions, there is no evidence that the Secretariat played a role in the making of Chinese foreign policy (with one possible exception to be discussed below).

The second heyday of the Secretariat was from 1980 to 1987, under Hu Yaobang's leadership. At that time, the Secretariat was extremely influential in administering China, at least partially supplanting the role of the CCP Politburo. Leading military figures also served on the Secretariat during this period as well. But with Hu Yaobang's purge in January 1987, the power, size, and prestige of the Secretariat were greatly reduced. Since that time, Party specialists have managed the activities of the Secretariat.[20]

Many military issues have been worked out through the regular military high command structure. At the pinnacle is the Central Military Commission, and under this body, the General Staff Department. There are other military organizations that formally are equal to the General Staff (the General Political Department, the General Logistics Department, and the Commission on Science and Technology for National Defense), but since 1958, the General Staff Department in effect has been in charge of foreign military activities.[21]

The formal structure of the military system was been in disarray at various (extended) periods in the 1960s and 1970s, and the Central Military Commission barely functioned (much like the FALSG). For about fifteen years, from the early 1960s until the end of the Mao period, the CMC was riven by factional and power politics, fierce disputes over priorities, and by the Cultural Revolution. It would be difficult to say that the CMC provided much central direction to military affairs.[22]

Two years after Mao's death, the chain of command was still not intact.

In April 1978, without the consent of the Military Commission, the Navy's principal responsible comrade at the time [either Xiao Jinguang or Su Zhenhua] arbitrarily decided to organize a major naval exercise . . . in Lushun. [Hua Guofeng] agreed to the exercise. When Comrade Yang Yong and I [Zhang Aiping] learned about this matter, we both deemed it inappropriate and immediately notified Comrade Luo Ruiqing [then secretary-general of the CMC]. . . . He too felt that such a large-scale mobilization of naval vessels, while termed an exercise, was actually tantamount to a naval show of force and was incorrectly motivated. Once it is staged, it would cause unnecessary international concern and result in adverse effects. Opposing such a move, he telephoned [Hua] to explain his views. However [Hua] refused to answer his call. Finally, with the support of Comrade [Deng] Xiaoping, this inappropriate exercise was eventually called off.[23]

Several remarks are pertinent here. First, April 1978 was a period of tension in Sino-Japanese relations concerning sovereignty over the Diaoyutai/Senkaku Islands. Thus, it appears that the effective commander of the navy wanted to stage an exercise in the Bohai Gulf that would serve perhaps to intimidate Japan. Bypassing the General Staff Department, headed by Deng Xiaoping, he went to Hua Guofeng, who was then chairman of the CCP, premier of the PRC, and chair of the CMC, and gained Hua's approval for the exercise. If, of course, Mao had made such a decision, no one would have dared to raise objections. But officials attached to the CMC may have felt that Hua's inexperience in foreign affairs was leading him to make a hasty decision, threatening China's international position. Their attempts to get Hua to reverse his decision illustrate Hua's limited authority. Those officials also (as officers from the ground forces) may have taken umbrage at the showboating by the Navy and the bypassing of the chain of command. Ultimately, with Deng's help, the exercises were called off. This incident suggests real tensions between the core leader and the CMC, particularly when it was staffed by powerful figures who were not dependent on the core leader for their positions and who were willing to challenge the decision, not just on military grounds, but on larger foreign policy grounds (or so it has been said in retrospect).

The incident may also be an indicator of what may happen to civil-military relations in China after Deng. One can only speculate why top naval figures went directly to Hua Guofeng, but it would appear that Hua's (and also Jiang Zemin's) limited authority may tempt, on the one hand, military figures to violate the chain of command, and on the other, strong members of the high command to oppose activities approved by the Chairman of the Central Military Commission. In short, although the Central Military Commission is probably the most important overall organization in the making of military policy, it, like all other organizations in China, has had its periods of ascendance and decline, and its degree of institutionalization is hard to assess.

Finally, with regard to military and national security policy, the center (the preeminent leader) has appointed ad hoc bodies to deal with major issues from time to time. Thus, in late 1962, the Party Politburo created a Central Special Commission that coordinated military industrial issues, especially of a high-tech nature. This body persisted into the late 1980s, and was chaired by the premier.[24] In early 1969, Mao appointed a special four-person committee to discuss and make recommendations about the nature of the international situation and China's policies. Mao appointed four PLA marshals for this task. Interestingly, all had come under attack during the Cultural Revolution, and all had been in opposition to the worst excesses of the Cultural Revolution. The activities of this group appeared to have played a catalytic role on the Chinese side for the Sino-American rapprochement of the early 1970s. It is also significant that Lin Biao, the minister of defense and Mao's nominal successor, was not appointed to this committee or did not involve himself in its activities.[25]

In terms of foreign trade management, the Ministry of Foreign Trade (now known as the Ministry of Foreign Trade and Economic Cooperation) and its foreign trade companies were the executive agents for most of China's foreign trade until the early 1980s. Foreign trade was largely planned, with the plans subject to approval by the State Planning Commission, following from national priorities. There were some linkages between the foreign trade system and the diplomatic and military systems, but foreign trade was more closely integrated into the domestic economic decision making system than were the other two systems. Since the beginning of the open door policy, tremendous variation and complexity has been introduced into foreign economic activity, making simple generalizations about the nature of the foreign trade system extremely difficult. Suffice it to say that there are few controls over Chinese exports, but the state does try to control, if not plan, imports.[26]

Thus, the structures at the heart of Chinese foreign policy making process can be identified, as can the leaders who make and supervise foreign policy actions. But although these individuals and structures can be identified, the interactions among individuals and organizations cannot be easily summarized. Organizations have been subject to attack. Ad hoc bodies to coordinate and organize activities have been created and then disbanded. The power and control of the top leader over foreign affairs has varied. In sum, there is a limit to what structures and individuals are able to tell us about the making of Chinese foreign policy.

Major Cases in the Making of Chinese Foreign Policy

This section will briefly survey some major decisions in the history of Chinese foreign policy and examine aspects of the policy process as revealed in these important cases. Most of the following examples are chosen on the basis of what they reveal about the operations of Chinese foreign policy, not because they necessarily were the most important issues in the history of the PRC's foreign relations.

China's Decision to Intervene in the Korean War

It is clear that Mao Zedong made the decision to intervene in the Korean War. Yet, he announced his decision after an extended series of meetings of the Politburo plus other invited attendees in early October 1950. Despite Mao's having opened the first Politburo meeting with the question of when should Chinese troops intervene (not whether the PRC should), there were heated debates at these meetings, and it appears that at times Mao and his supporters were in the minority. But over time, Mao's power and prestige, the logic of his argument, and his rhetorical abilities were sufficient to bring about apparent consensus within the leadership on the need to send troops to aid North Korea. Moreover, the decision appeared to have been contingent on Soviet air support and other aid. When Stalin either hesitated or reneged on earlier promises to support China's intervention, Mao also suspended plans to intervene. Ultimately, Mao concluded that Chinese national interests—domestic and foreign— necessitated Chinese intervention, even if Soviet support was not forthcoming. Stalin did supply assistance and limited air support, but at market rates.[27]

Although clearly Mao set the terms of debate with his initial agenda-setting question of when to intervene, the policy process here approaches the ideal of open-ended rational decisionmaking better than any other case in Chinese foreign policy. (There was free and frank debate, a significant number of voices were heard, and there was little or no hindrance on those advocating dissenting opinions.)

Policy Moderation in the Early 1960s

In the early 1960s, China was in the throes of an economic disaster. The Great Leap Forward had created an economic depression, and it is estimated that 20–30 million Chinese died as a result of the attendant famine caused by idiotic economic policies. In the summer of 1960, the Soviet Union ended its economic aid programs to China and recalled all its economic advisers. China was isolated and in dire straits.

In early 1962, Wang Jiaxiang, the head of the CCP's International Liaison Department, a member of the FALSG, the Party Secretariat, and a vice minister of foreign affairs, argued that China should not be so confrontational in its foreign policy, and in particular, China should not force conflict with the United States, the Soviet Union, and India. In addition, because of China's economic weaknesses, China should temporarily reduce its foreign aid. (Mao would later vilify this proposal as the "san he yi shao," or the three reconciliations and one reduction.) Wang gained consensus within the International Liaison Department for his views, and on February 27, submitted them to Zhou Enlai, Deng Xiaoping, and Chen Yi. The quasi-official PRC history for the period says that Mao rejected the ideas from Wang, but at least in scattered references in 1961 and 1962, Mao seemed to have somewhat similar views. Moreover, Wang's ideas coincided with a period when China peacefully concluded a number of treaties delimiting its borders with several neighboring states.[28]

This is the only known case of a distinct, concrete foreign policy line emerging from within China that was not clearly a product of Mao (and/or Zhou Enlai). Its impact on China's foreign relations is hard to assess. There was something of a lull in China's struggles with the United States, the Soviet Union, and India between late 1960 and mid-1962. But by late 1962, China had fought a border war with India, and coinciding with the Cuban Missile Crisis and Mao's late summer call to "never forget class struggle," China's rhetoric toward the two superpowers turned more aggressive and hostile. Nonetheless, peaceful border settlements were worked out with Burma, Afghanistan, Mongolia, Nepal, and Pakistan during the first half of the 1960s, perhaps implying some residual influence of Wang's ideas. In another context, economic planner Bo Yibo suggests that in some cases there was more rhetorical flourish to Mao's emphasis on class struggle in the early 1960s than there was to its effects on economic management.[29] This may also have been true in China's relations with the nonsuperpowers.

It is also interesting to note that Wang chose to address his recommendations to Zhou, Deng, and Chen. Deng was general secretary of the CCP, Chen was foreign minister, and Zhou, supervisor of overall foreign policy and premier. It is thus not at all clear which chain of command was primary in this case, and it may be that Wang hoped that more could be accomplished by approaching both Party and state authorities (or it may have been that Wang would have alienated any of the three individuals if he had ignored them). He was subordinate to all three officials.

This case indicates that alternative policy lines could emerge from within the bureaucracy, and that not every foreign policy initiative in China came from the preeminent leader. But it may also be the exception that proves the rule. There are no other cases that are as clear-cut as Wang's proposal, and by the summer or fall of 1962, Mao rejected it. Nonetheless, this case indicates that although the top leader has heretofore had the final say on Chinese foreign policy, it is possible for sharply drawn alternatives to appear on the agenda and have some influence.

The Third Front

The Third Front was one of the most significant developments in the history of the PRC, but until the mid-to-late 1980s it was all but unknown in the West.[30] In 1964, after reports from the PLA General Staff Department's Operations Division discussing China's strategic vulnerabilities to superpower air power, Mao single-handedly changed the policies of China's emerging Third Five Year Plan. Instead of a stable plan focusing on basic construction and economic needs of the population, Mao argued that defense industrialization was the key priority, and that in light of China's strategic vulnerabilities, most new investment should be located in remote interior regions, theoretically removed from the range of foreign aircraft.[31]

Mao's decision fundamentally affected the Chinese political economy and led to massive waste of resources. The legacy of the Third Front continues to plague China's economic reform, as the factories built during the Third Front period, almost universally inefficient, are at the same time central components of the industrial structure of provinces such as Sichuan, Guizhou, Gansu, and Shaanxi.

This decision indicates Mao's unilateral power to alter both domestic economic programs and set national security parameters for China. Although Mao's decision did not appear to come out of the blue (in light of the Operations Department report), there is no evidence that Mao discussed his ideas on the Third Front prior to announcing his decision. Mao made this decision at time when his power was widely viewed in the West as being challenged by moderate political leaders who opposed his radicalism. In short, it demonstrates Mao's superior political power, even in the aftermath of the Great Leap Forward. This pattern of absolute Maoist dominance of the national security agenda of China would persist until the end of his life in 1976, though, as discussed above, Mao could appoint special committees to investigate the international situation in 1969 and allow others to formulate ideas, subject to his approval or rejection (at potential political and physical cost to the proponents of such actions).

The Development of Foreign Trade in the Early 1970s

As noted above, the often asserted claim that China was isolated from the world prior to the reform period is an overstatement. Nonetheless, during the first four or so years of the Cultural Revolution decade (1966–1976), China's foreign trade was extremely limited, and the PRC approached self-sufficiency to the greatest degree in this period. Nonetheless, with Lin Biao's purge and the Sino-American rapprochement, China's leaders moved to import complete factories from the West and Japan to help modernize the Chinese economy. Such a policy emerged from the central bureaucracy, presumably with Mao's approval. Zhou Enlai was charged with executing these plans, but the great demands placed upon him and his declining health led him to recall Chen Yun to active service in the bureaucracy. Chen had been China's leading economic specialist until 1962 (he was under a political cloud from late 1957 to early 1959 and may have been ill from mid-1959 to late 1960), when he clashed with Mao about rural policy. He took sick leave and from then on was politically inactive.

From mid-1973 until the fall of 1974, the ever-cautious Chen promoted Chinese exports and urged that commodity exchange (market and comparative advantage) principles and other policies be employed to expand China's foreign trade and improve its efficiency. A number of these themes resonated with ones Chen had articulated in 1956 and the early 1960s and were to help inspire the open door policy of the late 1970s. But the "Gang of Four"—led by Mao's wife, Jiang Qing—increasingly objected to foreign trade, and the issue became more and more politicized, especially after Deng Xiaoping took over day-to-day policy implementation as Zhou's cancer progressively weakened him. The combination of political conflict and Chen's apparently poor health meant that he was no longer able to continue working on foreign trade issues after mid- to late 1974.[32]

Chen's role in foreign trade is another example of ad hoc procedures and processes used to make the system work, in this case (as in that of the four-man group in 1969) under conditions of political uncertainty and low levels of organizational stability. It also suggests several other things. First, although Mao dominated the policy process, undercurrents or alternative views were present in the system from the 1950s on, and they inspired or were the foundation for the reforms that emerged in the late 1970s and early 1980s, at least in the initial stages. Second, not only were there precursors to economic reforms in the Mao period, but also they were associated with specific views of Chen Yun, a leader of remarkable continuity in the upper reaches of the CCP. From 1978 until his death in 1996, Chen was probably the second-most-influential figure in the CCP. Third, foreign trade expansion grew out of a foreign policy initiative or development. But it appeared that foreign trade was handled through the domestic economic policymaking system. Thus, it was Zhou Enlai who brought Chen back into policymaking circles (with Mao's either tacit or explicit concurrence no doubt). But Mao played a more direct role in establishing the four-man small group in 1969 and in the rehabilitation of Deng Xiaoping in 1973. Given Mao's relative ignorance of economics and his general lack of interest in the subject, he delegated more responsibility in this field to Zhou than the top leader did in areas of greater concern to him.

China's Acceptance of the Comprehensive (Nuclear) Test Ban Treaty

In the summer and fall of 1996, the PRC stated that it would ratify the Comprehensive Test Ban Treaty (CTBT), which bans the testing of all kinds of nuclear devices. Given the recent nature of this announcement, little is known at this time about the actual decision processes involved. Many aspects of China's participation in this nascent regime and whether the regime itself will come into being remain unsettled. Nonetheless, certain insights might be gained and questions raised about the decisionmaking process here.

China had long expressed its dissatisfaction with the Partial Test Ban Treaty of 1968 and, along with France, continued to test nuclear weapons into the 1990s. Moreover, China seemed to be moving from a strategic posture of minimal deterrence to a posture more congruent with limited deterrence. In practice, this change meant greater willingness to consider the use of nuclear weapons as part of war fighting and meant upgrading, diversifying, and increasing the capabilities and numbers of China's nuclear weapons and delivery systems. Minimal deterrence required only a relatively small number of nuclear weapons with no great demands with regard to accuracy; these weapons existed only to deter nuclear blackmail of China. In short, they were not really incorporated in plans for war fighting.[33]

The change in doctrine appeared to coincide with improved weapons, with gradual modernization of parts of the PLA, and with the PLA being seen as playing a critical role in domestic politics as a result of its suppression of the Democracy Movement in 1989. In every year since 1989, the PLA's public budget has increased by more than 10 percent. Moreover, immediately prior to China's decision to ratify the CTBT, a number of analysts and Hong Kong sources argued that the military was promoting a more militant, assertive, and nationalist line in Chinese foreign policy, with a hard line toward the United States and Taiwan the specific areas of contention. Deng Xiaoping's health was so poor and he had become so infirm by early 1996 that it appears that he was not able to intervene in the Chinese political process at that time.[34]

In this context, it is hard to imagine how and why China could come to support the CTBT. Jiang Zemin was thought not to have great influence over military affairs, and although China was apparently moving in the direction of limited deterrence, it is not clear that it had developed the types of nuclear weapons needed for such a defense posture. In short, it appears that nuclear testing would or should have been central to continued pursuit of this stance. To be sure, Chinese leaders have never liked being completely isolated internationally, and after France in 1995 agreed to cease testing, China was the sole major nuclear power that upheld its right to test. But India, a one-time belligerent of China's, refused to ratify the treaty, and it had tested a "nuclear device" in 1974, giving China a possible reason to demur from the CTBT.

China's commitment to ratify the CTBT seems to fly in the face of the interests of China's military. Of course the CTBT may fall apart because of India's unwillingness to accept it, but China's cessation of testing may already have harmed some Chinese national security interests, and China would be under extensive pressure were it to be the only country to test nuclear weapons. From these considerations we might draw the following hypotheses about the policymaking process under Jiang Zemin. First, Jiang's political clout, both generally and vis-à-vis the PLA, is greater than is usually imagined. Second, given Jiang's limited interaction with the military hierarchy, the new commitment suggests that civil-military relations are more institutionalized than is commonly believed. The PLA follows the decisions of the central leadership. Somewhat mitigating against these two hypotheses is a third that suggests China was either able to develop indigenously or acquire from abroad the supercomputer and the advanced software that would allow computer simulations to substitute for actual nuclear testing. As in the United States, Chinese military figures probably prefer actual testing to computer simulations, but they may be willing to accept nuclear test simulations. In this case, China's commitment to the CTBT costs China and the PLA relatively little and earns them some international recognition and approval.

Until serious research is completed, these hypotheses are initial, approximate answers to what may have happened in this case. But China's signing on to the CTBT does appear discordant with many prevailing ideas about Jiang Zemin's power, the clout of the Chinese military, and China's growing "threat" to the world. It is such anomalies that should appropriately stimulate focused empirical and theoretical studies.

These five cases illustrate several aspects about the Chinese foreign policy making process. In general, they reveal the power of the top leader to control the agenda and set the basic terms of overall foreign relations. The cases also show that for the making and supervision of foreign relations, only a small number of high-ranking officials have been involved. If one can generalize from the Korean War decision, it would appear that the number of people involved in key decisions has declined over time and that "rationality" in the policy process may also have declined. The cases also suggest (and reinforce the view expressed above) that linkages across issue areas are relatively weak, and that for the most part, foreign policy decisionmaking is compartmentalized vertically.

These cases are not conclusive, and many other major decisions or activities have taken place in the history of the PRC's foreign relations. Moreover, just because certain patterns may have been present in the past does not mean that they will necessarily continue into the future. Nonetheless, as the hypotheses about the CTBT may indicate, there are reasons to believe that the core leader of the CCP may continue to dominate the formulation of Chinese foreign policy and that the existing organizational patterns of managing the whole gamut of Chinese relations with the outside world will persist.

The Future Evolution of the Chinese Foreign Policy Making System

China has finally passed out of the period of rule by those who made the Chinese revolution. Succeeding Chinese leaders will be better educated and probably less powerful, charismatic, and visionary than Mao or Deng (and their generations). China interacts with the world in more ways, in more depth, and with more complexity than it ever did under Mao and Deng. Limited government capacity and legitimacy color all policy developments. The economy has made extraordinary advances, but there remain many bottlenecks and areas of unsatisfactory performance. Very hard choices confront the leadership about further reform measures, particularly with regard to state-owned enterprises, the banking system, increasing tax revenues, and joining the World Trade Organization. In terms of politics, the succeeding generations of leadership will face the need to relegitimate the regime's position (or at least try to turn hostile feelings toward the regime to apathy or disinterest in the regime's activities to more active support). Given the breakdown of moral order caused first by Maoist radicalism and then the early stages of capitalism, such an effort to restore the regime's base of support is perhaps more difficult than further deepening of the economic reforms. How will these conditions likely affect the foreign policy making system?

The growing depth, complexity, and intensity of China's relations with the outside world have a number of functional consequences for the making of Chinese foreign policy. More Chinese citizens and more Chinese organizations will be involved in foreign-related activities. This involvement will place pressure on the system to develop better coordinating mechanisms to monitor and supervise what is going on and to formulate appropriate policies that fulfill regime interests. One might imagine, therefore, that the membership of the Foreign Affairs Leading Small Group will be expanded to incorporate a broader membership, including perhaps geographically based members (from Hong Kong, Guangdong, and maybe Shanghai) as well as members qualified by their functional specialties, such as the minister of state security.

Such changes in the membership of the FALSG are not likely to be very effective. Coordination will still take place only at very high levels in the system, but reforms have decentralized large amounts of resources and given greater discretionary authority to lower levels in the system. How can foreign-related issues be managed in this increasingly decentralized system? The current pattern might continue, with issues being bucked up to the top levels of the national system for resolution. But this pattern has severe costs in terms of the time it requires of the top decisionmakers, and the decisionmaking system may become overloaded if large numbers of relatively minor issues have to go to the central leadership to be resolved because no other institutional loci of decision and coordination exist. Although there is a clear need that some foreign policy decisionmaking and coordinating bodies at levels other than the top exist, it is not clear in light of China's political structures and culture what sort of organizations are possible and practical here. Moreover, this is hardly a problem confined to China. All states in the post–Cold War era are having trouble managing and coordinating their foreign policies in the context of the "delocalization" of economic production and the true globalization of international capital markets.

What sort of decision rules are likely to exist when foreign policy is made? The fifth case study presented here suggests that Jiang Zemin was sufficiently powerful to get the PLA to go along with a policy that it did not prefer. This case may suggest some continuity, with the core leader's having the final and decisive say on foreign policy issues. But for much of the history of the PRC, security policy was "trumps." The core foreign policy issues were related to security and territorial integrity. This emphasis on security and sovereignty is probably much less important today. Security issues may remain trumps, but the need to confront security issues may occur significantly less often than in the past. As economic and other

issues appear on the foreign relations agenda with more salience than security concerns, one might make the following predictions.

Foreign policy formulation will increasingly resemble domestic economic policy formulation, with extensive bargaining, negotiations, and
deal making. Issues will be more complex and potentially less zero-sum.
The time frame in which the decision must be made will be lengthened
and perhaps stretched indefinitely into the future. Compromise and consensus building will be the key political processes, and bureaucratic politics and interest politics will likely color the positions taken by actors in
policy debates. But the policymaking process for foreign policy is likely
to continue to represent more fully or overrepresent central bureaucratic
interests and underrepresent provincial and local interests.[35] Foreign affairs will remain an area of central government predominance in China
(as in all other countries). Indeed, foreign policy is a key component of
the resources available to the leaders of major powers in building their
domestic authority.[36]

This predicted pattern of policymaking may be only a temporary one.
Given China's size compared to all other countries (except India), if
China's economy continues to grow rapidly and its military continues its
gradual modernization, other countries in the Asia-Pacific will increasingly be forced to consider China the rising power in the region (if they
do not do so already). A number of Asian states have indicated that they
can or will accommodate the rise of Chinese power; others are deferring
a decision whether to accommodate or develop internal resources to enhance their military capabilities and seek external support to bolster their
security; and some are building up their defense capabilities and thinking about the nature of their relations with the United States. Japan seems
to be doing a little of all three. But an arms race or the rise of Chinese
power is likely to move China and the rest of the region back to a situation where security issues appear much more frequently on the political
agendas of all the states in the region. In China, this is likely to mean that
patterns of policymaking that incorporate the military dimension more
fully in the policy process, that limit the ability of leaders to compromise,
both internally and externally, and that have greater short-term consequences and short time frames are likely to predominate. The core leader
is likely to spend much more of his time on foreign policy issues, and his
position will weigh more heavily in the balance than is the case today.
The rewards of success and the costs of foreign policy failure will also be
more directly attributed to the top leader. Thus, the predicted extension
of the decision processes of the domestic political economy to the realm
of foreign policy is likely to be only temporary; the pattern would be
somewhat closer to that of the Mao period, but without the kind of dominance of the foreign policy process that Mao had.

Notes

1. The best of several important English works on these issues is Sergei Goncharov et al., *Uncertain Partners* (Stanford: Stanford University Press, 1993).

2. On the policymaking process generally, some of the best works include: Kenneth Lieberthal and Michel Oksenberg, *Policy Making in China* (Princeton: Princeton University Press, 1988); Kenneth Lieberthal and David M. Lampton, eds., *Bureaucracy, Politics, and Decision Making in Post-Mao China* (Berkeley: University of California Press, 1992); Kenneth Lieberthal, *Governing China* (New York: Norton, 1995), esp. chaps. 6 and 7; and Carol Lee Hamrin and Suisheng Zhao, eds., *Decision-Making in Deng's China* (Armonk, N.Y.: M. E. Sharpe, 1995). Important discussions on foreign policy making (in addition to some of the chapters in the edited works above) include: A. Doak Barnett, *The Making of Foreign Policy in China* (Boulder, Colo.: Westview Press, 1985); Carol Lee Hamrin, "Elite Politics and the Development of China's Foreign Relations," in Thomas Robinson and David Shambaugh, eds., *Chinese Foreign Policy* (Oxford: Oxford University Press, 1994), pp. 70–109; Lu Ning, *The Dynamics of Foreign Policy Decisionmaking in China* (Boulder, Colo.: Westview Press, 1997); Michael Swaine, *The Role of the Chinese Military in National Security Policymaking* (Santa Monica, Calif.: Rand Corporation, 1996); and Xu Jiatun, *Xu Jiatun Xiang Gang Huiyi Lu* [Xu Jiatun's Hong Kong memoirs] (Hong Kong: Lianhe Bao Yeshu, 1992).

3. See David Bachman, "The Limits of Leadership in China," *Asian Survey* 32:11 (November 1992): 1046–1062; "Succession, Consolidation, and Transition in China's Future," *Journal of Northeast Asian Studies* 15: 1 (Spring 1996): 89 106; and "Succession Politics and China's Future," *Journal of International Affairs* 49:2 (Winter 1996): 370–389.

4. Thomas J. Christensen, "Chinese Realpolitik," *Foreign Affairs* 75:5 (September-October 1996): 37–52; and Alastair Iain Johnston, *Cultural Realism* (Princeton: Princeton University Press, 1995), for an early period with resonances today.

5. On *waijiao*, meaning diplomatic interchange, see e.g., Han Nianlong, chief ed., *Dangdai Zhongguo Waijiao* [New China's diplomacy] (Beijing: Zhongguo Shehui Kexue Chubanshe, 1990); and Pei Jianzhang, chief ed., *Xin Zhongguo Waijiao Fengyun* [The storms of New China's diplomacy], 3 vols. (Beijing: Shijie Zhishi Chubanshe, 1990, 1991, and 1994, respectively).

6. Most of these campaigns are discussed in Zhou Keyu, chief ed., *Dangdai Zhongguo Junduide Junshi Gongzuo, shang* [The military affairs of contemporary China's army, Vol. 1] (Beijing: Zhongguo Shehui Kexue Chubanshe, 1989).

7. The nuclear, submarine, and missile programs are examined in John Wilson Lewis and Xue Litai, *China Builds the Bomb* (Stanford: Stanford University Press, 1988); idem, *China's Strategic Seapower* (Stanford: Stanford University Press, 1994); and John Wilson Lewis and Hua Di, "China's Ballistic Missile Programs: Technologies, Strategies, Goals," *International Security* 17:2 (Fall 1992): 5–40.

8. On foreign economic involvement prior to the open door policy, see Shen Jueren, principal ed., *Dangdai Zhongguo Duiwai Maoyi* [Foreign trade of contemporary China], 2 vols. (Beijing: Dangdai Zhongguo Chubanshe, 1992); *Chen Yun Wen Xuan, di san juan* [Selected works of Chen Yun, Vol. 3] (Beijing: Renmin chubanshe, 1995), pp. 155–159; 216–229; and Lewis and Xue, "China's Ballistic Missile Programs."

9. Background on these issues is found in Shi Lin, principal ed., *Dangdai Zhongguo de Duiwai Jingji Hezuo* [External economic cooperation of contemporary China] (Beijing: Zhongguo Shehui Kexue Chubanshe, 1989); Stephen Fitzgerald, *China and the Overseas Chinese* (Cambridge: Cambridge University Press, 1972); and Xu, *Xu Jiatun*.

10. Also see Lieberthal and Oksenberg, *Policy Making in China*; Lieberthal and Lampton, *Bureaucracy, Politics, and Decision Making in Post-Mao China*; Lieberthal, *Governing China*; and Hamrin and Zhao, *Decision-Making in Deng's China*; as well as Barnett, *The Making of Foreign Policy in China*; Hamrin, "Elite Politics"; Lu, *The Dynamics of Foreign Policy Decisionmaking*; Swaine, *The Role of the Chinese Military*; and Xu, *Xu Jiatun*. The account herein is particularly influenced by Lu and Swaine.

11. See Bachman, "The Limits of Leadership in China"; "Succession, Consolidation, and Transition"; and "Succession Politics and China's Future." On the centrality of the issue of the "core," see Tang Tsou, "The Tiananmen Tragedy," in Brantly Womack, ed., *Contemporary Chinese Politics in Historical Perspective* (Cambridge: Cambridge University Press, 1991), pp. 265–328, esp. pp. 287–295. Jiang Zemin is actually in the fourth generation of CCP leaders (those born in the 1920s). The real third generation (those born in the 1910s) have all retired, been purged, or died. They include Zhao Ziyang, Hu Yaobang, and Wan Li.

12. Although the Mao-Zhou relationship is well known, the roles being described here of "core" and chief lieutenant do not necessarily imply regular contact between core and lieutenant. Thus, in the last half of 1986, Deng Xiaoping only met with Zhao Ziyang twice, according to one of Zhao's former secretaries (personal communication). Jiang Zemin and Li Peng see each other much more regularly, though Li may see himself more as junior partner than chief lieutenant.

13. See Lieberthal and Oksenberg, *Policy Making in China*, esp. chaps. 3 and 4; Lieberthal, *Governing China*, pp. 192–208; Jonathan D. Pollack, "Structure and Process in the Chinese Military System," in Lieberthal and Lampton, *Bureaucracy, Politics, and Decision Making*, pp. 151–179; and Hamrin and Zhao, *Decision-Making in Deng's China*, pp. 3–129. An argument on the beginning of the breakdown of the vertical aspects of the overall system is found in Zhao Quansheng, "Domestic Factors of Chinese Foreign Policy," *Annals* 519 (January 1992): 158–175.

14. The following is taken from Lu Ning, *Dynamics of Foreign Policy Decisionmaking*, p. 107.

15. Lu, *Dynamics of Foreign Policy Decisionmaking*, p. 107; and Hamrin, "Elite Politics," pp. 110–112.

16. Personal communications about Jiang as FALSG head. Swaine reports on the Taiwan Affairs group: Swaine, *The Role of the Chinese Military*. The other positions are common knowledge.

17. Lu, *Dynamics of Foreign Policy Decisionmaking*, pp. 107–108, 187–190. Lu was a Foreign Ministry official, and his account of the foreign policy process emphasizes the role of that body.

18. On the evolving membership of the CMC, see Lei Yuanshen, "Zhongyang Junshi Weiyuanhui de Yan'ge" [The evolution of the Central Military Commission], *Zhonggong Dangshi Ziliao 34* [Material on CCP history, hereafter ZGDSZL] (Beijing: Zhonggong Dangshi Ziliao Chubanshe, 1990), pp. 218–237, esp. pp. 224–227.

19. On the membership of the Secretariat, see Ma Qibin et al., *Zhongguo Gongchandang Zhizheng Sishi Nian* [The Chinese Communist Party's forty years in power], rev. ed. (Beijing: Zhonggong Dangshi Chubanshe, 1991), pp. 587, 591, and 614

20. See Ma Qibin, *Zhongguo Gongchandang Zhizheng Sishi Nian*, p. 588. On the importance of the Secretariat under Hu, see Barnett, *Making of Foreign Policy in China*, esp. pp. 9–12.

21. *Zhonghua Renmin Gongheguo Jingji Guanli Dashiji* [Chronology of major events in PRC economic management] (Beijing: Jingji Chubanshe, 1986), p. 106. Technically, the CCP designated the Ministry of National Defense to undertake this role, but that ministry is largely an empty shell, and in fact, the General Staff Department handles the role. See Lu, *Dynamics of Foreign Policy Decisionmaking*, pp. 12–13, n. 17.

22. On the struggles in the CMC, see Lewis and Xue, *China Builds the Bomb*, esp. pp. 121–134; idem, *China's Strategic Seapower*, esp. pp. 33–39 and 75–88; Zhang Yunsheng, *Maojiwan Jishi* [A true account of Maojiwan] (Beijing: Chunqiu Chubanshe, 1988), passim; Ma Qibin, *Zhongguo Gongchandang Zhizheng Sishi Nian*, pp. 589–590; and Lei Yuanshen, "Zhongyang Junshi Weiyuanhui de Yan'ge," pp. 227–230. See also Frederick C. Teiwes and Warren Sun, *The Tragedy of Lin Biao* (Honolulu: University of Hawaii Press, 1996).

23. "Zhang Aiping Article Remembers Luo Ruiqing," in Foreign Broadcast Information Service, *Daily Report, China*, August 12, 1988, pp. 30–33, quotation on p. 32.

24. On the Central Special Commission, see Lewis and Xue, *China Builds the Bomb*, esp. pp. 126–134; and idem, *China's Strategic Seapower*, pp. 78–81, 262, n. 43.

25. On the four-man group, see Xiong Xianghui, "Dakai Zhong-Mei Guanxide Qianzou" [Prelude to the opening of Sino-American relations], ZGDSZL 42 (1992), pp. 56–96. Brief reports about this group and its role are in a variety of other sources.

26. For a quasi-official discussion of the planning process in foreign trade, see Shen Jueren, *Dangdai Zhongguo Duiwai Maoyi*, vol. 1, pp. 178–201. The best western assessment of the pre-reform system and some of the changes since 1978 is Nicholas R. Lardy, *Foreign Trade and Economic Reform in China, 1978–1990* (Cambridge: Cambridge University Press, 1992), chaps. 2 and 3.

27. See Goncharov et al., *Uncertain Partners*, pp. 176–187, among other sources.

28. Among materials on Wang Jiaxiang, see Cong Jin, *Quzhe Fazhan de Suiyue* [Years of tortuous advance] (Zhengzhou: Henan Renmin Chubanshe, 1991), pp. 500–502, 575–581; *Wang Jiaxiang Xuanji* [Selected works of Wang Jiaxiang] (Beijing: Renmin Chubanshe, 1989), pp. 444–445, 446–460; *Mao Zedong Waijiao Wen Xuan* [Selected diplomatic writings of Mao Zedong] (Beijing: Zhongyang Wenxian Chubanshe, 1994), pp. 421–435, 444–447, 470–471, 472–477, and 478–479; and Eric Hyer, "Defining China" (unpublished manuscript).

29. Bo Yibo, *Ruogan Zhongda Juece yu Shijian de Huigu, xia* [Recollections of certain important decisions and events, Vol. 2] (Beijing: Zhonggong Zhongyang Dangxiao Chubanshe, 1993), pp. 1103–1104.

30. The leading western studies are Barry Naughton, "The Third Front," *China Quarterly*, no. 115 (September 1988): 351–386; idem, "Industrial Policy During the Cultural Revolution," in William A. Joseph et al., eds., *New Perspectives on the Cul-*

tural Revolution (Cambridge: Harvard Contemporary China Series, No. 8, 1991), pp. 153–182; and Lewis and Xue, *China's Strategic Seapower*, chap. 4.

31. Major Chinese sources here include: Bo Yibo, *Ruogan Zhongda Juece yu Shijian de Huigu*, chap. 41; Cong Jin, *Quzhe Fazhan de Suiyue,,* pp. 461–469; Xiao Min and Kong Fanmin, "San Xian Jianshe de Zhengce, Buju, he Jianshe" [The policy, overall arrangement, and construction of the Third Front], *Jingji Kexue* [Economic Science], no. 2 (1989): 63–67, 40; *Mao Zedong Sixiang Wansui!* [Long live the thought of Mao Zedong] (n.p.: n.p., 1969), pp. 494–499; and "Liu Shi Niandai San Xian Jianshe Juece Wenxian Xuanzai" [Selected documents on the Third Front decisions of the 1960s], DDWX, no. 3 (1995): 33–41.

32. On Chen, see David Bachman, Chen Yun and the Chinese Political System (Berkeley: Center for Chinese Studies Research Monograph No. 29, 1985). On Chen's specific role in the early 1970s, see Chen Yun Wen Xuan, pp. 216–229; Sun Yeli and Xiong Lianghua, *Gongheguo Jingji Fengyunzhongde Chen Yun* [Chen Yun in the midst of the economic storms of the PRC] (Beijing: Zhongyang Wenxian Cubanshe, 1996), pp. 264–277. On the dynamics of the conflict over foreign trade in the final years of Mao's reign, see, among others, Ann Fenwick, "Chinese Foreign Trade and the Campaign Against Deng Xiaoping," in Thomas Fingar, ed., *China's Quest for Independence* (Boulder, Colo.: Westview Press, 1980), pp. 199–224.

33. These developments in China's military doctrine are discussed (in excellent fashion) in Alastair Iain Johnston, "China's New 'Old' Thinking," *International Security* 20, no. 3 (Winter 1995/96): 5–42.

34. On these developments, see Allen S. Whiting, "Chinese Nationalism and Foreign Policy after Deng," *China Quarterly*, no. 142 (June 1995): 295–316; John W. Garver, *Face-off* (Seattle: University of Washington Press, 1997); and Willy Wo-Lap Lam, *China After Deng Xiaoping* (Singapore: John Wiley, 1995), chap. 4. Swaine, *The Role of the Chinese Military*, pp. 12–18, questions the reliability of a number of the sources used by Whiting, Garver, Lam, and others.

35. On the domestic economic decision making process, see Lieberthal and Oksenberg, *Policy Making in China*, passim; Lieberthal and Lampton, *Bureaucracy, Politics, and Decision Making*, esp. pp. 1–58; and Susan Shirk, *The Political Logic of Economic Reform in China* (Berkeley: University of California Press, 1993).

36. On the importance of foreign policy for the leader's power and authority, see Franz Schurmann, "After Desert Storm," in Meredith Woo-Cumings and Michael Loriaux, eds. *Past as Prelude* (Boulder, Colo.: Westview Press, 1993), pp. 179–216.

3

International Structures and Chinese Foreign Policy

ALASTAIR IAIN JOHNSTON

It is true but trite to argue that Chinese foreign policy is a product of both international and domestic factors. What should interest us are the following questions: Which variables matter more than others? What are their interactive effects? What are the plausible hypotheses about causal relationships between these factors and behavior? How should we go about testing as rigorously and as reproducibly as possible? Since Chapter 2 looks at domestic sources of foreign policy, this chapter will focus on international sources. Specifically, it will examine the relationship between international "structures" and Chinese foreign policy.

Typically, Chinese foreign policy studies that focus on international "factors," "forces," and "pressures" argue that these constrain the policy options Chinese decisionmakers have to work with, most commonly by defining the kinds of threats China faces. But it is less common to find these arguments rooted in well-constructed, logical, and theoretically self-conscious models of what particular "factors" limit these options in which particular ways. The implicit, sometimes explicit, starting point is a fairly traditional balance-of-power perspective, where China responds to external threats in an obviously self-interested, security-maximizing way. Thus "leaning to the Soviet side" in 1950 was a predictable response to the external pressure the United States and the nationalists on Taiwan generated on a weak, new socialist state. And leaning to the U.S. side in the early 1970s was a predictable response to a real, growing Soviet threat. The problematic deviant case—the dual-adversary period of the 1960s—tends to be blamed on Maoist ideological interference in a "correct" reading of international signals.

There are, however, some major and frequent empirical anomalies in the history of state alliance behavior that raise doubts about this kind of "predictable" power-balancing behavior. Not all states balance through alliance: Some "bandwagon for profit"; some capitulate; some hide; some balance internally through arming. Some balance badly; some overbalance. Some misread the nature of these external threats and underestimate them. Some misread these threats and overestimate them. Some base their threat assessments on the military capabilities of other states. Some base their assessments on dominant interpretations of the nature or disposition or identity of the "aggressor" state, independent of its material capabilities. IR scholars heatedly debate the theoretical bases for what is clearly a very diverse set of empirical observations about state behavior.[1] This lack of agreement should be a signal that traditional balance-of-power arguments may also be problematic in the study of Chinese foreign policy.

What follows is a look at how a particular kind of international "factor" might affect Chinese foreign policy, namely, international "structure." In particular, there are two kinds of structures, the existence and effects of which are at the core of IR theory debates today: material power structures and normative structures.[2] The former refer to particular distributions of material power capabilities—typically the focus of analysis is on the number of poles. Polarity is one of the key ontological features of neorealist theory. The latter refer to particular patterns among states in what is considered socially appropriate behavior—typically the focus of analysis is on the content, strength, and distribution of injunctive or prescriptive norms. Norms are central to social constructivist claims about how and why states behave the way they do. That is, constructivists give ontological status to the social interactions by which norms are produced and diffused.[3]

International Structures: Some Definitional Issues

Before turning to these two kinds of international structures, we need to be clear about what international structures are not about. They are not about the discrete influence attempts of particular outside actors on China. There are many actors/entities/processes that are external to China. It is obvious that what Chinese leaders can or can't do is constrained, say, by the World Bank's conditions for loans. Structural analysis is not interested in who or what *is* outside China and how outside actors constrain Chinese options. It is interested in how these individual actors outside China interact with one another and with China so that the product of this interaction limits Chinese options.

Structural effects are, after all, the not-wholly-intended consequences of the interaction of members of a system, for each member. That is, system effects are constraints produced by unit interaction. Polarity is a result of the uneven distribution of material capabilities among states in the anarchical international system. The "invisible hand" of market forces is the product of the interaction among profit-maximizing firms in a perfectly competitive environment. Emergent international norms are the products of particular distributions of normative interests. The constraints these structural effects place on actors should not be confused with discrete influence attempts or "external pressure" from individual actors in the system.

Structural effects can be more or less severe and constraining. Few structuralists claim to be narrow determinists, who say that actors have no agency except to choose among the very narrowest range of options. Rather, actors choose among a narrowed range of alternatives, but within this range other, domestically grounded, independent variables may kick in and affect particular decisions. These boundaries may be narrower or wider, but they are passive, and they give agents some leeway. In Dessler's words, "Structure alone explains only the possibilities (and impossibilities) of action."[4]

Within this broad argument, however, one can discern a major fault line over the relative importance of actor intentions. There are those for whom intentions are generally unimportant. This kind of structuralist often points to all the unintended but important consequences of intentional behavior to suggest that a focus on the intentions of units is misguided if one wants to explain outcomes.[5] This lack of attention to intentions is particularly the case for those focusing on material power structures, such as neorealists. Many intentional actors, interacting, create many unintentional outcomes (namely, particular distributions of power) that constrain intentional behavior in the next iteration. The metaphors for this kind of structuralism are *a perfect market* and *the microeconomics of firm behavior.*

The second view argues there is a great deal of mutual influence between intentional actors and structural constraints. That is, agency matters. A system of great powers, or even a system where issue-specific power matters, is not a perfect market. The better analogy is an oligopoly, where the intended actions of a few have major effects on the market. That then raises questions and doubts about purely structural models that leave out actor characteristics, intentions, and purposes, as well as efforts to change the constraints under which they operate. These questions and doubts are the essence of critiques of neorealism that link realists such as Randall Schweller to constructivists such as Alexander Wendt. For Schweller, the effects of particular distributions of power under anarchy will differ for states, depending on whether the system is one of status quo actors or one of revisionist actors. In the former, states will be inclined to explore ways of reassuring others that they are not a threat and to codify the status quo. In the latter, states will be inclined to exploit one another and to compete both for security and for the power to distribute that which is valued in the system.[6] In a similar vein, Wendt notes that an anarchy of friends is very different from one of enemies. The difference is in the character of the history of social interaction among states—do they have a history of interaction that leads to identification as friends or enemies?[7] Both he and Schweller refer to these differences as alternative "distributions of interests"; different distributions of interest determine the effects of different distributions of material power.

There is, finally, the question whether structural approaches are even appropriate for explaining the foreign policy of particular actors. Neorealists say that they do not purport to offer a theory of foreign policy. Rather, they argue, their theory can explain only outcomes (war, peace, polarity), not the actions of individual units. Yet precisely because states worry about preserving autonomy and about the security disadvantages from unfavorable relative gains, they are likely to *intend to* act to prevent other states or coalitions from dominating the system.[8] It is hard to see how a balancing outcome would be produced if most of the major actors in the system refused to balance.[9]

Those who focus on normative structures are interested in how norms are produced at time t, diffused at $t + 1$, internalized at $t + 2$, and then reproduced or changed through the practice of states at $t + 3$. For constructivists, then, both outcomes (which norms dominate the international system at any particular time?) and discrete actions of states (how are norms internalized and then reproduced in practice by purposeful agents?) are of analytical interest. The interactive, feedback (or constitutive) relationship between norms and state practice and the prominent role given to agency and intentionality by constructivists lend constructivism a certain kind of foreign policy determinism. Although there is almost invariably some slippage between dominant international norms and the foreign policy practice of individual states, all behavior exhibits the influence of some norms and all norms exhibit some level of influence on behavior. That is because norms are ubiquitous. There is no behavior that is normless. This conclusion leads to some tricky methodological problems in observing and measuring the effect of norms, but these problems are no different from the problems in arguments that all behavior is a function of the rational pursuit of material interests.

In sum, structural approaches to Chinese foreign policy should focus on how the interaction of units (states for neorealists; states, international organizations (IOs), NGOs, individuals, indeed any actor with agency in IR for constructivists) creates external conditions that limit the policy options available to Chinese decisionmakers. The options can be delimited in at least four ways. The first is through socialization where certain options are simply dropped off the agenda or dramatically devalued, as value change deems them too costly or normatively inappropriate. Even mate rial structural approaches, such as neorealism, contend that fully social ized states are those that will pursue only balancing strategies. The second is through changes in internal politics. Structural pressures can affect do mestic balances of power, say, by undermining the position of soft-liners in the policy process or by building up certain constituencies with new in terests.[10] Alternatively, norms may affect the policy process through legis lation that embodies or institutionalizes these international norms.[11] Third, structures can place such severe physical constraints on states that certain options are simply impossible to implement. Finally, structures can alter the cost-benefit estimates of policy options without changing or narrowing the plausible range of options available. This chapter will not be able to examine these processes in much detail, but they are mentioned here because understanding structural effects doesn't require theorizing just about which ones exist and how they are produced, but about pre cisely how they are supposed to affect China's behavior.

Material Structures

The predominant arguments about material power structures in IR come from neorealist theory. Neorealism's influence on IR theory has been pro found. Not only has it nourished a couple of very rich generations of re search in security studies, but many of its basic assumptions underpin mainstream institutionalist approaches to international political econ omy as well. Neorealism starts from some very simple assumptions about the interplay of state interests and international structure and spins out the following logic: States are the basic units of analysis in the inter national system. States want to survive—this means their main goals are security and autonomy from others' control. States can be treated as ra tional actors—pursuing strategies that are most likely to maximize some measure of security and autonomy. Sovereign states interacting together operate under conditions of anarchy where there is no supreme authority governing their relationships. Thus there is a high degree of uncertainty in the system about the ability to survive. No one state can be sure an other isn't out to threaten its security and autonomy.[12] Under these condi tions, the prudent thing to do is to prepare for the worst, namely, to have the capabilities of ensuring security and autonomy through economic and military power.[13] Different states have different abilities to mobilize and extract resources (e.g., different resource endowments, levels of tech nology, levels of government efficiency), and the system will be charac terized by the uneven development and distribution of power. Thus the security and autonomy of any one state will be more or less threatened by different distributions in power in the system. That means states all have an interest in preventing the system's being dominated by any one state or coalition—a hegemon. Thus states have an interest in balancing against rising powers. Balancing can be done two ways—internally (relying on one's own resources to arm) and externally (relying relatively more on others' resources by allying and/or by pooling military power). Internal balancing is preferred because it maximizes autonomy (since alliances entail sacrificing some decision power to an ally and they raise the danger of being abandoned or entrapped).

From this logic, neorealists can come up with a number of fairly discrete predictions about the basic strategic behavior of a major but non-pole power such as China. Put simply, China ought to balance against whichever state constitutes the dominant or rising pole in the international system. Unfortunately, neorealists are none too clear about how states identify which one is a pole or how they measure the pace and direction of change in the relative power of prospective poles.[14] The difficulties of measuring change in distributions of power don't, however, undermine the basic prediction.

Fortunately, the normal ambiguities in measuring power and observing change in its distribution are ameliorated substantially in the case of the dramatic 1991 collapse of the USSR. There was a clear and rapid redistribution of material power in the international system, the kind one normally sees after major systemic wars. The United States emerged as the only superpower and the world entered a "unipolar moment."[15] As Figure 3.1 indicates,[16] the U.S. share of world military expenditures jumped dramatically with the collapse of the Soviet Union. In military power terms, the United States is the dominant actor. Thus it is plausible to assume for the purposes of testing neorealist balance-of-power theory that the end of the Cold War constituted a shift in polarity from a bipolar to a near-unipolar or highly asymmetrical multipolar system, where the United States is the one candidate hegemon.[17] From 1991 on, China therefore ought to have been balancing against the United States.

The evidence for balancing, however, is shaky. Some of the pathologies of balancing do not show up. For example, China's military expenditures have not risen in real terms at a rate one would expect if it had been trying to balance against U.S. hegemony. Although the statistics are inconsistent, the Pentagon has suggested that real growth in Chinese military expenditures (ME) has been around 40 percent from 1989 through 1994, or about 8 percent per year. The United States General Accounting Office estimates only a 6.4 percent real growth between 1987 and 1993, whereas Arms Control and Disarmament Agency (ACDA) figures for military expenditures in constant dollars also suggest relatively slow growth after 1989.[18] Military expenditures as a percentage of GDP and central government expendi-

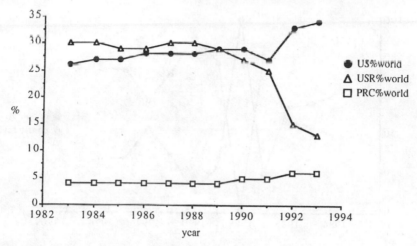

FIGURE 3.1   U.S., Russian, and Chinese Shares of World Military Expenditures
SOURCE: Arms Control and Disarmament Agency, World Military Expenditures,
1995 (Washington, D.C.: 1996).

tures also do not show an economy becoming increasingly militarized to deal with the shift in global power after 1991. Whether counting nominal or real military expenditures, one sees that these percentages have dropped over the 1980s and 1990s, showing no obvious reaction to the emergence of the United States as the sole remaining superpower.

A balancing state could also be expected to develop operational capabilities to deal with potential military threats from the system hegemon. Chinese military acquisition patterns after the collapse of the USSR do not indicate a particularly alarmed balancing directed at the United States. Rather, the PLA has been modernizing to deal with a range of contingencies, from border conflicts with India, to naval conflicts over the South China Sea, to operations against Taiwan. There is some discussion in military writings on modern high-tech war that suggest the United States, among other high-tech militaries, is the standard for which China should aim.[19] But these trends in doctrinal thinking were rooted in the "strategic decision" of 1985 to shift China's force posture away from dealing with a Soviet blitzkrieg and toward the management of local, limited high-tech wars. This shift was reinforced with more vigor after the Gulf War, but its origins are in the mid-1980s, not the post–Cold War redistribution of power.

Thus it seems that little internal balancing obviously directed at the U.S. consolidation of its post-1991 hegemony has been going on. What about external balancing? Neorealism suggests that states will also balance against the existing or emerging hegemon(s) by joining or construct-

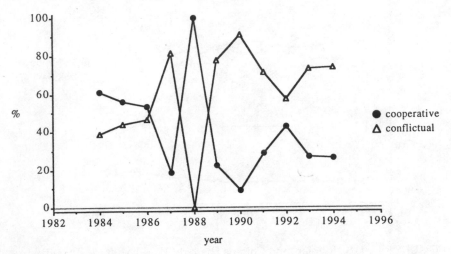

FIGURE 3.2   PRC Actions Directed at the United States: Cooperative and Con-
flictual Percentages
SOURCE: Kansas Events Data System/Protocol for the Assessment of Nonviolent
Direct Action (KEDS/PANDA) database.

ing security alliances aimed at containing the hegemon. At the same time
the state should try to loosen or undermine any alliance structures that
buttress the hegemon's power. That suggests that China ought to be
searching for allies and partners with which to coordinate in balancing
against the United States.

Certainly China has been acting less cooperatively toward the United
States since the end of the Cold War, as both quantitative events data (see
Figure 3.2)[20] and the stories of conflicts over trade, proliferation, human
rights, and the Taiwan question all suggest. There is also a moderate negative correlation between Chinese military expenditures in constant dollars
and the intensity ($r = -.26$) and proportion ($r = -.22$) of cooperative actions
directed toward the United States from 1984 to 1994, as one would have
expected if China had been balancing against the United States.[21]

However, as the percentage of cooperative and conflictual actions in
Figure 3.2 indicates, the precipitous drop in overall cooperative behavior
occurred in 1989, *prior* to the collapse of bipolarity. This shift was triggered primarily by the June 4 crisis and the effect this had in souring both
U.S. and Chinese perceptions of the intentions of the other in a range of
other issues. Structural change appears not to be the key causal variable
in this alienation in the relationship.

Even if the initial trigger of this decline in Chinese cooperative signaling occurred on June 4, did perhaps the emergence of the United States as
the dominant state in the system in 1991 inject new life into China's cal-

culus? If so, China should have tried to improve relations with potential adversaries of the United States and even to coordinate anti-U.S. policies with them. The principle ought to be a soundly realpolitik one—the enemy of my enemy is my friend. To be sure, China has worked hard to build up political and economic relationships with Iran and Iraq. But these relationships existed well before the emergence of the United States as the lone superpower. The Chinese had a number of motivations: to have at least some voice and presence in another region (as major powers must, in Beijing's view), to maintain good relations with radical Islamic states in order to understand better the sensitive political/strategic issue of Islamic fundamentalism on and within Chinese borders; to establish reliable energy supplies, as economic growth has changed China from an oil exporter to an oil importer; and to have an arms client that the United States doesn't especially like so that China can, if necessary, link its arms sales to the Middle East to U.S. arms sales to Taiwan.

China also ought to have been trying to consolidate relations with existing allies and strategic partners, particularly those whose relations with the United States have declined. The exemplar, of course, is Pakistan. But the dominant Chinese motivation in its security relationship is to arm Pakistan so that Pakistan will help divert Indian military resources away from China.[22] As for PRC relations with its one formal ally, a sworn adversary of the United States, North Korea, these have deteriorated, as China has used behind-the-scenes pressure to convince the North Korean regime to adopt an economic reform program, to rejoin the NPT, and to join four-party armistice talks. Indeed, despite the fact that China still has a military alliance with North Korea, Beijing has signaled that it does not consider this commitment to be particularly hard and fast. During Jiang Zemin's state visit to South Korea in 1995, a Chinese Foreign Ministry spokesperson stated that the alliance did not commit Chinese troops to defend North Korea.[23]

According to structural-balancing theory, we might also expect China to be trying to undermine U.S. relationships with other major players in the system, including U.S. allies. Since 1996 the Chinese government has become more publicly critical of U.S. bilateral alliances in East Asia—most notably the U.S.-Japan security treaty. But privately, many Chinese analysts and officials continue to indicate a preference for a continued, though constrained, U.S. security relationship with Japan so as to restrain Japanese military power, at least for the time being.[24] As for South Korea, another formal U.S. ally, China moved quickly to consolidate friendly political and economic relations with Seoul—establishing diplomatic recognition in 1992.

Sino-Russian relations have improved since 1991, despite Chinese invective directed at Yeltsin for undermining socialism in the former Soviet Union. The two countries have negotiated settlements for most of the disputed border areas, and in 1992 they concluded formal bilateral confidence building measures (CBMs) mandating the withdrawal of military forces along the border back by 100 kilometers. China has also made a couple of high-profile purchases of weapons systems—SU-27s, SA-10 SAMs (surface-to-air missiles), and two destroyers armed with long-range antiship missiles. However, none of this signals a concerted anti-U.S. security coordination between the two states. Indeed, the Chinese are worried about Russian-U.S. military collusion against China. The 1995 Clinton-Yeltsin communiqué pledging joint development of theater missile defense (TMD) systems raised concerns in Beijing. Moreover, there are serious perceptual problems in the Sino-Russian relationship, not the least of which are Russian fears that China is deliberately flooding Siberia with workers and businesspeople. Chinese exports to Russia as a percentage of Chinese exports to the United States stood at about 6 percent in 1994–1995. Chinese trade with Russia accounted for about 2 percent of China's total trade, as compared with 15 percent for trade with the United States.

Thus, there is little evidence of the kind of security coordination with U.S. adversaries directed at the United States that China developed with the United States and its allies and directed against the Soviet Union in the 1970s and 1980s. At the moment, China is not trying hard to manufacture an anti-U.S. united front, nor is it obviously trying to undermine U.S. security commitments to other states.

Finally, if China were balancing against the United States because of the change in polarity, one should also see China trying to reduce its economic dependence on the United States. If a state perceives that the relative gains of economic interaction may be used to develop the military power of potential adversaries, then it has an interest in reducing its trade with these adversaries and in diversifying its economic linkages with more strategically reliable partners.[25] That is especially the case if the asymmetry in trade dependence could be used as a political lever against the side relatively more dependent on trade. This has not happened, however. China's dependence on U.S. markets has increased, not decreased, since 1991. In the mid-1980s about 10 percent of China's trade was with the United States, according to PRC data. By 1993 the figure had reached about 14 percent, and for the period from August 1994 through August 1995, the figure was 15 percent.[26] Exports to the United States as a share of all China's exports jumped even more dramatically after 1991, from around 9 percent in 1991 to around 18 percent in 1993.[27] Chinese military expenditures are positively correlated with the percent of China's total trade that is with the United States ($r = .67$). In other words, even if increases in China's military expenditures in recent years were part of a balancing strategy against the United States, Beijing would be undermining its strategy by doing little to reduce the potentially negative security externalities of trade with its adversary. If China were truly balancing, there ought to be a negative correlation over time between trade dependence and military expenditures.

All this evidence against material structural-balancing arguments in a unipolar era raises an interesting question: Was China's reaction to bipolarity in the past similarly "autistic"? This is not an idle question. If material structural arguments are wrong about the 1990s, then they may also be wrong about the 1950s through the 1980s. If they are not wrong about the 1950s to 1980s, then either Chinese behavior in the 1990s is anomalous (and therefore requires explaining) or my analysis is wrong. If the material structural arguments are wrong, then this requires rethinking explanations for China's behavior in its relationships with the superpowers in the past. This is not the place for a rigorous retest of structural balancing theory on past Chinese foreign policy. What follows is a suggestive, more anecdotal reexamination of standard arguments about Chinese balancing behavior.

Michael Ng Quinn makes the case that the material structuralists were right about the past. Balancing options were limited by bipolarity.[28] As a weak state, China had no choice but to lean to one side, and it leaned to the side that was less powerful and less threatening. When it tried to stake out an equidistantly hostile position, it paid for it. It was diplomatically and economically isolated for much of the mid-1960s, when it pursued a dual-adversary strategy, and its security diminished appreciably, as it faced both a hostile United States in Vietnam and a hostile Soviet Union to the north.[29]

But the constraints of the international power structure, in reality, were not so straightforward. Balance-of-power theory gets a lot wrong—China should have stayed aligned with Soviets until early 1970s, as the United States was the dominant superpower from 1945 to 1972, according to Correlates of War data.[30] What is more, China should have staked out an equidistant position between the superpowers in the mid-1980s, when the United States and Soviet Union had stalemated (after the Reagan military buildup), or even leaned toward the Soviets when usable Soviet power atrophied under Gorbachev's new thinking. Yet, despite rhetoric about an "independent foreign policy," China continued, essentially, to cooperate with the United States on issues of strategic importance to China—Afghanistan and Vietnam. Well past the announcement of the independent foreign policy line, internal circulation materials continued to argue that the Soviets were the main threat to China, and that China would have to maintain closer strategic ties with the United States.[31] And, indeed, U.S.-Chinese overt and tacit cooperation in intelligence sharing, military-to-military ties, even on some arms control issues, deepened after the announcement of the so-called independent line.

Structural-balancing theory also predicts that a major power should try to increase its relative power *in response to* disadvantageous changes in distributions of power. China's most intensive push to increase relative power was the Great Leap Forward. Yet the Great Leap was only loosely connected to changes in international material structures—Mao's goal was primarily to compete for status (secondarily for security) with the great powers, to "surpass" Britain, to create the means to compete with the Americans, and to develop the material base to reduce reliance on the Soviets.[32] There was no change in the global distribution of material power that prompted this sudden push to increase status. Once a state's basic security is assured, there is nothing about international structure that says the state should be as powerful as the other major powers, or that it should play as important a role in world affairs. Here we are compelled to look at the interpretive lenses through which Chinese leaders viewed China's relationship to the rest of the world. Where did China's identity as a state deserving of great power status come from? This is a question of the nationalist historical legacy, the hubris inherited from the past myths of greatness and institutionalized in modern Chinese nationalist ideology. Indeed, Mao was even willing to behave in ways that *jeopardized* China's security in order to preserve or expand China's autonomy and independence as a major player. In 1958, for instance, he rejected closer coordination with Soviets on military affairs—at a time when U.S. policy had taken a more hostile turn toward China.[33] He alienated his Soviet allies to the point where they withdrew offers to transfer nuclear weapons know-how. And then when this mobilization of resources during the Great Leap led to a decline in relative power in the early 1960s—economic depression hit before China's nuclear deterrent was developed—Mao dealigned from the USSR and adopted a more hostile attitude toward the United States.

But what about rapprochement with the United States due to Soviet threat—isn't that a predictable and rational response to structural pressures, a realization the system (in this case increased Soviet threat) was punishing China for its decade of dual adversariness? Rapprochement was indeed a rational response, given the realpolitik assumptions of the Chinese leadership, but it was a response to a change in the direction of threat, not to a change in the distribution of power. Thus it is not behavior determined by material *structure*. The United States was still the dominant economic and military power in 1968–1969, and yet Mao began to explore a strategy of balancing with the United States. Moreover, the Soviet threat was a threat, to some extent, that Mao helped create. It was partly a result of failed diplomacy of the 1960s—a *failure* to balance as the system dictated with the weaker pole (USSR)—largely due to domestic political reasons related to Maoist ideology and Chinese nationalism, not to structural forces. The change in threat assessment had nothing causal to do with change in the relative power of the two poles—the relative power didn't change appreciably prior to 1968–1969.[34] Rather, the change was in Mao's assessment of Soviet intentions, given the Soviet invasion of Czechoslovakia and the Brezhnev doctrine. Threat perceptions changed, whereas capability distributions were essentially constant. The "signal" indeed came from the outside, but it was not a structural signal.

Moreover, the reaction to that signal was to adopt a policy of deterrence toward the USSR[35] and to seek rapprochement with the United States. Yet this doesn't exhaust the logical possibilities—why not accommodate or conciliate and buy time? What prevented China from pursuing this option? Mao was powerful enough to have gotten away with short-term accommodation in the late 1960s. He had been less politically powerful in 1950, and yet he gave away a humiliating degree of autonomy to the Soviets in the secret protocols to the alliance treaty, which gave the Russians extraterritorial rights in China.[36] Would he have been challenged in the late 1960s for accommodating the Soviets? Perhaps, but he probably would have been able to handle opposition. He was accommodating U.S. imperialism, after all (though in a less abject way), by exploring rapprochement, and he handled that opposition relatively harshly (e.g., the Lin Biao affair and the exclusion of the Gang of Four from most major foreign policy decisions of the 1970s).[37]

Put differently, to say that China balances against threats, not power, is probably accurate, but it is not a structural proposition. Many studies of Chinese foreign policy get this difference confused. Threat assessments are often highly subjective, and there is a lot of slippage between the appearance of new threats and changes in "objective" distributions of power. There was virtually no redistribution of material power between the Americans and the Soviets in the 1960s, yet Chinese threat assessments changed dramatically. Threats are created, not given by material structures alone. They are based on interpretations of these material structures, meanings given to structures by interpretative lenses that are ontologically separate from material structures—ideology, strategic cultures, normative preferences, and prior histories of social interaction.

This is evident in Sino–U.S. relations in the post–Cold War period. Changes in polarity did not dramatically increase Chinese skepticism of U.S. motives. June 4, 1989, the catalyst, was fundamentally a legitimacy crisis. Beijing viewed the U.S. response as a threat to the legitimacy of the regime. Similarly, the downturn in relations in 1995–1996 and the increasing tendency in both militaries to see the other as potential adversary are functions of the Taiwan problem. This problem too is a legitimacy issue for the regime in Beijing, a threat to its ability to manufacture and realize a particular vision of a sovereign, territorially complete great power. The international power structure does not dictate that China worry about Taiwanese independence. The political legitimacy of the China's political leaders dictates this. Indeed one could argue that China would be materially better off redirecting toward economic development projects the resources it devotes to Taiwan military scenarios. The international structure does not determine that the United States has to maintain a policy of strategic ambiguity toward Taiwan. U.S. domestic politics largely determines it.

Structuralists might argue that regardless of the adjustments in Chinese foreign policy, the range of options nonetheless are severely constrained. China has to align with one or the other superpower in bipolarity, or in the case of unipolarity, try to reduce the superpole's power.[38] Yet look at the range of behaviors China did pursue under bipolarity: tight balancing with the Soviets; "bandwagoning for profit" (e.g., during the late 1950s after Mao pronounced the East Wind to be prevailing, and in the mid-1980s, as Soviet power atrophied and Sino-U.S. strategic cooperation continued to evolve); status enhancement (empirically similar to internal balancing, but the goal is not, strictly speaking, to increase security); isolationism and/or multidirectional balancing (the 1960s); and active efforts to revise some of the rules of international relations (as in some applications of Maoist redistributive norms[39]) among others.

Neorealists are right, but not especially insightful when they argue that for all these different basic foreign policy strategies, the constant goal has been to maximize security and status. Clearly the definitions of security and the appropriate standards for status have varied in ways that are unattributable to change in polarity or distributions of material power. For instance, there was a time in the 1960s when China sought to enhance its status as the leader of a revolutionary bloc of states and, with Indonesia, toyed with the idea of setting up a revolutionary united nations. Now China is using membership in prominent international institutions to enhance its identity as a high-status major power. These two conceptualizations of status have had very different foreign policy implications. Yet there is nothing that changed in the international material power structure that might have determined why China held one conception of status in the 1960s and a different one in the 1980s and 1990s. If all the material structure does is compel states to seek security and status, leaving the definition of, and strategies for achieving, these ends unexplained, then it is not an especially interesting starting point for the study of foreign policy. That would suggest that material structures alone are far less determining than either the theorists or many students of Chinese foreign policy would have us believe.

Normative Structures

That the influence of material structures per se on foreign policy is often indeterminate does not mean that these structures are irrelevant. What gives them causal power are the interpretations or meanings given to them. These interpretations are functions of ontologically separate normative lenses through which actors/agents observe these material facts. Thus, for instance, if I meet someone carrying a baseball bat in a dark alley, whether I interpret these material conditions (dark alley, baseball bat) as constituting a threatening or nonthreatening situation depends, essentially, on whether I know this person to be a friend or an enemy. Thus the history of our social interaction, the identities I attribute to me and the other, determine how I interpret these material conditions.[40]

The following, then, is the fundamental insight from social constructivism: Distributions of material capabilities and their systemic effects are indeterminate; their effects are determined by intersubjective interpretation. Normative structures are the "shared expectations about appropriate behavior held by a community of actors."[41] This is a sociological approach, which contrasts with the economic approach at the heart of neorealism, where behavior involves a strict ends-means calculation on the basis of given material interests.[42] The interpretative categories that actors work with exist prior to their interaction with the system of actors. Social interaction creates conditions for socialization from which emerge common normative expectations and interpretative categories.[43] These categories define, constrain, delimit, and reformulate the interaction of the actors. They provide a guide not only to the meaning of structural pressures but also to how to deal with them.

As Dessler implies, even if one assumes that states are rational security maximizers, it is not obvious what behavior to expect from a state, say, with declining power—what its options are. There have to be some other preexisting rules of social communication and interaction that make it legitimate for this state, for instance, to seek alliances with other states or to allow it to pursue agreements to reduce the costs of decline (e.g., arms control). These rest on prior agreements among states on the rules and processes of treaty making, international law, and the legitimacy of diplomacy.[44] Action reproduces these rules, but at the same time reaction to constraints at time t can lead to behaviors at time $t + 1$ that reform or remold the structural constraints. Thus, because these interpretative categories are socially constructed, they are, in principle, mutable through purposive intentional action. So for constructivists, generally speaking, neorealists get only half the story when they refer to the constraining effects of structure. There are also enabling or empowering effects, where normative structures provide tools and incentives for actors to try to change, ameliorate, and alter the constraints.[45]

As is evident, constructivists work at the nexus of domestic and international levels of analysis. Unit-level identities both constitute and are constituted by normative structures at the international level. Actors bring already-formed identities, interests, and normative preferences into social interaction. The resultant normative structure and its effects, therefore, will reflect particular distributions of these identities and normative preferences.[46] An anarchy where colonialism is an appropriate behavior for major powers will be different from an anarchy where colonialism is illegitimate, undermined by predominant ideas of self-determination.

There are parallels here with the neorealist focus on particular distributions of power as defining the constraints under which states operate. Whereas neorealists categorize material structures by distribution of capabilities (polarity), constructivists might classify normative structures by the distribution of identities and norms (modality). In statistical language, modal points are places where the frequencies of some observed phenomena are greatest. Thus to say that different distributions of norms constitute different modalities is merely to say that at particular points in time and space certain normative preferences are more intensively and extensively accepted than others. For constructivists, then, different modalities have different effects on states. These modalities are not epiphenomena of material power distributions but have independent effects on behavior. Modes, being ideational constructs, need not be bounded by the nation-state (the way polarity is defined by concentrations of power in one or more states). Thus, for instance, the intensity and purity of market capitalist ideology are unevenly distributed globally and within national boundaries. Normative modalities, then, are arenas or communities of shared expectations about behavior that can cut across traditional nation-states.

Different normative structures therefore have different degrees of influence on actors. But these effects are, in principle, not permanent. Unlike neorealists, who contend that as long as anarchical structures persist, balancing behavior and conflict will be the enduring, primary feature of the system, constructivists hold out the possibility that actor agency can alter some of these effects. Like neorealists, constructivists argue that failure to heed these normative structures or persistent resistance to them incurs specific costs for actors. These could be social opprobrium (criticism and ostracism), inner psychological tension (guilt), and/or isolation (shunning by those who uphold the norm).

Given that different actors bring different identities and normative preferences to their interaction with others, there can be, in principle, quite a wide range of resulting normative structures, depending on who is interacting with whom. States are not the only actors in IR. Multinational corporations (MNCs), international organizations, epistemic communities, transnational organizations, even individuals in positions of moral or political authority, can affect the character of the normative structure that results from their interaction. Thus it is difficult to come up with a list of extant normative structures operating at any given time in any given territorial and ideational space in the international system. Some of the more obvious ones include: capitalism; sovereignty; anti-colonialism; human rights; nonproliferation; democratic security community; environmentalism; "postmaterialism." To the degree that these are internalized in the ideologies of decisionmakers and relevant publics, they establish the boundaries of legitimate behavior. Often they will be invoked for instrumental reasons. But they are also so internalized in some quarters that alternative normative models are considered beyond the pale or not considered at all. It would be inconceivable in most cases, for instance, for even the most economically depressed, politically weak, socially divided "failed" state to give up its sovereignty voluntarily in return for colonial status, even if this status ensured better internal order and faster economic development.

Before turning to Chinese foreign policy, a word about the ways in which normative structures can affect actor behavior. Essentially there are three ways.[47] In the first case, norms influence actors directly by changing identities and creating or modifying interests. That can be done through "teaching," dialogue, and persuasion where actors reconsider the normative categories with which they have defined their material environment.[48] Thus, for instance, international organizations and epistemic communities have been instrumental in diffusing new understandings about the rules of military conduct, definitions of development, arms control, and environmental protection.[49] These normative changes can also be a result of exogenous shocks, massive policy failures that push normally cognitively conservative actors to reconsider their cause-effect understandings of the external world. Indeed, normative change can be a combination of the two, where exogenous shocks open up political opportunities for national or transnational "ideas entrepreneurs" within state(s) policy processes.[50]

The second way is more indirect. Here an actor does not internalize new norms per se but is constrained by measures taken by other actors who have internalized them. These measures alter the instrumental cost-benefit calculus of the first actor in such a way that its behavior is more consistent with these new norms. An atheist in a community of religious fanatics may be compelled to obey the rules of the religion, not because they are internalized, but because disobedience is punished and obedience is rewarded by true believers.[51] Similarly, political leaders may be motivated solely by preserving their own perks and privileges as elites, but if the leaders are susceptible to recall in some form (either through election or coup), they will be receptive to the normative preferences of the relevant publics.

Finally, there can be a mixed sequential process: behavior pursued for instrumental, consequentialist reasons at time t can lead to outcomes that are institutionalized in legal or normative frameworks at time $t + 1$. These frameworks then become the environment in which actors at time $t + 2$ are socialized. Behaviors at time $t + 3$ are then followed because of their appropriateness, not their instrumental benefits.

A caveat before turning finally to how normative structures have or haven't affected Chinese foreign policy: Once we introduce normative structures that exist at the global level, then the "impact" of the system on units gets exponentially harder to measure because the objects of impact are no longer just the state or state policy. The behavior of regions, communities, social groups, and individuals can become the dependent variable because these actors can, in turn, shape the normative structure affecting other actors. Neorealists have it easy. The unit of analysis for material power distributions is the state. Only states can be poles. The unit of analysis for normative modality need not be spatially fixed, concentrated, or even recognized as legitimate by other actors. The relevant units of analysis for mapping the distribution and concentration of neoclassical economic ideology, for example, might be economics departments, central banks, MNCs, and IOs like the World Bank. One could, in principle, measure the concentration or intensity of this particular ideology relative to others by looking at the issue-specific power resources these actors can bring to bear. What follows is therefore an extremely simplified heuristic discussion of how normative structures appear to affect Chinese foreign policy. It is meant to provoke discussion and research, not to answer for all time the question of how normative or material structures affect Chinese foreign policy.

The impact of *some* normative structures on Chinese foreign policy is obvious. The basic and most important of these is sovereignty. There is almost universal acceptance that the only legitimate way of dividing the globe spatially and politically is into territorial states, the governments of which have sole authority over the exercise of power within their boundaries. That was not always the case, and the spheres in which governments can exercise authoritative power unchallenged by external actors has been shifting.[52] But if sovereignty were not considered universally appropriate, the interstate system either would not exist or would not be as stable as it is. This norm, globalized, deeply internalized, and reproduced through state practice, legitimizes certain behaviors and delegitimizes others. It legitimizes the practice of one-state, one-vote, in most international organizations, regardless of vast asymmetries in material power. Although it legitimizes the use of force for self-defense, over time it has delegitimized the use of force for conquest. As porous as state sovereignty has become in practice, states have increasingly been constrained by the universalization of the sovereignty norm: If this norm didn't matter, there would probably be much more conquering of the weak by the strong, a truly "Hobbesian" anarchy whose outcomes would be determined almost exclusively by power distributions. Yet micro states and failed states coexist with superpowers as equals in international law, in many IOs, and in general diplomatic practice precisely because of the strength of sovereignty norms.

China clearly is "constrained" by a particularly extensive and absolutist version of the sovereignty norm. It may be argued that China's version of sovereignty comes closer than most to the Westphalian ideal.[53] Much of Chinese foreign policy practice, particularly after 1989, has focused on the vigorous defense of China's own sovereignty and the sovereignty of others. Indeed, as an explanatory variable, the strength of Chinese adherence to the sovereignty norm provides more insights into Chinese foreign policy than any tendency to power balance in the neorealist sense. China has invoked the sovereignty norm to oppose interference in the internal affairs of states in the name of human rights. It has not been particularly supportive of the evolving practice of humanitarian intervention.[54] Sovereignty is a crucial test for determining whether an international regime should be supported and how much. It is a critical determinant of how to react to the influence attempts of other actors. It constrains perceived options on the Taiwan issue: China cannot accept any arrangement that hints of independence, since that would undermine its sovereignty and territorial integrity. In the South China and East China Seas disputes the strength of the sovereignty norm hinders China from dropping, modifying, or clarifying its territorial claims and from agreeing to multilateral demilitarization of the regions. The sovereignty norm prevents Chinese leaders from accepting international environmental commitments that are perceived to put constraints on economic growth rates (since that would undermine China's sovereign right to develop its resources as it sees fit), or that might involve more intrusive inspection of China's performance on compliance. Sovereignty is an normative obstacle to agreement on limits on weapons proliferation, since it is the sovereign right of a major power to make money and influence people, as the U.S. example amply demonstrates. Sovereignty is a norm that reduces China's support for intrusive arms control verification procedures, hence its effort to water these down in the Comprehensive Test Ban and Chemical Weapons Convention negotiations.

The fact that different states hold to the sovereignty norm more or less strongly, or hold to wider or narrower definitions of sovereignty regardless of their relative position in material power hierarchy,[55] suggests that there are competing normative structures that may place contradictory constraints on states—for example, human rights versus sovereignty, nonproliferation versus the legitimate right to self-defense. This suggests, as well, that identities vary across states, across time. China's concept of major powerhood has changed little since 1949: The model is of a maximally sovereign and autonomous political state that is both rich and strong. Yet this model is at variance with new visions represented by the "soft" (or softer) power of a Germany or Japan and is increasingly challenged by globalist voices inside China.[56] The old model was useful for a particular stage in economic and political development, as if it had been handed down to China in some normative product cycle, but now it is increasingly out-of-date and counterproductive for promoting the material and "postmaterial" welfare of its citizens.[57] It is not immutable, but it is powerfully reinforced through the way history is taught and through propaganda in the media. One puzzle for Chinese foreign policy studies is to figure out which international norms will prevail over others in constraining behavior and when. The predominance of sovereignty, combined with traditional realpolitik visions of major powerhood, means, for instance, that human rights or nonproliferation norms will be undervalued in policy process.

Sovereignty, therefore, is an example of a normative structure with a direct impact on Chinese foreign policy because the concept is deeply internalized and institutionalized in the decision process. How it got there is an exceedingly interesting question that needs more exploration. The answer may lie in how Chinese leaders, Nationalists and Communists alike, institutionalized China's history of weakness in domestic socialization processes and adopted the Westphalian model of a sovereign major power, the predominant model in the late-nineteenth and first half of the twentieth centuries, as *the* solution to this weakness.

There are other examples of normative structures affecting Chinese foreign policy through socialization and internalization, though the evidence is much harder to adjudicate at the moment. It appears, for instance, that China's involvement in the ASEAN Regional Forum and the plethora of Track II (nonofficial or semiofficial) security dialogues in the Asia-Pacific region may be helping to create the rudiments of a community of foreign policy specialists normatively committed to multilateralism. The evidence is only indirect.[58] ARF policy in China was put in the hands of the small Comprehensive Division of the Asia Department of the Foreign Ministry, with some input from strategic analysts from other government agencies. Initially, in ARF activities the Chinese representatives were unaccustomed to the give and take of debate and negotiation. They also came to the discussions with a watchful eye for developments that might impinge on sensitive security or domestic political issues. Over time, however, with experience in informal discussion, growing familiarity with the ARF norms of interaction, and more intensive interaction with committed multilateralists from other countries, these officials have become much more engaged, relaxed, flexible, and conceptually sophisticated. Most interesting has been their apparent endorsement, within limits, of multilateralism as being compatible with Chinese security interests. Some observers even suggest that the agenda of some of these officials is to tie China gradually into regional security institutions so that someday China's leaders will be bound by the institutions themselves. These officials see ARF involvement as a process of educating their own government and are evidently careful to frame information going back to Beijing about ARF discussions in ways that preclude the participation of certain potential critics in the policy process. According to one close observer of Chinese approaches to multilateralism, in their thinking, these individuals are groping toward variations of common or cooperative security. The main conduit for the infusion of these sorts of ideas has tended to be experience in Track I and II activities.

There are also examples where emerging normative structures indirectly constrain Chinese behavior. Two cases come to mind—the Comprehensive Test Ban Treaty and the land mines protocol to the treaty on inhumane weapons, both concluded in 1996. In the CTBT, China eventually agreed to the treaty, even though many of its military and nuclear weapons specialists were opposed, arguing that it would lock China into permanent inferiority in warhead design options. China bargained hard to minimize the constraints of the treaty but only managed to loosen somewhat the verification procedures.[59] In the land mines protocol negotiations China eventually agreed to certain technical restrictions on the kinds of land mines that can be deployed or sold so as to reduce the risk to noncombatants. Here again the military opposed the protocol, arguing that land mines were legitimate tools for the defense of sovereign states. In both cases, China agreed to constraints on its relative material capabilities in the absence of threats of material sanctions or side payments. In both cases it appears that a critical concern in Beijing was about being identified as an isolated spoiler of a treaty that had long been considered a pillar of the nonproliferation regime (CTBT) and an agreement that was part of the regime controlling "inhumane weapons" (land mine protocol). It appears, for instance, that on the latter issue the Ministry of Foreign Affairs arms control specialists eventually convinced senior decisionmakers in Beijing of the public relations disaster from upholding the PLA's preferred bargaining position.[60]

Why would a realpolitik actor, intensely worried about its relative power, care enough about public relations and image costs (and benefits) that they lead it to accept constraints on its relative power? The tentative answer is complex, but it has to do with the interplay of identity and normative structures.

The international public relations effects of behavior can only be a cost or benefit for an actor under two conditions: (1) when other actors, motivated by normative concerns, decide to materially punish or reward an actor for violating or upholding their norms; (2) when other actors, motivated by normative concerns, decide to expose an actor to "backpatting" or "social opprobrium" (praise or criticism), and when this other actor cares about social praise or criticism. The first case is obvious. There is some evidence, for example, that concessions China has made on missile sales and human rights issues in the 1990s have come in the face of sanctions threats from the United States.

The second case is more interesting. Traditionally analysts of strategic behavior and cooperation have downplayed the role of social sanctioning in state behavior. Yet it is clear that states, like individuals, in the absence of concrete material threats or rewards, sometimes go to great lengths to avoid criticism or to garner praise for their behavior. The causal process is not too clear, but one plausible argument is as follows: Cognitively conservative actors, concerned about reputations for consistency, become extremely uncomfortable when confronted with their own hypocrisy. Such criticisms challenge the legitimacy of the actor's self-identification. And if we are talking about a collective, such criticisms may undermine the legitimacy of the leadership of that group in relations with other groups and, in turn, in relations with others in the in-group. Thus they will be more inclined to modify behavior to reduce these sorts of criticisms. Conversely, social praise that reinforces the legitimacy of self-identification will be welcomed as well for its effect in boosting the internal legitimacy of leaders. Praise and criticism can cause an actor to double its efforts to establish its legitimacy as a member of a particular in-group. As new studies of the accession and compliance behavior of states suggest, in the absence of clear threats and promises, diffuse reputation—reputation that is not directly connected to the credibility of specific commitments—matters.[61]

Note two things: first, the "coercive" effects of concerns about diffuse reputation depend not just on the normative values of others but also on the self-identification of the target actor; second, the coercive effects will, in principle, be greater, the larger and more legitimate the audience with which an actor is interacting. The larger the audience, the greater the accumulation of social praise or opprobrium. Legitimacy here refers to the degree to which it is the social norms of this particular audience that matter, that have an effect on a potential free rider. If, say, an actor completely rejected the social norms of a particular group, then no matter what the size of that group, it could not generate backpatting or opprobrium effects. This audience, or institutional structure, is a forum where information about an actor's social performance is public, which means that the distance between an actor's behavior and socially approved standards is public. It is this distance that generates backpatting and opprobrium effects.

The argument about China, therefore, would be as follows: Over the 1980s and 1990s China's self-identification has undergone a change, a blurring. The traditional sovereign-centric, autonomous major power identity—rooted at the very least in the myths of modern Chinese nationalism—has been uneasily linked to a newer identity as a responsible major power, one whose status is measured in part by participation in institutions that increasingly regulate interstate behavior.[62] This linkage has created a tension in diplomacy between China's desire to show itself as an active, involved participant in international institutions (even those that offer no material obvious costs or benefits, or that indeed are somewhat costly), and the desire to minimize commitments and constraints that are required by this participation. But it has also meant that Chinese leaders are more sensitive to China's being portrayed as an isolated, obstructionist player in international institutions, since such accusations clash with this evolving new self-identity, an identity that is supported by other actors in the system.

In principle, the backpatting and opprobrium costs for China therefore ought to vary with the size and legitimacy of its international audience. China's participation in an institution brings it into social interaction with a particular audience. That means its behavior can be scrutinized or monitored by this audience, even though there are no material sanctions or rewards that might be triggered by this monitoring. Thus image concerns ought to play a more important role in eliciting cooperation in high-profile multilateral institutions than in bilateral relationships. That is why image calculations have figured more prominently in Chinese decisions to sign on to multilateral treaties and processes, even when they incur or may incur certain material power costs (e.g., CTBT, land mines), and why China has been more resistant to bilateral commitments to the United States on proliferation issues, even in the face of substantial U.S. criticism. Such criticism can be dismissed as expressions of U.S. power politics. Criticism from the developing states in the Conference on Disarmament, as oblique as they are at times, cannot be dismissed so easily. Conversely, the larger the coalition of states that supports China multilaterally, the greater the backpatting benefits for its position, and the less likely China will cooperate with its critics. Hence on human rights questions, the fact that China can garner support from a disparate group of states, from India to Singapore to Malaysia, against symbolic Western efforts to criticize China in multilateral forums, reduces the social opprobrium costs from its human rights stances.

The notion that backpatting and opprobrium matters for eliciting cooperation does not mesh easily with standard IR theories. For neorealists, for instance, reputation or image is at best instrumental and deceptive. Yet in interview after interview with arms control specialists and environmental specialists in recent years, a common response has been that China had to join such and such a treaty or process because joining was part of a world historical trend, because it was part of China's role as a responsible major power, or because it would help improve China's image.[63] These arguments show up, as well, in internal circulation documents on multilateral diplomacy. As one example, a State Council document outlining China's basic diplomatic postures for the Earth Summit in 1992 indicated that a primary goal of China's activities there was to improve its international image *(guoji xingxiang)*.[64]

This argument obviously requires more testing. But it is at least a plausible account of central feature of Chinese foreign policy—an acute sensitivity in discourse and practice to China's image and diffuse reputation, even when there are no material costs or benefits at stake. This account rests on the interplay of domestic normative structures (identities) and international normative structures.

Conclusion

In this chapter I have argued a number of things. First, structural effects on Chinese foreign policy are not the same as international pressure from particular actors. Rather, structural effects are pressures generated by the interaction of states and other actors in the international system.

Second, students of Chinese foreign policy have to be more explicit about the structural logics they employ and about the propositions and expectations these logics generate. I suggested that arguments about international material structural effects, most notably those made by neorealists and adopted to varying degrees by students of Chinese foreign policy, are problematic in accounting for much of China's foreign policy behavior. Material power structures alone—in particular polarity—do not constrain Chinese behavior in ways that are consistent with standard arguments. That is an interesting finding for IR theory and for Chinese foreign policy studies, and it is an example where the application of theory to the study of China can contribute to theory.

Third, this chapter has proposed that normative structures essentially determine the effects of material structures. And it indicated different ways in which Chinese foreign policy has been affected by the interplay of domestically generated and institutionalized identity and changing international norms. Except for the sovereignty norm, less-globalized normative structures appear to constrain primarily through indirect effects, either because of Chinese concerns about diffuse reputation, or image, or because other states, motivated by normative concerns, threaten to place material constraints on Chinese behavior. Testing these general propositions requires explicating microprocesses. How do norms affect policy? Through what channels and processes of socialization are norms more or less likely to be diffused into the policy process? What are the domestic normative, political, economic, and social preconditions for material structural effects to kick in?

We need to be perfectly clear here: This argument does not mean that the relative power means nothing to Chinese leaders or that they are unresponsive to it. Rather, the point is an obvious one, though perhaps made more strongly than it needs to be: Whose power matters and how China responds to it are not determined by polarity. They are determined instead by the fact that Chinese leaders have internalized a particular absolutist notion of sovereignty, and a realpolitik definition of the role of material power in world politics, but one that is increasingly in tension with an identity as a responsible major power. It is the interplay of these normative constructs that provides answers to whose power matters and how China ought to respond. These normative constructs generate threat assessments that may or may not correspond to changes in the material power environment. Since these constructs are not epiphenomena of material structures, they can, in principle, vary, even as the state system remains technically "anarchical" and polarity remains static.

To summarize, human agency—the power to act according to intentions—occurs within normative structural boundaries and within the meaning these structures provide to material "realities."[65] But these boundaries are produced by the interaction of agents acting intentionally. Therefore, we also need to focus on how China changes these structural constraints. In complex social systems, where agents are numerous and power unevenly distributed, the effects of one actor on the system are hard to gauge. But a truly complete answer to the question asked in this chapter would address how China's behavior affects and is affected by the system in a continuous, evolving feedback loop or mutually constitutive process.[66] There are, then, at least two major sets of questions that ought to be on the agenda of Chinese foreign policy studies. First, how has China's interaction with international structures—normative and material—changed these structures? What intended and unintended consequences have been generated in these structures by the rise of China, a state that operates uneasily with often conflicting identities as both a victim of superior power in a social-Darwinian world and as a great power with responsibility for maintaining key features of the global economic and political status quo? Second, how do global normative and material structures interact to move a China with these identities in particular directions? In short, how are norms of sovereignty and realpolitik reinforced or undermined by China's interaction with the rest of the international system?

Notes

1. See, for example, Dan Reiter, *Crucible of Beliefs: Learning, Alliances, and World Wars* (Ithaca: Cornell University Press, 1996); Randall L. Schweller, "Bandwagoning for Profit: Bringing the Revisionist State Back In," *International Security* 19:1 (Summer 1994), pp. 72–107; Paul W. Schroeder, "Historial Reality vs. Neorealist Theory," *International Security* 19:1 (Summer 1994), pp. 108–148.

2. This debate in theory is mirrored by the policy debate in the United States over whether a rising China is best constrained through its involvement in international institutions or through superior coercive power. So the theoretical debate is by no means irrelevant for the policy debate.

3. On social constructivist ontology in IR, see Alexander Wendt, "Collective Identity Formation and the International State," *American Political Science Review* 88:2 (June 1994).

4. David Dessler, "What's at Stake in the Agent-Structure Debate?" *International Organization* 43:3 (Summer 1989), pp. 453, 466–467.

5. Robert Jervis, "Systems Effects," in Richard J. Zeckhauser, ed., *Strategy and Choice* (Cambridge, Mass.: MIT Press, 1991), pp. 113–114.

6. See Schweller, "Bandwagoning for Profit." See also Charles Glaser, "Realists as Optimists: Cooperation as Self-Help," *International Security* 19:3 (Winter 1994).

7. Wendt, "Collective Identity Formation," p. 388. See also Alexander Wendt, *Social Theory of International Politics* (Cambridge, UK: Cambridge University Press, forthcoming).

8. Kenneth Waltz, *Theory of International Politics* (Reading, Mass.: Addison-Wesley, 1979), pp. 106, 127–28.

9. Colin Elman makes a far more eloquent and powerful argument that there is a theory of foreign policy in neorealism in "Horses for Courses: Why Not Neorealist Theories of Foreign Policy," *Security Studies* 6:1 (Autumn 1996), pp. 7–53.

10. John Vasquez, *The War Puzzle* (Cambridge, UK: Cambridge University Press, 1993).

11. James Davis and Andrew Cortell, "How Do International Institutions Matter? The Domestic Impact of International Rules and Norms," *International Studies Quarterly* 40:4 (December 1996).

12. Note that for pure material structuralists, objective and subjective threats are synonymous. That is, the rationality assumption means that states are generally able to accurately perceive the basic distribution of power in the system, and thus a rising major power is by definition a threatening power. Steve Walt's realism, by which in subjective terms the threatening power may not be the rising or dominant power, breaks this link between objective power distributions and threat. His theory is therefore not a material structuralist one per se and thus is not treated as one here. Stephen Walt, *The Origins of Alliances* (Ithaca: Cornell University Press, 1987).

13. There are variations within the neorealist camp about "how much is enough." For a summary of debate between defensive positionalists and offensive realists, see Fareed Zakaria, "Realism and Domestic Politics: A Review Essay," *International Security* 17:1 (Summer 1992).

14. Waltz notes simply that power is "difficult to measure and compare" and that how it is measured and distributed are "empirical" questions that "common sense can answer." Waltz, *Theory*, p. 131.

15. Christopher Layne, "The Unipolar Illusion: Why New Great Powers Will Rise," *International Security* 17:4 (Spring 1993).

16. If one uses the International Institute for Strategic Studies (IISS) data, the U.S. lead in military power increases still more. According to these data, in 1987 the United States accounted for 38.7 percent of world military expenditures (1985 dollars), the USSR for 17.0 percent and China 2.6 percent. In 1992 these shares stood at 43.5 percent, 7.1 percent and 4.0 percent respectively. (This calculation uses an unofficial revision of the IISS figures for China's official budget. As a rough rule of thumb the official budget may undercount by a factor of three.) This distribution doesn't quite fit Modelski's categorization of unipolarity either, since the United States has less than 50 percent and three or more states have more than 5 percent each, but it is closer to unipolarity than the Arms Control and Disarmament Agency (ACDA) figures indicate. Thompson calls this kind of distribution asymmetrical multipolarity or near unipolarity. See William Thompson, *On Global War* (Columbia: South Carolina University Press, 1988), pp. 209–210.

17. Because neorealists have been unwilling to commit to a firm and accepted measure of power, they offer few guidelines for determining when the system moves from one type of polarity to another. I rely for heuristic purposes on Modelski's measure: A state that possesses 50 percent or more of systemwide military expenditures is the unipole; two states that, combined, possess 50 percent or more of system capabilities, with each having 25 percent or more, are the two bipoles; and any other distribution is multipolar. George Modelski, *World Power Concentrations: Typology, Data, Explanatory Framework* (Princeton, N.J.: Princeton University Press, 1974). These criteria mean that the United States does not quite qualify for being the lone pole, but clearly the system is neither bipolar nor multipolar, given the clear lopsidedness— the United States would need only a few percentage points more for the system to be unipolar.

18. Department of Defense, *East Asia Strategy Report* (Washington: USGPO, February 1995); and General Accounting Office, "National Security: Impact of China's Military Modernization in the Pacific Region" (Report to Congressional Committees, GAO/NSIAD-95-84, June 1995), p. 3.

19. Guan Jixian, *Gao jishu jubu zhanzheng zhanyi* (Campaigns in high-tech limited wars) (Beijing: National Defense University Press, 1993).

20. I used the Kansas Events Data System/Protocol for the Assessment of Nonviolent Direct Action (KEDS/PANDA) data base. These events are machine-coded reports from Reuters wire service. From these data only official government statements and actions directed at the U.S. government actors/targets from 1984–1995 were chosen (N = 360), a very small proportion of the total number of "actions" directed by China at the United States. For caveats when using KEDS/PANDA, see Doug Bond and Joe Bond "Protocol for the Assessment of Nonviolent Direct Action (PANDA) Codebook for the P24 Data Set" (Unpublished paper, Program on Nonviolent Sanctions and Cultural Survival, Harvard University, May 1995).

21. Intensity refers to the mean yearly WEIS scores for Chinese actions directed at the United States (counting only WEIS scores over 1, so as to reduce error from coding ambiguous actions). As Chinese military expenditures increase, the scores drop, meaning its actions are less cooperative. The proportion refers to the per

centage of all actions that are coded cooperative, regardless of their weighted WEIS scales. As Chinese military expenditures increased, the proportion of cooperative actions decreased. The calculations use ACDA figures in 1993 dollars. If one uses official military expenditures the correlation coefficients increase to $r = -.53$ and $r = -.42$ respectively.

22. See "Nanya diqu junshi xingshi ji dui wo guo guofang zhanlue de yingxiang" [The military situation in the South Asia region and its influence on our national defense strategy], in China Military Future Studies Association, ed., *Ya Tai de xuanwo* [The Asia-Pacific vortex] (Beijing: Academy of Military Sciences, 1989), p. 205.

23. *Korea Times,* November 16, 1995, as reported in North East Asia Peace and Security Network Daily Report, November 16, 1995.

24. Thomas J. Christensen, "Structure, Perceptions and Aspirations in Chinese Security Policy" (Paper presented to Workshop on International Relations Theory and the Study of Chinese Foreign Policy, Harvard University, April 1995), p. 14; Andrew J. Nathan and Robert S. Ross, *The Great Wall and the Empty Fortress: China's Search for Security* (W. W. Norton, 1997), p. 79. This preference does not mean that the Chinese support any and all forms of U.S.-Japanese security cooperation.

25. Edward D. Mansfield and Rachel Bronson, "Alliances, Preferential Trading Arrangements, and International Trade" (Paper present to Olin Institute National Security Seminar, Harvard University, November 1995), pp. 2–3.

26. *China Monthly Statistics,* no. 9 (1995), pp. 35–39.

27. The data were drawn from *Almanac of China's Foreign Economic Relations and Trade,* 1988–1995.

28. Michael Ng Quinn, "International Systemic Constraints on Chinese Foreign Policy," in Samuel S. Kim, ed., *China and the World: Chinese Foreign Policy in the Post-Mao Era* (Boulder, Colo.: Westview Press, 1984), pp. 82–112. A number of other studies also use a balance-of-power perspective to analyze China's tendency to "lean" this way or that in the face of superior power or threat from one of the poles. For examples see Michael Yahuda, *China's Role in World Affairs* (New York: St. Martin's Press, 1978); Jonathan D. Pollack, "China and the Global Strategic Balance," in Harry Harding, ed., *China's Foreign Relations in the 1980s* (New Haven: Yale University Press, 1984); William T. Tow, "China and the International Strategic System," in Thomas Robinson and David Shambaugh, eds., *Chinese Foreign Policy: Theory and Practice* (New York: Oxford University Press, 1993), p. 120; and Nathan and Ross, *The Great Wall.* Most of these kinds of studies, however, tend to fudge the causal weight attributed to structural effects or balance-of-power considerations. Nathan and Ross, for example, begin from an avowedly neorealist perspective but rely on ideological and domestic political variables and, at one point, the very un-neorealist concept of obligation to international rules, to explain variation in Chinese behavior (see pp. 57, 235).

29. This assumes that Mao minded the costs prior to 1969. If he devalued these "costs," while China's existence as a state was never really in jeopardy, then it is hard to argue, as neorealists would have to, that the system was punishing China for misreading its signals.

30. The United States had the largest share of major power capabilities from 1945 to 1972. In 1972,the United States had 31.13 percent share, the Soviets 30.89

percent. In 1973, the U.S. share had dropped to 30.74 percent, whereas the Soviet share had risen to 31.02 percent. In other words, the Soviets surpassed the United States as the most materially powerful superpower. Balance-of-power proponents might reply that the Chinese perceptions of growing Soviet power shifted prior to 1973, in the late 1960s, even though the United States was materially the more powerful of the two. This is empirically accurate. But if it is perception of the balance of power that matters, then China should have leaned toward the United States in the late 1950s after Mao's speech at the Moscow Conference in November 1957, where he declared that the East Wind prevailed over the West Wind. Needless to say, if perceptions of polarity diverge from objective measures of it, and if one's explanation rests on the former, then one is not making a material structural argument.

31. See, for instance, Sha Ge, "Dui Zhong Su Mei guanxi zhong de ruogan zhanlue celue yuanze de tantao" [A discussion of several strategic and tactical principles in Sino-U.S.-Soviet relations], in *Shijie jingji yu zhengzhi neican* [Internal reference materials on World Economics and Politics], no.4 (1984), p. 5, and Li Yuanming, "Shitan Mei Su zhengba xin xingshi xia de wo guo dui wai zhengce" [Preliminary discussion of our country's foreign policy under the new conditions in the U.S.-Soviet struggle for hegemony], in *Shijie jingji yu zhengzhi neican* [Internal reference materials on World Economics and Politics], no. 11 (1983), p. 9. There is some evidence that the independent line was, in part, rhetoric designed to encourage the Soviets to pursue détente with China while allowing China to preserve its strategic relationship with the United States. See Shu's essay above for an outline of this strategy. Deng Xiaoping was not especially supportive of the "independent foreign policy" line rhetoric (which had been announced by Hu Yaobang at the Twelfth Party Congress in October 1982), as he believed China's security still rested on leaning more toward the United States. See Lu Ning, *The Dynamics of Foreign Policy Decisionmaking in China* (Boulder, Colo.: Westview Press, 1997), pp. 141–142.

32. Thomas J. Christensen, *Useful Adversaries: Grand Strategy, Domestic Mobilization, and Sino-American Conflict, 1947–1958* (Princeton: Princeton University Press, 1996).

33. Ibid., p. 210; and "Minutes, Conversation Between Mao Zedong and Ambassador Yudin, 22 July 1958," in *Cold War International History Project Bulletin 6-7* (Winter 1995–1996), pp. 155–159.

34. According to Correlates of War (COW) data, the Soviet share of major power capabilities from 1966–1969 was around 81–82 percent of the U.S. share.

35. And to deter by rather risk-acceptant signaling in 1968–1969. China adopted a more forward armed posture along the border, sent a signal of risk acceptance through a massive civil defense program and some well-timed nuclear tests, and by communicating a general willingness to fight a war with the Soviets. See, for example, Christian F. Ostermann, "New Evidence on the Sino-Soviet Border Dispute, 1969–1971," in *Cold War International History Project Bulletin 6-7* (Winter 1995–1996), pp. 186–189.

36. See Sergei N. Goncharov, John W. Lewis, and Xue Litai, *Uncertain Partners: Stalin, Mao and the Korean War* (Stanford: Stanford University Press, 1993), pp. 121–127.

37. See Robert S. Ross, *Negotiating Cooperation: The United States and China, 1969–1989* (Stanford: Stanford University Press, 1995).

38. Ng Quinn notes, "Constrained by bipolar international structure, Chinese foreign policy falls within a narrow range of possibilities." See "International Systemic Constraints," p. 97. See also Layne's expectation that under unipolarity eligible great powers such as China would strive to create a multipolar system (Layne, "The Unipolar Illusion," p. 3 n. 1, p. 9). Chinese foreign policy rhetoric has long stressed the desirability of a multipolar world, but the practice has not been entirely consistent with this goal.

39. See Samuel S. Kim, *China and the United Nations and World Order* (Princeton: Princeton University Press, 1979), pp. 49–93.

40. For an excellent example of how social interaction changes identification of self and other, and thus the definition of the relationship, see Hayward Alker, "Beneath Tit-for-Tat: The Contest of Political Economy Fairy Tales Within SPD Protocols," in Alker, *Rediscoveries and Reformulations: Humanistic Methodologies for International Studies* (New York: Cambridge University Press, 1996), pp. 303–331.

41. Martha Finnemore, *National Interests in International Society* (Ithaca: Cornell University Press, 1996), p. 22. Normative structures are roughly equivalent to what game theorists call common knowledge—a shared understanding that all players also believe others to share of the nature of the strategic game being played. Without this knowledge people couldn't act, since they could not predict the effect of their behavior, and hence they could not make rational choices. Similarly, without normative structures, actors cannot interpret the nature of the material environment within which they operate, preventing purposive action to change this environment. See Wendt, *Social Theory*, p. 190; and James Morrow, *Game Theory for Political Scientists* (Princeton, N.J.: Princeton University Press, 1994), p. 61.

42. See Dessler, "What's at Stake?"; and Paul Kowert and Jeffrey Legro, "Norms, Identity and Their Limits: A Theoretical Reprise," in Peter J. Katzenstein, ed., *The Culture of National Security: Norms and Identity in World Politics* (New York: Columbia University Press, 1996), pp. 451–498.

43. Common expectations are not necessarily cooperative ones. Actors can agree that their relationship is a zero-sum one just as they can agree it is positive-sum one, even as material conditions and distributions of power remain unchanged.

44. Dessler, "What's at Stake?" p. 459.

45. See Barrie Axford, *The Global System: Economics, Politics and Culture* (New York: St. Martin's Press, 1995), p. 91.

46. In contrast, by assuming states are undifferentiated units primarily interested in survival and autonomy, neorealists essentially believe that states bring nothing distinctive to their social interaction except particular power capabilities.

47. For a thoughtful discussion of how norms may or may not influence actors, see Kowert and Legro, "Norms, Identities and Their Limits." For a somewhat different conceptualization of the ways in which norms affect behavior see G. John Ikenberry and Charles Kupchan, "Socialization and Hegemonic Power," *International Organization* 44:3 (Summer 1990), pp. 290–292.

48. See Axford, *The Global System*, p. 69; the essays in Diana C. Muntz et al., eds., *Political Persuasion and Attitude Change* (Ann Arbor: University of Michigan Press, 1996); and Robert B. Cialdini, *Influence: The New Psychology of Modern Persuasion* (New York: Quill, 1984).

49. Finnemore, *National Interests;* Peter Haas, "Do Regimes Matter? Epistemic Communities and Mediterranean Pollution Control," *International Organization* 43:4 (Summer 1989), pp. 377–404.

50. See, for example, the explanations for the arms control and cooperative security features of Gorbachev's "new thinking" in Matthew Evangelista, "The Paradox of State Strength: Transnational Relations, Domestic Structures and Security Policy in Russia and the Soviet Union," *International Organization* 49:1 (January 1995), pp. 1–38; and Robert G. Herman, "Identity, Norms and National Security: The Soviet Foreign Policy Revolution and the End of the Cold War," in Katzenstein, ed., *The Culture of National Security*, pp. 271–316.

51. Note, however, that the atheist is also a normatively motivated actor. The contrast in the two sets of norms actually may generate even more coercive effects on the nonbeliever, since the community will be more vigilant about her/his behavior and the nonbeliever will be even more cautious about sending the provocative signals (if there is some other benefit from being a member of the community). The additional positive and negative constraints generated by the interactive effects of these two belief systems are important to remember when studying Chinese foreign policy. A case can be made that, ceteris paribus, the coercive effects of international criticism of Chinese behavior are enhanced precisely because China is so determined to represent its identity as a responsible major power.

52. Stephen Krasner, "Compromising Westphalia," *International Security* 20:3 (Winter 1995/6), pp. 115–151; J. Samuel Barkin and Bruce Cronin, "The State and the Nation: Changing Norms and the Rules of Sovereignty in International Relations," *International Organization* 48:1 (Winter 1994), pp. 107–130.

53. China's version also converges in many places with the version espoused by Republicans and isolationists in the United States. So it is not unique, but it is also not universal.

54. On this norm, see Martha Finnemore, "Constructing Norms of Humanitarian Intervention," in Katzenstein, *The Culture of National Security*, pp. 153–185.

55. Chinese definitions of sovereignty are more extensive and intrusive than Canadian definitions, even though the impact of Quebec's separation on Canada's relative power capabilities would be far greater than the impact of a symbolic declaration of Taiwan's independence on China's relative power.

56. See for instance, Wang Yizhou, *Dangdai guoji zhengzhi xilun* [Analysis of contemporary international politics] (Shanghai: People's Publishing House, 1995); Ma Shaolei et al., *Guoji guanxi xinlun* [New theories of international relations] (Shanghai: Social Science Academy Press, 1994); and Cai Tuo, *Dangdai quanqiu wenti* [Contemporary global problems] (Tianjin: People's Publishing House, 1994), pp. 561–565.

57. In an era where Chinese leaders themselves declare their external environment to be the most benign since 1949, a portion of the $30 billion or so devoted to the PLA could probably be used more constructively elsewhere for shoring up

the legitimacy of the regime (e.g., by paying civil servants more, in order to reduce incentives for corruption).

58. The following comes from interviews with: Canadian embassy officials, Beijing, April 12, 1996; a Singaporean embassy official, Beijing, April 22, 1996; a Chinese intelligence analyst involved in ARF policy process, Beijing, July 1996; a prominent Canadian academic involved in Track II activities, January 28, 1997; and from Gary Smith, "Multilateralism and Regional Security in Asia: The ASEAN Regional Forum and APEC's Geopolitical Value" (CFIA, Harvard University, June 1996, draft paper). This doesn't mean that everyone in Beijing who supports the ARF is a convinced multilateralist or true believer in cooperative security. There are other interests that converge on involvement: a "strategic" interest in observing U.S. relations with ASEAN up close; a diplomatic interest in presenting a good image so as to undermine "China threat" arguments, among others. To the extent that multilateralist ideology motivates the behavior of some actors in the policy process, however, socialization in the dialogue process raises the barriers to any Chinese pullout from these dialogues should the strategic and diplomatic interests change.

59. On China and the CTBT, see Banning Garrett and Bonnie Glaser, "Chinese Perspectives on Nuclear Arms Control," *International Security* 20:3 (Winter 1995/6), pp. 43–78; Alastair Iain Johnston, "Prospects for Chinese Nuclear Force Modernization: Limited Deterrence Versus Multilateral Arms Control," *China Quarterly*, no. 146 (June 1996), pp. 548–576; and Sun Xiangli, "Implications of a Comprehensive Test Ban for China's Security Policy" (Stanford University, Center for International Security and Arms Control occasional paper, June 1997).

60. Interview, July 1996.

61. On the role of praise, social opprobrium, and diffuse reputation in eliciting cooperation from egoist actors, see Abram Chayes and Antonia H. Chayes, *The New Sovereignty: Compliance with International Regulatory Treaties* (Cambridge, Mass.: Harvard University Press, 1996); Oran Young, "The Effectiveness of International Institutions: Hard Cases and Critical Variables," in James N. Rosenau and Ernst-Otto Czempiel, eds., *Governance Without Government: Order and Change in World Politics* (Cambridge, Cambridge University Press, 1992), pp. 160–194; Thomas M. Franck, *The Power of Legitimacy Among Nations* (New York: Oxford University Press, 1990); Cialdini, *Influence*, chap. 3. In contrast with Shih Chih-yu's study of Chinacentric psychocultural concepts of face (*The Spirit of Chinese Foreign Policy: A Psychocultural View* (New York: St. Martin's Press, 1990), the causal propositions in this chapter are more general, non–China specific, and suggest ways in which one can find variations in the constraining effects of social praise or opprobrium.

62. On this identity for major powers in general, see Chayes and Chayes, *The New Sovereignty*, p. 27. This identity might be considered an amalgam of what Kim calls "UN Charter" and "Neofunctionalist" visions of world order. See Samuel S. Kim, *China In and Out of the Changing World Order* (Princeton: Center of International Studies, Princeton University, 1991).

63. For example, interviews with military arms control specialists and specialists connected with military technology development, June 1996; with an environmental scientist in the National Environmental Protection Agency, July 1996;

and comments by senior environmental policy maker in discussions with Harvard environment specialists, May 1997.

64. State Council, *Wo guo guanyu quanqiu huanjing wenti de yuanze lizhang* [The principled position of our country concerning global environmental problems] (Beijing, China Environmental Science Press 1992, internal circulation), p. 11.

65. Dessler, "What's at Stake?" p. 443.

66. China's resistance to individual political/civil rights norms may generate a focal point for authoritarian Third World leaders determined to preserve their dictatorial regimes, but it also spurs efforts by NGOs to raise the profile of human rights in China, with consequences for the foreign policies of democracies. These efforts, in turn, may help reinforce these norms.

PART TWO

Interactions

4

Sino-American Relations: Practicing Damage Control

STEVEN I. LEVINE

The United States is China's biggest foreign policy problem, as it has been for most of the past fifty years. That is because the United States, the only true global power in the post–Cold War world, can do more to facilitate or hinder the attainment of vital Chinese foreign policy objectives than any other foreign country. These objectives range from enhancing national security and achieving territorial reunification (with Taiwan) to expanding prosperity and securing international recognition of China's great-power status. Since 1989 the Sino-American relationship has been wracked by contention over issues involving trade, human rights, arms transfers, and Taiwan. Both countries profess an interest in better relations and have recently made a start toward that end, but real conflicts of interest as well as misunderstanding and suspicion make this difficult to accomplish. In 1992 Chinese President Jiang Zemin, offering his prescription for Sino-American relations, said that the two countries should "increase trust, reduce troubles, strengthen cooperation, and avoid confrontation."[1] Addressing a meeting of Americans concerned with Sino-American relations in April 1997, Chinese Foreign Minister Qian Qichen called on them to "show strategic vision and courage . . . [in order to build] a sound, stable and steadily growing relationship between our two countries."[2] American leaders have made similar statements. On her first visit to China in February 1997, Secretary of State Madeleine Albright reiterated the administration's policy of comprehensive engagement with China and President Clinton's commitment to strengthening U.S.-China relations.[3]

Translating these fine sentiments into reality will not be easy. At a minimum, it will require a level of sustained commitment by national leaders on both sides who are willing to pay the domestic political price that compromise entails. Nothing less than the security and prosperity of the Asia-Pacific region in the coming decades is at stake in the Sino-American relationship. A hundred years ago, the United States was first coming of age as a world power and China was a powerless victim of predatory international politics. On the eve of the twenty-first century, the United States is the dominant power and China a rising great power in an increasingly interdependent and multipolar world.[4] A Sino-American relationship tilted toward cooperation rather than competition or confrontation could be a vital element in the structure of regional and global politics in the next century.

Many American as well as Chinese observers forecast a rocky future for Sino-American relations. For example, in *The Coming Conflict with China,* journalists Richard Bernstein and Ross Munro assert the likelihood of conflict because "China during the past decade has set goals for itself that are directly contrary to American interests, the most important . . . to replace the United States as the preeminent power in Asia."[5] Criticizing this perspective, several noted Chinese international affairs scholars, drawing lessons from history, have responded that the United States, as the dominant world power, is trying to suppress a rising China, but they add that Sino-American conflict is by no means inevitable.[6] It is not without reason that Chinese leaders believe that the United States, accustomed to having its way in international affairs, is unsympathetic to and even apprehensive of China's growing international power.

Among China's specific concerns is the fear that the U.S. alliance with Japan, originally designed to contain Soviet expansionism, could become the keystone of an anti-China containment structure. U.S. support of Taiwan continues to frustrate Beijing's reunification policy, as it has for decades. China's recent prosperity is partly dependent upon easy access to American consumers. If provoked, however, Washington might deny China access to the lucrative U.S. market, China's largest, inflicting serious injury on the livelihood of tens of millions of Chinese. American criticism of Chinese human rights practices and political repression, merely an irritation to Beijing at present, could become a serious threat should the Communist Party encounter another challenge on the scale of the one it crushed during the spring 1989 Democracy Movement. These are some of the many reasons why China can no more afford to ignore the United States than the tide can ignore the moon.

Although the making of Chinese foreign policy is considerably more complicated now than during the era when Mao Zedong was in command (1949–1976), China's policy toward the United States is a matter of strategic importance that engages the attention of China's top leaders (see Chapters 2 and 3). As China becomes increasingly active in regional and global affairs, however, it becomes more and more difficult for Beijing to coordinate all the domestic and foreign policy decisions that impact on relations with the United States, particularly since Washington takes an interest in questions such as human rights, Taiwan, and Tibet that Beijing considers domestic issues. Nevertheless, compared to the baroque complexity of American politics where Congress, numerous interest groups, and public opinion vie with the executive branch for control over China policy, China's U.S. policy is relatively straightforward. It can still best be understood using a rational-actor model according to which China's top leaders chart policy toward the United States in accordance with their own understanding of what constitutes China's national interests.[7]

Despite American awareness of China's growing economic, military, and political clout, a considerable gap exists between China and the United States in the weight each country attaches to Sino-American relations. If the United States is often on China's mind, the reverse is not true. China is rarely at the top of the foreign policy agenda of the United States, a global power prone to the complacent parochialism that privileged position often engenders. Congress and the American public display a merely episodic, if occasionally intense, interest in China and know little about a country that U.S. media portray in a mostly negative light. The press amplifies the problems in the Sino-American relationship while overlooking positive interactions. By contrast, because the United States has long functioned as both a positive and a negative symbol in Chinese political discourse, many ordinary as well as well-educated citizens among China's growing urban population take an interest in Sino-American relations that is unreciprocated by most Americans.

Despite the asymmetry in levels of interest, Chinese and American elites recognize the importance of the Sino-American relationship in bilateral, regional, and global terms. For most of the 1990s, however, neither side made much effort to address fundamental problems in the relationship. On the U.S. side, President Bill Clinton failed to provide effective leadership with respect to China policy. On the Chinese side President Jiang Zemin's preoccupation with consolidating his own power precluded any initiatives on his part in the realm of Sino-American relations. Not until October 1997, five years into the Clinton administration, did the U.S. and Chinese presidents hold their first substantive summit meeting, although they had talked briefly several times before, in connection with multilateral meetings. In the vacuum of leadership, the tenor of Sino-American relations in the early and mid-1990s was set by lower-ranking officials on both sides; they often traded accusations and engaged in mutual recriminations as they wrangled over the details of trade, arms transfers, human rights, and other contentious issues.

In 1996, after a troublesome episode in the Taiwan Strait, Washington finally began to implement its three-year-old policy of comprehensive engagement with China that was intended to restore high-level contacts with Chinese officials, promote a strategic dialogue, and accelerate China's integration into the world community.[8] By then, however, much valuable time had been lost and disillusionment toward the United States had permeated Chinese popular consciousness. This feeling was reflected in the enthusiastic public response to *China Can Say No*, published by three young journalists in May 1996.[9] An immediate best-seller in China, this collection of essays attacked the shallowness of American popular and materialist culture and lambasted Chinese intellectuals who fawn on the United States. Meanwhile, in the United States, a swelling anti-China mood was fed by a stream of media reports detailing a variety of Chinese human rights abuses, repression in Tibet, and alleged Chinese efforts to influence the outcome of U.S. elections through money politics.

To the historian of Sino-American relations, the present moment is merely the latest in a Sino-American cycle of positive and negative swings that can be traced back well over a century.[10] Never before, however, have relations between the two countries been as important as they are now, when China is emerging as a major actor in world affairs and the United States is the dominant power. It is unfortunate that China and the United States have been running out of patience with each other precisely at a time when patience and understanding are needed to cope with present problems and future challenges.

A Glance Backward

The present state of Sino-American relations is the product of fundamental changes in the international environment as well as specific aspects of the domestic politics of both countries. The end of the Cold War, which had structured Sino-American relations since 1949, spurred policymakers in both Beijing and Washington to reexamine their international relationships as they struggled to come to terms with a fluid global environment. Weak leadership in China and the United States impeded the search for a new Sino-American paradigm.

In the early 1970s, parallel concerns about the rise of Soviet power led Chairman Mao Zedong and President Richard Nixon to end more than twenty years of Sino-American confrontation, dating from the 1949 victory of the CCP in China's civil war.[11] A common interest in combating the "Soviet threat"—the focus of the shared obsession of the United States and China—served as the *creation myth* of Sino-American relations, sanctioning the development of an elaborate network of economic, political, military, cultural, academic, and scientific and technological exchanges. As the relationship expanded beyond its original strategic focus, the mutual suspicion that had originally permeated this marriage of convenience between two oddly matched partners gradually dissipated. Post-Mao China's acceleration on the fast track of economic reform coincided with the establishment of diplomatic relations between China and the United States in 1979. "Normalization," as it was called, facilitated a decade of explosive growth in every area of interaction.[12] By the late 1980s, however, the restoration of amicable Sino-Soviet relations and the end of the Cold War had eliminated the anti-Soviet strategic basis for Sino-American alignment and posed the question of the durability of Sino-American relations once the strategic foundation on which it had rested had crumbled.

In practical terms, Sino-American political, military, economic, cultural, and other links had expanded so rapidly during the 1980s that there should have been no question about either the durability or the resilience of the overall relationship. A dense network of interwoven common interests bound the two countries together, and the plurality of interests operated like independently suspended shock absorbers cushioning the vehicle of Sino-American relations from the bumps and potholes in the road. By the mid-1980s, U.S. interest in promoting China's modernization had replaced strategic cooperation as a mutually acceptable basis for Sino-American relations.[13]

Throughout the 1970s and 1980s, however, serious disagreements persisted between the two countries, the most difficult of which concerned Taiwan. Chinese and American diplomats engaged in a series of difficult and sometimes contentious negotiations, attempting to stabilize what was an inherently difficult relationship.[14] These efforts bore fruit because national leaders, realizing the importance of good Sino-American relations, put their political weight behind ambiguous compromises crafted by the diplomats, even though these compromises failed to satisfy either side completely. At this time, even China's more hidebound Communist leaders, although uneasy with the effects of American culture on China's educated youth, saw no immediate threat from the United States to the hegemony of the CCP, and understood that the United States could make a substantial contribution to the development of China's economy.

In the United States, China policy rested on shifting sands. In order to be acceptable to Congress and the public, the policy had to be grounded in an explicit and easily understood rationale consistent with the informal ideology or the political value system.[15] Initially, the U.S. global contest with the USSR, marketed to the public as an anti-Communist ideological crusade, provided a rationale for Nixon's strategic alignment with China, which was generally accepted as a necessary exercise in realpolitik. Deng Xiaoping's market-oriented reforms in the 1980s persuaded many Americans that the PRC was abandoning communism in all but name and was launched on a trajectory toward capitalism and democracy. The age-old dream of transforming China into the American image, which derived from both religious and commercial missionary impulses, provided an alternative rationale for U.S. China policy. When huge student-led demonstrations filled Tiananmen Square, China's symbolic center, in the spring of 1989, Americans watching on television eagerly anticipated the Second Coming of Chinese Democracy. But the brutal armed suppression of the popular movement on June 4, 1989, punctured U.S. illusions and knocked the props out from under the Sino-American relationship.[16]

In retrospect, it is clear that neither the creation myth (the anti-Soviet strategic rationale of the 1970s) nor its replacement (the proreform rationale of the 1980s) provided a stable foundation within the United States for long-term Sino-American ties. Rather, by disseminating such simplifying notions, U.S. political and public opinion leaders, especially the mass media, obscured the complex realities of China, fostering exaggerated and unrealistic expectations that the Sino-American relationship could not possibly fulfill. In the 1990s, in the absence of a persuasive, clearly articulated, and frequently reiterated explanation by national political and opinion leaders of why good relations with China were essential to the United States, U.S. China policy became increasingly fragmented and contested both within and outside official Washington. On the one hand, many global-minded business interests became advocates for China, seeing the world's fastest-growing economy as an enormous opportunity that the United States cannot afford to cede to foreign competitors. On the other hand, human rights groups, religious groups, supporters of Tibet and of Taiwan, arms control advocates, and others condemned China as an authoritarian state that abuses human rights, suppresses Tibetan culture, threatens Taiwan, and flouts international arms control agreements.

The fragmentation of U.S. China policy and the proliferation of American interest groups asserting claims in the China policy arena represented a dilemma to Beijing, which prior to 1989 had been accustomed to dealing primarily with the White House and only secondarily with Congress. In the aftermath of June 4, 1989, it was Congress that forced President George Bush to impose a series of tough sanctions on China including a cutoff of high-level visits with China, an end to arms transfers and military-related sales, and the suspension of financial credits and economic assistance. In President Bush, who took a strong personal interest in Chinese affairs, Beijing nevertheless had a powerful partner who was intent upon checking the free fall of Sino-American relations.[17] For the remainder of his term, Chinese leaders, never comfortable with Congress's wild-card foreign policy role, looked to the White House as a bulwark against efforts on Capitol Hill to influence China's conduct via punitive legislation. Even when the president gradually toughened his stance toward the PRC during his final year in office, authorizing the sale of 150 F-16 fighter planes to Taiwan in violation of a Sino-American agreement, Chinese leaders were slow to criticize him.

The victory of Democrat Bill Clinton in the 1992 presidential election raised questions about the future of Sino-American relations similar to those that Ronald Reagan's victory had posed in 1980. Like Reagan, the new president had sharply criticized his predecessor's China policy during the campaign and had promised new policy directions. Once in office, however, Reagan rapidly adjusted his views to accord with the prevailing bipartisan China policy consensus. The problem in the early 1990s was that there was no longer any U.S. consensus on China policy. Beijing was uncertain whether Clinton would choose the path of political realism, by which they meant refraining from interfering in Chinese domestic affairs and treating China with respect, or would embark on an anti-China crusade, which an unusual coalition of congressional liberals, human rights lobbyists, and conservative anti-Communist ideologues favored.[18]

In the event, Clinton did neither. Inclined during his first term to play the role of a domestic-policy president, the president virtually ignored China. Warren Christopher, who served as secretary of state during the first Clinton administration, likewise devoted very little time to dealing with China policy issues. During those years the administration as a whole failed to implement a well-defined and consistent policy toward Beijing. Interaction over issues ranging from trade to human rights took place in what was effectively a policy vacuum.

If Clinton had little interest in China policy, Chinese President Jiang Zemin was not himself in a position to take the lead in the realm of Sino-American relations. China's U.S. policy tended to be reactive rather than initiatory. Elevated to the top leadership position in 1989 by Deng Xiaoping, Jiang was a cautious centrist who focused on building the domestic political networks he lacked on coming to power. His primary concern may have been to legitimize his rule in the eyes of the People's Liberation Army, the standard-bearer for China's reasserted national pride. Nevertheless, when in 1996 the United States finally signaled its readiness to upgrade relations with China by agreeing to an exchange of state visits between Jiang and Clinton, it was the Chinese president who urged Washington to consider Sino-American relations from a strategic, long-range perspective, looking toward the creation of a healthy, good, and stable relationship for the twenty-first century.[19]

China and the United States in the Post–Cold War World

Throughout the Cold War, Chinese leaders viewed the United States in the context of an international system defined by the competition of the superpowers for global hegemony. China, although significantly weaker than either of the superpowers, became adept at extending its own influence in international politics beyond the limits of its tangible power by playing upon American and Soviet hopes and fears. The end of the Cold War and the collapse of the Soviet Union terminated this game. China then faced the question of how to position itself in an international system dominated, at least temporarily, by the United States, a country still vastly more powerful than China. It is no surprise that Beijing and Washington approached the global context of their relationship very differently.

The United States defined the problem as one of how to integrate China, a state that had long been on the periphery of world politics, into a well-established, albeit constantly evolving, system of international institutions, norms, and regimes. As the dominant power, of course, the United States had played a key role in the design, construction, and operation of this system. In scrutinizing China's qualifications and behavior, Washington functioned like a self-appointed Credentials Committee that had the power to accept, reject, or grant probationary membership in the international club to an applicant of uncertain respectability. Should Beijing behave in ways of which Washington disapproved, for example, by assisting Pakistan's clandestine nuclear weapons program, the United States could consign the PRC to the category of "rogue states."

Beijing also wanted to integrate China into the international system but resented being treated like a Rottweiler in the waiting room of an obedience school. Wary of the new Western dogma of interdependence, which seemed a pretext for foreign intervention in Chinese domestic affairs, China vigorously wielded its sovereignty as a shield against unwanted attention from the outside world. As realists, Chinese leaders were well aware of U.S. power, but Chinese observers believed that the habits of domination Washington called global leadership exceeded its actual capabilities. Throughout the 1990s, Chinese argued that over the longer term the United States would be unable to achieve its hegemonic global aspirations because of the inherent multipolarity of world politics as well the limits imposed by domestic American problems.[20] In this respect, the ambitions and limitations of the Clinton administration were no different from those of its predecessors. "The strategic plan of the United States is to exploit its economic and military might, plus diplomatic efforts, to deal with perceived threats to its national security and economic interests, and strengthen its supremacy in the world."[21] Chinese analysts believed that international opposition to American policies on the part of many states in Europe, Asia, and the Middle East plus domestic opposition from conservative Republicans and disaffected liberal Democrats act as significant constraints upon U.S. foreign policy.

China has adopted a multipronged approach to managing its strategic relations with the United States. In bilateral terms, Chinese leaders frequently emphasized their desire for improved Sino-American relations and denied that any fundamental conflicts of interest existed between the two countries. In the 1990s, Beijing signed the Nuclear Non-Proliferation Treaty and the Comprehensive Test Ban and acceded to the international conventions on biological and on chemical weapons. China likewise cooperated with the United States and other countries in international efforts to end the civil war in Cambodia and to reduce tension on the Korean peninsula. Tacitly acknowledging the anxieties of some of its neighbors, China participated as a dialogue partner in the security discussions of the ASEAN Regional Forum (ARF), which it saw as an initial step along the road toward new forms of security cooperation in the Asia-Pacific region.[22]

Such reassuring gestures, however, have gone hand in hand with redoubled efforts to upgrade China's conventional military capacity via domestic investments and the purchase of modern weapons systems from abroad, particularly from Russia, which again became China's major foreign arms supplier, as it had been in the 1950s. China's active diplomacy vis-à-vis its major Asian neighbors—Japan, Vietnam, Korea, and India—also strengthened its claim to Asian great power status and implicitly challenged Washington's globalism. Chinese leaders were quick to take advantage of their new economic muscle by making clear that political considerations would be employed in awarding large contracts and other economic favors to foreign firms. That produced the desired effect of enlisting foreign business interests as advocates of pro-China policies.

China and the United States are both major components of the emerging multipolar structure of international power and share parallel interests in wanting to maintain a peaceful environment in the Asia-Pacific region. But their interests are by no means identical. China is not yet a status quo power like the United States. In addition to its desire to reintegrate Taiwan, China has staked out large claims to the islands and waters of the South China Sea, which bring it into potential conflict with several of its Southeast Asian neighbors. Beijing professes its desire for a peaceful resolution of territorial disputes even as it uses military means to strengthen its position in the disputed territories.

Progress toward multilateral security arrangements in the Asia-Pacific region lags well behind the economic dynamism that has characterized the region for several decades. Many of the bilateral security arrangements that Washington forged during the Cold War remain in place, providing the foundation for U.S. power in the region. Chinese power is likely to grow incrementally over the coming decades, since China will be unconstrained by multilateral regional security obligations and unlikely to enter into restrictive bilateral arrangements. But the freedom of action that Chinese leaders might expect from their enhanced power is severely limited by the existence of more powerful states, in particular the United States. That is the context for Chinese objections to the U.S.-Japan Joint Declaration of April 1996 regarding the enhanced role of the U.S.-Japan alliance in the twenty-first century. Although China prefers to see Japan harnessed to the United States rather than developing its military power unilaterally, references in the declaration to a shared interest in the peaceful resolution of regional problems arouses Beijing's suspicion that Washington and Tokyo might assert an interest in Taiwan that could hobble Beijing. A strengthened U.S.-Japan alliance also weakens China's position vis-à-vis each of the two countries.[23]

Americans who advocate containment as a way to deal with a current or prospective "China threat" argue that China is pursuing the goal of hegemony in Asia in the twenty-first century. This perspective suggests an ignorance of Asian power realities that no Chinese leader could possibly betray. The growth of Chinese power is only one factor in a complex security environment. The United States will remain a significant factor in the regional security equation by virtue of its technical and economic prowess as well as its military presence and alliances. Regional security will increasingly be decided among the states of the region itself without reference to an overarching global struggle that disappeared with the Cold War. Numerous factors contribute to the Asianization of Asian-Pacific security politics. In addition to China's emergence as a comprehensive regional military power are Japan's slowly growing foreign policy assertiveness, the appearance, sooner or later, of a unified Korea, the end of Vietnam's international isolation and its membership in ASEAN, and the possibility of a revitalized Russian role in Asia in line with Moscow's historic interests. These developments may stimulate the reappearance of historic rivalries that were muted in the past half century.

How China and the United States relate to each other under such circumstances will very much depend upon how each of them relates to other states in the region. For example, should China decide to use its air and naval power to enforce its expansive territorial claims in the South China Sea, other claimants, including Vietnam, might look to Washington to counter Chinese power. Should Japan someday veer away from its security relationship with the United States in the direction of armed unilateralism, Beijing and Washington might conceivably draw together to contain Tokyo.[24]

Of more immediate concern to both countries is the question of Taiwan, which Beijing defines as the major issue between the United States and China.[25] This is a chronic problem with major implications for regional security. In 1950, the United States intervened to protect the Chinese Nationalist government, which had taken refuge on Taiwan after losing the Chinese civil war. Until its abrogation by Washington in 1980, the U.S.-Republic of China Mutual Security Treaty guaranteed Taiwan against the threat of military action from the Communist mainland. After Washington switched diplomatic recognition from Taipei to Beijing in 1979, what purported to be unofficial relations between the United States and Taiwan were governed by the Taiwan Relations Act (TRA), passed by Congress in 1979. This act renewed in different language the security guarantees of the abrogated treaty, pledged to supply Taiwan with defensive weapons, and authorized the president to take appropriate measures to deal with military and other threats to Taiwan's security.

Beijing has always considered the TRA to be inconsistent with Washington's pledge to abide by a "one-China" policy, but for many years China and the United States managed to avoid a collision over Taiwan through the adroit diplomacy of "creative ambiguity"—employing diplomatic formulas that each side interpreted as it chose. From Beijing's perspective the bedrock of Sino-American relations was the three core U.S.-China communiqués carefully negotiated between 1972 and 1982. These agreements precariously balanced Beijing's assertion that Taiwan was a part of China with Washington's determination to supply defensive weapons to the island and assert an interest in its security. The formulas contained in these agreements combined strength with elasticity, like garments that hold their shape even when stretched. What these agreements had not anticipated was the magnitude of political change in Taiwan in the 1980s and 1990s that undermined Beijing's strategy for eventual reunification.

When the United States severed diplomatic ties with Taiwan in 1979 in order to normalize relations with the PRC, Deng Xiaoping gambled that growing international isolation would eventually force Taiwan to accept integration into the PRC on Beijing's terms. That has not happened. Political and economic developments on the island have confounded Beijing's expectations and created a vibrant society that increasingly asserts its right to participate in international affairs like any other state. Taiwan's claims on U.S. sympathies, originating in Cold War anticommunism, have been reinvigorated by the democratic transformation of the island's political system over the past dozen years. President Lee Teng-hui has spearheaded an energetic campaign of "pragmatic diplomacy" designed to counter Beijing's attempts to isolate Taiwan in the international community. Chinese leaders mistrust Lee, believing that he is pursuing a "two Chinas" or "one China, one Taiwan" policy aimed at steering Taiwan toward independence.

That is why China exploded in anger in 1995 when the White House, under goading from Congress, reversed its earlier position and granted

Lee Teng-hui an American visa to give the keynote address at the graduation ceremonies of Cornell University, where he had received his doctorate. Few Americans understood why the Chinese made such a fuss about an apparently innocuous visit. But Beijing read Washington's approval of Lee's trip as proof of U.S. duplicity and a serious violation of the core Sino-American agreements. Beijing's attempts in July–August 1995 and again in February–March 1996 to pressure Lee Teng-hui and intimidate Taiwan's voters on the eve of their first direct presidential election by conducting large-scale offensive military exercises, including test firing of live missiles in Taiwan's coastal waters, tested Washington's commitment under the TRA. To Beijing's further outrage, Clinton responded by dispatching two powerful aircraft carrier battle groups to the waters off Taiwan, sending an unmistakable signal to Beijing that the U.S. commitment to Taiwan remained firm.[26]

Beijing's scare tactics vis-à-vis Taiwan reopened the question in the United States whether Washington should make its security commitment to Taiwan more explicit than the language of the TRA. Although the administration thought it unwise to do so, House Speaker Newt Gingrich, on a trip to China in March 1997, flatly stated, "We want you to understand, we will defend Taiwan. Period."[27] In reality, that is far from certain. To reassure China, the United States has frequently reiterated its adherence to the three core Sino-American agreements, in which the United States acknowledges the Chinese position that Taiwan is a part of China. Washington's position is that it is interested in ensuring that any change in Taiwan's current status occur peacefully as a result of dialogue and agreement among the parties concerned rather than through the unilateral application of military force.

One effect of the face-off over Taiwan was heightened U.S. interest in the status of Hong Kong after Great Britain's handover of the territory to China on July 1, 1997, in accordance with the terms of the Sino-British agreement of 1984. Washington's interest in the political future of Hong Kong, asserted via the U.S.-Hong Kong Policy Act passed by Congress in 1992, was regarded by Beijing as unwarranted meddling in Chinese affairs. U.S. attention focused on the question of whether the new government of the Hong Kong Special Administrative Region would honor its pledge to respect the democratic freedoms and political rights of its citizens. Most American commentators expressed grave doubts on this score. Martin Lee, the outspoken leader of Hong Kong's Democratic Party, was given a more respectful hearing in Washington than was Tung Chee Hwa, the shipping magnate whom Beijing designated as chief executive. China's treatment of Hong Kong, both President Clinton and House Speaker Gingrich suggested, would be considered an important indicator of whether China could be trusted to abide by its commitments.[28]

If the intensified U.S. interest in Hong Kong was partly connected with Taiwan, Washington's interest in China's arms transfer and nuclear weapons policies was linked to regional security and world order questions. Beijing and Washington have frequently been at odds over Chinese arms sales, to the Middle East in particular, and its supplying of nuclear reactors and technology to Pakistan, Iran, North Korea, and Algeria. With respect to conventional weapons sales, China accused the United States, the world's largest arms dealer, of hypocrisy in objecting to Chinese sales, far smaller in value. In recent years, as China's share in the international arms market has declined, this issue has faded. China's special relationship with Pakistan, based on Beijing's desire to support a regional counterweight to India in South Asia, has been a core element of Chinese foreign policy since the late 1950s. For years Beijing deflected Washington's intermittent pressure on it to stop supplying nuclear weapons technology and nuclear-capable missiles to Islamabad, which, with clandestine Chinese help, has achieved its goal of developing nuclear weapons. In May 1996, in response to additional pressure from Washington, China agreed to refrain from transferring nuclear technology and equipment to facilities not under safeguards drawn up by the International Atomic Energy Agency. China's support of the Comprehensive Test Ban Treaty and the indefinite extension of the Nuclear Non-Proliferation Treaty has allayed U.S. fears that China might play the role of a "rogue" nuclear state.

In 1993 China and the United States resumed their security dialogue, which Washington had suspended in 1989 to protest the PLA's role in suppressing the Democracy Movement. Beijing followed suit in 1995 to protest Lee Teng-hui's visit to the United States. The resumption of the dialogue in 1996 following the Taiwan Strait crisis underlined the importance of regular Sino-American communication between military officials and security managers on both sides, particularly given the power and autonomy of the Chinese military in the post-Deng era. Like most countries, China's penchant for secrecy is particularly strong when it comes to military matters. Through a continuing dialogue with their Chinese counterparts, U.S. security managers hope to encourage China to adopt a policy of greater transparency with respect to defense expenditures, which the official budget probably understates by a factor of four or five, and by promoting such confidence-building measures as providing China's neighbors advance notice of military exercises.[29]

A focus on points of contention between Beijing and Washington with respect to security issues should not obscure the fact that the countries share an interest in promoting a stable and peaceful environment in the Asia-Pacific region. Cooperation between the United States and China was instrumental in crafting a settlement of the civil war in Cambodia and facilitating a solution to the problem of North Korea's nuclear weapons program. The volatile situation on the Korean peninsula necessitates ongoing Sino-American dialogue and cooperation. With respect to the larger issue of the growth of Chinese military power, it would be folly to suppose that Beijing will ever allow Washington, or any other foreign capital, to dictate terms on issues concerning Chinese national security. The modernization of China's armed forces inevitably discomfits China's neighbors, large and small, but they are not without the means of individual and collective defense should China assume an aggressive stance toward them. There is no good reason to suppose that twenty-first-century China will follow the late-nineteenth-century path of imperial expansion that Meiji Japan or Wilhelmine Germany pursued or the path that the Soviet Union followed after World War II. The pertinent question in terms of Sino-American relations is whether the United States will invoke misleading historical analogies to adopt containment-style policies vis-à-vis China, the actual purpose of which may be to perpetuate U.S. domination rather than counter a real Chinese threat.

Economic Relations

In a stunning reversal of its historical fantasies about the China market, the United States has become the largest overseas market for Chinese goods since the beginning of China's export-oriented economic reforms. Although China represents a rapidly growing market for U.S. products, a mushrooming trade imbalance has joined the list of American complaints against China. In 1995, the U.S. trade deficit with China, which had mounted steadily since 1983, approached $34 billion, according to official U.S. statistics, and was continuing to climb.[30] China, which uses a different method of calculation, disputes these figures, which it says greatly inflate the size of the deficit.[31] Chinese exports to the United States consist largely of a wide variety of inexpensive consumer goods, such as apparel, toys, sports equipment, footwear, and consumer electronics. Chinese imports from the United States consist largely of aviation and aeronautical equipment, heavy machinery, chemicals (fertilizers), raw materials, and agricultural commodities.

By the late 1980s, the growth of Chinese exports to the United States, which followed the earlier trajectories of Japanese, Korean, and Taiwanese goods on the U.S. market, began to elicit accusations of unfair trading practices similar to those that Americans have regularly voiced since the 1970s against their other major Asian trading partners. By 1996, China's trade surplus with the United States had rivaled, and in some months, exceeded Japan's. To accusations that China was dumping goods on the U.S. market, that is, selling at below production cost in order to gain market share, were added complaints that China had become one of the main international violators of intellectual property rights and was costing the U.S. software and entertainment industries between $2 and $3 billion in lost revenues by illegal copying of computer software, CD-ROMs, videos, audiocassettes, and films. When earlier intellectual property rights agreements signed in 1992 and 1995 failed to substantially improve the situation because of lax Chinese enforcement, U.S. trade negotiators threatened to impose exorbitant tariffs on selected Chinese goods and Beijing threatened retaliation in kind. Washington's high-profile strategy of economic brinksmanship, in which negotiations took place under the gun of U.S.-imposed deadlines, reinforced Chinese feelings about high-handed American behavior.

The United States has also pressured China to cut tariffs, eliminate most of the quotas, and drop other import-licensing restrictions on U.S. goods as well as to publish hitherto secret trade laws, statutes, and regulations that had long frustrated American companies. The protracted negotiations among China, the United States, and other countries over China's application to join the World Trade Organization also centered on these and related questions. By mid-1997, differences over conditions for Chinese membership had narrowed considerably, and it seemed only a matter of time before China was finally admitted.[32]

The Chinese market for American goods has been growing rapidly, and certain companies, e.g., Motorola in the field of cellular phones, have done extremely well in garnering the lion's share of the Chinese market, as has Boeing in the field of commercial aircraft. By the mid-1990s, U.S. companies had invested $26 billion in China, placing the United States just behind Japan among foreign investors. U.S. companies lobbied hard in Washington against imposing political conditions, especially those concerning human rights, on trade with China.[33] The most visible evidence of U.S. commercial success in China is the fast-food industry. That the world's largest McDonald's and KFC franchises are located in the heart of downtown Beijing is, of course, more of a cultural than a culinary statement. The Chinese, who, it may be argued, possess the world's finest cuisine, are eating American culture, although it bears noting that fast food is most attractive to Chinese children, for whom Maidanglao Shushu (literally Uncle McDonald, aka Ronald) is fast becoming as familiar an icon as Mickey Mouse and Donald Duck. Another sign of American chic is the chain of spotless Chinese restaurants offering that perfect marriage of the familiar and the exotic—steaming bowls of so-called California beef noodles—a dish that most Californians would fail to recognize as part of their cuisine. Meanwhile, Coca Cola, which many Chinese used to think tasted like bad medicine, has grown to dominate the Chinese soft drink market, and Budweiser and Pabst Blue Ribbon compete with premier Chinese beers like Tsingtao and Five Star.

Undoubtedly the most frequent source of irritation in Sino-American economic relations in recent years has been the question of Most Favored Nation (MFN) status. MFN, a misnomer for normal trading relations, is routinely granted by the United States to all but a handful of its trading partners and was extended to China in 1980. But because it was considered a "nonmarket economy," China's status comes up for annual congressional review. MFN was routinely extended until 1990 when congressional and other critics of China's crackdown on dissent argued that MFN for China should be conditioned on the easing of political repression and improvements in China's abysmal human rights record.[34] President Bush thought otherwise, arguing that the revocation of MFN would destroy Sino-American trade, which was not only was mutually beneficial but also indirectly helped the cause of Chinese reform by accelerating the growth of the nonstate sector. Although for three consecutive years (1990–1992) large majorities in the House and the Senate voted for various forms of conditionality, Congress was unable to muster the two-thirds majority needed to override Bush's vetoes. As a presidential candidate in 1992, Bill Clinton roundly criticized Bush for caving in to the Chinese and promised to make human rights a priority of his administration's China policy.[35]

Facing contradictory pressures when the issue of MFN extension came up in the spring of 1993, Clinton characteristically waffled between business groups, which lobbied hard to protect MFN, and human rights groups, most of which favored either revoking MFN or imposing tough conditions on extending it. Clinton finally opted for extension but stipulated that China would have to make "consistent overall progress" in several specified areas of human rights during the coming year or face the loss of MFN next time around. By this action, the president merely deferred making a tough choice and wedged himself into a corner from which only the Chinese could extricate him if they acceded to his stipulations. Naturally, Beijing rejected conditionality and demonstrably refused to play ball with Clinton on human rights despite wheedling and cajoling by Secretary of State Christopher and others. Ultimately, Clinton was forced to eat crow. On May 26, 1994, he announced that he was delinking human rights from MFN once and for all.[36] Claiming that the policy of conditionality had served its purpose, Clinton asserted that it was no longer a useful policy tool. Beijing and the United States business community applauded the president's decisions, whereas human rights groups accused Clinton of betraying both his promise and the cause of human rights in China.

Since 1994 the annual extension of MFN has again become mostly a formality, although it provides an opportunity for Congress to vent its displeasure with China. Meanwhile, the hope entertained by China and the U.S. business community that China would be granted permanent MFN status has not been fulfilled. The Clinton administration, on the defensive because of accusations that Democrats received illegal Chinese campaign contributions in 1996, does not want to take on a controversial issue in a climate in which it has nothing to gain from making an unreciprocated gift to Beijing. Eventually, implementation of China's new policy of converting most state-owned enterprises into joint stock companies, adopted at the Fifteenth CCP Congress in September 1997, will present an opportunity for Washington to change the anachronistic classification of China as a "nonmarket economy," facilitating the granting to China of permanent MFN status.

Human Rights and the Role of Values in U.S.-China Relations

What role do political and cultural values play in Sino-American relations? Does raising value-oriented issues such as human rights jeopardize the relationship by needlessly introducing irreconcilable perspectives? Proponents of Sino-American reconciliation in the 1970s considered values irrelevant to the pursuit of their strategic objectives. China's massive abuse of human rights during the later Maoist era was largely ignored, denied, or excused by most Americans. The June 4, 1989, Beijing massacre reawakened Americans to the repressive side of Chinese-style socialism. Enjoying greater access to Congress and the media, human rights groups like Human Rights Watch-Asia, Amnesty International, and Human Rights in China succeeded in placing political repression, imprisonment for political activities, torture, prison labor exports, and other human rights abuses on the agenda of U.S.-China relations. The imprisonment and brutal treatment of Wei Jingsheng, the martyr of Chinese democracy, and Wang Dan, a thoughtful leader of the 1989 student movement, received considerable attention in U.S. media. Americans also took sympathetic notice of the long struggle of Tibetans, inside and outside their homeland, to defend their culture against harsh, colonial-style Chinese rule. When China threatened financial retribution if the Disney Corporation proceeded to make a film sympathetic to the Dalai Lama, Hollywood defied Beijing's cultural commissars. The Dalai Lama is a celebrity in the United States and Free Tibet a rallying cry on college campuses.[37] In 1997, a broad coalition of American religious organizations pushed for passage of the Freedom from Religious Persecution Act, which would apply economic sanctions on countries engaging in religious persecution. Powerful rightist Christian groups were particularly active in this effort. In sum, the issue of human rights has become a core item on the agenda of U.S.-China relations, which Beijing cannot wish or wave away.

China has fought an increasingly active campaign in response to human rights pressure from the United States. As Chapter 10, on human rights, clearly demonstrates, Chinese authorities believe that the United States has brandished the issue of human rights as a cudgel to attack Chinese socialism. Yet the variety of Chinese responses James Seymour delineates reflects alternate assessments by different Chinese political leaders of how best to handle these issues. China itself has participated over the years in international efforts to develop an international human rights regime focused on economic and social rights. At the same time, China has repeatedly rejected foreign criticism of its human rights record as constituting unacceptable interference in its internal affairs. China has also aggressively defended its own human rights record, arguing that Chinese socialism has done a superior job in guaranteeing vital social and economic rights that are neglected in the United States.[38] China has foiled U.S. efforts to persuade the UN Commission on Human Rights to examine China's human rights record and has made common cause with other non-Western countries that resent what they perceive as meddlesome American moralizing.

For a time, Beijing rather grudgingly accepted a dialogue on human rights with U.S. officials as well as representatives of U.S. nongovernmental organizations, but after President Clinton delinked human rights from the MFN issue, Chinese leaders correctly concluded that they could hang tough because U.S. business interests had trumped human rights. Their calculation is only partly correct. The issue of human rights may recede at times but will not go away, because it is deeply rooted in U.S. political culture and basic values. If that is true, the question then becomes one of how to manage American and Chinese differences over human rights.

Many thoughtful Chinese and American observers worry that the fragile structure of Sino-American relations may collapse under the weight of value dissonance. Ideological conflicts between Chinese state socialism and U.S. liberal capitalism should be set aside in line with former premier Zhou Enlai's injunction to "seek common ground while reserving differences" (*qiu tong cun yi*). Unfortunately, past experience suggests that ignoring the essential differences between China's still essentially Leninist system and the U.S. democratic political system is a defective formula for Sino-American stability.

In order to win long-term acceptance by Congress and the American people, U.S. policy toward China must be rooted in democratic political culture, which accords a high value to human rights, particularly political and civil rights. That is realism, not idealism. Furthermore, rather than being an incitement to ideological warfare or an excuse for restricting relations, the affirmation by each side of its own values can be the point of departure for a new and much-needed realism. Stripping away the sentimentalism and phony friendship of "special relationships" of any sort facilitates the search for real common interests as well as the sober discussion and prudent management of real points of conflict. It thereby reduces mutual expectations to realistic proportions.

Democratic political and civil rights are not the parochial expression of U.S. culture even if Americans sometimes believe it to be their peculiar birthright. They are universal values that are recognized and implemented by culturally diverse members of the international community. The most powerful challenges to Chinese Leninism have come, not from the outside world, but from within China itself where the official ideology of state socialism is ignored or even mocked by many members of the CCP. Wei Jingsheng's may be a unique voice, but it is undoubtedly Chinese.[39] Chinese political culture has evolved away from authoritarianism enough to be compatible with the value system and attitudes that underpin democratic polities.

Arguing that the U.S. approach to human rights in China has failed, Harry Harding suggests that the United States and China should make a fresh start aimed at promoting cooperation rather than confrontation in the area of human rights.[40] The U.S. side should expand its definition of human rights to include the social and economic rights that China emphasizes and should adopt a long-term perspective on democratization in China. The Chinese side should reaffirm and strengthen its commitment to the international human rights regime and should commit itself to a long-term process of political reform that values representative political institutions. Both sides should work together to promote human rights in their societies. Unfortunately, these sensible prescriptions are unlikely to make much headway in an atmosphere charged with mutual resentment and suspicion, but they could eventually become the basis for progress at some later time.

For the present, the inclusion of values such as human rights on the agenda of Sino-American relations serves to legitimate U.S. China policy to Americans, to encourage realism by clarifying the limits and possibilities for interactions, and to promote universal values. It also challenges both sides to improve their performance and acknowledges the pluralism of Chinese and American society, in preparation for a range of future political contingencies.

Since the early 1970s, cultural, educational, scientific, and technical exchanges have been an important component of Sino-American relations. U.S. popular culture and consumerist ideology and democratic ideas have been a potent force for change in Chinese society. Mickey Mouse and Donald Duck quickly became widely disseminated Chinese cultural icons; their individualism, irreverence, and pleasure ethic implicitly challenged such paragons of socialist virtue as the nerd soldier Lei Feng.[41] American rock music inspired cultural iconoclasts such as the rock singer Cui Jian, whose daring lyrics probed the personal and political despair of contemporary Chinese society.[42] Even though most Chinese intellectuals remain committed to the idea of serving China, they are increasingly cosmopolitan, and many are drawn to Western notions of intellectual autonomy, unfettered criticism, and democratic norms.[43]

Conclusion

Years of inattention by high-level officials in Washington and Beijing have taken their toll on Sino-American relations, enabling professional doomsayers in both countries to seize the high ground and propagate the message that for ideological or geopolitical reasons, conflict rather than cooperation is certain to dominate the Sino-American relationship for years to come. Yet even in the 1970s, when the political, social, and economic gap between China and the United States was considerably wider than it has since become, Chinese and Americans managed to cooperate in many different areas. The technological superiority and greater wealth enjoyed by the United States since the nineteenth century has often infected Americans with the germ of condescension based on the assumption that China needs to learn from the United States. Patriotic Chinese, equally proud of their cultural heritage and achievements, have bristled in response. Such attitudes are an impediment to engaging in the hard work that cooperation entails.

Chinese leaders are well aware that the United States no longer has it in its power to isolate China as it attempted to do, with only limited success, in the 1950s and 1960s. A U.S. effort to apply a policy of containment toward China, under whatever name, would lead to the isolation of the United States and is unlikely to be attempted for that very reason. At the same time, China cannot dislodge the United States from the Asia-Pacific region. Chinese and U.S. versions of the agenda of Sino-American relations differ in particulars, but both countries realize the need to cooperate in addressing such issues as regional security, environmental protection, natural resources, terrorism, and trade, to name just a few. China and the United States must learn to live with each other's differences even as they engage in the hard work of cooperation. The main danger is that for domestic political reasons, both sides may push disagreements over basic values, economic advantage, international politics, Taiwan, and other issues on which they differ beyond the limits of their capacity to work out compromises. It will take concerted efforts by Chinese and American leaders to recognize this danger and avoid senseless and provocative actions that could indeed cause irreparable harm to the Sino-American relationship.

Notes

1. *Renmin Ribao* [People's daily], overseas ed., December 1, 1992.

2. "Toward a China-U.S. Relationship for the Twenty-First Century," *Beijing Review* 40:20 (May 19–25, 1997), 11.

3. Secretary Albright's press conference in Beijing, February 24, 1997, Department of State press release.

4. For an incisive analysis of the ambiguities surrounding the notion of China as a great power, see Samuel S. Kim, "China as a Great Power," *Current History* 96:611 (September 1997), 246–251.

5. Richard Bernstein and Ross H. Munro, *The Coming Conflict with China* (New York: Knopf, 1997), p. 11.

6. "Scholars Refute Book's Views on U.S.-China Relations," *Beijing Review* 40:22 (June 2–8, 1997), 1012.

7. For a recent book using this approach, see Andrew J. Nathan and Robert Ross, *The Great Wall and the Empty Fortress: China's Search for Security* (New York: Norton, 1997).

8. See David Shambaugh, "The United States and China: Cooperation or Confrontation," *Current History* 96:611 (September 1997), 242–244.

9. Song Qiang et al., *Zhongguo keyi shuo bu* [China can say no] (Beijing: Zhonghua gongshang lianhe chubanshe, 1996).

10. See Michael H. Hunt, *The Making of a Special Relationship: The United States and China to 1914* (New York: Columbia University Press, 1983).

11. For a stimulating set of historical essays on Sino-American relations, see Rosemary Foot, *The Practice of Power: U.S. Relations with China Since 1949* (Oxford: Clarendon Press, 1995).

12. Harry Harding, *A Fragile Relationship: The United States and China Since 1972* (Washington, D.C.: Brookings Institution, 1992), pp. 138–172.

13. Ibid., p. 215.

14. Robert S. Ross, *Negotiating Cooperation: The United States and China, 1969–1989* (Stanford: Stanford University Press, 1995).

15. For this concept, see Michael H. Hunt, *Ideology and U.S. Foreign Policy* (New Haven: Yale University Press, 1987).

16. See Stephen R. MacKinnon, "The Role of the Chinese and U.S. Media," in Jeffrey Wasserstrom and Elizabeth Perry, eds., *Popular Protest and Political Culture in Modern China* (Boulder: Westview Press, 1992), pp. 206–214. For a fine if unconscious example of the fatuousness of American reporting, see the book by CNN's then–Beijing correspondent, Mike Chinoy, *China Live! Two Decades at the Heart of the Dragon* (Atlanta: Turner Publishing Co., 1997).

17. See "President's Report on MFN Status for China," *U.S. Department of State Dispatch* 2:24 (June 7, 1991), 430–432. In 1974–1975, when Secretary of State Henry Kissinger directly controlled U.S. China policy, Bush served as head of the U.S. Liaison Office in Beijing. That was prior to the establishment of formal diplomatic relations between the two countries.

18. Early in Clinton's second term, conservative columnist George Will, urging a U.S. offensive against "Chinese tyranny," wrote: "The strategic aim of U.S. policy is, and must be seen to be, the subversion of the Chinese regime. It is China's turn." *Durham Herald-Sun*, April 17, 1997, p. A13.

19. *Renmin Ribao,* July 10, 1996, p. 1.

20. Wang Haihan, "Meiguo de quanqiu zhanlue mianlin yanzhong tiaozhan" [American global strategy faces fundamental challenges], *Guoji wenti yanjiu* [International Studies], no. 4 (October 1992), 19–24.

21. Xue Heming and Wang Haihan, "U.S. Foreign Policy: Goals and Characteristics," *Beijing Review* 40:26 (June 30–July 6, 1997), 9.

22. *Beijing Review* 40:33 (August 18–24, 1997), 6–7.

23. For a fuller discussion, see Banning Garrett and Bonnie Glaser, "Chinese Apprehensions About Revitalization of the U.S.-Japan Alliance," *Asian Survey* 37:4 (April 1997), 383–402.

24. For further discussion, see Ronald N. Montaperto, "Whither China? Beijing's Policies in the 1990s," *Strategic Review* 20:3 (Summer 1992), 23–33.

25. The following paragraphs are based on Steven I. Levine, "The United States and China: Managing a Stormy Relationship," in William A. Joseph, ed., *China Briefing: The Contradictions of Change* (Armonk, N.Y.: M. E. Sharpe, 1997), pp. 239–242.

26. For an authoritative Chinese view of the crisis, see Chen Qimao, "The Taiwan Strait Crisis: Its Crux and Solutions," *Asian Survey* 36:11 (November 1996), 1055–1066. For a stimulating discussion of the larger issues, see Edward Friedman, "Chinese Nationalism, Taiwan Autonomy and the Prospects of a Larger War," *Journal of Contemporary China* 6:14 (March 1997), 5–32.

27. *New York Times* (National edition), March 31, 1997, p. 1.

28. *New York Times* (National edition), May 1, 1997, p. A10.

29. Transparency of military forces was one of ten "principles of conditional engagement" recommended in a recent Council on Foreign Relations study of U.S.-China relations. Among other principles relating to security matters were: no unilateral use of military force, peaceful resolution of territorial disputes, freedom of navigation, moderation in military force buildup, and nonproliferation of weapons of mass destruction. See James Shinn, ed., *Weaving the Net: Conditional Engagement with China* (New York: Council on Foreign Relations Press, 1996), pp. 12–30.

30. For a comprehensive overview of Sino-American economic relations, see Julia Chang Bloch, "Commercial Diplomacy," in Ezra F. Vogel, ed., *Living with China: U.S.-China Relations in the Twenty-First Century* (New York: Norton, 1997), pp. 185–216.

31. Nicholas Lardy, a leading China scholar, has estimated that U.S. figures exaggerate the trade deficit by as much as 40 percent. *China in the World Economy* (Washington, D.C.: Institute for International Economics, 1994), pp. 73–79.

32. For alternate perspectives on this issue, see Robert Ross, "Enter the Dragon," *Foreign Policy*, no. 104 (Fall 1996), 18–25; and Greg Mastel, "Beijing at Bay," ibid., 27–34.

33. See Ken Silverstein, "The New China Hands: How the *Fortune 500* Is China's Strongest Lobby," *Nation*, February 17, 1997, pp. 11–16.

34. See David Zweig, "Sino-American Relations and Human Rights: June 4th and the Changing Nature of a Bilateral Relationship," in William T. Tow, ed., *Building Sino-American Relations: An Analysis for the 1990s* (New York: Paragon House, 1991), pp. 57–92.

35. The following paragraphs are based on Levine, "The United States and China," pp. 230–231.

36. See *U.S. Department of State Dispatch* 5:22 (May 30, 1994), 345–346.

37. See "Lama Chic," *Far Eastern Economic Review,* January 16, 1997, pp. 36–37.

38. See Nathan and Ross, *The Great Wall,* pp. 179–184.

39. See Wei Jingsheng, *The Courage to Stand Alone: Letters from Prison and Other Writings,* ed. and trans. Kristina M. Torgesen (New York: Viking Press, 1997).

40. Harry Harding, "Breaking the Impasse over Human Rights," in Vogel, *Living with China,* pp. 165–184.

41. See James Lull, *China Turned On: Television, Reform, and Resistance* (London and New York: Routledge, 1991).

42. Andrew F. Jones, *Like a Knife: Ideology and Genre in Contemporary Chinese Popular Music* (Ithaca, N.Y.: Cornell University, East Asia Program, 1992).

43. Perry Link, *Evening Chats in Beijing* (New York: Norton, 1992); also H. Lyman Miller, *Science and Dissent in Post-Mao China: The Politics of Knowledge* (Seattle: University of Washington Press, 1996).

5

Sino-Russian Relations

JOHN W. GARVER

The Normalization of Post-Soviet Sino-Russian Relations

An irony of history of the late twentieth century is the rapid development of cordial relations between the state emerging out of the most important anti-Communist movement of the century—the Russian Federation, which formally replaced the Union of Soviet Socialist Republics (USSR) in December 1991—and the sole remaining major Communist-led state, the People's Republic of China (PRC). Whereas the CCP defended its monopoly of state power with violent military force in June 1989, the Russian anti-Communists led by Boris Yeltsin founded a new state predicated on liberal democratic ideals. Yet those two states quickly came together to pick up and develop the cordial relations that had begun during the late Soviet period and were symbolized by the May 1989 summit meeting of Deng Xiaoping and Mikhail Gorbachev.[1]

China's willingness to set aside ideological differences and develop friendly relations with the newly independent Russian Federation arose out of several considerations. One was the deterioration of China's relations with the United States and other Western powers following June 1989. Beijing responded to Western sanctions by courting virtually all countries other than the United States, including especially neighboring and other Asian countries. Russia was important on two counts. First, it was a large, neighboring country; that proximity would greatly complicate China's situation if Russia went along with Western criticism of China. Second, Russia was still a major world power with permanent membership on the UN Security Council and a large nuclear arsenal; thus Russia had some potential for mitigating Western hostility. Both Beijing and Moscow also recognized the importance of foreign trade in fostering economic development and saw considerable potential for bilateral cooperation in this regard.

As Lowell Dittmer has pointed out, the U.S.-led victory over Iraq in early 1991 created movement "toward an ideologically based [Russo-Chinese] affinity without formal alliance," a movement aborted, however, by the August 1991 coup in the USSR.[2] A critical transition in Russo-Chinese relations came at the end of 1991 and in early 1992 when leaders in the two countries decided to set aside ideological differences—including CCP support for the CPSU over the past two years and deep CCP distaste for Yeltsin's politics—and continue developing amicable relations.[3] On December 7, 1991, the day after representatives of Belarus, Ukraine, and Russia founded the Commonwealth of Independent States (CIS), a Russian parliamentary delegation arrived in Beijing and delivered a letter from Russian President Yeltsin to PRC President Yang Shangkun saying that Russia would take over the foreign policy of the USSR and would continue to implement treaties and agreements signed by the PRC and the USSR. The head of China's parliament, Wan Li, reciprocated, saying that "China's economic development needs a peaceful international environment. Therefore, China is willing to live on good terms with all other countries." On December 25, the day that Gorbachev resigned as president of the USSR, China recognized Russia as independent successor to the USSR in the UN Security Council. (China also recognized the independence of the remaining former-Soviet republics.) Beijing also agreed to continue carrying out all agreements and treaties in force between the USSR and the PRC. Russia promised to "respect and support" Beijing's position on Taiwan. This did not prevent Moscow from moving toward establishing in Taipei an "unofficial" Russian representative office modeled after that of the United States.

Throughout the first half of 1992, although Sino-Russian economic ties advanced rapidly, political relations developed very slowly. Foreign affairs took a low priority for the leaders of the newly founded Russian state. Only later in 1992 did Russian and Chinese leaders begin to recognize that common interests of the two countries in containing Islamic fundamentalism in Central Asia required closer political cooperation. The way to this cooperation was opened in September 1992 when Yeltsin signed a presidential order abolishing the representative office in Taiwan and strictly limiting Russia's future links with Taiwan. This move opened the way for Yeltsin's first visit to China in December 1992. Throughout the development of the new Sino-Russian relationship China demanded and Russia gave satisfaction on the Taiwan issue.

The joint declaration issuing from the December 1992 Yeltsin–Jiang Zemin summit was the first element in what would become over the next five years an impressive edifice of Russo-Chinese agreements. The December 1992 communiqué explicitly stated the new Russian state's "recognition" that Taiwan was an "integral part of Chinese territory" and its pledge to maintain only nongovernmental relations with Taiwan. The communiqué also provided: "Neither party should join any military or political alliance directed against the other party, sign any treaty or agreement with a third country prejudicing the sovereignty and security interests of the other party, or allow its territory to be used by a third country to infringe on the sovereignty and security interests of the other party."[4] Implicit in these words was a Russian promise not to join with the United States against China on various issues that Beijing deemed prejudicial to its "sovereignty and security interests." In early 1991 Moscow (then representing the USSR) had supported U.S. efforts in the United Nations to punish Iraq. Now Russia promised Beijing it would not join a comparable effort directed against China. Similarly this clause excluded Russian support for India or Vietnam against China. Throughout the late Cold War era the Soviet Union had been those countries' major backer against China. The 1992 communiqué also contained an "antihegemony clause" declaring China and Russia's common opposition "to hegemonism and power politics in any form." Similar clauses in Sino-American and Sino-Japanese declarations of the 1970s had been generally understood as code for opposition to the Soviet Union. By making such a clause a basis of Russo-Chinese relations, the 1992 communiqué implicitly excluded a repetition of a 1970s-style alignment when China acted as a "quasi-ally" of the Western alliance to contain the USSR.

During the immediate post-Soviet period, Beijing was deeply apprehensive that Russia's aspirations of becoming a Western, democratic state would lead it into partnership with the United States. Chinese commentary predicted, however, that a clash of Russian and U.S. interests would derail such cooperation. According to Chinese commentary, this contest of Russian and American interests began to intensify in 1993. In any case, early in 1994 Yeltsin sent a letter to Jiang Zemin proposing a "constructive partnership" between the two countries geared to the twenty-first century. China's Foreign Affairs Small Group headed by Premier Li Peng was very receptive to Yeltsin's proposal. A state visit by President Jiang Zemin to Russia in September 1994 was one result of the mutual desire for closer ties. The most prominent element of the communiqué issuing from this (the second) Jiang-Yeltsin summit was agreement that neither side would be the first to use nuclear weapons against the other, and neither would target nuclear weapons at the other.[5] This agreement did not mean much in practical terms, as Russian rockets, at least, could be swiftly retargeted. Nor did there appear to be any protocol for verifying the detargeting commitment. Yet detargeting and declaration of "no first use" were important symbolic gestures.

Further additions to the edifice of Russo-Chinese agreements came during the third Yeltsin-Jiang summit in April 1996. Arriving in Beijing on April 24, Yeltsin came just after the U.S.-PRC confrontation in the Taiwan Strait, in the weeks preceding Taiwan's late March presidential election. This was the first Sino-American military confrontation since the end of the Vietnam War and sent a chill through capitals around the world. Sino-American relations were still quite tense when Yeltsin arrived in Beijing. In this context Yeltsin's visit was itself a potent manifestation of the December 1992 pledge not to join a hostile bloc with other powers. Yeltsin's visit was a demonstration that however much Sino-American or Sino-Japanese relations might deteriorate as a result of conflict over Taiwan, Russo-Chinese relations would develop normally. As if to eliminate any question, Russia reiterated in the April 1996 communiqué its position that "Taiwan is an inalienable part of the Chinese territory." As a quid pro quo, Beijing gave its "support" to "measures and actions" adopted by the Russian Federation on the question of Chechnya.[6] The communiqué of also pledged the two sides "to develop a strategic cooperative partnership (*zhanliie xiecuo huoban guanxi*) of equality, mutual confidence and mutual coordination." The Sino-Russian relationship thereby advanced from "constructive partnership" to "strategic cooperative partnership."

The fifth Jiang-Yeltsin summit, in April 1997, produced a lengthy declaration "On the Multipolarization of the World and the Establishment of a New International Order."[7] It put the two countries on record as opposing "enlarging and strengthening military blocs." Differences in social systems and ideologies were not to interfere with normal state-to-state relations, and nations were not to use economic sanctions against others. The declaration also called for elimination of "discriminatory policies and practices in economic relations" and criticized the tendency for "other international organizations" to replace the United Nations. Between the lines one could locate the real referents of these generalities. The relevant "military blocs" being expanded and strengthened were the North Atlantic Treaty Organization (NATO) and the U.S.-Japan alliance. Interference on the basis of social system and ideologies arose when Western countries criticized others. The most egregious of the "discriminatory economic policies" was exclusion of both Russia and China from the General Agreement on Tariffs and Trade (GATT) and its World Trade Organization (WTO) successor. And the most notable international organization that excluded China and Russia was the Group of Seven (though Russia was invited to join the Group of Seven as an observer in June 1997). The declaration left the drawing of such conclusions to others, however, and included the disclaimer that the Sino-Russian strategic partnership was "not directed against any third country."

The Logic of the "Strategic Cooperative Partnership"

The unstated premise underlying the Sino-Russian "strategic cooperative partnership" is that the United States is a hegemonistic power driving for global domination via "unipolarity" and trying to achieve this goal by weakening both China and Russia. The "partnership" of those two countries is directed toward thwarting American hegemonistic efforts. An array of Chinese sources confirm the antihegemonistic purposes of the "strategic cooperative partnership." During President Yeltsin's April 1996 visit to Beijing (when the "strategic cooperative partnership" was announced), *Wenhui bao* explained:

> Some countries maintain that a unipolar world should be established. Through implementing a high-handed policy, they intend to force other big nations to dance to their batons, and accept their political, economic, and legal systems. ... Most countries believe ... [that] they must not use the method of putting pressure on others to compel them to submit. They must not impose their social systems and values on others.[8]

Premier Li Peng made the same point in more subtle terms. The newly proclaimed "strategic cooperative partnership" was "in line with the general trend toward a multipolarization of the world," Li told Yeltsin. This trend was "much better than for a country to issue orders."[9] A briefing on the "strategic cooperative partnership," prepared for high-ranking cadre by the Peace and Development Institute of Shanghai in early 1997, explained that both China and Russia "advocate development of the world in the direction of multipolarity." U.S. global preeminence would continue for some time. "To realize its scheme of sole hegemony over the world [the United States] will continue to implement its policies of hegemonism and power politics around the world, containing China's and Russia's development." China and Russia "oppose hegemonism and power politics" and are victims of "the 'containment' policies of the United States and other western nations." This creates "common interests and increasing mutual need" between them. As "relatively weak countries," China and Russia need the support of one another. "Russia needs to utilize China as a balancing strength in order to achieve its objective of great power status," whereas China needs the support of Russia to "develop, resist provocations, and achieve greater international maneuvering room."[10]

In the fall of 1995, to cite another example, thirty Russian and Chinese international relations specialists convened to discuss the relationship between their two countries. According to an authoritative account of those proceedings, the Chinese participants maintained that both countries face common international pressure. In the international realm at present there is a certain type of force [*yi zhong shili*] which looks upon China and Russia as "strategic rivals" or "latent threats," and thus implements policies to weaken and contain China and Russia, to interfere in their internal politics, injure the security of those two countries, and prevent them from developing and becoming powerful.[11]

Virtually every Chinese analysis of the Sino-Russian strategic partnership contains an apparently politically de rigueur disclaimer to the effect that the "strategic cooperative partnership" is "not confrontational, not an alliance, not a united front, and is not directed against any third country," but merely "involves coordination whenever confronting foreign pressure in the international sphere"[12] or "opposes power politics in international affairs or efforts to monopolize international affairs by a small group of nations."[13] This insistence on the innocuous nature of the partnership is based on apprehension of possible adverse American reaction to it. As the vice director of the Russian Institute of the Chinese Academy of Social Science says:

> A Sino-Russian alliance or unity to oppose a third country is not in accord with the basic interests of both countries, and is also not in accord with trends after the Cold War. The establishment of a strategic partnership between China and Russia will not influence the development of their relations with any other country, including their relations with the United States and other Western countries.[14]

"The lesson of the Sino-Soviet alliance [of 1950] shows," according to another authoritative source, "that regardless of its form, an alliance is by its nature directed against a third country and will bring about that third country's opposition, spoiling the international environment for economic construction."[15] In more straightforward terms, China's leaders fear that overplaying the Russian card could lead to adverse American reaction—perhaps to restriction of access to U.S. markets, capital, technology, and so on. American leaders are to be made apprehensive by Chinese-Russian solidarity, but not scared enough to adopt forceful countermeasures.

Russian Assistance to China's Military Modernization

Beijing clearly sees advantages in persuading Washington (and other members of the Western alliance) of the possibility of a Russo-Chinese bloc. Apprehension over such a possibility would help make those capitals less willing to offend Beijing; ignoring the interests of China too egre-

giously might force China and Russia together. It can be argued, however, that to foster such apprehensions, Beijing has been engaging in
many highly symbolic visits and agreements of limited significance plus
effusive rhetoric—"gong clanging," as it is sometimes called—but that
there is little substance to the putative "partnership." It thus remains to
analyze the degree of substance in the new Russo-Chinese strategic partnership. It that partnership largely illusory and symbolic? Or is there real
substance to it?

Important substance to the "strategic partnership" is found in the transfer of Russian military technology to China.[16] During the 1990s China has
undertaken the most sustained and successful technological modernization of the PLA since the 1950s. Russia has emerged as China's major partner in that modernization effort. This is an extremely important, indeed a
truly "strategic," dimension of the Russo-Chinese partnership.

Russian cooperation in China's recent military modernization effort
may be traced back to June 1990, when a delegation led by then–Central
Military Commission (CMC) vice chair and Politburo Standing Committee member Liu Huaqing visited Moscow. That was twelve months after
the Beijing massacre and the suspension of Western military links with
China. At that point the PLA was especially interested in obtaining an advanced fighter aircraft to remedy a serious shortcoming in PLA capabilities, which sustained efforts at indigenous development had been unable
to overcome. Russia proved willing to accommodate Chinese demands
and agreed to sell twenty-four Sukoi-27 (Su-27), a highly sophisticated
aircraft comparable to the U.S. F-15. Further sales followed. By 1996
China had bought seventy-two Su-27s. Production of Su-27s was also licensed to China. Many more transfers followed over the next several
years, including: ten Il-76M heavy transport aircraft; RD-33K turbo fan
engines for use in a new Chinese fighter; two dozen M-17 high-altitude
transport helicopters; sophisticated radars for installation in Chinese
warplanes; a hundred SA-10 air defense missiles incorporating phased-
array radar with multitarget capabilities; extremely potent SS-N-22 antiship missiles; fifty T-72 main battle tanks; infantry fighting vehicles and
the assembly lines for these weapons; airborne refueling systems; specialized technology for manufacturing titanium structural elements for
airplanes; four Kilo-class submarines, including two of technical specifi-
cations equivalent to boats supplied to the Russian navy itself; two
highly sophisticated Sovremenny class destroyers; and upper-stage
rocket engines for intercontinental ballistic missiles. Many of these deals
involved transfer of production technology. Such acquisitions represented major technological gains for the PLA, substantially narrowing
the technological gap between itself and its potential adversaries. By the
early 1990s China had emerged as the largest buyer of Russian weapons.

Between 1991 and 1994 China bought an estimated $4.5 to $6 billion in Russian military hardware and technology. In 1997 negotiations were reportedly under way over the sale of mine-laying boats, landing craft, missile cruisers, air tankers, MiG-31 interceptors, airborne warning and command system (AWACs) aircraft, supersonic Tu-22 Backfire attack bombers, plus Su-30 and Su-35 aircraft not yet supplied to the Russian military. Close links also developed between Chinese and Russian military research and development centers.

Russia's willingness to provide wide access to state-of-the-art military technology was a major boost to PLA modernization efforts. Since the mid-1980s, PLA doctrine had envisioned short high-intensity wars along China's borders fought by relatively small forces armed with high-tech weaponry and seeking swift, decisive victory. A major liability for the PLA had been its distinct technological inferiority relative to several of its probable opponents in these "partial wars," as they were called. This situation meant that for China to prevail, it would have to win in the old-fashioned way, through sheer weight of numbers and protracted attrition of enemy strength. That would potentially be very disruptive of China's economic development. Throughout the 1980s the PLA had sought to upgrade its technological level and made some significant progress in this respect. The new partnership with Russia represented a quantum leap. For the first time China gained access to numerous integrated military technology and weapons systems. Chinese personnel were sometimes involved in research and development of the next generation of military technology. In short, China gained broad cooperation of a leading military power in the development of its military technological capabilities.

The motives behind this Russo-Chinese military relationship are complex. On the Russian side the primary motives are financial, although some top leaders (such as Foreign Minister Yevgeny Primakov) have openly justified the sales as helping to create a new balance of power in the Asia-Pacific region, which lessens the influence of the United States, thereby benefiting Russia. On the Chinese side too economic factors loom large. By 1992 China's economy was booming and the government—and more especially the PLA, many of whose enterprises generated substantial extrabudgetary funds—had money to address some of the PLA's long-standing deficiencies. Globally, post–Cold War cutbacks in defense budgets had created a buyer's market in munitions. Chinese leaders also hoped that Russian technology would be easier to assimilate than the American, Israeli, and French technology acquired by the PLA during the 1970s and 1980s. Too often full assimilation of Western technology had been limited in spite of considerable effort. PLA leaders may have concluded that Russian technology, in contrast, was more fundamentally similar to China's own and therefore easier to assimilate.[17] Having recognized this importance of economic factors, one should still be aware of the strategic component in China's new military partnership with Russia. Russian assistance substantially enhances PLA capabilities vis-à-vis Taiwan and the United States, thereby strengthening China's position should it feel compelled to use military force against Taiwan while deterring or defeating U.S. intervention in a cross-Strait war.

Transformation of the Border Regime

As Beijing and Moscow began moving toward a more cooperative relationship, transformation of the border regime became imperative. Unless this could be done, suspicions would remain deep, and both sides would necessarily rate more highly the possibility of renewed conflict. Conversely, resolution of the border issue would allow both countries to focus their energies away from each other and toward other theaters along their periphery. It would also free up resources for economic modernization. The objective lauded by Russia and China since 1989 has been to transform their long border into a nonmilitarized and open border of peace and cooperation, through a combination of force reductions, confidence-building measures (CBMs), delineation and demarcation of the boundary, and institutionalization of a more open administration of the border plus encouragement of cross-border economic cooperation.[18]

Reduction of the Soviet military presence on China's borders was one of the "three obstacles" to better Sino-Soviet relations pinpointed by Deng Xiaoping in 1979, and it became a central component of Gorbachev's effort to normalize relations with China in the late 1980s. During his meeting with Deng in May 1989, Gorbachev detailed Soviet plans to demobilize 120,000 troops facing China. China's response to Gorbachev's gesture was initially cool, but following Western sanctions after the Beijing massacre, China grew increasingly positive. Border demilitarization talks began in November 1989. By April 1990 they had advanced sufficiently for Premier Li Peng to sign during a visit to Moscow a statement of principles on "Mutual Reduction of Military Forces in Sino-Soviet Border Areas and Guiding Principles of Enhancing Trust in the Military Sphere." Subsequent agreement on major troop reductions along the border was more difficult. One difficulty had to with the asymmetrical pattern of troop deployment on the two sides of the border. The Chinese were also reluctant to allow Soviet observers to watch PLA exercises or to provide information on Chinese military affairs to the Soviet/Russian side. Nor did either side have the money to pay for major redeployment of troops away from the border.

Talks over CBMs to reduce tension along the border proceeded parallel to force-reduction negotiations. In July 1994 Defense Minister Chi Haotian and his Russian counterpart, Pavel Grachev, finalized agreement on the first set of CBMs. Talks between China and the four CIS states sharing borders with China (Russia, Kazakhstan, Kyrgyzstan, and Tajikistan) over border CBMs had begun in November 1992. In April 1996 these talks bore fruit, with a five-power agreement signed by the five presidents in Shanghai. The agreement provided that military forces on either side of the borders of the five signatory states would not attack or aim their military exercises against one another. Observers were to be invited to observe military exercises and prior notice was to be given of any major military activities within 100 kilometers (63 miles) of the border.[19] Within that zone the armed forces of the signatory powers would not carry out military activities affecting the peace and stability of the border region. The Five-Power Agreement should *not* be interpreted as an attempt by Beijing and Moscow to establish a Central Asian buffer zone between them. The agreement did not provide for the withdrawal of Russian forces in Tajikistan and Kazakhstan, thus leaving such forces stationed in those two countries. Nor did the agreement modify the 1992 Russia-Kazakhstan treaty of friendship and cooperation, which extended the Russian nuclear umbrella to Kazakhstan. The 1996 agreement was, however, a Russo-Chinese effort to cooperate in minimizing tension along sensitive inner-Asian frontiers.

Regarding resolution of the border issue, talks had begun in February 1987 and by September 1988 an aerial survey of the eastern sector had been completed. In May 1991, during CCP Secretary General Jiang Zemin's visit to Moscow, Foreign Ministers Qian Qichen and Alexander Bessyrtnich signed an agreement resolving all but two relatively minor problems in the eastern sector—one involving the islands lying below Khabarovsk at the confluence of the Ussuri and Amur Rivers, and the other involving several islands on the Argun River. Although agreement between the central authorities of the two governments came relatively easily with the May 1991 treaty, the execution of that agreement was far more difficult. Indeed, as of mid-1997 the agreement had still to be fully implemented. The May 1991 agreement involved a net transfer of more than 1,500 hectares (3,706 acres) from Russia to China in three areas along the land border. These "adjustments" (as they were called in deference to Russian nationalist sentiment) are illustrated in Figure 5.1. They proved extremely unpopular in the Russian Far East (RFE), an unpopularity sometimes fanned by local politicians. The decision of Moscow authorities to conclude an agreement involving a net transfer of land to China, and to stand by that agreement after the unpopular Soviet government that signed it had fallen and after the treaty had come under mounting criticism from ambitious politicians in the RFE, reflected a high-level political decision to build a positive relationship with China, overriding parochial opposition if necessary.

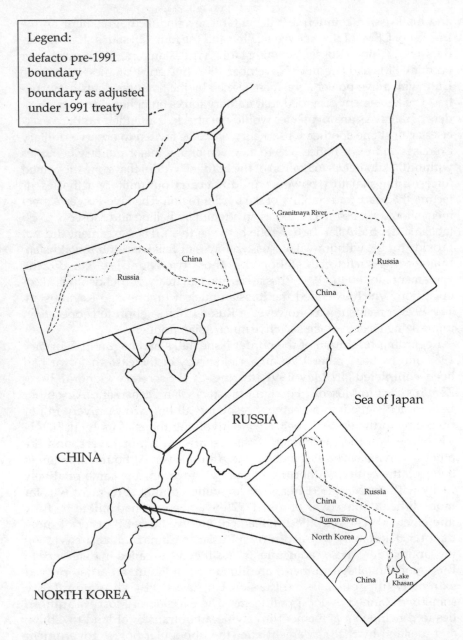

Legend:

defacto pre-1991 boundary

boundary as adjusted under 1991 treaty

FIGURE 5.1   Adjustments in Russo-Chinese Far Eastern Land Border Under the 1991 Treaty

The Immigration Crisis of the Early 1990s

As the border issue was moving toward resolution, another drama was unfolding, one that aroused some of the very apprehensions the resolution of the boundary issue had been intended to quiet. In July 1988 the Soviet and Chinese governments adopted a system of visa-free travel for short-term business and tourist travel. The purpose of this move was to foster cross-border economic cooperation. In that aim it was successful. Between 1988 and 1993 trade between China and Russia tripled, leaping from U.S.$2.55 billion to U.S.$7.67 billion. By 1993 China had become Russia's third-largest export market and its second-most-important supplier of imports. The liberalization of the border regime had the unanticipated consequence, however, of facilitating illegal and virtually uncontrolled Chinese immigration to Russia.

In discussing the issue of Chinese immigration to Russia in the early 1990s, it is essential to distinguish between the ascertainable facts of that immigration and its political impact within Russia. Whereas there was, in fact, a dramatic increase in the movement, legal and illegal, of Chinese into Russia during this period, the political impact of that immigration can be understood only with reference to the profound crisis Russian society was then undergoing. Exact and reliable figures about the size of Chinese immigration are impossible to come by. In 1993, when the issue had become highly politicized, the Russian Foreign Ministry estimated the total number of Chinese nationals, legal and illegal, resident in Russia as 500,000 to 600,000. The Russian mass media gave far higher numbers—up to 2 million, or even 5 or 6 million—settled in the RFE alone.

The movement of Chinese into the RFE shot up after Deng Xiaoping's southern tour of January 1992, when China entered a period of renewed reform and opening. During 1993, 15,000 Chinese entered Primorski Krai each month, with a large portion remaining illegally in Russia.[20] During one month in early 1994, fourteen groups of Chinese "tourists" entered Russia via a border post in Primorski Krai. Of the 361 people in those groups, only 48 returned to China within the legally specified time. Many of the Chinese companies ostensibly engaged in border trade also facilitated illegal immigration. In a few towns and areas of the RFE, Chinese residents actually came to outnumber the Russians. There were also isolated instances of Chinese mobs clashing with Russian police and of riot police having to be called in to quell the disturbances.[21] Still other elements of the immigration crisis were added by the seeming incompetence of Russia's post-Communist government, which seemed to be losing control over Russia's borders and territory. Russians began to ask whether the Russian Far East was undergoing de facto sinization.

Chinese leaders recognized the sensitivity of the immigration issue and acted swiftly. In January 1994 at Russia's request the two sides reinstituted a visa system to regulate cross-border travel. During his visit to Moscow in September of that year, Jiang Zemin discussed the issue frankly, reassuring Russian leaders of China's benign intentions and its willingness to cooperate in measures satisfactory to Russia. In a public speech in Moscow, Jiang said that the problems that had emerged along the border resulted from the actions of individuals and a lack of proper administrative order on both sides of the border—not from government policy. The Chinese government had always opposed and struck hard against illegal immigration, Jiang said, and problems arising from this matter should not affect the development of positive, cooperative relations between the two countries. Over the next several years Chinese and Russian officials worked closely to suppress illegal activity in border areas. Police, customs officials, and border police increasingly assisted in the investigation of criminal activities on the other side of the border. On the Russian side, there were roundups and expulsions of illegal immigrants, a large portion of whom were Chinese. More than 9,500 Chinese were deported from Primorski during the course of 1994.

Economic Cooperation

Russia ranks in the second tier of China's trading partners. According to Chinese customs statistics, in 1996 Russia was China's eighth-largest trading partner, roughly in the same category as Singapore, Australia, and Italy but far behind such leaders as Japan, the United States, Hong Kong, and Taiwan. In that year Russo-Chinese two-way trade was 11 percent of Sino-Japanese and 16 percent of Sino-American trade. Nor was expanding trade with Russia a major factor behind the phenomenal growth of China's foreign trade in the 1990s. Although Russo-Chinese trade did grow rapidly during that period, the base was so low that the increase paled in significance when compared to China's exploding trade with South Korea and Taiwan. China's trade with the latter two areas leaped from virtually zero in 1989 (again according to customs statistics) to around U.S.$20 billion for each in 1996; China's trade with each was about three times the total volume of Russo-Chinese trade in that year. But even though economic cooperation with Russia is of second-rank importance in national terms, it is highly important to regions of China adjacent to Russia—Heilongjiang, Jilin, and Xinjiang. These landlocked provinces are among China's poorest and are deeply envious of the rapid growth achieved by China's coastal provinces. If China's landlocked interior is to emulate the coast's successes, it must look to its landward neighbors. From Beijing's perspective, this is a cheaper more preferable solution than increased subsidies from the central government. Economic cooperation with Russia is also important for Beijing because that cooperation is less likely to be adversely affected in the event of a crisis in Sino-American relations than are China's economic links with Japan and Western Europe.

China's $1.7 billion in exports to Russia in 1996 consisted of a diverse mix of light-industrial and agricultural products. Leather goods and wool products were the largest category of Chinese exports, representing 22 percent of the total (see Table 5.1). Textiles were not far behind, followed by animals and animal products, umbrellas and hats, and so on, and foods, beverages, and tobacco. China's imports from Russia were more concentrated. A whopping 33 percent of imports were nonprecious metals such as steel, copper, nickel, aluminum, lead, zinc, and tin. Another 28 percent were represented by chemicals such as fertilizers and industrial chemicals. The latter fed China's booming industrial sector. Another 15 percent was made up of automotive, navigation, and aviation parts and equipment. In short, China largely exported consumer goods and imported products from and inputs for heavy industry. China also bought nearly three times as much as it sold to Russia, running a deficit of nearly $3.5 billion in 1996. This deficit was probably acceptable because a large component of China's imports, one not visible in regular customs data, was high-tech weapons and military technology. Weapons and military technology represent what is probably the largest single, and certainly the most politically significant, component of Chinese-Russian trade. According to one Russian source, Sino-Russian military trade reached $2.1 billion in 1996.[22] That would represent 41 percent of the amount of China's imports from Russia, as reported by China's customs.

During the 1980s some analysts argued that Soviet industrial manufacturing machinery would prove attractive to Chinese industry because it was relatively cheap, simple, and similar to the machinery reverse-engineered from Soviet models by Chinese design bureaus during the 1960s and 1970s. With a few exceptions (including defense industry, electrical generation technology, petroleum mining, and aerospace) that does not seem to have been the case. China's imports of machinery and equipment from Russia in 1996 were only 3 percent of all imports from Russia in that year. This amount was between 27 and 31 percent of China's machinery and equipment imports from Taiwan, the United States, or Germany, and less than 1 percent of similar imports from Japan. China's imports of machinery and equipment from Russia were about half of such imports from Thailand, and a less than imports in this category from Denmark! The conclusion is obvious: Chinese enterprises generally look not to Russia but to more technologically advanced capitalist countries for supply of industrial equipment and machinery.

TABLE 5.1   Composition of Sino-Russian Trade, 1996

	As % of Total Chinese Imports from Russia	As % of Total Chinese Exports to Russia
Animals and animal products	4	14
Plant products	<1	8
Fats and edible oils	<1	<1
Foods, beverages, and tobacco	1	7
Mining products	5	3
Chemical products	28	2
Plastics and rubber products	3	1
Leather and wool products	<1	22
Wood and wood products	1	<1
Paper and paper products	5	1
Textiles	1	19
Umbrellas, hats, shoes, artificial flowers, etc.	<1	11
Glass and ceramics	<1	1
Pearls and precious metals	<1	<1
Nonprecious metals	33	2
Machinery and equipment	3	6
Automotive, aviation, navigation items	15	2
Instruments, optical, medical	<1	1
Weapons	1	N.A.
Miscellaneous manufactured items	<1	4
Total value (U.S.$)	5,153,356,000	1,692,762,000

SOURCES: *Haiguan tongji* [Customs statistics], General Administration of Customs of the People's Republic of China (December 1996), pp. 44–45, 66–67.

The rapid expansion of Russo-Chinese economic cooperation has not been without tension. During the early 1990s problems were many and rather severe, especially in the booming Wild West–style border trade. Neither Russia nor China had a strong legal or market-regulatory system. When conflicts arose, there were few ways to arbitrate them. Contracts could not be enforced. Cases of fraud and outright theft proliferated. Standardized business practices and banking arrangements common in other countries and devised precisely to minimize such problems were absent in the Sino-Russian border trade. Deals were often in barter, an arrangement that made simultaneous exchange of possession of goods difficult to arrange. Banks did not have branches or corresponding institutions across the border. There were no procedures for settlement of debts between Russian and Chinese banks. Typically a South Korean or a Japanese bank would have to be brought in to execute such a function. Many traders preferred not to deal with banks. Nor were there arrangements for insurance.

During 1990–1992, as the centrally planned economy of the USSR was disintegrating, Russian consumers were starved for goods and welcomed China's cheap exports. Within several years, however, popular anger over poor quality and defective Chinese goods became quite strong. Local Russian governments also became concerned that raw materials, construction materials, and precious metals and animal furs were being taken (legally and illegally) out of Russia in large quantities, sometimes driving up the cost of those products in Russia or depriving Russians of the opportunity to sell these lucrative products to Japanese, Europeans, or Americans. Russia was being plundered, economic nationalists asserted. Worst of all, from this perspective, was the fact that the Chinese population of the RFE was growing rapidly.

Late in 1993 Russia moved to regain control of the increasingly chaotic border. Moscow slapped heavy duties on the export of fertilizer, steel, and construction materials. China responded by imposing duties on a long list of Russian manufactured goods. Most important, Russia reinstituted, as we have seen, a rigorous visa system to control cross-border movement. Border trade dropped 21 percent in 1994 to $1.6 billion.[73] It began to revive in 1995. Meanwhile the two governments began addressing the manifold problems. Efforts were made to encourage large and medium-sized firms to become involved in Sino-Russian trade—the idea being that these firms were less likely to be dishonest. Many of the firms that had been active in the pre-1994 boom were very small. Chinese authorities began an inspection of these firms and many were closed for lacking adequate assets. Chinese and Russian police began cooperating more closely, and in June 1995 an extradition treaty was signed. Procedures were established to inspect the quality of goods traded. More-regular methods of supplying credit and clearing debts were implemented.

The Significance of the Russo-Chinese "Strategic Cooperative Partnership"

The evolution of international history in the twentieth century culminated in a dominant coalition of immense power and influence. In the early 1990s North America, an increasingly united Europe, Japan, South Korea, and Australia remained a coherent alliance and possessed collectively an immense store of the instruments of power, financial, industrial, technological, and purely militarily. Ideologically, the set of ideas that justified that coalition's exercise of power—liberalism—had by century's end achieved a position of global dominance perhaps unparalleled in human history. This ideological hegemony may well prove to be transitory, as critics of Francis Fukuyama maintain, but few would deny that the failure of both Fascist and Communist experiments in the twentieth century has left liberal ideology nearly unchallenged at century's end.

Nations that had substantial power and self-concepts of greatness but that were left outside this coalition felt deep apprehension. The two major powers in this category were Russia and China. This common pariah status alone might have been adequate to impel them toward formation of a countercoalition, but other factors reinforced their status. The fact that the two countries shared a long border conferred immense strategic advantages on both in dealing with dominant coalition adversaries. If the substantial resources devoted to confronting each other along that border could be freed for deployment elsewhere, both countries would be in a stronger position vis-à-vis dominant coalition powers along their peripheries. Moreover, robust economic transactions across the Sino-Russian border would guarantee supply routes to rear areas in the event of a confrontation between either country and a dominant coalition power. In fact, the two countries have a tradition of cooperation (against Japan and/or the United States—in 1896–1904, 1924–1927, 1937–1945, and 1950–1960) plus foreign policy elites steeped in the tradition of triangular maneuver. Given the continuing coherence of the dominant coalition, the formation of a countering Russo-Chinese coalition was highly likely. Once the dominant coalition began adopting policies contrary to the interests of Russia and China, formation of a countercoalition was virtually certain.

The Russo-Chinese partnership has already had a significant impact on East Asia. Russia's broad assistance to China's military modernization drive is one of the most important factors contributing to the success of those ambitious efforts. The rapid improvement of PLA capabilities has, in turn, permitted China to take a much more forceful approach toward Taiwan—as during its campaign of military coercion in 1995–1996. Greater Chinese military capabilities have also significantly reduced the qualitative superiority of U.S. forces vis-à-vis the PLA. The U.S. superiority would be crucial in a Chinese decision to risk conflict with the United States over Taiwan and to a U.S. decision to risk conflict with China by standing firm with respect to Taiwan. By providing the PLA with much-improved technology and thus a substantially better chance of striking effective blows against U.S. military forces in East Asia, Russian assistance to China makes it more likely that China's leaders will conclude they can secure an acceptable outcome in a war with the United States.

The potential significance of the Russo-Chinese entente becomes apparent when one ponders the role of that alignment in the event of a Sino-American conflict over Taiwan. Such a war would almost certainly lead to a U.S. embargo or blockade of China. The critical question would then become, would U.S. allies fall in line to support those measures? Although much would depend on how such a conflict came about and on the caliber of U.S. diplomacy, the most likely result would be a rallying of American allies around Washington. Of all the major powers, only Russia would probably remain supportive of China. Russia could be expected to supply China with whatever materials it had and China could pay for. Strategic materials bound for China might circumvent U.S. domination of the seas by traveling over Russian roads and rail lines.

Short of such extremes, the Russo-Chinese entente may be the beginning of a new quadrilateral alignment in East Asia in which a "continental" Russo-Chinese bloc balances a "maritime" American-Japanese bloc. Parallel with the formation of the Russo-Chinese entente in the mid-1990s was a cooling of both Chinese-American and Chinese-Japanese relations plus a reinvigoration of the Japanese-American alliance. Russo-Japanese relations also remained very cool, almost unchanged from Cold War days. One unspoken assumption underlying the Russo-Chinese entente seems to be a convergence of views regarding the dangers inherent in an increased Japanese military-political role in Asia. The United States, however, looks to a more vigorous Japan to help balance China.

Notes

1. Regarding the last period of Sino-Soviet relations, see Lowell Dittmer, *Sino-Soviet Normalization and Its International Implications, 1945–1990* (Seattle: University of Washington Press, 1992).

2. Lowell Dittmer, "China and Russia: New Beginnings," in Samuel S. Kim, ed., *China and the World*, 3rd ed. (Boulder, Colo.: Westveiw Press, 1994), p. 96.

3. Regarding Sino-Russian relations at this juncture, see Roxane D. V. Sismanidis, "China, the Soviet Collapse, and the Post-Soviet States," *Washington Journal of Modern China* 1, no. 2 (Spring 1993), pp. 53–83; Hung P. Nguyen, "Russia and China: Genesis of an Eastern Rapallo," *Asian Survey* 33, no. 3 (March 1993), pp. 285–299; and John W. Garver, "The Chinese Communist Party and the Collapse of Soviet Communism," *China Quarterly*, no. 133 (March 1993), pp. 1–26.

4. Foreign Broadcast Information Service, Daily Report: China [hereafter, FBIS, *DRC*], Dec. 18, 1992, pp. 7–9.

5. The joint communiqué is in FBIS, *DRC*, Sept. 6, 1994, pp. 19–21.

6. The 1996 communiqué is in FBIS, *DRC*, Apr. 25, 1996, pp. 14–17.

7. *Beijing Review*, May 12–18, 1997, pp. 7–8.

8. *Wenhui bao*, Apr. 26, 1996, in FBIS, *DRC*, Apr. 26, 1996, pp. 10–11.

9. Xinhua, Apr. 25, 1996, FBIS, *DRC*, Apr. 26, 1996, p. 13.

10. Li Jiyu, "Zhong E fazhan mianxiang 21 shiji de zhanlüe xiecuo huoban guanxi" [The development of the Sino-Russian strategic partnership for the twenty-first century], *Heping yu fazhan* [Peace and development], no. 1 (1997), p. 7.

11. "Xin xingshi xia de Zhong E guoji hezuo wenti—guoji xueshu yantaohui jiyao" [The problem of Sino-Russian international cooperation under new international conditions—summary of an international academic conference] *Xiandai guoji guanxi* [Contemporary international relations], no. 1 (1996), p. 16.

12. Li Jiyu, "Zhong E fazhan," p. 13.

13. "Xin xingshi xia de Zhong E guoji hezuo wenti," p. 7. See also Zheng Yu, "Zhong E zhanlue xiezuo huoban guanxi pingxi" [Analysis of the Chinese Rus-

sian strategic partnership], *Guoji jingji pinglun* [Commentary on international economics], no. 5–6 (1996), p. 40.

14. Li Jingjie, "Shilun Zhong E zhanlue xiecuo huoban guanxi" [Preliminary investigation of the Chinese-Russian strategic partnership], *Dong ou zhong ya janjin* [East Europe and Central Asian research], no. 2 (1997), p. 8.

15. Li Jiyu, "Zhong E fazhan," pp. 3–4.

16. Bates Gill and Taeho Kim, *China's Arms Acquisitions from Abroad: A Quest for Superb and Secret Weapons*, SIPRI Research Report No. 11 (New York: Oxford University Press, 1995). See also Stephen J. Blank, *The Dynamics of Russian Weapon Sales to China*. U.S. Army War College, Strategic Studies Institute, March 4, 1997. Gill and Kim provide a full chronology of Russo-Chinese military interactions between 1989 and 1995. Regarding more recent sales, see Kathy Chen, "Latest Big China-Russia Arms Deal Could Raise Concern in Asia and U.S.," *South China Morning Post*, Jan. 14, 1997; Simon Beck, "Sino-Russian Ties Worry Washington," *South China Morning Post*, Jan. 25, 1997, p. 7.

17. Rajau Menon, "The Strategic Convergence Between Russia and China," *Survival* 39, no. 2 (Summer 1997), pp. 101–125. See also Tai Ming Cheung, "Ties of Convenience: Sino-Soviet/Russian Military Relations in the 1990s" (Paper prepared for conference on "The PLA and the New World Order" convened by the Chinese Council on Advanced Policy Studies, June 26–28, 1992, Taipei, Taiwan); and Blank, *Dynamics of Russian Arms Sales.*

18. Tai Ming Cheung, "Ties of Convenience, p. 2. James Clay Moltz, "Regional Tension in the Russo-Chinese Rapprochement," *Asian Survey* 35, no. 6, (June 1995), pp. 511–527.

19. The Five-Power Agreement is in FBIS, *DRC*, Apr. 26, 1996, p. 22.

20. Peter Kirkow and Philip Hanson, "The Potential for Autonomous Regional Development in Russia: The Case of Primorski Krai," *Post-Soviet Geography* 35, no. 2 (1994), p. 74.

21. *Izvestiya*, Feb. 4, 1994; quoted in *Russia in Asia Report*, no. 17 (July 1994), p. 44.

22. *Rossiyskaya Gazeta*, Moscow, Oct. 5, 1996. Global Newsbank (http://www.library.Yale.edu).

23. Pei Jianfeng, "Sino-Russian Border Trade to Regain Glory," *China Daily Business Weekly*, July 16–22, 1995, p. 1.

6

Japan and Europe in Chinese Foreign Relations

DONALD W. KLEIN

This chapter describes and analyzes China's relations with Japan and Europe, with a primary focus on the middle-to-late 1990s. The emerging "New World Order" of the 1990s suggested that China would continue to pursue its already elaborate economic ties with Japan and Europe, but this may be altered by China's more aggressive military posture, which might conflict with its desire to achieve overall economic goals.

Until the epochal Kissinger-Nixon visits to China in 1971–1972 and China's entry into the United Nations in 1971, Beijing's relations with both Japan and Europe ranged from hostile to chilly. In the 1950s, China viewed both Europe and Japan as contemptible U.S. lackeys. These countries challenged China's legitimacy in that most of them continued to recognize Taiwan and with few exceptions supported the United States in keeping Beijing out of the United Nations.

In the 1960s, relations improved somewhat in the wake of the Sino-Soviet split. Not only had Beijing lost the Soviet defense connection and foreign aid, but both Sino-Soviet trade and Soviet technology transfer to China rapidly declined. Seeking new trade partners, China began to bolster its commercial links to both Japan and Europe. And thus by 1966 (notwithstanding the Cultural Revolution's turbulence), seven of China's ten top trade partners included European countries, Canada, Australia, and Japan. These seven represented 44 percent of China's total foreign trade, even granting that trade amounted to a modest $1.9 billion. Three decades later, the percentage of China's trade with the industrialized nations (excluding the United States) had dropped slightly, but the $1.9 billion level of 1966 had soared to $108 billion in 1995. The increased links to both Japan and Europe are very important elements in China's rapid rise

133

as a major trading nation—rising from a very modest $4 billion when Nixon visited China in 1972 to an impressive $290 billion in 1996.

Soon after the 1972 Nixon visit to China, Japan established formal diplomatic relations with Beijing (Japan simultaneously broke its formal—but not its informal—ties with Taiwan). Meanwhile, China moved swiftly to establish diplomatic relations with a flock of industrial nations and by 1979 had formal relations with *all* of Western Europe. China moved gingerly in terms of its military relations with Europe. Beijing apparently wanted to strike a balance between reminding the then-very-hostile Soviet Union that military ties with Europe were possible and not inflaming Moscow. China began to talk favorably about NATO and sent numerous arms-purchasing missions to Europe. In the event, few arms were bought (they were too expensive), and after Mikhail Gorbachev took power in 1985, China's need to play the "European card" sharply diminished.

If important links to Japan and Europe took place in the late Mao era, even more important ones occurred after his passing in 1976. In terms of foreign aid, China abandoned its "self-reliance" policy to become an eager recipient of Western economic aid. From a mere $17 *million* in official development assistance (ODA) in 1979, the figure rose to $3.5 *billion* in 1995.[1] Most of this ODA comes directly (or indirectly through multilateral organizations) from Japan and Europe.

In addition to foreign aid, post-Mao China has witnessed massive amounts of foreign direct investments (FDI). By 1996, cumulative, actualized FDI totaled $177 billion.[2] One study reported that China, in addition to receiving the greatest amount of FDI of any country in the developing world, ranked third in the 1985–1994 period (after the United States and the United Kingdom [UK]) among *all* nations receiving FDI.[3] Most of this has come from Overseas Chinese in Hong Kong and Macao, but both Japan and Europe stepped up their investments in the mid-1990s.

Still other post-Mao developments include the spectacular leap forward in that tens of thousands of Chinese students and scholars were sent abroad. It's true that the largest number have gone to the United States,[4] but thousands have gone to Japan and Europe. China has also earned vast sums from tourism, amounting to $10 billion in 1996.[5] Chinese from Hong Kong and Macao represent the largest contingent, but among non-Chinese the peripatetic Japanese have led the way.

The Tiananmen massacre of 1989 put a damper on China's ties to Europe and Japan. But at least in economic terms, the damage was relatively short-lived. Perhaps more important, by the 1990s China had become more militarily secure than it had been since the Communists took power in 1949. The Gorbachev visit to China in May 1989 largely settled the long-term Sino-Soviet dispute. Moreover, the Soviet collapse has meant that Vietnam lost its Kremlin support, thus forcing Hanoi to come to terms with China.

Measuring the Costs and Benefits of China's Relations with Europe and Japan

Europe

In political-diplomatic terms, China has sought to institutionalize its ties to Europe since the 1970s by sending its most senior officials there. For example, the three premiers since Zhou Enlai's death in 1976 (Hua Guofeng, Zhao Ziyang, and Li Peng) have all traveled there, Li Peng most recently in 1996. Party leader Jiang Zemin visited European capitals four times in the mid-1990s. On the European side, virtually all European countries sent senior leaders to China in the 1970s and 1980s. These visits were briefly halted after Tiananmen, but in 1990 they had been renewed without fanfare. China's leaders' visits to Europe were also halted after Tiananmen. But again, less than two years after Tiananmen, senior Chinese officials were visiting Europe. It's no exaggeration to say that top-level visits in both directions had become routinized by the early 1990s.

In terms of economic ties, Europe has been an increasingly fruitful partner for China. For the past three decades, China's trade with the European Economic Community/European Union (EEC/EU) has ranged from 10 to 20 percent of Beijing's total trade. The sheer volume is more impressive than the percentages. China-EEC trade in 1986 was $11.8 billion, a figure about double the amount for 1983. It reached $14.9 billion in 1989 (the Tiananmen year). One might have expected that the outrage occasioned by Tiananmen would have caused a drop in 1990 and thereafter. In fact, trade rose markedly (see Table 6.1). In the first half of the 1990s China has run a fairly modest trade deficit (in the $2-3 billion range) with the EEC/EU.

The EU is the world's largest trading unit, and thus it's no surprise that the percentage of its export trade to China is far less than China's export trade to the EU. In point of fact, Europe's "Big Four" (Germany, France, the UK, and Italy) have had only 1 to 2 percent of their trade with China in recent years. Yet given current trends, further increases seem almost inevitable. From Beijing's perspective, Europe is an ideal alternative to Japan or the United States, putting China in a good position to get good trading terms or long-terms loans, which are virtually a form of foreign aid. China's economy and the EU's economies are essentially complementary, so there's less likelihood of the sort of trade disputes that often darken the commercial horizon between Japan and Europe. European financial institutions apparently agree in their optimism regarding EU-Chinese economic ties. By 1996, the Big Four nations had established eighty-six financial firms in China (e.g., banks, insurance firms).[6]

TABLE 6.1   China's Trade with the EEC/EU, 1990–1996

	Total Trade[a]	Trade with EEC/EU[a]	Trade with EEC/EU[b]
1990	116.8	15.4	13.2
1991	135.8	16.4	12.1
1992	167.3	18.9	11.3
1993	195.2	28.0	14.3
1994	236.4	34.0	14.4
1995	280.8	40.4	14.4
1996	289.9	39.8	13.7

[a]Billion U.S.$.
[b]Percentage of total trade.
SOURCE: International Monetary Fund, *Direction of Trade Statistics: Yearbook* (Washington, D.C.: IMF, various years).

In recent years, Germany has been by far China's leading EU trade partner, and the Germans have been the largest EU aid donor to China. Aid amounted to only $100 million 1991 but rose to almost $700 million by 1995 (or roughly half the amount of Japanese aid to China).

Closely related to trade is the matter of technology transfer. Europeans have regularly taken out patents in China, and large numbers of Europeans (especially from Germany, Britain, and France) have worked in China as economic and technical experts.

However, European investments in China have fallen far short of Chinese expectations. Investments did increase during the early 1990s, but by the middle of the decade EU members still had only a 4 percent share of investments in China.

China's disadvantages in dealings with Europe seem relatively few. At the most basic level, Europe clearly poses no strategic danger. A deterioration in Sino-American ties might cause Washington to pressure its European allies to lessen their China ties, but in the post–Cold War era it seems increasingly unlikely that Europe will bend to U.S. pressures. Should China begin to act in a draconian fashion toward Hong Kong (which it took over in 1997), then Sino-European (and especially Sino-British) relations might deteriorate. On balance, this seems unlikely.

Taiwan might pose a problem for Sino-European relations. In recent years, Taiwan-EU trade has roughly matched PRC-EU trade, although by 1995 China's EU trade was about one-fifth larger than Taiwan's. In any case, the Europeans have a large stake in continuing their trade with Taiwan. Virtually all European nations have so-called unofficial trade offices in Taiwan, and Taiwan has counterpart offices all over Europe. Beijing has grudgingly accepted this situation as long as commercial ties have not moved to formal diplomatic recognition of Taiwan. From time to time, European officials have made "unofficial" trips to Taiwan. Beijing typically registers an "official" objection, but there the matter rests.

Not surprisingly, China is more sensitive when Europeans have sold (or begun negotiations to sell) weaponry to Taiwan. The most important case occurred in 1992 when France (perhaps emboldened by the U.S.-Taiwan agreement of November 1992 to sell 115 American F-16 jets to Taiwan), agreed to sell 60 Mirage 1000-5 jet fighters and 1,000 missiles (worth $2.6 billion) to Taiwan. Beijing declared that it would "react strongly." In fact, it didn't, and in the late spring of 1997 the first batch of the 60 Mirage jets arrived in Taiwan (ironically only a few days before French President Jacques Chirac's state visit to China).[7] Beijing's acquiescence to these sales may relate to the fact that by the mid-1990s several EU countries had begun to ignore the Tiananmen-related ban on military sales by selling China ostensibly "nonlethal" military equipment.[8]

Notwithstanding the Tiananmen troubles and possible further European weapon sales to Taiwan, most other signs point to a continuing good relationship with Europe. The relationship has been in the main an economic one. In this regard, it's worth emphasizing that China has relatively little economic leverage to use against the Europeans. By way of a rough comparison, Japan's 1996 trade with the EU was almost three times that of China-EU trade, and U.S.-EU trade was over seven times greater than China's trade with the EU. It's quite possible—indeed it's probable—that within a very few years China will close these trade "gaps," for the simple reason that it has already closed them substantially in the first half of the 1990s.

Asia-Europe relations received a boost in March 1996 when the first Asia-European Conference was held in Thailand. It was attended by leaders from China (represented by Premier Li Peng), Japan, South Korea, and seven members of the Association of Southeast Asian Nations, and all fifteen EU countries. The Chinese press gave positive coverages to the meetings but did note that EU investments in East Asia were "sorely deficient, accounting for less than 1 percent of its total overseas investments."[9]

Japan

In considering Sino-Japanese relations, it's worth stressing that Japan is vastly more important to China than any European nation. Except for the United States and perhaps Russia, China's most important bilateral relationship is with Japan. Some would argue that by the early twenty-first century Japan might well surpass the United States in importance. For well over a century, East Asian interstate relations have hinged largely on Sino-Japanese affairs—and the relationship was generally bad (indeed, often disastrous) from China's viewpoint.

Sino-Japanese problems certainly exist today and indeed may worsen in the years ahead. Still, it should be emphasized that the relationship has been better in the late 1990s than at any time in well over a century. Moreover, it is likely that Japan will play *the* most significant role of any nation to aid in China's long and arduous quest for economic modernization.

One would be hard-pressed to find two major nations with more complementary economies. China has many natural resources that Japan needs; Chinese labor costs are a fraction of those in Japan (thus inducing Japanese manufacturers to operate in China); and, of course, there is the vast potential Chinese market. Japan has the technology and money to assist China and a rich market for Chinese goods. Proximity adds another positive element by holding down transportation costs.

Japan replaced the USSR as China's top trading partner in 1965 and held that position until 1987 when it was displaced by Hong Kong. Sino-Japanese trade during the 1965–1986 period was usually much greater than China's trade with the number-two contender (which for many years was Hong Kong). For most of this period, Sino-Japanese trade was usually about 50 percent larger than China's trade with West Europe. By the late 1980s, China's trade with Japan and Europe was roughly the same, but in the mid-1990s Japan again outpaced the EU. A different pattern characterizes a comparison of China's trade with Japan and the United States. As recently as the mid-1980s, Beijing's trade with Japan was about double its trade with the United States. By the late 1980s the trade was roughly equal, and then in the first half of the 1990s, U.S.-China trade surpassed Sino-Japanese trade. Finally, note must be taken of the importance of Sino-Japanese trade from Japan's side. Throughout the 1970s and 1980s, oil-exporting Saudi Arabia was Japan's number-two trade partner (after the United States). The Saudis were displaced by China in 1985. The PRC slipped back to fifth or sixth place for the next few years but emerged again in 1994 as Japan's second-most-important trading partner. The odds are likely that China will retain this position for many years to come.

As noted, China ran a trade deficit with the EU of $2–3 billion a year during the 1990s. But with Japan, China has had surpluses ranging from $3 to $19 billion during the 1990s. China's trade with the EU and Japan together rose from almost 29 percent in 1990 to 35 percent in 1996. (See Table 6.2.)

By the mid-1990s, the composition of China's exports was moving steadily toward more and more manufactured goods. For example, almost a third of its $151 billion in exports consisted of machinery and electric products, and over 29 percent consisted of textile products, garments, and footwear.[10] In 1995, China exported far more textile products to Japan than to any other country. It ranked third in the export of electrical machinery to Japan and fourth in the export of chemicals.[11] In terms of imports, China bought nearly $18 billion worth of Japanese machinery and electronic products in 1996.

Problems naturally arise when the sheer trade volume reaches Sino-Japanese levels, which in 1996 hit $62 billion (about a fifth of China's to-

TABLE 6.2   China's Trade with Japan, 1990–1996

	Total Trade[a]	Trade with Japan[a]	Trade with Japan[b]
1990	116.8	18.2	15.6
1991	135.8	22.8	16.8
1992	167.3	29.0	17.4
1993	195.2	38.1	19.5
1994	236.4	46.3	19.6
1995	280.8	57.8	20.6
1996	289.9	62.2	21.4

[a]Billion U.S.$.

[b]Percentage of total trade.

SOURCE: International Monetary Fund, *Direction of Trade Statistics: Yearbook* (Washington, D.C.: IMF, various years).

tal foreign trade). Yet these problems don't obscure the central fact that it has been highly profitable to both sides (even granting that many Japanese firms have had numerous problems in their dealings with China). Accordingly, although China can be expected to avoid an overdependence on Japan, we can also expect a continued very high volume of commodity trade well into the twenty-first century. To put foreign trade in its broadest perspective, among the world's bilateral trading partners, by 1995 China's trade with Japan ranked twelfth.

Beyond trade, other economic links testify to Japan's importance to China. Beginning in 1982, China for the first time became the top recipient of Japan's official development assistance. In subsequent years China has been the number-one or number-two recipient of Japanese ODA, and during the 1993–1995 period it received annual funds ranging from $1.4 to $1.5 billion.[12] To put this in another perspective, in 1994 Japan supplied 62 percent of *all* China's bilateral ODA. China has also received large loans from the Asian Development Bank (ADB), an organization that gets the lion's share of its fund from Japan. Between 1986, when China joined the ADB, to September 1996, China received $5.6 billion in ADB loans and led all borrowers in 1996, to the tune of $1.1 billion.[13]

Japanese aid was predictably "suspended" in the wake of Tiananmen—in part because of Western (especially United States) pressure. Tiananmen was obviously a human rights violation, but given Japan's guilt over its own wartime human rights violations, Tokyo is always reluctant to push this point vis-à-vis China. The Japanese also argued that it was in no one's interest to isolate China. Accordingly, Tokyo urged its Western allies to lift the ban on aid to China. In any event, Japanese aid was back in the pipeline by 1990, and late that year the two countries signed documents for Japan's third loan, worth about $7 billion, for the 1990–1995 period. The renewal of "normalized" relations was punctuated in mid-1991 when Japanese Prime Minister Kaifu Toshiki became the first head of state among the industrialized nations to visit China since the Tiananmen events two years earlier. Even though Japan has been a major advocate for economic aid to China, Tokyo—reflecting Japan's well-known sensitivity regarding nuclear weapons—did suspend grant aid (a small part of Japan's overall aid to China) in 1995 to protest China's nuclear weapons' testing. A year later, grant aid was resumed.[14]

China has been particularly eager to attract foreign direct investments from Japan's business community. Into the early 1990s, Beijing often complained about the relative paucity of these investments. By early 1992, Japan's cumulative, realized investments amounted to $3.4 billion—a hefty sum, but only about 1 percent of Japan's global investments. Thereafter, Japan rapidly boosted its FDI, which reached $13 billion by the fall of 1996. To put this in perspective, note that in 1996 Japan's investments in Hong Kong were $14 billion and those in Taiwan came to $6 billion.[15] The jump in FDI from $3.4 billion in 1992 to $13 billion in 1996 is notable. Nevertheless, it still remains a tiny fraction of Japan's global investments and is also a very small portion of the total cumulative, actualized investments in China, which rose to $177 billion through 1996.[16]

Beijing has been generally dissatisfied with Japan's willingness to transfer technology to China. Yet in terms of longer-range technology transfer, that is, the training of Chinese in Japanese universities, 40,000 Chinese had studied in Japan by 1994, of whom 15,000 had returned home after completing their studies. By 1995, the Japan-China Science, Technology, and Cultural Centre had arranged for 4,500 technicians to work in Japan.[17]

Japanese tourists add another increasingly important flow of funds to China. In the last "pre-Tiananmen" year (1988), 477,000 Japanese visited China. Tiananmen obviously scared off visits for a few years. But after the early 1990s, the numbers rose rapidly, and in 1995, 865,000 Japanese enriched the Chinese by an estimated $1.5 billion.[18] Estimates for 1997 were that China would earn $10 billion from *all* visitors.[19] The $10.9 billion that tourists spent in Hong Kong in 1996 presumably adds another reason why it behooves Chinese officialdom to ensure that the 1997 takeover process runs as smoothly as possible.[20]

Sino-Japanese ties are regularly reinforced by visits between the two countries' cabinet-level ministers. Virtually all senior Japanese leaders, including the staunchly conservative Liberal Democratic Party chiefs, have visited China. Beginning with Prime Minister Tanaka Kakuei in 1972, nine Japanese prime ministers during the years 1979 through 1997 have visited China (Tanaka, Ohira Masayoshi, Suzuki Zenko, Nakasone

Yasuhiro, Takeshita Noboru, Kaifu Toshiki, Hosokawa Morihiro, Murayama Tomiichi, and Hashimoto Ryutaro). On China's side, paramount leader Deng Xiaoping visited Japan in 1978 and 1979, followed by visits in 1980, 1982, and 1989, respectively, by Premiers Huo Guofeng, Zhao Ziyang, and Li Peng. Also, former Communist Party general secretary Hu Yaobang visited Japan in 1983, and the current general secretary, Jiang Zemin, was there in 1992 (the first top-ranking Chinese to visit Japan after Tiananmen). The United States has roughly matched these high-level exchanges, but no European nation comes close to official Japanese contacts with China. In a word, senior-level Sino-Japanese contacts have been fairly well routinized over the past quarter century.

Despite the extensive economic linkages and regularized contacts between political leaders, problems do exist—and by the late 1990s, some of these problems had seemed to be getting more serious. Some are essentially bilateral in nature, whereas others are part of the larger Asian geopolitical scene. A few cases are illustrative. In 1982, changes in school textbooks, in effect, whitewashed Japan's invasion and predatory occupation of China during the 1930s and 1940s. Japan promised to rectify the situation only in the face of strenuous Chinese objections. Three years later, Prime Minister Nakasone angered Beijing by visiting Tokyo's Yasukuni Shrine—the burial place of Japan's military men. China saw this as a visit to the graveyard of war criminals and vigorously protested. Eleven years later, Prime Minister Hashimoto Ryutaro also visited the shrine, and once again China reacted sharply—Hashimoto had "dared" to do so, and thus this was a "serious development" and "outrageous act," demonstrating that "Japan has failed to repent that period of history and settle its war crimes."[21] In reviewing world events for 1996, Beijing listed Hashimoto's visit as one of the "Ten World Events" in 1996.[22]

Although impossible to prove, it may be that Beijing almost welcomes these inept blunders as a way of keeping a kind of psychological upper hand in dealing with Japan. In any case, China shows no reluctance in reminding Japan of its past war crimes. There are many examples of this. A recent one took place in 1995—a year the Chinese used to mark two "anniversaries": the hundredth anniversary of the end of the Sino-Japanese War of 1894–1895 and the fiftieth anniversary of the end of World War II. In two consecutive issues of *Beijing Review,* aside from detailed commentaries, many pictures of appalling and very vivid atrocities (beheadings, rapes, and so on) were featured.[23]

Taking note of this tactic, a former cultural attaché of Japan in Beijing commented that the new Japanese generation has a weaker sense of historical guilt, and thus "China may not be able to continue with this stratagem for long."[24] Along these same lines, two Western scholars have written that "personal testimony of many Japanese officials and scholars is that they are getting very tired of China's insistence on repeated apologies and the Japanese government's 'diplomacy of apology' in East and Southeast Asia."[25] Similarly, two other Western scholars, based on extensive interviews in China, quoted one Chinese official as saying, "Attitudes toward China in Japan are no longer guided by the 'sense of guilt toward China' that Japanese felt when their memories of World War Two were fresh."[26]

Other problems derive from the very different political systems. For example, Japan has an independent judiciary, whereas China doesn't. The ownership of a student dormitory in Kyoto, Japan (claimed by both China and Taiwan), has languished in Japan's courts for many years. To Beijing, it is purely a political case—a manifestation of "certain circles" in Japan that foster a "two China" policy. To the Japanese, it's a legal matter for the courts. (The case is still undecided.) Similarly, it appears that Chinese officialdom has grown apprehensive about the direction of Japanese politics since the collapse of Liberal Democratic Party rule in mid-1993.[27]

Some of the geopolitical problems that long troubled Beijing-Tokyo relations have sharply diminished in the post–Cold War era. For example, Japan recognizes only South Korea but has moved cautiously to improves relations with North Korea. China, of course, has long had formal relations with North Korea and for many years viewed South Korea as an enemy state. But then in the late 1980s, strong Sino–South Korean economic ties were developed, leading to the establishment of formal diplomatic relations in August 1992. In this regard, it's interesting to note that when Jiang Zemin made a state visit to South Korea in late 1995, he joined Korean President Kim Young Sam at a new conference in rebuking Japan for its refusal "to recognize that [the Pacific War] was an act of aggression."[28]

Similarly, the "Soviet issue" is far less troublesome than it was a few years ago. China resented Japan's fairly active trade ties with Moscow. For example, in 1985 China's trade with the Soviet Union was less than half of Japan's trade with Moscow, but a decade later Russo-Japanese trade was only marginally greater than China's trade with Russia. In any event, Beijing has essentially made its peace with the Russians, so this issue has been deflated.

The most troublesome issue in Sino-Japanese relations involves military and strategic issues. Until the Cold War ended, China tended to see itself as part of a three-way informal alliance with Japan and the United States as a means of countering the Soviet Union. But since the late 1980s, China has increasingly expressed its concern about Japanese "militarism," including Japan's security treaty with the United States. And during these same years, China has made concerted efforts to modernize the People's Liberation Army (PLA).

In 1987, China issued some sharp remarks when Japan's defense budget slightly passed the self-imposed (since 1976) 1-percent-of-GNP "barrier." Similar remarks were made in 1991 during the Persian Gulf crisis when Japan's parliament considered a bill to allow Japanese military forces to be dispatched abroad. Beijing, however, has difficulty in claiming the higher moral ground on this issue, because China's military forces are vastly larger than Japan's and because of the recent surge in China's defense spending. Moreover, China has been buying huge amounts of advanced weaponry from the Russians in recent years—a trend that appears to be continuing.

Sino-Japanese problems remain unresolved concerning jurisdictional disputes over the continental shelf that involve fishery questions and oil-drilling rights. The most important of these is about sovereignty over the uninhabited Senkaku Islands (Diaoyutai in Chinese), not far north of Taiwan. (Taiwan also claims these islands.) Back in 1978, Deng Xiaoping told the Japanese that this dispute could be settled peacefully at some future time. But the issue has not gone away, and by the 1990s had grown worse. In late 1990, Japan built a lighthouse on one of the islands. Then in February 1992 China escalated the problem by passing a law that explicitly listed the islands as part of its territorial waters and further asserted the right to use military force to repel any foreign incursions. Japan's embassy in Beijing lodged a verbal protest, claiming that the islands were "without doubt" Japanese territory.[29] Another flare-up occurred in the spring of 1997 when several prominent Japanese political leaders planted a flag on one of the islands. In this case, Japan's prime minister criticized this provocative action.[30] In any event, the dispute continues to trouble Sino-Japanese relations, especially because of the potential relationship of Senkaku/Diaoyutai to China's overall claims to the Spratly Islands in the South China Sea—a vital sea lane for Japan's massive oil imports from the Middle East.[31]

The most potentially explosive issue in Sino-Japanese relations concerns the linkage (in Chinese eyes) of the U.S.-Japan security treaty and the "two China" issue. The best scenario from China's perspective would be a continuation of the U.S.-Japan Security Treaty in order to check Japan's presumed ambitions to become a regional hegemon and to curb any Japanese military buildup. The most "worrisome scenario" was aptly described as "the prospect of American and Japanese forces cooperating under the umbrella of the U.S.-Japan alliance in response to use of force by [China] . . . to prevent Taiwan from becoming independent."[32]

The following is an overview of Japan's important economic ties with Taiwan. As with South Korea, China in recent years has developed very extensive economic ties with Taiwan and is thus less inclined to badger Japan for having equally extensive economic links with Taiwan. Moreover, many senior members of Japan's powerful (and conservative) Liberal Democratic Party hold pro-Taiwan views, and public opinion polls reveal a Japanese public that hopes Taiwan can remain, in effect, independent. Beijing has presumably concluded that Japan's important business establishment is unlikely to budge on this issue—all the more so since Taiwan is Japan's fourth-largest trading partner (a trade that reached to $41 billion in 1996).

In brief, the "two China" issue in Sino-Japanese relations is not much of a problem in *economic* terms. But from China's perspective, a *military-strategic* problem has arisen in recent years—a period in which Japan has seemingly become more assertive and in which key members of Japan's elite have openly discussed such previously "unthinkable" matters as a revision of the famous "peace" constitution.

A turning point occurred in April 1996 when U.S. President Bill Clinton and Japanese Prime Minister Hashimoto Ryutaro issued a joint declaration on the U.S.-Japan security alliance. Among other things, they called for a review of the guidelines for U.S.-Japan defense—with a view to strengthening the existing security framework in Asia.[33] Predictably, both sides insisted that this effort to revitalize the security treaty was not directed at any particular nation. But just as predictably, China regarded itself as the target of these endeavors and that they were a possible prelude to the worst-case scenario noted above. One Chinese commentator concluded that if U.S.-Japan "cooperation moves beyond the bilateral range, new complications enter the picture which will undoubtedly affect stability and development in the region."[34]

Basing their analysis on extensive interviews in China in the 1995–1997 period, two American scholars wrote: "Most Chinese leaders, officials, and think-tank analysts have long judged that on balance, continuation of the U.S.-Japan alliance serves Chinese interests."[35] Another American analyst (also as a result of interviews in China) has written that although the Chinese "harbor suspicion toward the United States, they view Japan with even less trust and, in many cases, with a loathing rarely found in attitudes toward America." He also found among Chinese analysts a "basic consensus that Japanese power would be more threatening than American power and that the status quo in the U.S.-Japan security arrangement—without upgrades—is desirable."[36] In Chinese eyes, the "upgrades" are now under way. Chinese officialdom, according to American analysts, foresees "potential Japanese naval intervention in conjunction with the United States in a South China Sea conflict involving China. Of greatest concern to the Chinese, however, is the possibility that the U.S. and Japan will tacitly include Taiwan within the alliance's zone of coverage."[37]

China's unease was heightened by the Japan Defense Agency's 1996 white paper that cited China as a security concern. A Chinese commentator, indignantly and with Japan-bashing sarcasm, responded that with "expanding military cooperation with the United States, Japan put China on top of its so-called enemies list." He concluded: "With rightism and nationalism running rampant, many Japanese choose not to confront their history of aggression. Propped up by a sense of racial superiority, . . . [the Japanese] increasingly look down upon other Asian nations."[38]

The situation was exacerbated in August 1997 when a very senior Japanese leader (Chief Cabinet Secretary Kajiyama Seiroku) bluntly stated that the Taiwan Strait would be an area for U.S.-Japan cooperation under the revised U.S.-Japan defense cooperation guidelines. In fact, the guidelines do not list any specific areas. Nonetheless, the damage was done. Predictably, Chinese officials (including Premier Li Peng) sharply condemned Kajiyama's statement, and with equal predictability Kajiyama's deputy issued a clarification that clarified nothing.[39]

From Japan's point of view, China is not the "injured innocent" it makes itself out to be—endless in its litany about sovereignty and the five principles of peaceful coexistence. China's actions and inactions in foreign affairs have obviously played their part in Japan's unease concerning its huge neighbor. One analyst summarized recent Chinese actions as follows: The unilateral claim to sovereignty regarding the Senkaku/Diaoyutai Islands; "gunboat diplomacy" in the South China Sea; an "active role in the global arms trade, both as buyer and seller"; "perfidious behaviour on a host of arms control and disarmament issues, including nuclear testing and proliferation"; and human/rights and environmental conditions in China.[40] All of these Chinese actions are of deep concern to Japan's leaders. Elites aside, there are signs that the Japanese public is also uneasy about China's growing power. The *Yomiuri Shimbun* (Japan's largest daily) polled the public on Chinese issues. In 1994, 18 percent felt that China was a military threat, yet in a mere three years the figure had risen markedly to 40 percent.[41]

The military-strategic problems in Sino-Japanese relations have occurred during a period in which both nations have exhibited a rising nationalism, and as history instructs us, strident nationalism can lead to xenophobic tendencies. China's extraordinary economic growth in recent years and its increasing military muscle have led to claims for a greater voice in East Asian affairs that will brook no interference from the United States or Japan. As a Chinese commentator wrote in early 1997: "Without China's involvement, it is impossible to resolve any international dispute in the Asia-Pacific region."[42]

In early 1997, a Chinese commentator wrote a hard-hitting piece entitled "After the Cold War, Where Is Japan Headed?" He noted that a "conspicuous phenomenon" in Japan's "current political landscape is rising *nationalistic* sentiment, which . . . has led to repeated efforts to gloss over

Japan's war crimes." He also mentioned that Japanese cabinet members had a "penchant for making scandalous speeches through their twisting of historical truth," and he described Japan's efforts to increase ties with the Association of Southeast Asian Nations (ASEAN) as a move "to counter China's influence." Japan, according to this author, was "itching to walk out on America" and to follow its own diplomatic path.[43]

On the more positive side, the 1990s have witnessed the emergence of two multilateral organizations in which both China and Japan participate: the Asia-Pacific Economic Cooperation (APEC) meetings and the ASEAN Regional Forum (ARF). Hitherto, aside from the UN, virtually all Sino-Japanese relations were conducted bilaterally. Now both sides (which always send top officials) can discuss regional issues across a broad range of affairs in an atmosphere that has been quite positive in nature. It's too early to judge the effectiveness of these meetings, but there's reason to think that they might serve both sides' interests.[44]

Concluding Remarks

Setting aside what appears to be the relatively short-term damage resulting from Tiananmen, China has profited enormously—especially in the economic realm—from the elaborate linkages to Europe and even more so from those to Japan. Both Europe and Japan on the one side and China on the other have huge stakes in good relations, and all would suffer should these relations flounder. Moreover, the crucial geopolitical changes of recent years have also greatly benefited China. From the 1970s through the 1990s, China emerged from a partial isolation to become an acknowledged member of the world community, and its links to Japan and Europe certainly contributed to this emergence. To repeat, China is today more strategically secure today than at any time in the past century and a half.

What lessons, if any, about Chinese foreign policy can be drawn from this analysis of China's ties to Europe and Japan? An important one is that despite much Chinese rhetoric about hegemonism, imperialism, and so forth, Beijing quite relentlessly pursues its ties to Europe and Japan. There have been many zigs and zags, to be sure, but the basic links—especially the economic ones—remain in place and continue to expand. Once again ignoring Chinese "self-reliance" rhetoric, the willingness, indeed the eagerness, to accept Western and Japanese aid seems to be an enduring policy. The same applies to foreign investments, a point emphasized in Premier Li Peng's government work report in March 1997.[45] Foreign analysts often dwell on real or fancied Chinese "sensitivity" to Western criticism. The Chinese were certainly badgered about Tiananmen—and most of this hectoring came from the Western world. Call it opportunism or whatever, but in retrospect it's clear that China has been willing to absorb much verbal punishment in order to maintain its economic links with the West.

Still, it's important to remember that the most striking element of Chinese policy is volatility. In its five-decade history, China has had extreme swings of policy with *every* important nation with which it has dealt. During this half-century it has had very good and very bad relations with the (former) Soviet Union, the United States, India, and Vietnam— having met all four on the battlefield. China's willingness to use force was again demonstrated in March 1996 when it fired ballistic missiles quite near Taiwan's two most important ports. In the words of one analyst, this firing was "designed to underscore Beijing's long-standing commitment to use force should Taipei declare independence."[46]

Such "missile diplomacy" damages Beijing's relations with the United States and also has the potential to hurt China's relations with the ASEAN countries, all of which have ever-growing ties to both Japan and Europe. Japan's close ties with ASEAN are familiar, but in recent years the EU states have rapidly increased their commercial links with ASEAN. ASEAN-EU trade, for example, reached no less than $100 billion in 1995, or well over double China-EU trade. Were it not for the South China Sea—where China not only asserts its sovereignty but has used military force[47]—Sino-ASEAN relations could be described as quite solid in the 1990s. Aside from being one of the world's most important sea-lanes, the South China Sea contains petroleum riches that both China and several ASEAN countries hope to exploit.[48]

These issues aside, what other domestic or foreign considerations should command our attention? In domestic affairs, the 1980s and 1990s have centered on achieving the Four Modernizations—the policy to modernize industry, agriculture, science and technology, and national defense. Virtually all signs point to a continuation of this policy into the twenty-first century, and it's unlikely that these goals can be achieved without Japanese and European cooperation. Beijing's leaders clearly know that the lion's share of direct and indirect aid comes from Europe and even more so from Japan. They are equally aware that a very substantial share of China's trade is with Japan and Europe—35 percent in 1996, worth over $100 billion. Could China's relations with Japan and Europe weather another Cultural Revolution? China's economic ties to Japan and Europe remained largely intact not only through the Cultural Revolution but also through the Vietnam War, the "Gang of Four" radicalism in the mid-1970s, and even the Tiananmen crisis. (Of course, the intensity of economic links today is vastly greater than in the years from the 1960s to the early 1980s.) Occasional flurries of strident nationalism might well inflict limited damage on China's ties with Europe and especially those with Japan. But both

Europe and Japan have some of the world's most experienced business executives, who are accustomed to such excesses from governments ranging from left or right around the world.

A few years ago one might have speculated on possible ideological clashes between the communism of China and the capitalism of Europe and Japan. At the close of the twentieth century this appears to be much less likely, on the seemingly safe assumption that nationalism has replaced communism as the guiding "ism" driving Chinese foreign policy. Yet it can be argued that nationalism could be disruptive of China's relations with Europe and, especially, those with Japan. Nationalism, after all, destroyed the great Western colonial empires, and we have seen the power of nationalism in the dismemberment of the "worldwide Communist movement," not to mention the former Soviet Union. The capitalist nations, however painfully, have adjusted to this development, so it seems unlikely that ideology will significantly damage China's future ties with Europe and Japan.

Finally, at the most basic strategic level, do Europe and Japan threaten China? Distance alone answers the European question. Japan is the only conceivable threat. Yet in this case, China does not stand alone. Several Asian nations are apprehensive about Japanese remilitarization. They tend to see the U.S.-Japan Security Treaty as a means of containing China, but also as a barrier to a Japan that might move toward a rapid rearmament should the security treaty be terminated. Japan's ruling elites are fully aware of these anxieties. Accordingly, Japanese military action against an increasingly militarily powerful China seems no more likely than a renewal of French-German hostilities in Europe. Yet, as Voltaire said, "Doubt is not a very agreeable state, but certainty is a ridiculous one."

Notes

1. *Geographical Distribution of Financial Flows to Aid Recipients* (Paris: OECD, 1997), p. 77.

2. *Beijing Review* (hereafter *BR*) 39:12 (March 18–24, 1996): 12; and *BR* 40:14 (April 7–13, 1997): 28. In 1996 alone, FDI totaled over $42 billion. The latter source also noted that an additional $16 billion in foreign loans was utilized in 1996.

3. *Financial Market Trends* 64 (Paris: OECD), June 1996: 54.

4. See David Zweig and Chen Changgui, *China's Brain Drain to the United States* (Berkeley, Calif.: Institute of East Asian Studies, 1995).

5. *BR* 40:17 (April 28–May 4, 1997): 28.

6. *U.S.-China Business* (Los Angeles) 1:A (Spring 1996): 45.

7. *Far Eastern Economic Review* [hereafter *FEER*], May 15, 1997, p. 15.

8. *FEER*, April 24, 1997, p. 25.

9. *BR* 40:15 (April 14–20, 1997): 28.

10. *BR* 40:17 (April 28-May 4, 1997): 27. Economic Intelligence Unit, *Country Report, China,* 1st Quarter 1997, p. 42, and ibid., 2nd Quarter 1997, p. 42.

11. Japan Institute for Social and Economic Affairs, *Japan 1997: An International Comparison* (Tokyo: 1997), 42–45.

12. For an article suggesting that Japan may be in the process of cutting back on ODA to all countries, see *FEER,* May 22, 1997, p. 77.

13. Economic Intelligence Unit, *Country Report, China,* 1st Quarter 1997, p. 44; *FEER,* May 15, 1997, p. 62.

14. *FEER,* November 7, 1996, p. 95.

15. *FEER,* September 26, 1996, p. 23.

16. See the useful article by Eric Harwit, "Japanese Investment in China," *Asian Survey* 36:10 (October 1996): 978–994. See also Roy Grow, "Sino-Japanese Economic and Technical Relations," in Denis F. Simon and Hong Pyo Lee, eds., *Globalization and Regionalization of China's Economy* (Seoul, Korea: Sejong Institute, 1995), 75–108.

17. Diana Betzler and Greg Austin, "Gulfs in Sino-Japanese Relations: An Evaluation of Japan's Cultural Diplomacy Toward China," in *Journal of East Asian Affairs*: 11:2 (Summer/Fall 1997): 583–585.

18. *FEER, Asia Yearbook 1996,* p. 118; Japan Institute for Social and Economic Affairs, *Japan 1997,* 60.

19. *BR* 40:11 (March 17–23, 1997): 37.

20. *FEER,* May 8, 1997, p. 51.

21. *BR* 39:34 (August 19–25, 1996): 9.

22. *BR* 40:2 (January 13–19, 1997): 11.

23. *BR* 38:33 (August 14–20, 1995): 14–22; and *BR* 38:34 (August 21–27, 1995): 8–15.

24. Kazuaki Kotake, "A Sense of Place," *Look Japan* (Tokyo), no. 437 (August 1992): 7. In this regard, note that Prime Minister Hashimoto (who visited Yasukuni in 1996) is the first Japanese prime minister who had not even reached his teens (he was eight years old) when the war ended in 1945.

25. Betzler and Austin, "Gulfs in Sino-Japanese Relations," p. 591.

26. Banning Garrett and Bonnie Glaser, "Chinese Apprehensions About Revitalization of the U.S.-Japan Alliance," *Asian Survey* 37:4 (April 1997): 398.

27. Banning Garrett and Bonnie Glaser, "China and the Great Powers in the Asia-Pacific: Perspectives from Beijing," paper prepared for the U.S. Army War College's Seventh Annual Strategy Conference on China into the Twenty-First Century, April 23–25, 1996, p. 2.

28. B. C. Koh, "South Korea in 1995," *Asian Survey* 36:1 (January 1996): 59.

29. Samuel S. Kim, "China as a Regional Powers," *Current History,* September 1992: 249; *FEER,* March 12, 1992, pp. 8–9; *Japan Quarterly* 39:2 (April-June 1992): 282.

30. *FEER,* May 15, 1997, p. 15.

31. For an excellent article on this issue, see Lam Peng Er, "Japan and the Spratlys Dispute: Aspirations and Limitations," *Asian Survey* 36:10 (October 1996): 995–1010.

32. Garrett and Glaser, "Chinese Apprehensions," pp. 385–386.

33. The interim report of the new guidelines, issued in June 1997, is summarized in the July 1997 issue of *Japan Now,* a publication of Japan's embassy in Washington.

34. *BR* 39:19 (May 6–12, 1996): 9.

35. Garrett and Glaser, "Chinese Apprehensions," p. 385.

36. Thomas J. Christensen, "Chinese Realpolitik," *Foreign Affairs* 75:5 (September-October 1996): 41, 44. This echoes some of the themes in Allen S. Whiting, *China Eyes Japan* (Berkeley: University of California Press, 1989).

37. Garrett and Glaser, "Chinese Apprehensions," p. 390.

38. *BR* 39:39 (September 22–29, 1996): 8–9.

39. *Yomiuri Shimbun*, August 20, 21, 23, 1997; *New York Times*, August 24, 1997, p. 9.

40. Samuel S. Kim, "China's Pacific Policy: Reconciling the Irreconcilable," *International Journal* 50:3 (Summer 1995): 471–472.

41. *Yomiuri Shimbun*, March 17, 1997, p. 10. For another assessment of the rise of Chinese and Japanese nationalism, see Stuart Harris, "The China-Japan Relationship and Asia Pacific Regional Security," *Journal of East Asian Affairs* (Seoul, Korea): 11:1 (Winter-Spring 1997): esp. 143–145.

42. *BR* 40:14 (April 7–13, 1997): 7.

43. *BR* 40:9 (March 3–9, 1997): 9. Italics added.

44. It's interesting to note that in mid-1997 a Chinese journal featured a glowing account about ARF. See *BR* 40:33 (August 18–24, 1997): 6–7. At about the same time, the usually conservative *Far Eastern Economic Review* commented: "ARF is becoming an important forum for handling the region's security problems." *FEER*, August 7, 1997, p. 26.

45. *BR* 40:13 (March 31-April 6, 1997): VI.

46. Paul H. B. Godwin, "From Continent to Periphery: PLA Doctrine, Strategy and Capabilities Towards 2000," *China Quarterly* 146 (June 1996): 486.

47. Kim, "China's Pacific Policy," pp. 478–479.

48. See *FEER*, April 3, 1997, pp. 14-16, for a good article dealing with this issue.

7

China and the Third World: Patterns of Engagement and Indifference

PETER VAN NESS

China is a country, and a developing country as well. China belongs to the Third World. . . . China is not a superpower, nor will she ever seek to be one. . . . If capitalism is restored in a big socialist country, it will inevitably become a superpower. . . . If one day China should change her color and turn into a superpower, if she too should play the tyrant in the world, and everywhere subject others to her bullying, aggression and exploitation, the people of the world should identify her as social-imperialism, expose it, oppose it and work together with the Chinese people to overthrow it.

—*Deng Xiaoping, speech at the UN General Assembly, April 1974*[1]

Throughout the history of the People's Republic of China, since its founding in 1949, Beijing's foreign policy rhetoric (or what some analysts call "declaratory policy") has given high priority to China's relations with the countries of Asia, Africa, and Latin America—usually referred to collectively as the "Third World." But Beijing's actions (or "operational policy") have demonstrated, by contrast, a shifting pattern of engagement and indifference. This contrast between what China has said and what is has actually done with respect to the Third World raises some fundamental questions. Do China's leaders really see their own country as part of the Third World? Or does China aspire instead to emerge from the Third World to become a global superpower? Does Beijing really care about the countries of Asia, Africa, and Latin America? What does China want to achieve in its relations with the Third World?

In the mid-1970s when Mao Zedong sent Deng Xiaoping to the United Nations to expound Mao's "three-worlds theory," Deng's lecture ended with the assurances quoted in the opening of this chapter. However, neither that speech nor the many subsequent assurances given by China's post-Mao leadership have provided convincing answers to these questions. The reason is that there has been a fundamental contradiction between China's rhetorical role as a champion of Third World causes and Beijing's own search for wealth and power in the global system. Claiming to support the objectives of the former colonial countries of Asia, Africa, and Latin America (the have-nots of the non-Western world), China throughout has principally sought to win Third World endorsement for policies designed to achieve the PRC's fundamental strategic and economic goals.

Whether Beijing's policy of the moment focused on revolutionary "national liberation" struggles, as in the 1960s; "self-reliant development," as during the 1970s; or "Asian values," as in the human rights debate today, the underlying logic has been to mobilize Third World diplomatic support for key Chinese objectives. Typically, China has sought to use its relations with the Third World to enhance its position vis-à-vis the United States (or the Soviet Union before its collapse). For example, both Mao's "three-worlds theory" in the past and the current policy of opposing U.S. post–Cold War "hegemonism" have been designs for building Third World coalitions to limit superpower influence. Now, in the late 1990s, China has once again launched an activist Third World diplomacy, including official visits by President Jiang Zemin to ten African and Asian countries in 1996 and by Premier Li Peng to six countries in Africa in May 1997 and to Singapore and Malaysia in August 1997.

This chapter examines four topics: (1) how to define and to understand the concept of "Third World," especially after the collapse of the bipolar, Cold War world; (2) patterns in the history of China's relations with the Third World and the various strategies that Beijing has employed to mobilize support among the countries of Asia, Africa, and Latin America; (3) recent initiatives and the reasons for the PRC's renewed interest in the Third World in the late 1990s; and, finally, (4) some conclusions about the relationship, focusing on the factors that appear to be the main determinants of PRC policy toward the Third World.

What Do We Mean by "Third World"?

Historically, the idea of a Third World emerged out of the independence struggles of societies dominated by Western imperialism. The French apparently coined the term *tiers monde* in the mid-1950s, after the first conference of Afro-Asian states at Bandung, Indonesia, in 1955.[2] The French term originally emphasized the idea of a third force, or a group of states between, and distinctively apart from, the two major alliances of that time, the West and the socialist camp. The Chinese concept of a Third World has similarly envisaged a grouping of states opposed to the two major world power centers: the United States and the Soviet Union.

There are six separate criteria often used by analysts to identify countries of the so-called Third World: history (previously colonized by the West), economics (poor and/or underdeveloped), race (non-white), culture (non-Western), geography (situated in Asia, Africa, and Latin America), and politics (nonaligned). Today, after the collapse of the Soviet Union, formerly a superpower second only to the United States, the idea of a Third World in the sense of third force has lost its political meaning. However, we can still identify this grouping of nations empirically in terms of the other criteria.

The *Human Development Report 1996* (hereafter referred to as *Report*) of the United Nations Development Program (UNDP) divides the countries of the world into two groups: "industrial countries" and "developing countries."[3] The 1996 *Report* analyzes 174 countries and categorizes 47 as industrial and 127 as developing. Roughly speaking, the 127 developing countries meet the selection criteria already discussed for identifying the Third World. I will take those 127 countries to constitute "the Third World" for the purposes of this study.[4]

Obviously, this is a very diverse group, representing important differences with respect to wealth, education, religion, history, and political influence. For example, the richest, Qatar, had a per capita gross domestic product in 1993 (in purchasing-power-parity or PPP terms) of $22,910, whereas the poorest, Ethiopia, had a per capita GDP of only $420. Nonetheless, understood in Kishore Mahbubani's distinction between "the West and the Rest,"[5] they are "the Rest": the global have-nots, all of them sharing historical memories of domination by Western imperialism. Beijing targets these key distinguishing features of national identity in its efforts to mobilize the Third World into a global political force.

In some respects one might argue that the term *Third World* no longer has any significant political meaning. For example, since the collapse of the Soviet Union, there is no longer an opportunity to attempt to play the role of a third force in a bipolar, Cold War world. Also, the issues that divide this group of 127 countries one against another are often much more salient for them than problems that might give them common cause to oppose the West. Note as examples the postindependence history of wars between India and Pakistan, Iran's hostilities with Iraq, and the genocidal conflict between Tutsis and Hutus in central Africa.

Moreover, several Third World countries, especially in East Asia, ranked among the world's most effective and competitive players in the global marketplace, at least until the financial crisis of 1997,[6] whereas by contrast, others are experiencing negative growth, and in several especially tragic cases (e.g., Somalia and Liberia), states have collapsed and chaos ensued.[7] Generally, as countries participate more in the global economy, it seems that they tend to see one another more as economic competitors (e.g., in offering low-cost labor incentives to attract scarce foreign direct investment) rather than as political allies in some broader strategic relationship.

Nevertheless, Beijing has continued to attempt to mobilize these developing countries on the basis of their common experience with Western imperialism and their relative have-not status. China's approach to the Third World has been built largely on the notion of a dichotomized, the Rest versus the West, approach. For example, during the spring 1997 deliberations in the UN Human Rights Commission on a resolution expressing concern about the human rights situation in China, PRC representatives charged that Western countries were attempting to use the commission as a "courtroom" to judge developing countries and to force Western values upon them. PRC Ambassador Wu Jianmin said, "We appeal to developing countries who genuinely care for human rights, because what happens to China today may well happen to them tomorrow."[8]

Yet, is China itself really a Third World country in the way that I have defined that term? Nominally, yes. But do China's leaders actually identify as "Third World"? Probably not.[9] China fits many of the criteria: history (victim of Western imperialism), culture (non-Western), race (non-white), and economy (still largely underdeveloped and poor).[10] But all Chinese know that their country is special, exceptional, in a category all its own. For some four thousand years, the Chinese people produced one of the world's great civilizations. Pride in that tradition and historical memory of the power and prestige of China's past set a standard for Beijing's contemporary performance, which places China apart from the rest of the Third World.

There is much debate in China and abroad about what contemporary world role would be most appropriate to the stature of China's preindustrial past and the ambiguous sense of national identity that defines what it means to be Chinese today.[11] The world's most populous country and the third-largest economy (after the United States and Japan), China today has the largest standing army in the world, although most of its equipment is obsolete despite recent modernization. The PRC joined the select nuclear club with its first test in 1964 and since 1971 has enjoyed the status of being one of five permanent members of the United Nations Security Council (with the United States, Russia, France, and Britain). Hence, in terms of international influence and military power,[12] China is hardly a country typical of the Third World.

Patterns in PRC Relations with the Third World, 1949–1997

What is it that China wants from the Third World, and how has that changed over time? Obviously, there are particular economic and strategic concerns in China's relations with each country. Neighboring Third World countries, for example, usually receive the highest priority for security reasons including the problems of shared borders and sometimes territorial disputes.[13]

There are, however, several consistent patterns in China's Third World policy: a desire to establish beneficial trade relations with the Third World; the objective of gaining a more influential role for the PRC in the United Nations thanks to Third World voting power; and an intention to isolate Taiwan diplomatically, both within the UN and elsewhere. The most consistent pattern, however, has been an effort to win Third World diplomatic support for China in its relations with the world's superpowers, the United States and the Soviet Union before its collapse.

The intellectual roots of CCP ideology regarding the Third World are to be found principally in Mao Zedong's concepts of "new democratic revolution"[14] and "intermediate zones."[15] Mao argued that Communist-led revolutions in colonial and semicolonial countries would have to be quite different from revolutions in the industrialized countries of the West, and that strong coalitions of countries at the margins of world politics (i.e., in the Third World) could be decisive in Cold War confrontations. For Mao, to be "Third World" meant to share a common sense of deprivation and exploitation at the hands of the rich and powerful.

The Third World line in PRC foreign policy sought to shape the have-nots of Asia, Africa, and Latin America into a revolutionary force to overturn the global status quo. These supposedly backward and powerless nations, Beijing argued, could be fused into a powerful revolutionary force by adopting the Chinese experience as their guide. Lin Biao, Mao's closest political ally during the Cultural Revolution, published an essay on "people's war" in 1965 that painted an apocalyptic vision of the Maoist revolutionary model projected on to a global canvas. There the Third World "rural areas of the world" would surround the Western "cities of the world" in a revolutionary struggle to transform the globe. "In the final analysis," Lin argued, "the whole cause of world revolution hinges on the revolutionary struggles of the Asian, African, and Latin American peoples."[16]

Mao's strategy emphasized building political coalitions in the Third World at two different levels: that of the revolutionary movements and that of the newly independent governments. At the revolutionary movement level, China supported "national liberation struggles" both to force out the remaining colonial regimes and to overthrow those independent Third World governments that were most closely allied with the West. For example, in 1965, at the peak of China's Third World foreign policy line, Beijing endorsed ongoing armed struggles in twenty-four countries, eighteen of which were pro-Western, independent states.[17] Meanwhile, at the government-to-government level, Beijing attempted to build close, cooperative relations with the rest of the independent Third World governments, urging them to reject the West. The most comprehensive theoretical statement of the PRC approach to Third World governments was Mao's three-worlds theory.[18]

As the Sino-Soviet dispute deepened, Mao tried to create a truly third-force coalition among the developing countries of Asia, Africa, and Latin America to oppose both superpowers simultaneously, targeting not just U.S. imperialism but also Soviet social imperialism. But when PRC policy toward the superpowers changed, Beijing's Third World policy changed, too. Increasingly fearful that the Soviet Union might launch a "surgical strike" against China's nascent nuclear weapons capability, Mao Zedong negotiated an accommodation with the Nixon administration in 1971–1972 in order to help deter a possible Soviet attack. For Maoists abroad, this was like making peace with the devil. Gradually, Beijing gave up its support for Third World revolutionary movements, and Maoist ideology and the Chinese model lost their influence in the Third World.

After Mao died in 1976 and Deng Xiaoping emerged as China's paramount leader, China once again turned its back on the Third World. As a part of Deng's Four Modernizations strategy and the opening of China to the world market, announced in 1978–1979, international economic policies that had been anathema to Mao were embraced by Beijing: joining the World Bank and the International Monetary Fund, the two key multilateral institutions linking the capitalist industrialized countries with the Third World; inviting foreign multinational corporations to invest in China; accepting long-term foreign loans; building a foreign tourist industry; and sending thousands of Chinese students and scholars abroad for academic training in capitalist countries.

China's attempt during the 1960s and early 1970s to shape Third World have-nots into a third force in international politics opposed to both of the two superpowers failed. But under Deng Xiaoping's leadership, Beijing seemed to give up entirely on taking collective action with Third World countries. The Third World rhetoric continued, but Deng was no longer preoccupied with trying to build alliances among the have-nots, but rather sought to join the haves as quickly as possible by making a separate peace with the global status quo. If anything, China had by the late 1980s shown that it wanted desperately to escape from being a Third World country.

Beijing's Renewed Interest in the Third World

The West's condemnation of China after the PLA's suppression of the 1989 student-led demonstrations in Tiananmen Square and the subsequent collapse of the Soviet empire and global communism prompted a renewed Chinese interest in the Third World. Despite the continued success of the development strategy initiated by Deng Xiaoping, linking domestic market reforms with an opening of China to global capitalism, Beijing faced the danger that China's Communist government might become politically isolated or, worse yet, designated the West's new enemy in the post–Cold War world.

The worst-possible-case scenario that Beijing was working to avoid was that China, despite its rapidly growing economic and military power, might come to be seen as a global pariah: (1) ideologically, one of a handful of Communist party holdouts following the collapse of the Soviet Union; (2) politically, a dictatorship and abuser of human rights (e.g., the Beijing massacre) in an era of democratic transformation,[19] and (3) internationally, an expansionist, aggressive power seeking hegemony (e.g., as alleged in the debate over the "China threat" following the PRC's 1995–1996 missile exercises designed to influence Taiwan's presidential election).

By the mid-1990s, China was being left out of major strategic decisions affecting global power relationships. The U.S.-Japan Security Treaty was revitalized, with the threat from China as its unstated new rationale. The Group of Seven richest capitalist countries, meeting in Denver in June 1997, transformed itself into the Summit of Eight after inviting Russia's President Yeltsin to participate, but China was not invited. And NATO decided to expand its membership (initially to include the Czech Republic, Hungary, and Poland) with Moscow's acquiescence, but without need to consult with China.[20]

Official Chinese visions of the post–Cold War world insisted that the emerging global order was a multipolar system consisting of competing power centers; but the realities of the global system increasingly looked like a U.S.-led hegemonic order with China on the outside looking in. Acknowledged in the 1990s to have the world's third-largest economy, China was nonetheless not a member of the Group of Seven, nor was China yet a member of the World Trade Organization. Beijing conducted an exchange of summit meetings with Moscow to negotiate a "strategic partnership" with Russia in 1996–1997; but President Yeltsin seemed much more interested in cooperating with Washington, despite the expansion of NATO, than in joining China to oppose the Western alliance.

As in the past when China faced isolation, Beijing turned to the Third World for support. In the months following the Chinese "missile exercises," China undertook an active diplomacy at the highest level. During the period from March 1966 through May 1997, PRC officials of the rank of vice premier or above (including the official visits by President Jiang Zemin and Premier Li Peng) paid official calls on no fewer than twenty-eight countries in Asia, Africa, and Latin America. Leaders of several other Third World countries (e.g., Singapore, Ivory Coast, and Guinea) were invited to pay official visits to China.

China, the Third World, and Human Rights

China's Third World diplomacy addressed many issues, but to illustrate the way that Beijing has cultivated the Third World to gain support on issues that were perceived as vital to the PRC, let me briefly describe the role of the Third World member-states on the United Nations Commission on Human Rights in their annual deliberations regarding resolutions on human rights abuse in China, where Beijing's effort to defeat those resolutions has been dependent upon Third World support.[21] I will focus on the votes in April 1996 and April 1997.[22] As Samuel Kim noted, this is a politics of collective legitimation and delegitimation.[23]

Responding to the sanctions imposed by the West in 1989 after the Beijing massacre, Beijing devised an elaborate human rights diplomacy designed to lift the sanctions and to refute the stigma of being called the "butchers of Beijing."[24] In 1991, the PRC, having invited delegations from Australia, France, and Switzerland to investigate the human rights situation in China, published a white paper on human rights. Chinese scholars were encouraged to research human rights issues; and Chinese officials engaged in what has become a vigorous human rights debate.[25]

The Third World, especially the countries of Asia, became the focus of China's human rights diplomacy.[26] In 1993, the United Nations convened a World Conference on Human Rights in Vienna. Prior to the Vienna meeting, preparatory conferences were held in different parts of the world. Chinese diplomacy focused on the Asian preparatory meeting held in Bangkok, where Beijing won support for a declaration that challenged the Western position, prompting a debate about "Asian values" versus universalism.[27]

At the Vienna Conference, Vice Foreign Minister Liu Huaqiu endorsed the Universal Declaration of Human Rights but placed special emphasis on collective rather than individual rights (e.g., the right of self-determination of nations against colonialism, racism, apartheid, and foreign invasion and occupation) and on the economic, social, and cultural agenda (i.e., problems of poverty, starvation, and disease). Liu insisted that "the concept of human rights is a product of historical development. It is closely associated with specific social, political, and economic conditions and the specific history, culture, and values of a particular country."[28]

Thus, although Liu Huaqiu nominally endorsed the principle of universality, he insisted on culturally relativist human rights standards for each country, depending on its history and culture, stage of development, and the character of the social system (e.g., socialist, capitalist). The thrust of the Chinese position was to argue that each country had its own standards, and no one else had any right to interfere. "If the sovereignty of a state is not safeguarded, the human rights of its citizens are out of the question, like a castle in the air," Liu argued.

Each year since Tiananmen (except 1991 when the United States needed China's acquiescence in the UN Security Council to pursue the Gulf War), a resolution on China has been proposed to the UN Human Rights Commission, whose fifty-three members are overwhelmingly from the Third World. The Chinese delegation thus far has been successful in defeating the resolution, usually by means of a no-action motion. China's face-saving effort is totally dependent on Third World support in the commission. During 1996 and 1997, China won on a no-action motion: in 1996, the vote was 27 for, 20 against, and 6 abstentions; in 1997, 27 for, 17 against, and 9 abstentions. In each of those years, all but two of the votes supporting the Chinese position were cast by Third World countries (the other two were countries from the former Soviet Union: Belarus and Ukraine).[29]

Beijing worked hard to consolidate its position among the Third World members of the commission. Western countries were using the UN commission "as if the United States is the master of the world and all countries have to listen to it," insisted Li Baodong, a PRC representative.[30] Among the six African countries that President Jiang visited in May 1996, four (Ethiopia, Egypt, Mali, and Zimbabwe) were members of the commission. All four supported China in the commission's April 1997 vote. Similarly, all four Asian countries that President Jiang visited in November–December 1996 were members of the commission. In this case, Beijing won the support of three (Pakistan, Nepal, and India) and lost one (Philippines).

A commentary published in China's authoritative *People's Daily* shortly before the commission's vote in 1997 stated Beijing's position quite bluntly: "It must be emphasized that a lot of the fuss over human rights has nothing to do with human rights at all, but is merely a smoke screen for legalizing interference in other countries' internal affairs, openly practicing hegemonism and power politics, and disseminating Western values worldwide." The article continued: "This serious fight in the realm of human rights represents essentially an encounter between developed and developing countries over interference and counter-interference, containment and counter-containment. . . . It is a continuation of the anti-imperialism and anti-colonialism struggle and constitutes a major contribution to the cause of promoting and safeguarding human rights and preserving world peace and stability."[31]

During the 1997 commission deliberations, China succeeded for the first time in undermining the Western coalition, which, since Tiananmen in 1989, has pressed the commission to examine the human rights situation in China. First France, and later Germany, Italy, Spain, Greece, Australia, Japan, and Canada, accepted either explicitly or implicitly the Chinese characterization of the issue as one of "confrontation versus cooperation." Using the lure of China's potentially immense market to win Western governments over to the PRC position of bilateral dialogue, and thanks to its overwhelming Third World support, Beijing seems to have defeated the commission's ability to undertake multilateral deliberations on human rights in China.[32]

Taiwan and "China Threat"

Two other key issues for Beijing in China's relations with the Third World are (1) PRC attempts to isolate Taiwan diplomatically as part of its effort to gain control over the island and (2) Beijing's desire to refute allegations of the "China threat." The two issues have become linked in contradictory ways for Beijing.[33]

China's threat to use force against Taiwan, the "missile exercises" begun in July 1995 and sustained until the presidential elections on the island in March 1996, were counterproductive not only in failing to prevent President Lee Teng-hui's election victory but also in prompting the United States to send two aircraft-carrier battle groups to deter the PRC, and in producing heightened fears in the region of an expansionist, potentially aggressive, China.

For China, Taiwan is an internal Chinese affair, and Beijing has consistently refused to renounce the use of force as a means to reunify Taiwan with the mainland. Diplomatically, countries recognizing the PRC have acknowledged Beijing's position that reunification is a domestic issue, but they have been much more ambivalent about use of force. The United States, for example, has tried unsuccessfully for the past twenty-five years to convince Beijing to renounce the use of force in its policy toward Taiwan. A military conflict over Taiwan could shatter the political stability of East Asia, which has been a vital precondition for the series of "economic miracles" achieved by Third World countries in the region.[34]

Since 1949, Taiwan has been a central preoccupation of PRC Third World diplomacy. During the years before the UN recognition of the People's Republic as the sole legitimate representative of China in October 1971, Beijing worked to win votes away from Taipei and to gain diplomatic recognition throughout the Third World. Since then, the PRC has sought to complete the diplomatic isolation of Taiwan, especially in recent years in response to an activist diplomacy by President Lee Teng-hui, designed to achieve a more substantial international role for the island.[35] As of June 1997, only 26 of the 127 countries identified here as "Third World" maintained formal diplomatic ties with Taipei.

Beijing faces a dilemma between standing up for China's rights with respect to Taiwan and the vital need to avoid international isolation, between taking action deemed appropriate to reunifying the country and refuting charges of a "China threat." Especially at a time of leadership transition after Deng's death and in response to strong nationalistic currents running in the country, in part prompted by government manipulation,[36] Taiwan remains a difficult problem for China's Communist leadership.[37] A decision to use force or once again to threaten the use of force would have a marked effect on international perceptions of China, especially among its Third World neighbors.

During a visit to China by UN Secretary-General Kofi Annan in May 1997, President Jiang Zemin took pains to reassure him that China would not practice hegemonism and had no plans for expansion. He called fears of a threat from China "totally groundless." President Jiang insisted that growing Chinese power threatened no one. "China has proved that it is possible for a developing country to improve its situation in a relatively short period of time," noted President Jiang.[38]

China and ASEAN

In the face of Washington's attempts to shape the post–Cold War world to its own design, Chinese diplomacy in the late 1990s focused on encouraging alternative centers of power to counter U.S. initiatives. China's objective was a multipolar world, rather than an all-roads-lead-to-Washington U.S. hegemonic system. As we have seen, Beijing negotiated a strategic partnership with Russia and sought to play the United States and its European allies against each other, using the attractions of the potentially immense Chinese market. A financial crisis that struck first Thailand in mid-1997 and later other East Asian countries (including Malaysia, Indonesia, and the Philippines) provided Beijing with an opportunity to strengthen its ties with one of the most important regional groupings of Third World countries, the Association of Southeast Asian Nations (ASEAN).

China's relations with ASEAN illustrate the general point that it is Beijing's preoccupation with certain specific issues or foreign policy problems that prompts it to take an interest in a particular country or group of Third World countries at any particular time. ASEAN's nine member-countries constitute probably the most important group of Third World nations for China because of three factors: their strategic location, neighboring China and controlling access by sea from East Asia to the Indian Ocean; their high rates of economic growth and the modern military capabilities that they can afford to purchase;[39] and the success of ASEAN as a multilateral organization in East Asia, a region, unlike Europe, where there is very little multilateral institutional structure to support state-to-state cooperation. The large Overseas Chinese communities resident in Southeast Asia (for example, Singapore has the largest Chinese community in percentage, at 76 percent of the total population), and the fact that several of the members of ASEAN (Vietnam, the Philippines, Malaysia, Indonesia, and Brunei) contest China's territorial claims in the resource-rich South China Sea, make relations with ASEAN additionally sensitive for China. Total trade between China and ASEAN in 1996 was $20.4 billion.[40]

Although many Western financial analysts were shocked when Malaysian Prime Minister Mohamad Mahathir denounced foreign currency speculators and briefly introduced trading restrictions in August 1997 in response to heavy selling on the Malaysian stock market and the weakening of the ringgit, China stepped in to help support ASEAN economies, first by offering a $1 billion loan as part of a package organized by the International Monetary Fund to help Thailand, and later in announcing a $1.5 billion investment in a Malaysian pulp and paper mill, China's largest overseas investment. As Western investors pulled out of ASEAN equity markets, Chinese Premier Li Peng visited Singapore and Malaysia to underline China's support.[41] Trade between China and Malaysia had reached a high of $3.6 billion in 1996, eight times the total of 1986.[42]

The Malaysian prime minister has often challenged Western positions in international politics, especially when the United States and the other richest industrialized countries (as he put it) "have decided that they, and they alone, should determine the fate of every country" in the world.[43] For many years, Mahathir pressed for the establishment of an East Asian Economic Caucus (EAEC), a grouping of East Asian countries that, unlike the Asia-Pacific Economic Cooperation forum (APEC), which includes both Asian and Western countries, would limit its membership exclusively to Asian nations. Also, about the same time that he was denouncing George Soros, founder of the $10 billion Quantum Fund, and other "rogue speculators" who, he charged, had sabotaged the Malaysian economy by undermining its currency and stock market in July 1997, Mahathir proposed a review of the Universal Declaration of Human Rights, originally adopted by the United Nations in 1948. He asserted that it "was formulated by the superpowers which did not understand the needs of poor countries."[44] Allen Whiting's research, undertaken before the financial crisis, showed how ASEAN was attempting to position itself independently between the Washington and Beijing, avoiding "tight alignment with or forced submission to either capital." He argued that, on democracy and human rights, ASEAN takes the side of China; but on the issue of PRC use of force, "ASEAN sides with the U.S. policy as the mainstay of peace and stability in East Asia."[45]

ASEAN scheduled a summit meeting with China, Japan, and South Korea for December 1997 as a part of its strategy of attempting to balance the power of China, Japan, and the United States in the East Asian region. Although some American analysts discuss the feasibility of trying to reshape ASEAN into a military alliance to contain a potentially expansionist China,[46] the ASEAN Regional Forum, established in 1994, is constructed on the basis of a very different strategic concept: cooperative security.[47] By inviting all of the major powers in the region (the United States, China, Japan, and Russia) to discuss strategic issues with it,[48] ASEAN is attempting to include all those countries vital to maintaining strategic stability in the region, rather than to exclude, much less to construct a military alliance against, any of them. Specifically with regard to relations with China and the United States, Jusuf Wanandi of Indonesia's Center for Strategic and International Studies observed: "The main worry in East Asia is that by default, and because of misunderstanding and faulty domestic debates in the U.S. and elsewhere in the West, China will be demonized and seen as the next 'enemy No. 1' replacing the Soviet Union."[49]

Prompted in part by China's threat to use force against Taiwan during the "missile exercises" of 1995–1996, the United States and Japan have redefined the security treaty between them.[50] The U.S.-Japan Security Treaty is designed to serve as both a nuclear "umbrella" to ensure the national security of Japan and as a "leash" to assure that Japan never again becomes a military threat to Asia; therefore the treaty is of major concern to every country in East Asia. But in its new redefinition, the treaty is designed mainly to balance the growing power of China.[51] Relations with ASEAN provide one of Beijing's best opportunities to temper a possible realignment of East Asian international relations against China. "If the U.S. is not careful, it will drive ASEAN and China much closer together and both will be increasingly antagonistic towards the U.S.," Dewi Fortuna Anwar, an Indonesian strategic analyst, has observed. It is in this connection, as Mak Joon Nam of the Malaysian Institute of Maritime Affairs has noted, that "China wants support [from ASEAN] in its foreign-policy initiatives."[52]

Conclusions

China could, as President Jiang has suggested, propose its own experience since 1978 as a model for development, as an exemplar of how a Third World country could best use the global capitalist system to its own advantage in its search for wealth and power. No country has gotten more capital, technology transfer, and access to foreign markets with fewer political strings attached than China has since the advent of Deng Xiaoping's market reforms less than twenty years ago.[53]

But the factors that have enabled China to manipulate the system so effectively are unique to China and therefore not replicable by other Third World countries. They are (1) the attractions of its potentially immense market of 1.2 billion consumers for foreign investors and exporters; (2) its military and strategic power (as one of the five permanent members of the UN Security Council and one of five acknowledged nuclear weapons powers); and (3) the resources of the Overseas Chinese, a vital source of investment capital, technology transfer, management expertise, and access to foreign markets. Moreover, the PRC competes with all other developing countries for the limited number of grants and loans available from multilateral institutions and individual aid-donating countries, and therefore China's success in some respects is at the expense of the rest of the Third World.

There is a strong movement in many Third World countries to counter the more exploitative aspects of capitalist globalization,[54] but it is difficult for China's leaders to demonstrate a convincing connection with this movement when they are working feverishly to exploit globalization for China's own benefit. Ironically, it is those characteristics that distinguish the PRC most sharply from the typical Third World country (its huge potential market, strategic power, and the overseas Chinese) that give Beijing the power to benefit from, rather than be victimized by, globalization.

In the end, PRC foreign policy is shaped by its relations with the most powerful states in the global system. It is the Group of Seven and Russia that most influence China's search for wealth and power. Only those countries have the military and economic capabilities sufficient to threaten China's national security and the capital, technology, and foreign markets indispensable for China's economic modernization. Hence, the PRC's policy toward the countries of Asia, Africa, and Latin America twists and turns in response to the perceived needs of Beijing's strategy for dealing with the United States, Europe, Japan, and Russia.

Despite Beijing's rhetoric to the contrary, China is in truth only a "fair weather friend" of the Third World. During the 1960s, Beijing supported revolutions to overthrow newly independent Third World governments, but today, China has become a champion of state sovereignty and defender of noninterference in the internal affairs of those same Third World countries. In the 1970s, Mao preached Third World solidarity to reshape radically the global status quo, but since Mao's death, Deng and his successors have worked hardest of all to join that global establishment. In short, PRC policy toward the Third World is always subject to change, even making 180-degree changes, when Beijing decides to take a different approach to achieving wealth and power in its relations with the most influential states in the system.

Notes

1. Translated in *Peking Review*, April 19, 1974, pp. 6–11.

2. Paul Robert, *Dictionnaire alphabétique et analogique de la langue française* (Paris, Sociéte du nouveau Littré, 1969), s.v. *"tiers monde."*

3. United Nations Development Program, *Human Development Report 1996* (New York: Oxford University Press, 1996), pp. 135–145.

4. The 127 countries included under my definition of "Third World" are roughly equivalent to the membership of the so-called Group of 77, which, as of July 1997, had 131 member-states. Alternatively, the Non-Aligned Movement (NAM) includes many but not all of the Third World countries among its 101 member-countries. The principal benefit of using the *Human Development Report* for the purpose of identifying "Third World" is that each annual *Report* also provides both data and analysis of the individual countries that can be useful for the investigation of North/South and other development problems.

5. Kishore Mahbubani, "The West and the Rest," *National Interest*, Summer 1992, pp. 3–12.

6. World Bank, *The East Asian Miracle: Economic Growth and Public Policy* (New York: Oxford University Press, 1993).

7. The poorest of the Third World countries (over half of them had a GNP per capita in 1993 of less than $1,000) have serious problems of nutrition, basic literacy, and public health. For example, UNDP has estimated that within twenty-five years almost one-quarter of Malawi's present population of some 2.5 million people will have died of AIDS. "Malawi Is Ravaged by AIDS, UN Says," *International Herald Tribune*, July 11, 1997, p. 6.

8. "China constantly emphasized the dividing line between the West and the developing world, while asserting its position as the leader of the latter," wrote Béatrice Laroche in "Dodging Scrutiny: China and the U.N. Commission on Human Rights," *China Rights Forum*, Summer 1997, pp. 28–33.

9. Peter Van Ness, "China as a Third World State: Foreign Policy and Official National Identity," in Lowell Dittmer and Samuel S. Kim (eds.), *China's Quest for National Identity* (Ithaca: Cornell University Press, 1993).

10. China's world ranking in the "human development index," or HDI, was number 108 among the 174 countries ranked by the United Nations Development Program in 1996, roughly in the middle of the 127 Third World countries. *Report*, pp. 144–145.

11. For examples, see the debate prompted by the 1988 TV documentary series on China, *He Shang* or *River Elegy*; the various contributions to Dittmer and Kim, *China's Quest for National Identity*; and Chalmers Johnson's argument that "China is East Asia's natural hegemon" in his *Nationalism and the Market: China as a Superpower*, Japan Policy Research Institute Working Paper, July 1996, p. 12.

12. For a recent assessment, see "A More Assertive China," in International Institute for Strategic Studies, *Strategic Survey 1996/97* (London: Oxford University Press, 1997), pp. 161–174. See also pp. 246–251.

13. For example, Burma, Thailand, and Bangladesh have become more important for China in recent years not only because of new trade opportunities but also because of their strategic location as China seeks access to the Bay of Bengal.

Michael Vatikiotis, "A Friend in Need: Thailand Cosies Up to China and India—With Strategic Implications," *Far Eastern Economic Review*, July 10, 1997, p. 29.

14. Mao Zedong, *Xin minzhu zhuyi lun* [On new democracy] (Yenan: Liberation Association, 1940).

15. See John Gittings, *The World and China, 1922–1972* (New York: Harper and Row, 1974), chaps. 11, 12, and Conclusion. For an example of the concept applied, see *Renmin ribao* [People's daily], January 21, 1964, p. 1.

16. Lin Biao, "Long Live the Victory of People's War!" translated in *Peking Review*, September 3, 1965, pp. 9–30.

17. Peter Van Ness, *Revolution and Chinese Foreign Policy: Peking's Support for Wars of National Liberation* (Berkeley: University of California Press, 1970), esp. chaps 4 and 6.

18. *Peking Review*, April 19, 1974, pp. 6–11.

19. For an attempt to measure political freedom empirically, see the annual reports from Freedom House in New York, available on the Internet at: http://www.freedomhouse.org. The 1995–1996 report covers 191 countries (including 112 of our 127 Third World countries), assessing political rights and civil liberties in each, ranking them on a seven-point scale, and categorizing each country as free, partly free, or not free.

20. "Alliance Votes to Accept Poland, Hungary, and Czech Republic," *International Herald Tribune*, July 9, 1997, p. l. See also Madeleine Albright, "Enlarging NATO: Why Bigger Is Better," *Economist*, February 15, 1997, pp. 17–19.

21. Ann Kent, "China and the International Human Rights Regime: A Case Study of Multilateral Monitoring, 1989–1994," *Human Rights Quarterly* 17, no. 1, February 1995, pp. 1–47.

22. Laroche, "Dodging Scrutiny."

23. Samuel S. Kim, "Human Rights in China's International Relations," a paper for the Marquette University conference on "What If China Does Not Democratize?" July 1997, Milwaukee, Wisconsin.

24. Michael J. Sullivan, "Development and Political Repression: China's Human Rights Policy Since 1989," *Bulletin of Concerned Asian Scholars* 27, no. 4, October-December 1995; Andrew Nathan, "Human Rights in Chinese Foreign Policy," *China Quarterly*, no. 139, September 1994; and Wenhui Zhong, "China's Human Rights Development in the 1990s," *Journal of Contemporary China*, no. 8, Winter-Spring 1995.

25. The leading PRC official articulating China's position on human rights is a veteran propagandist, Zhu Muzhi, former minister of culture and head of the New China News Agency. He serves as president of the "nongovernmental" China Society for the Study of Human Rights. "Beijing Open to Rights Talk," *International Herald Tribune*, July 17, 1997, p. 4.

26. For analyses of PRC concern about human rights as a threat to the regime's security, see Peter Van Ness, "China and the World: The Transnational Challenge," *Chinese Social Sciences Quarterly*, no. 1, November 1992, pp. 135–147; and Denny Roy, "Human Rights as a National Security Threat: The Case of the PRC," *Issues and Studies* 32, no. 2, February 1996.

27. For a text of the Bangkok Declaration, see Michael C. Davis (ed.), *Human Rights and Chinese Values: Legal, Philosophical, and Political Perspectives* (Hong Kong: Oxford University Press, 1995), pp. 205–209.

28. Liu Huaqiu, "Proposals for Human Rights Protection and Promotion." *Beijing Review*, June 28–July 4, 1993, pp. 8–11.

29. Voting data supplied by Béatrice Laroche, Human Rights in China.

30. Laroche, "Dodging Scrutiny," p. 30.

31. "A North-South Struggle over Human Rights," translated in *Beijing Review*, April 14–20, 1997, pp. 7–10. Kim, in "Human Rights in China's International Relations," made the important point that the fundamental differences on human rights that emerged were not so much between Western and Asian governments as they were between some Asian governments and human rights NGOs from Asia. He wrote: "The chief divide is no longer, if it ever was, between the states of North and South but between states, and more particularly between authoritarian south and southeast Asian states, and their human rights non-governmental organizations" (p. 10).

32. Laroche, "Dodging Scrutiny." It should be noted that the Chinese position is by no means universally supported in the Third World. South Africa, for example, voted against China in 1997. Moreover, South Africa's Truth and Reconciliation Commission is setting an example for the world, both the industrialized and the developing countries, in its effort to hold the winners as well as the losers responsible for their human rights atrocities in a domestic civil conflict. Suzanne Daley, "Party Led by Mandela Now Owns Up to Atrocities," *New York Times*, May 13, 1997, p. A7.

33. See, for example, the special issues on Taiwan: *China Quarterly*, no. 148, December 1996; and *Journal of Contemporary China* 6, no. 15, July 1997.

34. Peter Van Ness, "The Impasse in U.S. Policy Toward China," *China Journal*, no. 38, July 1997.

35. "'Face Reality,' Taipei Tells Beijing," *International Herald Tribune*, July 22, 1997, p. 4.

36. Note, for example, the debate and series of books prompted by the publication of *Zhongguo keyi shuo bu: Lengzhan hou shidai de zhengzhi yu qinggan jueze* [A China that can say no: Political and emotional choices in the post–Cold War era] (Beijing: Zhonghua Gongshang Lianhe Chubanshe, 1996).

37. You Ji, "Making Sense of War Games in the Taiwan Strait," *Journal of Contemporary China* 6, no. 15, July 1997, pp. 287–305.

38. "China No Threat to the World, Jiang Tells UN Chief," *Beijing Review*, May 26–June 1, 1997, p. 5.

39. Desmond Ball, "Arms and Affluence: Military Acquisitions in the Asia-Pacific Region," *International Security* 18, no. 3, Winter 1993/94, pp. 78–112.

40. *International Herald Tribune*, August 27, 1997, p. 18.

41. "Imperial Intrigue. China Takes Advantage of Southeast Asia's Economic Woes to Foster Closer Ties and Head Off American-led Containment," *Far Eastern Economic Review*, September 11, 1997, pp. 14–15.

42. *China Trade Report*, September 1997, p. 14.

43. Quoted in Frank Ching, "Is UN Declaration Universal?" *Far Eastern Economic Review*, August 28, 1997, p. 32.

44. Ibid.

45. Allen Whiting, "ASEAN Eyes China: The Security Dimension," *Asian Survey* 37, no. 4, April 1997, p. 301.

46. James Shinn (ed.), *Weaving the Net: Conditional Engagement with China* (New York: Council on Foreign Relations Press, 1996).

47. See David Dewitt, "Common, Comprehensive, and Cooperative Security," *Pacific Review* 7, no. 1, 1994, pp. 1–15.

48. The ASEAN Regional Forum (ARF) also includes Canada, South Korea, Australia, New Zealand, Papua New Guinea, Cambodia, the European Union, and India as members.

49. Quoted in Michael Richardson, "ASEAN Aims to Test Balances of Power," *International Herald Tribune*, August 2–3, 1997, p. 4.

50. Just prior to an official visit to China by Japanese Prime Minister Hashimoto in September 1997, a dispute erupted within Hashimoto's Liberal-Democratic Party about whether U.S.-Japan security cooperation would extend to a conflict in the Taiwan Strait. Nicholas D. Kristof, "Japan Agonizes over Its Role in Event of Conflict over Taiwan," *International Herald Tribune*, August 25, 1997, p. 4.

51. Steven Lee Myers, "Risking China's Wrath, the U.S. Bolsters Military Ties to Japan," *New York Times*, September 24, 1997, p. A5.

52. Both analysts as quoted in "Imperial Intrigue," p. 15.

53. Nicholas R. Lardy, *China in the World Economy* (Washington, D.C.: Institute for International Economics, 1994).

54. See, for example, the publications of the Third World Network in Penang, Malaysia, like the periodical *Third World Resurgence*. See also Jeremy Seabrook, *Victims of Development: Resistance and Alternatives* (London: Verso, 1993).

PART THREE

Policies and Issues

8

Force and Diplomacy: China Prepares for the Twenty-First Century

PAUL H. B. GODWIN

China's Strategic Culture and Beijing's Security Policy

As Beijing makes abundantly clear, China is about to enter the twenty-first century more secure from major external military threats than at any time since the early nineteenth century. Rapprochement with the USSR in the late 1980s and the Soviet Union's ultimate disintegration in 1991 terminated the threat that had been the focus of Beijing's military preparations from the late 1960s on. Furthermore, two decades of reform have transformed China into a major participant in international trade and commerce and a leading diplomatic power in the world. China's remarkable recovery, however, has not been accompanied by the kind of self-confidence that contributes to an open and forthcoming relationship with the international community. Rather, Beijing still views much of the world with suspicion and doubt, fearing that whatever weaknesses it displays will be exploited by potential adversaries.

In large part, this distrust stems from what Chinese refer to as "the hundred years of humiliation," extending from the first Opium War of 1839–1842 until the victory of the Chinese Communist Party (CCP) over the Kuomintang (KMT) in the civil war of 1946–1949. In these years, because internal political decay and division, technological backwardness, and economic weakness left China without the means of effective defense, it fell victim to Western and Japanese imperialism and the loss of great power status, sovereignty, and territory. As a consequence, core elements of Beijing's present strategic culture are the drive to build a powerful economy and the military strength to restore and preserve China's territorial integrity and reinstate China's status as a great power. With such objectives, it is no surprise that the slogan of China's mid–nineteenth century reformers has come back into fashion: *fu guo qiang bing* (a wealthy country, a strong army).

The pervasive sense among Beijing's security elites that China must develop the national strength to redress the evils inflicted upon it by nineteenth-century imperialism and ensure China's status as great power in the next century creates a major dilemma for Chinese security policy. Beijing perceives its armed forces as weak and ill prepared for the twenty-first century military environment. Across Asia and in the United States, however, Beijing's programs designed to modernize China's conventional and strategic nuclear forces are viewed as potentially destabilizing the region's military balance over the next two decades.[1]

Anxiety over China's defense modernization programs is fueled by a number of factors. In 1985, Beijing directed the Chinese People's Liberation Army (PLA), as the armed services and their branches are collectively named, to prepare for local, limited wars on China's periphery, including defense of its maritime territories, claims in the South and East China Seas, and the possibility that Taiwan may have to be recovered by force of arms. Since 1988, the PLA has been receiving increased resources to fund acquisition and training programs designed to enhance its ability to conduct such wars. Much of the increase was necessary to offset the erosion of defense funding over the years 1979–1987 caused by budgets that did not match the high levels of inflation that accompanied the first decade of China's economic expansion. Nonetheless, Beijing's annual budget reports do not, it is believed, reflect actual expenditures on defense, which are generally assumed to be at least three or four times the official figure. In 1997, such estimates transform the official budget of U.S.$9.76 billion (renminbi 81 billion) to funding in the range of U.S.$30 to U.S.$40 billion.

China's growing arms and military technology linkage with Russia heightens concern over Beijing's increasing defense allocations. Moscow appears willing to transfer and grant licensed production for weapon systems, components, equipment, and military technologies at levels of sophistication the Western industrialized powers would not sell in the years before the Tiananmen tragedy brought about an arms embargo on China. China's image as an emerging great power whose dynamic economy is supporting an ever-increasing military capability therefore contrasts sharply with Beijing's perception of China as a weak power with serious domestic development problems demanding the highest priority in resource allocation.

The Origins of China's Post–Cold War Security Strategy

Despite military preparations to defend against a possible attack by the Soviet Union, in the early 1980s China's long-term security strategy was based on the assumption that a multipolar world would gradually emerge as the two superpowers' mutually debilitating competition reduced their global influence. This gradual decline of superpower influence would occur while China was building its economic and military strength to a level where Beijing would play a major role in the emerging multipolar international system.[2] The unexpected extinction of one of the two superpowers over the years 1989–1991 abrogated Beijing's strategic logic; moreover, the United States demonstrated its diplomatic leadership and military power when it used the UN Security Council to establish a broad coalition opposing Iraq's occupation of Kuwait and bind together a military coalition of Western and Islamic states that swiftly and decisively defeated Iraq's seemingly strong military forces. In Beijing's eyes, the Cold War concluded with the United States as the world's "sole superpower."

U.S. preeminence came on the heels of an American led program of punitive sanctions designed to punish Beijing for its use of lethal military force to suppress political expression around Tiananmen Square during the night of June 3–4, 1989. The sanctions, especially those on the transfer of military goods and technologies, meant that to the West, and particularly the United States, the luster of Deng's reforms had faded. China's international image was transformed overnight from that of a modernizing, liberalizing regime to a pariah state, one that reflected the worst aspects of Communist totalitarianism.

Beijing thus entered the post–Cold War era militarily more secure than at any time since the first Opium War, but facing U.S.-led condemnation and punitive sanctions from the Western powers and a reluctant Japan. Beijing's perception that its relationship with Washington had been transformed from Cold War cooperation, no matter how fragile that collaboration had been, to post–Cold War contention was confirmed in the fall of 1992 when the United States sold 150 F-16s to Taiwan. Selling such a large number of advanced fighters was viewed by Beijing as a breach of the 1982 Sino-American agreement limiting U.S. arms sales to Taiwan and as a signal of Washington's intent to use its new status in the world to seek "hegemony" through "power politics."

Thwarting Isolation: China's Diplomatic Offensive

Beijing launched a diplomatic offensive in response to the post-Tiananmen diplomatic quarantine sought by Washington.[3] The strategy's essence was to build "good neighbor" relations with all the states on China's periphery. China normalized relations with Singapore, Malaysia, Vietnam, and South Korea, as well as Israel, and a total of fifteen states established full diplomatic relations with China in 1992 alone. Trade and commerce with Asia expanded, and Japan restored the official development aid (ODA) it had suspended under U.S. pressure in response to the Tiananmen slaughter. Indeed, the most significant symbolic event of the year was a state visit by Japan's Emperor Akihito in October—the first visit of any emperor of Japan to China.

Even as Beijing saw success in its diplomatic strategy, relations with the United States began yet another decline. In 1993, the new Clinton administration linked future extension of most-favored-nation (MFN) trading privileges directly to improvements in China's human rights record; charged Beijing with transporting poison gas components to Iran, with violating its earlier agreement to abide by Missile Technology Control Regime (MTCR), and with illegally transporting chemical weapons precursors on the vessel *Yinhe*. Moreover, the U.S. Congress passed a resolution calling on the International Olympic Committee to deny Beijing's bid to host the 2000 Olympic Games. Beijing saw these acts as flagrant examples of "hegemonism and power politics."

Although the United States explicitly de-linked human rights with MFN extension in 1994, the summer of 1995 saw Sino-American relations continue their downward spiral when the United States reversed a long-standing policy rooted in Washington's commitment to "one China" and granted Taiwan's President Lee Teng-hui a visa for a private visit to Cornell University, his alma mater. Beijing responded to President Lee's visit by suspending the military-to-military relations reopened by the United States in November 1993; by shelving its "unofficial" cross-Strait talks with Taipei; and by holding a series of military exercises in the Taiwan area designed to coerce Taipei from making further steps toward what Beijing perceived as de jure independence. As 1995 drew to a close, the United States and China faced each other with no little hostility. In Beijing's view, the United States was continuing to exploit its post–Cold War status as the world's sole superpower. This perception was reinforced in the spring of 1996 when in response to a second series of Chinese military exercises designed to intimidate Taipei, including unarmed missile launches into target areas close to Taiwan's major ports of Keelung and Kaohsiung, the United States dispatched two aircraft carrier battle groups into the Taiwan area. An October summit meeting between Presidents Jiang Zemin and Bill Clinton in New York defused the immediate crisis but failed to resolve the Taiwan dilemma or any other issues driving the United States and China apart.

China Views Its Current Security Environment

China has eased much of the earlier tension that existed along its inner-Asian frontiers. Border issues are in the final stage of resolution, and rapprochement with the former Soviet Union initiated in the late 1980s has progressed to the point where the April 1997 joint communiqué issued by Presidents Jiang Zemin and Boris Yeltsin at the conclusion of their Moscow summit declared that China and Russia had formed a "strategic cooperative partnership" for the twenty-first century.[4] This same summit saw China, Russia, Kazakhstan, Kyrgyzstan, and Tajikistan sign an agreement on the mutual reduction of forces along their border areas, building on the April 1996 military confidence and security-building measures (CBMs) signed in Shanghai. China's other troublesome inner-Asian border has been with India. Over the years since Prime Minister Rajiv Gandhi's 1988 visit to Beijing, Sino-Indian relations have been normalized and their border disagreements subject to extensive negotiations. These negotiations culminated in a series of political and military CBMs agreed upon during President Jiang Zemin's visit to New Delhi in 1996. The CBMs were designed to maintain a peaceful border until the territorial disagreements could be resolved.[5] Normalization of relations and efforts to ease the potential for a border conflict do not imply that the strategic divergences between New Delhi and Beijing have dissolved, but that a repeat of the 1962 Sino-Indian border war is now extremely unlikely.

Secure along its major inner Asian borders, Beijing perceives a more disturbing environment in East Asia, where Taiwan and the South China Sea represent extremely intense issues of sovereignty for China. Although not containing a binding, multilateral security infrastructure such as Europe's NATO, East Asia does have a core security structure built around a series of bilateral and multilateral ties centered primarily on the United States and Australia. These bilateral ties link the United States with Korea, Japan, the Philippines, Thailand, Singapore, Australia, and informally with Taiwan. Multilateral ties link the British Commonwealth countries of Australia, Malaysia, Singapore, and New Zealand with the United Kingdom through the Five-Power Defense Arrangement (FPDA). New post–Cold War security arrangements now link Australia to Indonesia and the United Kingdom with the Philippines, thereby potentially expanding the FPDA's security structure. Although the FPDA is not overtly directed against China, Beijing does face a complex security infrastructure embracing all the major states of East Asia.

Beijing's reaction to these arrangements has been mixed. All of them, especially the U.S. defense treaty with Japan, bring to the region a security stability from which China benefits by its participation in the dynamic economic growth this stability has encouraged. Additionally, given the history of Japan's imperialist conquests of China that began in 1895, the U.S.-Japan security link has Beijing's support to the extent that it is seen as limiting Japan's military capabilities and ensuring that Tokyo will have no reason to return to the militarism of its past.[6] American treaty commitments and deployment of forces in South Korea also serve Beijing's interests, for they restrain North Korean military adventurism at a time when Pyongyang's regime is facing great internal stress and external diplomatic pressures to become more open in its relations with the outside world it fears. In this sense, Beijing, not wishing to disturb a security system benefiting China's economic and military security, is a status quo power.

U.S. defense arrangements, although they serve China's immediate interests, are also viewed by Beijing as sustaining American "hegemonism" in Europe and Asia.[7] NATO expansion is characterized by Beijing as part of a strategy to contain Russia's revival, whereas with respect to Asia, revitalized U.S. security ties with Japan and Australia are viewed as part of a strategy seeking "to consolidate U.S. dominance in the region."[8] Expanding the U.S.-Japanese security treaty's scope in 1996–1997 from the defense of Japan to a more open commitment for cooperation across the Asia-Pacific region received extremely pointed censure. This criticism became even stronger when Prime Minister Hashimoto specifically cited Taiwan and the Spratly Islands as areas of joint U.S.-Japanese concern.[9] Beijing realizes that should a military confrontation occur over Taiwan or the South China Sea territorial disputes, U.S. forces would require use of Japanese base facilities to conduct operations related to these conflicts. China had just such an example during its March 1996 military exercises designed to intimidate Taipei, when the first of two U.S. carrier battle groups dispatched to the Taiwan area, ironically led by the aircraft carrier *Independence*, was home-ported in Japan. Any extensive American military operations in the West Pacific would involve the use of Japanese bases; thus China's intense, nationalistic commitment to its sovereignty and territorial integrity comes into conflict with Beijing's security interest in sustaining an alliance viewed primarily as preventing Japan's return to the path of militarism.[10] Currently, the ambiguity in Beijing over the future value of the U.S.-Japan Security Treaty to China's security arises from this dilemma. Beijing's support for the alliance is based upon the restraint it places on Japan. An alliance that increases Tokyo's military capabilities and extends military cooperation with the United States beyond defense of Japan itself is viewed with suspicion and receives Beijing's condemnation.[11]

Southeast Asia's security arrangements have become more complex in recent years, and much like Tokyo's apprehension over Beijing's future policies, the region's long-term focus is on China.[12] In addition to Australian and American agreements in 1996 revitalizing their security pact, the FPDA has shown increased potency with the twenty-day Flying Fish South China Sea military exercise conducted in the spring of 1997. This exercise involved 10,000 troops, 36 ships, and 160 fighter aircraft from the FPDA's members (Australia, Britain, Malaysia, New Zealand, and Singapore), including a British aircraft carrier and a nuclear-powered submarine.[13] The maneuvers, the largest and most complex ever conducted by the FPDA, served to underscore the expanding regional defense links seen in Australia's 1995 security and defense cooperation agreement with Indonesia, and Britain's defense cooperation memorandum signed with the Philippines in 1996. Although the U.S. military presence, supported by access agreements to regional naval and air bases in the region, is recognized as most important, expanding security arrangements and more-frequent military exercises involving forces from Southeast Asia often joined with Australian units are a clear indicator of regional preparations for any potential confrontation with China. As a Malaysian scholar observed in discussing the FPDA exercises, "It's a benign security environment—there isn't anyone out there that's going to invade." He saw the exercise location, however, as demonstrating that "increasingly, there is a certain strategic orientation toward threats in the South China Sea."[14] Such preparations are no doubt seen by the ASEAN states as a form of deterrence: they demonstrate the sophistication of armaments, training levels, and interoperability among regional militaries and their allies.[15]

ASEAN's long-term security concerns are, nonetheless, not uniform.[16] Thailand has no territorial disputes with China and is least fearful of Beijing's intentions. Vietnam, the Philippines, Singapore, and Indonesia are the most skeptical, and China's 1995 occupation of Mischief Reef and the missile firings used to intimidate Taiwan raised Malaysia's concern to a much higher level than in previous years. Given the diversity in the degree of concern over Beijing's long-term intentions, the ASEAN states, seeking not to confront China, have individually and collectively balanced the "hard power" of their improving military capabilities with the "soft power" of dialogue and trade. ASEAN states engage China in security dialogue through the ASEAN Regional Forum (ARF) and have extensive trade and investment connections with China. None see any imminent military threat from China, and all see the intervening years—a decade or more—before Beijing's armed forces have the capability to sustain military operations far from China's mainland as a period they can use to alleviate Beijing's potentially aggressive intentions.

China's Post–Cold War Security Policy

Beijing sees the emerging security environment as marked by two characteristics. The first is a global shift to multipolarity, and the second is the U.S. effort to resist this transition and use its status as the sole remaining superpower to enforce American leadership on the world. As "Commentator" in the PLA-connected China Institute for International Strategic Studies (CISS) journal defined the issue in January 1997, the "trend of global and regional multi-polarization is more evident. However, the world is in a trial of strength over whether it will be multi-polar or uni-polar."[17]

Beijing is convinced that at the heart of U.S. strategy is the intent to delay, if not prevent, China's emergence as great power in the twenty-first century; that the United States views China as the principal contender for the predominant position of the United States in Asia. It is this conviction that leads Beijing's security analysts to conclude that the United States seeks to "contain" China, even if it is only a "soft" containment, and to interpret many if not all U.S. policies toward East Asia as part of a containment strategy. China thus views the United States as the single most important barrier to be overcome as it seeks its rightful place in the world. The United States does not simply stand alone as a major political, economic, and military power in East Asia. In Beijing's eyes, U.S. superpower status depends on its extensive diplomatic, economic, and military engagement throughout the Asia-Pacific region. The obstacle perceived by Beijing in the American presence is consequently not simply the forward deployment of U.S. military forces, but also the web of influence that Washington has created over the decades since the conclusion of World War II and that it is intent on sustaining. This intention is recognized by Beijing when it protests Washington's reinvigoration of U.S. security linkages with Japan and Australia, combined with American insistence that its forward-deployed forces will remain at their current level for at least the near future. These forces exemplify East Asia's continuing reliance on the United States for reassurance that the region's peace will not be disturbed. Beijing understands that within the region China is perceived as the most likely power to disturb the peace in the coming century.

Force and Diplomacy: China's Defense Policy Dilemma

Widespread apprehension of a potentially aggressive China stems in large part from the reorientation of Beijing's defense policy in 1985 and the military modernization programs designed to support a new military strategy.[18] The consequences of this change for the PLA's military strategy and modernization were extensive and ultimately raised apprehensions across Asia. In the early 1980s, defense against the Soviet Union relied upon the sheer size of the PLA to block an attack initially and, if necessary, to retreat to China's interior and exhaust the adversary through protracted war. The new national military strategy was designed to respond to short, limited, potentially highly intensive wars that could erupt around Beijing's extensive maritime territories and its lengthy land borders. The military strategists' primary concern was that if these potential wars were short and intense, as they expected, then the PLA's military operations had to shift from principles based upon protraction and attrition to operations based upon speed, mobility, and lethality.[19] Quality and readiness had to replace sheer numbers, for it was essential to maintain standing forces trained and equipped for quick, effective responses to crises involving the threat or application of military force.[20]

Responding to the new defense guidance, China's armed forces were reorganized and drastically slimmed down. An army's strength, the PLA's chief of staff declared in 1985, "is not determined by the number of troops, but by the quality of its commanders and fighters, the quality of its arms, and the degree of rationality of its systems and foundations."[21] As the Cold War drew to its close in the late 1980s, the organizational and doctrinal changes required to implement the new national military strategy were well under way. China's eleven military regions were reduced to seven; the PLA's thirty-six army "corps" were being restructured into twenty-four combined arms group armies (*jituanjun*); the headquarters of the Artillery and of the Armored Corps were transformed into subdepartments of the PLA General Staff Department; and major reductions were made in headquarters staff. These organizational changes were integral to the reduction in the PLA personnel, from 4.238 million to 3.235, including civilian positions. Reorganization and personnel cuts were accompanied by the elimination of much obsolescent equipment: 10,000 artillery pieces, more than 1,100 tanks, 610 naval vessels, and some 2,500 aircraft were reportedly taken out of service.[22] A "leaner, meaner" PLA began to emerge, accompanied by a new system of recruitment, promotion, and professional military education designed to build a younger, better-educated officer corps, competent in the demands of modern, combined arms, joint service warfare.

Revised naval missions arising from 1985 CMC meeting focused on Taiwan and the South China Sea, both of which were perceived as containing the seeds of military conflict. Beyond these requirements, China's 11,160 miles of coastline and some 1,060,000 square miles of territorial waters containing numerous islands to defend led to a review of China's maritime defense requirements.[23] Naval analysts called for a change in strategy from coastal defense (*jinhai fangyu*) to offshore defense (*jinyang fangyu*). In essence, they wanted the navy's defense perimeter to be extended from coastal waters out to between 200 and 400 nautical miles, and even farther in defense of territorial claims in the South China Sea. PLA Navy (PLAN) strategists sought an offshore-capable navy by 2000, and a "blue water" navy (*yuanyang haijun*) by 2050. These missions would require increased fleet-replenishment ships, improved amphibious-warfare capabilities, and air cover to protect patrols and sea actions extending some 600 miles from China, and even farther in terms of blue water operations. In the late 1980s,

PLAN capabilities were so inadequate in all these areas that meeting the new requirements was many, many years into the future.

Major exercises testing the PLA's capabilities to respond quickly and effectively to border clashes and local wars were conducted in 1988,[24] introducing forces that were to attract considerable attention as the years passed and more of these units were trained. Special forces, or "fist" (*quantou*) units, undertook commando-like operations during the exercises, and "rapid-reaction" (*kuaisu*) units appeared for the first time. The Fifteenth Group Army (Airborne) was designated as a rapid-reaction unit,[25] as was the PLAN Marine Corps headquartered with the South Sea Fleet in Zhanjiang, Guangzhou Province.[26] Deployment with the South Sea Fleet clearly identified PLAN marines as the rapid-reaction unit for operations in the South China Sea. Soon, each of China's seven military regions was reporting the development of fist and rapid-reaction forces.

China's nuclear deterrent strategy also came under review as questions about its viability in the twenty-first century were raised. Military research centers assessed the possible need to modify Beijing's nuclear weapons doctrine,[27] especially as theater and national missile defenses (TMD/NMD) become more plausible in the twenty-first century. Their analyses indicate that some military strategists are conceiving of a shift from "minimum deterrence," where a relatively small number of single-warhead missiles capable of inflicting considerable countervalue damage in a second strike are viewed as sufficient for nuclear deterrence, to a strategy of "limited deterrence." Limited deterrence requires a far larger number of increasingly accurate strategic weapons than China currently deploys, because both counterforce and countervalue targets must be threatened, and theater nuclear weapons (TNW) must be available to strike battlefield targets in order to ensure escalation control in the event of a nuclear war.[28] China's current deployment of perhaps seventeen intercontinental ballistic missiles (ICBM) and seventy intermediate-range missiles (IRBM)[29] is insufficient to support any strategy beyond minimum deterrence. The single nuclear-powered ballistic missile submarine (SSBN) with twelve weapons should not be included in this count, because it is not known to have test-launched a missile in a decade and is almost certainly no longer operational, if it ever was. A more important point is that military strategists, by reconsidering Beijing's basic approach to nuclear deterrence, demonstrate a lack of confidence that China's current nuclear strategy and force structure will suffice as a deterrent in the twenty-first century.

Defense Policy and Military Technology

China's new national military strategy underscored the PLA's earlier recognition that its obsolescent weapons and equipment were simply not capable of supporting the kinds of military operations required for contemporary warfare. However, sanctions applied to China following the Tiananmen tragedy had suspended European and American, but not Israeli, arms and technology sales just as planning and training for the kinds of military operations required for the new <u>limited-war defense</u> guidance were highlighting the PLA's technological inadequacies. Normalizing relations with the USSR enabled Beijing to sidestep these sanctions and initiate a defense technology linkage with Moscow in 1990 that continued after the USSR's collapse.[30] Severe financial needs within the former Soviet Union's defense industries combined with Moscow's desire to affirm a cordial relationship with China led to what became Beijing's most fruitful military technology connection. Russian cooperation came at a time when the military operations fought by the U.S. armed forces in the 1991 Desert Storm campaign were seen by Chinese military analysts as demonstrating technology's supreme importance in contemporary and future warfare. Following that campaign, the rubric under which the PLA prepared for war changed from preparation for local, limited war to "local, limited war under high-tech conditions" (*gaojishu tiaojian jubuzhan*).

Reservations about the Chinese armed forces' capabilities of conducting this type of war were expressed by China's senior military official in 1993, when General Liu Huaqing declared that the PLA "fails to meet the needs of modern warfare and this is the principal problem with army-building."[31] His model for modern warfare was specifically the Persian Gulf conflict, and General Liu pointedly stated that neither the PLA's weapons nor its training was adequate to conduct combat operations in the manner now required for success in war. His commentary served to underline the fact that negotiations with Moscow begun in 1990 had resulted in the sale of advanced weaponry to China.

Initially, a regiment of 26 Su-27 interceptors (Russia's functional equivalent of the U.S. F-15), 10 Il-76 heavy-lift transport aircraft, some 24 Mil-17 helicopters, and perhaps 100 to 150 S300 (SA-10 Grumble) air defense missiles with U.S. Patriot capabilities were purchased. In 1995, an additional regiment of Su-27s and 4 Kilo-class diesel-electric submarines (SSK) were ordered. Two Sovremenny guided-missile destroyers (DDG) were ordered in 1997 for delivery in two or three years. These known purchases were accompanied by reports that China was considering a variety of Russian weapons and equipment, including airborne warning and command system (AWACS) equipment or complete aircraft, aerial refueling aircraft or technologies, MiG-29/MiG-31 fighters, licensed production of advanced jet engines for combat aircraft, and a wide variety of other types of equipment. Moscow's agreement to license Chinese production of Su-27s is viewed by many as an indicator that Russia is willing to sell the most advanced military equipment and armaments in its inventory. Regardless of what limitations Moscow may choose to place on its military technology transfers to Beijing, it is clear that Russia has already agreed to sell technologies and complete weapon systems far more advanced than any the United States and the Western powers had transferred prior to the Tiananmen sanctions.

Speculation about future purchases stem from President Yeltsin's declaration during his December 1992 visit to Beijing that Russia was willing to sell China "the most sophisticated armaments and weapons" and Moscow's acknowledged sales that year of U.S.$1.2 billion.[32] Yeltsin's commitment was followed by a 1993 five-year military cooperation accord signed in Beijing by Russian defense minister Pavel Grachev, and yet another Sino-Russian defense technology agreement signed in December 1995. Russian arms sales to China in 1996 amounted to at least U.S.$2.1 billion—perhaps 70 percent of Beijing's global weapons and equipment purchases.[33]

China and Russia have become sensitive to the concerns raised in Asia and the United States over what is clearly an expanding defense-technology relationship. A Chinese spokesman reflected this apprehension when he observed that the 1993 agreement "did not relate, in any way, to the subject of cooperation in military production and arms sales."[34] Similarly, in April 1997, just prior to President Jiang Zemin's Moscow summit meeting with President Yeltsin, defense minister Rodionov defended Moscow's arms sales during a speech at the PLA Academy of Military Science. He insisted that "all weapons are for defensive use only," and that all sales would comply with the arms control agreements to which Russia was signatory.[35]

Chinese purchases from Russia have been accompanied by an expanding defense technology relationship with Israel, most particularly the J-10 advanced-fighter program under development with the Chengdu Aviation Industrial Corporation in Szechuan Province.[36] The Chengdu plant also produces the J-7, a variant of the MiG-21 that has benefited from European technology transfers of the 1980s. It is generally assumed that Tel Aviv's assistance to the J-10 includes technology and designs from Israel's canceled Lavi advanced-fighter program, and that the power plant will be obtained from Russia.

In addition to acquisitions from Russia, China's naval forces have been undergoing modernization programs utilizing technologies that had been imported from France, the United Kingdom, Italy, and the United States prior to the Tiananmen sanctions. Production of two new classes of surface combatants, the Luhu-class guided-missile destroyer (DDG) and the Jiangwei-class guided-missile frigate (FFG), has begun, and the first of the new Song-class diesel-electric submarines is undergoing sea trials. These ships are being joined by the production of fleet-replenishment vessels and new amphibious-warfare ships. Naval construction is, however, slow. Only one of two Luhu DDGs constructed and four Jiangwei FFGs are in service, and all other ship building is proceeding at an equally unhurried pace. Given this leisurely tempo, the PLAN's surface warfare backbone will continue to be the seventeen older Luda destroyers and thirty Jianghu frigates. These ships are being upgraded with technologies and weapon systems acquired from Europe before the Tiananmen sanctions were applied. Major improvements include more sophisticated missile and gun fire–control systems, more effective anti-ship missiles (AShM), better antisubmarine warfare (ASW) capabilities, including onboard helicopter facilities. Even with these improvements, all of China's surface combatants, including the new ships, lack effective defenses against air attack and sea-skimmer antiship missiles.

Acquisition of Kilo SSKs underscored the obsolescence of China's submarine force. Although Beijing retired around 50 percent of PLAN submarines over the past decade, with the sole exception of the single Song-class, the remaining fifty-four submarines are based on the 1950s Soviet Romeo design, including the twelve Romeo-derived Ming-class. These conventionally powered ships are supplemented by five Han-class nuclear-powered submarines (SSN) based on older technologies, and therefore undoubtedly very noisy and easily targeted by modern antisubmarine warfare systems.

Modernization programs enhancing China's conventional general purpose forces are paralleled by improvements in strategic and short-range ballistic missiles.[37] Upgrading the strategic forces is considered essential in order to provide a survivable, quicker-reacting deterrent in an era when the United States and Russia continue to deploy thousands of strategic weapons and when ballistic missile defense is on the horizon. Improved survivability is sought through tactical mobility, with both the new solid-fueled 7,500-mile range DF-41 (Dongfeng–East Wind) and 5,000-mile-range DF-31 designed to be road and/or rail mobile. Solid propellants are more reliable and provide quicker reaction time but provide less boost than liquid fuels. Changing to solid fuels therefore has required smaller warheads with greater yield-to-weight ratios. Smaller warheads are also being developed in preparation for the time when China masters multiple-reentry vehicle technologies allowing a single booster to carry independently targeted warheads and penetrations aids to deceive ballistic missile defenses. Initial operational capability for the DF-41, which is to replace the aging DF-4 and 5A, is not anticipated before 2010. The DF-31 could begin replacing the DF-3 in 1999 or shortly thereafter. China's new submarine-launched weapon, the JL-2 (Julang–Big Wave), is derived from the DF-31 and has identical range and warhead capacity. When a new SSBN will replace or supplement the single, old Xia-class ship that entered service in 1983 is not known. Development of these strategic systems was accompanied by the introduction of two solid-fueled, tactically mobile short-range ballistic missiles designed for battlefield use with conventional warheads. Both the M-9 and the M-11 were originally developed for the export market. The M-9, known as the DF-15 when deployed by the PLA, has a range of 370 miles with a 500-kilogram warhead; it was used to intimidate Taiwan in China's 1995 and 1996 military exercises. The M-11 reaches out some 185 miles with a 500-kilogram warhead.

Although the various strands of PLA modernization and training are directed at improving its combat capabilities, shortcomings that will take many years to overcome exist. Only a small number of new weapon systems are being acquired or built, and the vast majority of the PLA's major armaments remain derivatives of Soviet designs from the 1950s. Limitations inherent in obsolescent arms and equipment join with logistical support and command and control inadequacies to severely hinder Beijing's ability to project and sustain forces beyond China's continental boundaries for any length of time. These overall deficiencies have led the PLA to define its core weakness as "short arms and slow legs."[38] The implications of the "Revolution in Military Affairs" (RMA) for future wars serve to compound existing problems. PLA strategists show great concern over the RMA's ramifications, but China's R&D infrastructure is currently incapable of responding effectively to the technological demands of this new type of warfare.[39] Thus, Beijing's planners see their military modernization programs as far from fulfilling China's twenty-first-century needs and inadequate for any near-term contingencies that could arise in the South China Sea or related to Taiwan.

Nonetheless, it was Beijing's more systematic, although slow, modernization of PLA armaments, combined with the expanding military technology relationship with Russia, that led many in Asia and the United States to become concerned about the long-term effect of China's programs on Asia's security and stability. For the past several years Beijing has adamantly denied that its military modernization programs were anything but defensive. Beijing, however, looks out on an Asia undergoing major military renovation that in many areas exceeds the PLA's current capabilities and will continue to exceed them for at least a decade and more.

China and Asia's Military Modernization Programs

Defense modernization programs under way throughout Asia are a major source of Beijing's concerns.[40] Notwithstanding Tokyo's long-standing security relationship with the United States, including the protection provided by American nuclear forces and continuing discussions about join-ing the U.S. theater missile defense program, Japan's Self-Defense Forces (SDF) form the largest technologically advanced military in the region and are supported by Asia's most sophisticated defense industrial base.[41] Japan's Maritime Self-Defense Forces (MSDF) constitute the region's largest modern navy, with 63 major surface combatants and 17 sub-marines, many armed with the most advanced military technology in the world, including 2 large Aegis-equipped Kongo-class guided-missile de-stroyers displacing 7,000 tons—China's new Luhu displaces only about 4,000 tons. Trained and equipped to operate out to 1,000 nautical miles from the home islands, this navy is supported by an air arm deploying cutting-edge antisubmarine and antiship warfare weapons in 110 aircraft and 99 armed helicopters. Japan's Air Self-Defense Forces (ASDF) are equally powerful, deploying 70 American F-4Es and 189 domestically produced models of the U.S. F-15 (considered to be world's finest inter-ceptor), all supported by AWACS aircraft.

The People's Liberation Army Air Force (PLAAF), in contrast, may have received 50 Su-27s of the 72 ordered, and as yet has no AWACS ca-pabilities. China's naval and air forces cannot match their Japanese coun-terparts, for they do not deploy as many modern combatants. Although the newly acquired Kilo-class SSKs may individually match Japanese submarines, China has ordered only 4. The PLAN will have no surface combatants matching those of the MSDF until it takes delivery of the 2 Sovremenny-class destroyers from Russia in 1998 or 1999, and it will take three to four years following delivery before they become operational. Furthermore, Tokyo's current plans call for continued modernization of its air, land, and sea forces within a defense budget that, when measured in U.S. dollars, is the third largest in the world. Tokyo's intent to sustain Asia's most powerful navy and air force is made even more evident to the Chinese defense establishment when it recalls that the PLA and Japan's SDF began their modernization programs at about the same time. Tokyo's National Defense Program Outline (NDPO) that guided the SDF to their current status was announced in 1976, and Deng Xiaoping's mili-tary reforms were initiated in 1979. In the two decades that China and Japan have been modernizing their armed forces and defense industries, Tokyo has clearly made the greater amount of progress—an equipment and defense industrial edge that will continue into the foreseeable future.

Even apart from Japan, most East Asian defense establishments have been modernizing their armed forces at a rapid rate, adding advanced-technology combat aircraft, ships, and submarines, with Thailand about to deploy the region's first aircraft carrier—the Spanish-built *Chakkrinareubet*. Although displacing only about 11,500 tons, with planned missions of search-and-rescue and humanitarian operations, this ski-jump carrier can operate a small number of helicopters and Harrier V/STOL aircraft, representing East Asia's first sea-based airpower. Within Southeast Asia, maritime forces are being acquired that, in combination with air forces that are modernizing and deploying a variety of advanced U.S. and Russian combat aircraft, will be able to better defend territorial and maritime interests,[42] as the Flying Fish exercise demonstrated.

In response to China's programs, Taiwan is extensively upgrading its air and naval forces, including air defense capabilities. Sixty advanced French Mirage 2000s and 150 U.S. F-16s are being acquired together with 4 E-2 AWACS aircraft. These sophisticated and capable aircraft are being joined with 130 less capable but still very effective IDF (Indigenous Defense Fighter) interceptors designed and built in Taiwan with technologies imported from the United States. Ground-based air defense systems include U.S. Patriot and Stinger surface-to-air missiles (SAM). Taiwan's naval forces are being improved with the purchase of 6 French Lafayette-class frigates, the construction under U.S. license of 6 improved Perry-class frigates, and the lease of 6 modernized U.S. Knox-class frigates, augmenting 22 updated older American destroyers. These ships all out-class China's surface combatants in antisubmarine warfare, in defense against air and cruise missile attack, and in antiship cruise missiles. With the exception of the 2 yet-to-be-delivered Russian Sovremenny DDGs, on a ship-to-ship basis Taiwan's navy can outshoot China's. Taiwan's development of a formidable defensive capability is possible only because of U.S. support. Beijing has taken punitive actions, including economic sanctions, against other major suppliers such as France to eliminate or curtail future sales of military equipment and weaponry to a territory it considers part of China.

Beijing Responds to the "China Threat"

Beijing is now fully aware that it has become the focus of the region's long-term security concerns. Although it continues to condemn the United States for distorting China's intentions, contending that Washington can sustain its position as the world's superpower after the collapse of the USSR only by creating a new enemy,[43] Beijing recognizes that this posture has failed to convince fearful Asian capitals. In recent years, Beijing has conducted a carefully orchestrated campaign seeking to reassure East Asia of its peaceful intentions. This diplomatic effort includes an intensified program of military-to-military diplomacy designed to ease regional concerns over China's defense policy and military modernization programs, publication of Beijing's first defense white paper, and the presentation of a "new model" for regional security.

As part of its military-to-military diplomacy, in 1996 Beijing sent "scores" of high-ranking delegations to more than fifty countries, includ ing senior members of the Central Military Commission, the chief of the PLA General Staff Department, heads of PLA General Political and Lo- gistics Departments, and the commanders-in-chief of the navy and air force. These delegations have been complemented by regular PLAN ship visits, to Malaysia, Thailand, and the Philippines in 1997. In return, more than thirty high-ranking delegations led by deputy prime ministers, de- fense ministers, commanders-in-chief, and thirty-six other military dele- gations from Asian countries visited China.[44]

After several years of unremitting criticism of the lack of transparency in China's defense policies, in November 1995 the State Council re- sponded with the release of *China: Arms Control and Disarmament*. Al- though far from meeting the standards of openness established by de- fense white papers from countries such as Australia, Japan, or the Republic of Korea, Beijing's response was a first step, albeit a very small one, toward greater transparency. Publication was prompted by Assis- tant Secretary of Defense Joseph Nye's November 14-18, 1995, visit to Beijing; it was designed to counter the pervasive image of a potentially dangerous China sharpened by Beijing's attempts to intimidate Taiwan in the summer of 1995 and the clash with Manila over Mischief Reef ear lier in the year. The document was also undoubtedly intended as a ges- ture manifesting some forward motion on long-standing American de- mands that Beijing establish a more rigorous process to monitor the transfer of dangerous military and dual-use technologies, and for greater defense transparency.

These initial, tentative steps toward transparency were accompanied by Beijing's presentation of a new approach to regional security to re- place the existing system of U.S.-dominated alliances. Beijing touted China's April 1997 accords with Russia, Kazakhstan, Kyrgyzstan, and Tajikistan as a "brand new model for safeguarding regional security."[45] This "model" is presented as distinctly different from the method of "hegemonism and power politics" used by "some forces." In contrast, Beijing noted, the accord with its neighbors was negotiated over a seven- year period, during which time "mutual understanding and cooperation helped find an eventual solution to the complicated and sensitive issues" involved in developing CBMs and mutual force reductions.[46] In present- ing its new model as a replacement for the Cold War military alliances and security agreements that currently mark Asia's security system, Bei- jing has to cope with the consensus across most of East Asia that a signif- icant American military presence, including the mutual defense treaties and other nontreaty arrangements that make this presence possible, must be retained to offset or hedge against China's growing military power.

Force and Diplomacy: Retrospect and Prospect

The only potential "local, limited wars" Beijing perceives possible in the near future are to prevent Taiwan's independence by force of arms and to defend China's territorial claims in the South China Sea. Apart from these contingencies, the primary purpose of Beijing's defense modernization programs remains ensuring that in the twenty-first century China cannot be intimidated by superior military strength and that Beijing's foreign policy will not be constrained by military weakness, as it was during the disastrous nineteenth century and the first half of the twentieth century.

Beijing clearly fears that the United States, with probable Japanese collusion, seeks to prevent China from achieving the long-term purpose of its defense modernization programs. Beijing would take careful note of the statement by Lieutenant General Patrick Hughes, director of the Defense Intelligence Agency, testifying before the U.S. Congress in 1997: "China is one of the few powers with the potential—political, economic and military—to emerge as a large-scale military threat to U.S. interests within the next 10–20 years."[47] China believes containment, even if a "soft containment" *(ruan e zhi)*, is sought by Washington through its reinvigoration of its Cold War alliances and through its policy of comprehensive engagement, which Beijing interprets as aspiring to "integrate China into an international system dominated by Western states."[48] China's strategic culture, especially the influence of the "hundred years of humiliation," impels Beijing to reject such a system.

In East Asia, Beijing seeks what it has achieved in inner Asia: the status and consequent influence of a principal rule maker in determining the region's post–Cold War security architecture.[49] Over the long term, Beijing seeks to substitute nonalliance bilateral and multilateral cooperation and confidence-building measures for the military alliances that yet order East Asia's security and sustain U.S. preeminence. For the near term, China does not seek to displace the United States or eliminate its alliances as long as these alliances contribute to regional stability while a new security architecture is being constructed. Within this perspective, Beijing does not want the U.S. security link with Japan ended as long as the treaty restrains Japan's military power and is strictly limited to the defense of Japan. Increasing Japan's treaty commitments to what Beijing views as "out of area" cooperation and incorporating Japan into a theater missile defense system that erodes China's nuclear deterrent would expand rather than limit Tokyo's military power in the region. Beijing, however, is seeking to diminish U.S. influence over East Asia's security even as most of the region desires to sustain the American-led alliance structure and formulates additional pacts and understandings in response to China's increasing military power and aggressive nationalism.

Beijing's diplomatic strategy to alleviate concerns over the long-term implications of China's defense programs for East Asian security will fail to ease apprehension until the strategy is accompanied by greater transparency in defense policies and acquisitions, and until Beijing restrains its extreme nationalism on issues of sovereignty and territorial integrity. Especially sensitive to the region are settlement of the South China Sea territorial disputes and the future of Taiwan. Here China must resolve the contradiction between the demands of its strategic culture that place highest priority on national autonomy and sovereignty, and the post–Cold War's renewed emphasis on the peaceful resolution of territorial disputes. Such a choice places Beijing's political and military elite in an onerous position, for sovereignty and nationalism have replaced Marxism-Leninism as critical ingredients in the cement holding China's polity together.

Despite the policies of engagement now pursued by China, East Asia, and the United States as they face their mutual future, there is little confidence within the region that a future confrontation can be avoided without some compromise by China. The areas of compromise are unfortunately in those realms most sensitive to China's tragic modern history and strategic culture. For the near term, therefore, East Asia faces a continuation of the potentially destabilizing frictions created by the region's acceptance of U.S.-led alliances as a hedge against China's rising power, and Beijing's perception of these same arrangements as part of a strategy to contain China and restrain it from regaining what Chinese elites see as China's rightful place in the world. The uncertainty and consequent insecurity that marks China's perception of its security environment is inauspiciously mirrored in much of East Asia's and the U.S. perception of China.

Notes

The views expressed in this chapter are the author's and are not to be construed as those of the United States government.

1. Robert G. Sutter, *China as a Security Concern in Asia: Perceptions, Assessment, and U.S. Options,* CRS Report for Congress 94-32 S, Congressional Research Office, The Library of Congress, January 5, 1995.

2. See, for example, Zong He, "Changes and Developmental Trends in the International Situation," *Shijie Zhishi,* no. 11 (1983), in Foreign Broadcast Information Service, *Daily Report: China* [henceforth FBIS-*China*], July 21, 1983, pp. A1-5.

3. James C. Hsiung, "China's Omnidirectional Diplomacy: Realignment to Cope with Monopolar U.S. Power," *Asian Survey,* no. 35, no. 6 (June 1995), pp. 573-586.

4. Beijing, *Xinhua,* "Text of Sino-Russian Joint Statement," April 23, 1997, in FBIS-*China,* April 23, 1997.

5. Surjit Mansingh, "India-China Relations in the Post–Cold War Era," *Asian Survey* 34, no. 3 (March 1994), pp. 285–300; and Timothy Mapes, "Nervous Neighbors," *Far Eastern Economic Review*, vol. 159, no. 50 (December 12, 1996), pp. 16–17.

6. Allen S. Whiting, *China Eyes Japan* (Berkeley: University of California Press, 1989); and Thomas J. Christensen, "Chinese Realpolitik," *Foreign Affairs* 75, no. 5 (September-October 1996), esp. pp. 40–45.

7. Zhang Dezhen, "Strengthening Military Alliances Does Not Conform with Trend of the Times," *Renmin Ribao*, January 31, 1997, in FBIS-*China*, January 31, 1997, pp. 1–2.

8. Ibid., p. 1.

9. Beijing, *Xinhua* Domestic Service, April 30, 1997, in FBIS-*China*, May 1, 1997, pp. 2–3; and Tokyo, NHK General Television Network report, "Japan: Hashimoto on Review of the Japan-U.S. Defense Cooperation," April 9, 1997.

10. Banning Garrett and Bonnie Glaser, "Chinese Apprehensions About Revitalization of the U.S.-Japan Alliance," *Asian Survey* 37, no. 4 (April 1997), pp. 383–402.

11. Liu Wenyu, "The Dangerous Trend of Japan-U.S. Military Cooperation," Beijing, *Xinhua Domestic Service*, April 30, 1997, in FBIS-*China*, May 1, 1997, pp. 1–2.

12. Allen S. Whiting, "ASEAN Eyes China: The Security Dimension," *Asian Survey* 37, no. 4 (April 1997), pp. 299–322.

13. Charles Bickers, "Frolics at Sea," *Far Eastern Economic Review* 160, no. 20 (May 15, 1997), p. 26.

14. Quoted in ibid.

15. On the importance of the FPDA exercise demonstrating the sophistication of weapons, equipment, and command and control in joint, combined operations, see M. Jeffri Razali, "Malaysia: Minister Sees Need for British, U.S. Military Presence," *New Straits Times* (Kuala Lumpur), April 16, 1997, in Foreign Broadcast Information Service, *Daily Report: East Asia* [henceforth FBIS-*EAS*], April 16, 1997.

16. Whiting, "ASEAN Eyes China," esp. pp. 303–318.

17. Commentator, "New Trends in the Current International Strategic Situation," *International Strategic Studies* (Beijing), no. 1 (January 1997), p. 1.

18. Nan Li, "The PLA's Evolving Warfighting Doctrine, Strategy and Tactics 1985–95: A Chinese Perspective," pp. 443–463; and Paul H. B. Godwin, "From Continent to Periphery: PLA Doctrine, Strategy and Capabilities Toward 2000," both in *China Quarterly*, no. 146 (June 1996), pp. 443–487.

19. Two of the more interesting analyses are Jia Wenxian et al., "A Tentative Discussion of the Special Principles of Future Chinese Limited War," and Jiao Wu and Xiao Hui, "Modern Limited War Calls for Reform of Traditional Military Principles," both in *Guofang Daxue Xuebao*, no. 11 (November 1, 1987), in JPRS *China Report*, July 12, 1988, pp. 47–51.

20. Jia Wenxian et al., "A Tentative Discussion," p. 48.

21. Yang Dezhi, "A Strategic Decision in Strengthening the Building of Our Army in the New Period," *Hong Qi*, no. 15 (August 1985), in FBIS-*China*, August 8, 1985, p. K3.

22. *China: Arms Control and Disarmament* (Beijing: Information Office of the State Council, People's Republic of China, November 1995), p. 8.

23. John W. Lewis and Xue Litai, *China's Strategic Seapower: The Politics of Force Modernization in the Nuclear Age* (Stanford, Calif.: Stanford University Press, 1994), pp. 219–230.

24. Xing Jingyao, "1988: A Year of Reform for the Chinese Army, *Liaowang* [overseas edition—Hong Kong], no. 3 (January 16, 1989), in FBIS-*China*, January 24, 1989, p. 36.

25. Tan Jun and Hong Heping, "A Fist Battalion of a Certain PLA Airborne Unit, *Jiefangjun Bao*, June 1, 1988, in JPRS-*China*, August 9, 1988, p. A2.

26. Deng Huaxu and Li Daoming, "A Visit to the PLA Marine Corps," *Renmin Ribao* [overseas edition], August 2, 1988, in FBIS-*China*, August 3, 1988, p. A2.

27. Alastair I. Johnston, "China's New 'Old Thinking,'" *International Security* 20, no. 3 (Winter 1995), pp. 41–77; and his "Prospects for China's Nuclear Force Modernization: Limited Deterrence Versus Multilateral Arms Control," *China Quarterly*, no. 146 (June 1996), pp. 548–576.

28. Johnston, "Prospects for Chinese Nuclear Force Modernization," pp. 554–558.

29. Unless indicated otherwise, all military holdings are taken from appropriate sections of: The International Institute for Strategic Studies, *The Military Balance 1996–97* (London: Oxford University Press, October 1996).

30. Tai Ming Cheung, "Ties of Convenience: Sino-Russian Military Relations in the 1990s," in Richard H. Yang (ed.), *China's Military: The PLA in 1992/93* (Boulder: Westview Press, 1993), pp. 61–77.

31. Liu Huaqing, "Unswervingly March Along the Road of Building a Modern Army with Chinese Characteristics," *Jiefangjun Bao*, August 6, 1993 (originally published in *Qiushi*, no. 15 (1993), in FBIS-*China*, August 18, 1993, p. 18.

32. Lena Sun, "Russia, China Set Closest Ties in Years," *Washington Post*, December 19, 1992, p.10.

33. Aleksey Baliyev, "Great Friendship Growing Through Kalashnikovs," *Rossiskaya Gazeta*, October 5, 1996, in Foreign Broadcast Information Service, *Daily Report: Central Eurasia* (henceforth FBIS-CE), October 5, 1996, p. 12.

34. Quoted in *Agence France Presse* (AFP) report, Hong Kong, November 11, 1993, in FBIS-*China*, November 12, 1993, p. 2.

35. Hong Kong, AFP, April 15, 1997, in FBIS-*China*, April 15, 1997, p. 1.

36. Kenneth W. Allen, Glenn Krumel, and Jonathan Pollack, *China's Air Force Enters the Twenty-First Century* (Santa Monica, Calif.: Rand Corporation, 1995), pp. 146–161.

37. John W. Lewis and Hua Di, "China's Ballistic Missile Programs: Technologies, Strategies, Goals," *International Security* 17, no. 2 (Fall 1992), pp. 5–40.

38. *Jiefangjun Bao* has used this phrase since at least May 1994. See, for example, *PLA Activities Report* (Hong Kong), May 1994, p. 17.

39. For a useful collection of translations on this topic see Michael Pillsbury (ed.), *Chinese Views of Future Warfare* (Washington, D.C.: National Defense University Press, 1996).

40. Desmond Ball, "Arms and Affluence: Military Acquisitions in the Asia-Pacific Region," *International Security* 18, no. 3 (Winter 1993–94), pp. 78–112.

41. Michael W. Chinworth, *Inside Japan's Defense: Technology, Economics and Strategy* (Washington: Brassey's (U.S.), Inc., 1992).

42. David Dewitt, *Arms Embrace? Proliferation Management in Southeast Asia*, CAPS Paper No. 15 (March 1997), Chinese Council of Advanced Policy Studies, Taipei, Taiwan; and Captain Bernard D. Cole, USN (ret.), "Asia at Sea," *Proceedings*, March 1997, pp. 36–39.

43. See, for example, the text of Foreign Minister Qian Qichen's April 29, 1997, speech before the Council of Foreign Relations, the U.S.-China Business Council, and the National Committee on U.S.-China Relations released by the Embassy of the People's Republic of China, May 12, 1997, p. 2; and Yan Xuetong, "Economic Security, Good Neighbor Policy Emphasized in Post–Cold War Security Strategy," *Xiandai Guoji Guanxi*, no. 8 (August 20, 1995), in FBIS-*China*, October 16, 1995, pp. 8–13.

44. Beijing, *Xinhua*, "Yearender: Active Military Exchanges Yield New Achievements," December 19, 1996, in FBIS-*China*, December 19, 1996.

45. Beijing, *Xinhua* Commentary, "Five Nation Accord a Fresh Model for Security," April 24, 1997, in FBIS-*China*, April 24, 1997, p. 5.

46. Ibid.

47. Quoted in Nigel Holloway, "That T-word Again," *Far Eastern Economic Review* 160, no. 8 (February 20, 1997), p. 18.

48. Zhu Chen and Xie Wenqing, "The U.S. China Policy and Sino-American Relations Moving Toward the Twenty-First Century," *International Strategic Studies* (Beijing), no. 1 (January 1997), p. 36.

49. See, for example, Tang Guanghai, "An Analysis of Post–Cold War Security," *Shijie Zhishi*, no. 19 (October 1, 1996), in FBIS-*China*, October 1, 1996.

9

[In][ter]dependence in China's Post–Cold War Foreign Relations

THOMAS W. ROBINSON

In the 1970s and 1980s, it became fashionable to speak of interdependence as one of the major determinants of international, and therefore foreign, relations. As a result principally of the two oil crises of the 1970s, the manifestation of various global issues, and the emergence of a global trading regime, decisionmakers discovered that more than the Cold War was important to global affairs. This notion—and the several assumptions and ideas at its base—were applied by theorists and statesmen alike to China.[1] Beijing's post-Mao turn toward rapid economic development and the associated foreign policy of peace and opening toward the outer world was coterminous with this new emphasis. Analyses of Chinese foreign policy thus incorporated the assumption that Deng Xiaoping and his associates were equally susceptible to these global currents and equally eager to modify China's foreign policy in the benign directions pointed out by the interdependence thesis. Overall foreign policy moderation appeared to supply proof that China's reentry into the family of nations would be reasonably gentle and that China would end up with the same domestic structure (market democracy) and foreign policy (peace and internationalism) as other developed nations.

The 1989 Tiananmen massacre, the 1990 breakup of the Soviet empire and the resultant end of the Cold War, and the 1991 collapse of the Soviet Union and the American-led victory in the Gulf War called seriously into question at least some of the underpinnings of this way of thinking. Tiananmen made clear that the road to democracy would be much longer and more difficult that initially presumed. The subsequent Chinese retraction of some of the market reforms gave pause to those who argued that full Chinese marketization was inevitable and that, therefore, the influence of foreign trade (and the cultural currents that came with it) would make China fully interdependent, in the economic sense, with the rest of the world. The end of the Cold War, of the Soviet empire, and of the Soviet Union itself at first indicated that interdependence within the West would now extend itself to the former Communist states, but the checkered nature of that transition and the near-collapse of the Russian economy and polity brought that line of thinking to a halt. And the Gulf War appeared to be but the preview of a new international system dominated by the "sole remaining superpower," the United States, and hardly the new era of multilateralism and compromise-based cooperation in international affairs that interdependence proponents had assumed.[2]

Moreover, after 1991, although China did resume its course of rapid economic growth and at least some further reformist impulse remained, several new aspects appeared. Most important, the economics-driven growth of Chinese power emboldened Beijing to assert itself internationally, to resist attempts of Americans and others to change China domestically according to their own notions of how that country should be ordered, and to project Chinese power—mostly economic but increasingly militarily—outside the nation's geographic boundaries. In addition, Beijing renewed its stress on foreign policy independence, as opposed to the previous grudging acceptance of the necessity, if not the desirability, of interdependence.[3] Further, along certain dimensions (as will be discussed below), it was not even evident that China was moving toward interdependence; renewed or continued dependence appeared to be the rule. Finally, Chinese foreign policy analysts (if not their decisionmaker superiors) were, with others, coming to understand that interdependence was no longer an accurate description of all that was occurring across national boundaries: Many new concepts were springing up to describe the exploding nature of post–Cold War international reality. Globalization was the most popular of the new terms, so interdependence was no longer the locus of analytic attention or diplomatic interest and concern.

That was not to say that interdependence had lost its utility, for China and for students of Chinese foreign policy. In a number of spheres, there was still something "real" behind various measures and opinions. The combination of Beijing's policy of opening to the outside world, the expansion of Chinese power and hence of its catalogue of interests, and the vast complexity and dynamism of international life all guaranteed that along several dimensions, some old and others new, the nation would find its foreign relations best described by that term. That was particularly the case in China's foreign economic relations, but interdependence had relevance to many other spheres, as detailed below. Nonetheless, the term was increasingly the victim of its own success, as perhaps too many complex phenomena and trends were made to fit within its boundaries. It was thus time to take the term apart and inquire whether this portion of China's foreign relations would not better be described and analyzed by several different terms.

General Ideas Concerning Interdependence

Interdependence has always been a fact of human activity, as people and institutions depend on each other to survive and achieve their goals. Interdependence is also a fact of international relations and foreign policy. But differences in interpretation or emphasis do arise. Is interdependence sometimes inequitable, so that the "balance of dependence" too heavily favors one partner? Does not the spillover of economic interdependence into the political-military and cultural spheres greatly complicate equity calculations as well as engender dangers of overall dependence when gross national power differences are too great? Interdependence is clearly multifaceted, yet it cannot be numerically assessed, since the units of calculation differ between fields, since some fields—for instance, the cultural—entirely lack quantitative measurement capability, and since even within traditional fields—for example, the military—there is no agreed on set of measures. How, in the face of these problems, can decisionmakers make policy on important matters of national security and foreign relations?

There are two general sets of answers to these questions. The first stems from economic theory, where the idea of interdependence has been developed most highly. The second set emerges from latter-day international relations theory, analyses of national security issues, and other diverse arenas of international activity. In each case, the ideas can be applied to China's foreign relations and have, at some time or other, also been recognized by Chinese policy analysts. In economic theory, four reasonably distinct "schools" exist.

Traditional international trade theory[4] concentrates on the idea of mutual advantage. Attention centers on comparative specialization, terms of trade, the consequent linking for mutual benefit of internal economies, and distortions that tariffs and other government restrictions bring. Nations are assumed to be rational and trade only when their self-interests so dictate. The terms of trade, set by the marketplace, are by definition mutually advantageous, even if internal markets are severely affected and even if specialization leads some countries to remain permanently underdeveloped. So traditional theory does not concern itself with many of the issues that have led to international concern about China's trade policies—beggar-thy-neighbor policies, for instance—simply because they are either passing phases in a much broader historical change or can with relative ease be accommodated by natural, market-force-driven adjustments in exchange rates, balance of payments, commodity composition, and the like.

Dependencia[5] in contrast argues that the terms of trade between more and less developed nations are by nature unequal because they retard industrial growth in the latter. The supply of raw materials or low wage goods for industrial countries consigns underdeveloped nations to permanent dependence. Industrial countries assure the continuation of this relationship by use of transnational corporations, support of authoritarian governments, undue interference in internal affairs, and use of superior power, knowledge, and wealth. This otherwise self-perpetuating system can be ameliorated only by deliberate trade concessions to the less-developed nations, artificially hiking raw materials prices, expanding concessionary capital transfers, and reducing foreign control of the domestic economy through nationalization or regime control of foreign trade. Trade must therefore be subordinated as a value to equity and development. In particular, the assumed alliance between "imperialist" Western capitalist governments and local authoritarians to keep the people in a servile position must be broken. That means the end of colonialism and "neocolonialism," of which interdependence is a species. Genuine interdependence is thus impossible until political and economic equality has been attained everywhere.

Developmentalism[6] starts with the same factual base but draws optimistic conclusions. The removal of economic and political barriers naturally generates industrial growth through the market mechanism. The crucial impediments are internal—traditional attitudes, customs, and institutions—and they must be removed for progress. The goal is Western-style capitalism, which should be universally embraced. The important internal prerequisite is political and social stability, best supplied by authoritarian governments. They can best westernize their societies through free trade, gradual elimination of economic barriers, encouraging foreign investment, and technology transfer. Internationalization of the economy and interdependence thus become synonymous, with the Japanese economy between 1868 and 1931 being the best example.

Export-led growth[7] straddles the space between *dependencia* and developmentalism, claiming to have discovered a middle way between political-economic servitude and the dangers of too-rapid development. It combines state capitalism, forcible maintenance of very low wages, the alleged necessity of authoritarianism, high barriers against manufactured imports, massive acceptance of foreign loans and investment, controlled exchange rates, and aggressive marketing in wide-open Western markets. A high balance-of-payments deficit is deliberately run, financed by new loans and investment and a constant decline of the exchange rate, until sufficient sales in developed countries reestablishes equilibrium. Once a reasonably high gross national product is attained, economic barriers can be lowered, authoritarianism can change to democracy, and interdependence achieved. Interdependence thus becomes a long-term goal, not a means. This strategy has supposedly been followed by the four Asian "mini-dragons"—South Korea, Taiwan, Hong Kong, and Singapore.

In international relations theory, two orientations, with subvariants, exist. Both acknowledge the existence of interdependence but differ on its importance. (Neo)realism,[8] the latter-day successor to classical realism, continues to emphasize the state as the most important international actor, centers analysis on power and interest more or less objectively defined, points to the anarchy as the most important characteristic of international relations, regards security and not economics as the leitmotiv of foreign policy, de-emphasizes the contribution of domestic factors to foreign policy formulation, and regards international institutions and regimes as subordinate elements in the continuous struggle for power within a balance of power-centered system. Interdependence therefore shrinks to a minor and dependent element of the more fundamental state-centered (interest, power, and security) and system-centered (anarchy, war, and crises) aspects of this approach.

(Neo)liberalism,[9] the contemporary, expanded version of liberal-idealistic internationalism, begins with acknowledging the same facts of international relations as neorealism but underlines all those factors that neorealism treats lightly. Thus, economics takes precedence over security; the organizational and institutional aspects of international activity overlay (if not entirely replace) anarchy, the power struggle, and the balance of power; foreign policy is more the product of domestic, bureaucratic, and individual inputs than capabilities and interests; nations cooperate as much as compete; and extranational relations are looked on as a single interdependent activity composed as much of a globalized economy, environmental and other global issues, and mutually interactive domestic societies as of wars, arms races, and crises. Interdependence, in this view, expands to encompass a large portion of the totality of domestic and international life, and the term is increasingly replaced with descriptions and analyses of these processes or is reserved only for economic interdependence. Given this emphasis, most of the work in this field has been undertaken by theorists on this side of the great divide among international relationists.

Within neoliberalism, several more-particular and useful ideas relating to interdependence have emerged. The idea of *international regimes*[10] emphasizes the changes wrought by construction of the many institutions and processes that have become a central element in recent international relations. Nations become more interdependent to the extent that they participate in such regimes or to the extent that the latter impinges upon their foreign relations. Studies of *dependence* and *dependency*[11] give rise to the notion of a spectrum from dependence through independence to interdependence and encourage the analyst to ask whether a nation might simultaneously be interdependent along some dimensions, dependent along others, and independent in still other regards, what the relation is among them, and what the net outcome is when all three are "added up." Interdependence is further dissociated by the emergence of the category of *epistemic communities*[12]—subnational groups of knowledge-based experts influencing, both within and across national boundaries, the formulation and execution of foreign policy. To the extent that such foreign policy-related interest groups exist in post-1992 China, the prior near-exclusive handling of foreign relations by a small group within the Party and Foreign Ministry must be modified and, with it, Beijing's former emphasis on independence (and avoidance of dependence) and not on interdependence.

A more general idea is *cooperation*,[13] be it in the security, the economic, or other realms, and the derivative emphasis on *engagement*.[14] In the post–Cold War world, where the structure of international relations is inchoate, a balance of power is lacking, and "global issues" rise in prominence, there is more room for working together on common problems and taking a non–zero sum approach to issues, especially conflict avoidance. Interdependence then becomes a complex of activities in many fields, not just the economic, that progressively breaks down the boundary between subnational, foreign policy, and international levels of analysis. Interest has fastened especially on the presumed positive relationship between cooperative engagement and the decline of international conflict, with interdependence as an intervening variable, and on the "rule" that democracies, being interdependent as well as ideologically compatible, do not wage war against one another. Finally, and by way of summing up these various ideas, is the notion of *globalization*.[15] Although principally referring to international economic activity and to the idea that national economic boundaries are being swept away by regional and global economic integration, globalization also points to the ease with which societal, ideational, cultural, scientific-technological, educational, and communications ideas and processes cross national boundaries and thus must be included in any evaluation of a nation's foreign relations. Globalization is the universalization of interdependence.

Somewhat outside of these neoliberal derivatives is the continuing relevance, for interdependence analysis, of *modernization*.[16] The basic idea, extant for several decades, is that an interrelated complex of processes—industrialization, urbanization, education, communication, mobilization, and higher-order political institutions (e.g., democracy)—eventually and inexorably takes hold in every traditional society, transforming it into a variant of a common model. Foreign policy and international relations, regarded as generally dependent variables, also evolve in a single, reasonably well-defined direction, eventuating supposedly in a relatively conflict-free system composed of market democracies, all mutually interdependent. It is only necessary to locate particular societies (and thus nations) on the path to modernization to determine their foreign policies and their degree of interdependence. And, in case of slippage (e.g., warlike behavior, self-imposed isolation, or ideas and institutions left over too long from the traditional era), it is desirable for other, more modernized states, to give a little push to those not yet exhibiting all the positive qualities of fully developed societies. Given time and such effort, the world, and hence relations among its constituent parts, will become a pleasant, comfortable, and peaceful place in which to live. Interdependence, like international relations itself, is something that evolves, in this case in an ever-better (i.e., more commanding) direction.

Looking at economic and international relations notions of interdependence together, it is possible to draw a number of conclusions relevant to China:

1. *Interdependence* is no longer the term of choice to describe many aspects of China's relations with other nations and the several components of post–Cold War relations. Interdependence should perhaps be limited to the economic realm, but even there the emergence of globalization has pulled that restricted meaning apart as well.

2. The term *interdependence* needs to be expanded greatly to include many domestic and cross-boundary elements of China's contemporary existence. Although no balance of [in][ter]dependence is possible because of the disparate nature of those elements, it is still possible to list, analyze, and draw lines of connection between them.

3. As far as economic interdependence is concerned, neither traditional international trade theory nor *dependencia* appears to be an accurate reflection of China's post–Cold War situation. Residual aspects of both continue to be relevant (emphasis on balance of payments in the former case, residual Marxism in the latter, for instance). More in line with reality is some combination of developmentalism and export-led growth.

4. Even these cases do not entirely fit recent Chinese experience. Thus, the Chinese leadership is not anxious to remove internal political and cultural barriers to development and is only partially interested in eliminating economic barriers. Nor, in the case of export-led growth, is there any stated or implied intent to move eventually to democracy, although most other aspects of that model do fit the Chinese case reasonably closely.

5. As concerns the various international relations approaches to interdependence, neorealism, so obviously congruent with Chinese foreign

policy before 1979, was much less congruent once economic modernization became the chief element of that policy. Neoliberalist elements had
to be inserted in that "model" thereafter. Nonetheless, Beijing's excessive
(in terms of the post–Cold War world) concern for military security and
the rise of Chinese cultural nationalism, among other trends, indicate the
continuing relevance of the neorealist approach for China. Best is some
complex mixture of aspects of both approaches.

6. Particular neoliberal ideas are useful for investigating (the now dissociated term) *interdependence* in China's case. China participates in many
international regimes, both formal and implied. There is clearly a spectrum of dependence-interdependence-independence across many Chinese trends and processes, domestic and cross-boundary. Beijing is simultaneously dependent in certain regards, interdependent in others,
and independent in still others, as the substantive analysis of this chapters demonstrates. This variation occurs despite China's well-known de-
clarative emphasis on an independent foreign policy. Attention to epistemic communities (scientists, students, academics, businesspeople, for
example) is a useful departure, alerting the analyst to developments and
influences well before they "surface" in overt foreign policy planks, although in China's case the regime takes particular care to control or suppress such groups when it feels necessary.

China may be increasing its cooperative international behavior in net
terms, but it seems still to lag behind other major states in that regard and
also appears to be quite reluctant to participate in such manner in many
important arenas, such as security. The same may be said for engagement: foreign nations appear eager to pull Beijing into interdependent relationships, but that can hardly be said for China, which continues to resist such policies and surely does not include engagement in its asserted,
implied, or enacted policies. As for globalization, it is probably accurate
to state that China is, like other nations, subject to the influences, and
thus the effects, of globalization. But Beijing continues to resist them and
thus deliberately lags behind others, is not a leader in many of its
processes (for instance, cultural interpenetration, instantaneous cross-
border communications, sudden and sensitive susceptibility to worldwide economic and fiscal changes), and is a reluctant participant at best.

7. The modernization "model" appears still to be applicable to China.
But, as with the other process that have an interdependent component,
Beijing continues to resist the noneconomic aspects of modernization.
China, and thus its foreign policy, may eventually become "modern" in
the full sense of the term, and thus join the emerging comity of nations,
but probably only after those aspects (which Beijing treats as undesirable
side effects) evolve into an interdependent complex of cross-border
processes that that regime can no longer deny.

These propositions, and the economic and international relations ideas behind them, become guideposts for investigating the current and projected future status of China's interdependence. We turn now to ask to what extent these ideas are reflected in Chinese post-Tiananmen writings about interdependence; that is, what are Chinese views of interdependence?

Chinese Views of Interdependence

Contemporary Chinese attitudes are strongly conditioned by the country's historic relationship to the outside world. During the long dynastic period, Chinese looked on foreigners, their countries, and their products as interesting but inferior. That attitude produced the well-known tributary relationship, which was hardly a species of interdependence. This approach changed only gradually in the nineteenth and twentieth centuries, under Western pressure, in the direction of equality in international relations. But as China fell increasingly far behind the West militarily and as the dynasty declined, it could only become increasingly dependent, penetrated by foreign ideas and practices, and lacking in national self-respect.[17] A positive orientation toward trade, foreigners, cooperative exchanges, and outside investment and technology transfer stood no chance of emerging. The natural conclusion was to strengthen the country by taking from the West, build a powerful state through China's own efforts, and shun nonmaterial Westernism as inherently evil. This attitude continued under the Nationalists.

The Communists acted in the same manner, adding only the ideological justification of opposing "neocolonialism," praising self-reliance, and stressing supposed anti-imperialist unity among socialist countries and solidarity between China and the Third World. These were the leitmotivs of Chinese foreign policy during the Mao era, and interdependence could have no currency then. With the 1978 Deng-led reforms, however, interdependence was more positively regarded, since the reforms stressed investment, trade, technology transfer, and scientific exchanges. But not always: The 1980s campaigns against "spiritual pollution" and "bourgeoise liberalization"[18] favored self-reliance, opposed the concept and practices of interdependence, and viewed it as a one-way street. The West was supposed to provide benefits without imposing political, economic, military, and cultural costs. The upshot until the mid-1980s was for the Chinese to adopt a combination of the *dependencia* and neorealist approaches to interdependence.

The peak of pre-Tiananmen reformism brought a pronounced tilt toward interdependence and its benefits. Now analysts recognized the necessity of keeping open the door, the close connection between internal economic reform and external interdependence, the necessity of joining regional and global international economic organizations, and the negative effects of autarky and excessive self-reliance. Interdependence was mutually beneficial, so other nations' development was innately desirable and not threatening to China. Nations, through interdependence, could pursue common interests.[19] Export-led growth, admixed with neoliberalism, became the Chinese model.

Tiananmen dealt a setback to positive Chinese inclinations toward interdependence, as the regime reverted to extreme emphasis on self-reliance and resistance to Western cultural "pressure." Even so, some realized that China could no longer isolate itself. Chinese spokespersons asserted that China had become too important to the world economy—as a supplier of raw materials, a locus for Western investment, and a major trading nation—for American-led attempts to punish and isolate the country to succeed. Chinese pronouncements evolved toward developmentalism and cooperation by stressing the responsibility of developed nations toward Third World countries like China. Now the stress was on resolving the debt crisis, reversing the flow of financial resources, eliminating developed countries' trade barriers, and raising growth rates. Thus, the year and a half after Tiananmen posed only a temporary setback to the evolution of Chinese views generally supporting interdependence.[20]

Thereafter, from early 1991 to late 1992, Chinese statements became increasingly favorable, reflecting the following positions:

- Interdependence was not only a fact but also indispensable to China's development. Economic cooperation, capitalist investment, international cooperation in production, and subnational (but official) cooperation were all favored.
- Interdependence included the international division of labor: internationalization of production, economic regionalism, linked growth rates, and parallelism in interest rates.
- Interdependence promoted peace and security by breaking down barriers between economics and national security and by promoting diplomatic cooperation.
- To the five principles of peaceful coexistence—always somewhat anti-interdependence—were added the idea of a new international economic order as innately good and the principle of cooperative prosperity.
- North-South relations were viewed as mutually benefiting from exchange of Chinese resources, investment sites, inexpensive labor, and markets for other countries' capital, technology, and expertise. Chinese writers also recognized the mutual interpenetration of stabilized commodity prices and debt

repayment in the global South, and combating protectionism, lowering interest rates, and raising growth rates in the North.

- Post-Tiananmen sanctions, particularly removing most-favored-nation treatment, were criticized as anti-interdependence.
- The "North" owed a debt to the "South" stemming from the historical inequity between the two groups. This inequity was explicitly manifested in environmental protection, like all "global issues," inherently interdependent. For a solution, developed nations should provide developing nations, including China, with added assistance. Moreover, environmental matters could not interfere with the inherent right of developing nations to grow at as fast a rate as possible.[21]

From 1993 to 1997, further evolution occurred concerning interdependence:

- Economic interdependence was accepted in all details, along with such new descriptive terms as globalization.
- As a freestanding term and explanation, *interdependence* was used much less frequently, being replaced by description and analysis of its many components and processes, especially security, domestic determinants, regionalization, multipolarity, and global issues. When used, the term was linked with such other descriptors as *complex*.
- A more sophisticated understanding emerged of all such processes and their relation to the declared bases of Chinese foreign policy: development, peace, security, and close attention to the United States. Concomitantly, emphasis on an independent Chinese foreign policy faded in favor of independence as a basis for interdependence.
- The national security and economic cooperation components of complex interdependence received equal attention.
- North-South relations and peaceful coexistence were given continuing attention but with declining emphasis.
- No hint appeared of familiarity with latter-day theoretical literature on interdependence and its sequelae in economic or international relations theory. In the latter case, classical realism continued its hold on Chinese analysts, although modernization theory was understood.[22]

The Facts of China's Interdependence

All nations are interdependent to some degree. Thus, for China neither isolation nor dependence nor independence are workable or desirable policies. So Beijing had to walk a middle ground between these extremes, hoping to maximize their respective benefits and minimize their risks. Isolation had long since been jettisoned, and throughout the 1990s, independence was progressively less emphasized, leaving Beijing with an admixture of dependence and interdependence amid a residual declaratory independent policy. In practical terms, its entire modernization program, and thus its foreign policy, rested on its ability to tap the international environment for monetary, technological, and human resources, that is, on interdependence. Nonetheless, along several dimensions China remained dependent on other nations' policies and on the structure and processes of the international system. For analytic purposes, the facts of China's [in][ter]dependence are usefully divided into two categories, economic and all other.

Economic Interdependence

Several measures existed of Chinese economic interdependence. One was the very large growth of Chinese foreign trade since the late 1970s. From 1970 to 1996, exports grew from about $10 to $151 billion, while imports grew from about $11 to $139 billion. Another was the degree to which China permitted foreign investment, including foreign equity participation and foreign management of Chinese plants. By the end of 1996, direct foreign investment in China totaled $3.67 billion, representing some 283,000 projects. Yet another was China's willingness to borrow from foreign commercial and multilateral institutions. China minimized the risk of giving foreigners a say in domestic economic affairs by borrowing less than "safe" limits for developing countries and adeptly managed its external debt. The Chinese debt-to-GNP ratio (1.8 in 1996) and debt service as a percentage of exports (9.9 in 1996) were well below the norm for such countries. That hardly made China independent economically but did allow enough freedom of maneuver for Beijing not to worry excessively about dependence.

China was also not highly interdependent as measured by exports or imports as a percentage of gross national product. Neither figure was much above one-sixth of the total, although both were rising. But if economic interdependence is defined as the sum of imports and exports as a percentage of gross domestic product, China's degree of "trade dependence" rose greatly, from less than 10 percent in 1978 to over 35 percent in 1996, with a high of over 43 percent in 1994. These figures, illustrated in Table 9.1, can be compared with similar numbers for other relevant economies. Thus, United States in 1996 was about 19, Japan 16, Hong Kong greater than 100, Taiwan 80, Germany 42, and South Korea 58 percent trade dependent, as per Table 9.2. So by this definition, China was in the middle range of trade dependence (which of course was a vast change from its degree of historical trade dependence, less than 5 percent).[23]

TABLE 9.1   China's Foreign Trade Dependence, 1978–1996 (billion U.S.$)

	GNP	Exports	Imports	Exports + Imports	Exp. + Imp. as % of GNP
1978	225.7	10.1	10.3	20.4	9.04
1979	266.5	13.7	14.3	28.0	10.51
1980	288.4	18.9	19.1	38.0	13.18
1981	279.9	21.6	21.6	43.2	15.43
1982	274.3	21.9	18.8	40.7	14.84
1983	294.0	22.1	21.3	43.4	14.76
1984	299.2	24.9	26.6	51.5	17.21
1985	291.8	27.4	42.2	59.6	20.42
1986	281.7	30.9	42.9	73.8	26.20
1987	305.1	39.4	43.2	82.7	27.11
1988	376.5	47.5	55.3	102.8	27.30
1989	419.3	52.5	59.1	111.7	26.64
1990	332.5	62.1	53.3	115.4	34.47
1991	406.3	71.9	63.8	135.7	33.40
1992	487.4	84.9	80.6	165.5	34.31
1993	601.2	91.7	104.0	195.7	32.55
1994	540.8	121.0	115.6	236.6	43.75
1995	697.7	148.8	132.1	280.9	40.26
1996	816.9	151.1	138.8	289.9	35.49

SOURCES: *International Financial Statistics; Zhongguo Jinrong* (Chinese Finance): [China] State Statistical Bureau, *Monthly Bulletin of Statistics;* World Bank, *World Tables; UNCTAD Trade Figures;* International Monetary Fund, *Direction of Trade Statistical Yearbook; China Statistics Yearbook; China Statistics Monthly; China Economic News; Far Eastern Economic Review;* and *China Business Review.*

Nevertheless, China's imports supplied a critical input to its overall modernization, which was not always the case for these other nations. Those at a high level of industrialization produced a larger portion of their equipment at home. Those that were hard currency economies, unlike China's, had less difficulty purchasing needed goods abroad. Therefore, trade dependency figures must be modified accordingly. Although there are many measures of economic modernization, for trade dependence purposes the percent of population engaged in nonagricultural pursuits is perhaps acceptable. The United States employed more than 98 percent of its people in that manner, whereas the Chinese figure was probably not more than one-third, a nearly 3:1 ratio. Thus, China was much more trade dependent than the United States even though neither nation was near the top of the scale in terms of percent of gross national product devoted to trade. China was closer to Germany but still less than the four Asian "tigers." So some multiplier needs to be attached to trade dependence figures to take into account the difference in modernization between China and the advanced economies. But that multiplier could

TABLE 9.2   Trade Dependence of China and Selected Countries, 1996 (billion U.S.$)

	GNP	Imports	Exports	Imports + Exports	Imp. + Exp. as % of GNP
China	816.9	138.8	151.1	289.9	35.5
United States	7,630.0	822.0	625.1	1,447.1	19.0
Japan	4,599.3	349.2	410.9	760.1	16.5
Hong Kong	154.8	198.6	180.7	379.3	245.0[a]
Taiwan	273.1	102.4	115.9	218.3	79.9
Germany	2,353.1	455.7	521.1	976.8	41.5
S. Korea	484.8	150.3	129.7	280.0	57.8

[a]Hong Kong's imports and exports are both larger than its gross national product because of its role as an entrepôt for China. When re-exports to and from China are taken into account, Hong Kong's trade dependence drops significantly, probably to close to 100 percent.

SOURCES: *International Financial Statistics; Zhongguo Jinrong* (Chinese Finance); [China] State Statistical Bureau, *Monthly Bulletin of Statistics;* World Bank, *World Tables; UNCTAD Trade Figures;* International Monetary Fund, *Direction of Trade Statistical Yearbook; China Statistics Yearbook; China Statistics Monthly; China Economic News; Far Eastern Economic Review;* and *China Business Review.*

not be as high as 3:1, which would place China's trade dependence as high as 80 percent, because China remained a large continental economy that mostly produced and consumed its own wealth.

Considering the global regions with which it traded, China was clearly linked with the developed countries of Asia, Europe, and North America in both import and export terms, as shown in Table 9.3, but not with Third World nations in Africa, Asia, and Latin America. That may explain declining Chinese attention to North-South issues. Finally, the regions of China were differentially interdependent with other nations. The southern and eastern coastal provinces since 1978 increasingly joined the international market, which in the 1990s spread to the coastal Northeast. Thus, interdependence became a feature of large sectors of China, but less so of the Northeast and least so of the inland provinces, which were still largely left out. There was thus a danger of economic bifurcation into a modern, foreign trade–oriented, interdependent coastal sector and a traditional, internally oriented, semi-isolated inland sector. But the mid-1990s reforms, centered around construction of a "socialist market economy," further extended the modern sector and could eventually convert China to full interdependence.[24]

Interdependence in Other Areas

Measurement makes Chinese economic [in][ter]dependence explicit. That is not so in many other areas, where composite evaluation is much

TABLE 9.3   Direction of China's Foreign Trade: Value of Exports/Imports, 1978–1996 (billion U.S.$)

	Industrial Nations[a]	Africa	Asia[b]	Southern/ Eastern Europe	Middle East	Latin America	USSR/ CIS and Others
1978	6.1/8.1	.5/.2	.7/.4	.5/.5	.6/.1	.1/.5	1.2/1.2
1979	8.7/11.8	.6/.3	1.0/.5	.6/.7	.8/.2	.2/.8	1.4/1.6
1980	12.7/16.6	.7/.4	1.5/.9	.8/.8	1.0/.4	.4/.7	1.3/1.6
1981	15.4/16.5	.7/.4	1.5/.8	.7/.7	1.0/.3	.5/.6	.8/.9
1982	15.2/14.5	.8/.3	1.4/1.1	.5/.6	2.7/.2	.5/.6	.7/1.2
1983	15.7/16.3	.5/.3	1.3/.9	.5/.6	2.7/.3	.4/1.3	.9/1.3
1984	18.2/20.8	.5/.3	1.6/1.2	.5/.8	2.4/.3	.5/.9	1.1/1.4
1985	20.6/34.8	.4/.2	1.5/2.1	.8/1.3	1.8/.2	.5/1.8	1.8/1.9
1986	23.6/35.0	.6/.3	1.6/2.1	1.0/1.6	2.1/.2	.4/1.6	2.1/2.5
1987	29.6/35.5	1.2/.2	2.1/1.9	1.1/1.4	2.6/.3	.4/1.2	2.2/2.3
1988	37.2/43.5	1.6/.2	2.6/2.7	1.1/1.5	2.1/.6	.2/1.9	2.7/3.3
1989	42.6/45.8	.6/.4	3.2/2.8	1.0/1.4	1.4/.6	.3/2.2	2.9/3.0
1990	51.1/40.2	1.2/.4	5.3/5.8	.5/.8	1.4/.5	.6/1.3	2.8/2.2
1991	59.1/50.1	.8/.4	6.9/7.9	.5/.5	1.6/.8	.6/1.4	2.7/2.5
1992	69.4/59.8	.8/.4	7.3/12.2	.5/.5	2.0/1.0	.9/1.7	3.7/4.5
1993	71.9/67.5	1.2/0.7	9.3/222.7	.9/1.3	2.6/1.7	1.6/1.7	4.0/6.5
1994	96.6/76.6	1.4/1.8	13.7/26.8	1.2/.9	2.9/1.4	2.3/2.1	2.7/5.2
1995	115.4/84.7	2.0/1.4	20.0/32.4	1.8/.5	3.4/2.2	3.0/2.8	2.9/5.4
1996	118.1/84.2	2.1/1.4	19.7/37.1	1.8/.4	3.5/3.1	3.0/3.5	2.9/6.7

[a]North America, Japan, industrial Western Europe, Hong Kong, Singapore, Australia, and New Zealand.

[b]All East, Southeast, and South Asia, except Japan, Hong Kong, and Singapore.

SOURCE: International Monetary Fund, *Direction of Trade Statistics Yearbook,* [annually from] 1979–1997.

more difficult. Generally, it seems reasonable to conclude that modernization increases the degree of interdependence for China. But given the isolated and only quasi-modern nature of the country until 1978, as well as Beijing's insistence on an independent foreign policy thereafter, it should be expected that interdependence was only partial in many areas, that dependence may have actually increased in others, and that China remained independent in still others. Many areas need exploration:

Communications and Transportation.   In communications and transportation, China opened its doors wide for the first time since 1949. The advent of satellites and computers, together with government acquiescence, made possible the infusion of radio, television, and the Internet broadly into China. By the mid-1990s, China had allowed many world airlines and shipping companies direct access to its ports. But Beijing was not thereby more interdependent, for the country depended mostly on others for these links, whereas most communications were inbound, carried by foreign-owned systems. All electronic communications into and out of

China were still subject to censorship, as the Party leadership sought to continue the country in semi-isolation. The woefully outdated Chinese air traffic control system was being modernized only through international assistance, and China did not put up its first communications satellites until in 1995. The "balance of dependence" here favored the outside world.

Science and Technology.   In science and technology also, China became more dependent, on balance, even as the country experienced an unprecedented upsurge in foreign contacts. By the mid-1990s, more than 200,000 students and scholars had gone abroad for training, whereas only a comparative trickle came to China. A huge volume of scientific data was imported, and although some Chinese scientists worked on international research teams, attended international conferences, and participated in scholarly interchange, the forefronts of scientific research were all occupied by other nations. China continued to try to overcome the damage done by the Cultural Revolution and earlier Communist rule. A China-domiciled Chinese had yet to win a Nobel prize. Technology transfer, one of the engines of Chinese modernization, remained a one-way, inbound street in both kind and level. International patents were still not being taken out by Chinese inventors in noticeable numbers, and China regularly was accused of wholesale patent infringement and theft of other nations' technology. In the post-Tiananmen period the amount of technology transferred to China in various manners—much to be sure as concomitants of foreign investment—was truly stupendous. Were this flow to decline greatly or cease, China's economic development would slow or even reverse. The degree of China's technological dependence was clearly evident in military research, development, and procurement: Although some progress was made in space, airframes, and missiles, China remained significantly, perhaps increasingly, behind the advanced industrial nations and was constrained to import relatively old technology and weapons systems from Russia to modernize its defense industry. Dependence, not interdependence, was the rule in this arena.

Education.   Between 1978 and 1996, China sent abroad over 200,000 students, the majority to American colleges, totally reversing the isolationist situation of the Cultural Revolution. And even though a large portion of those students remained abroad, at least temporarily, after Tiananmen, the flow continued throughout the 1990s. The counterflow of students and scholars to China remained very low by comparison, perhaps a few thousand per annum (up, to be sure, from zero previously). As education is the most efficient means of acquiring technology and ideas from abroad, China became quite dependent on other nations' largess and access to their facilities. China translated a large number of texts in many fields for teaching purposes and depended on foreign teachers to sketch out the basic concepts and current ideas of many fields. Except in Chinese-language studies, the reverse was not true. Funds earmarked for Chinese education continued to enter China, but there was no known instance of Chinese organizations or individuals funding education in foreign lands. Here also, therefore, China was surely not interdependent with, but was undoubtedly at least partially dependent on, the outside for development of its modernization program. Beijing's foreign policy thus had to bend to assure continuation of that process.

Culture. In culture, the situation was mixed. Chinese culture was an important influence in certain nations, mostly Asian neighbors with a Confucian heritage. In certain other areas, for example, Chinese cuisine, Chinese global cultural influence was growing. But taken as a whole, Chinese cultural influence was not great and declined rapidly with distance from Chinese borders. Moreover, in terms of music, literature, and the performing arts, China had yet to make its mark (although Chinese artists in the mid-1990s were beginning to enter the world stage and in certain instances—film, for instance—Chinese standards were ascending to world-class levels, albeit against Party wishes). In contrast, cultural influence from the outside—whether from such Chinese-speaking entities as Hong Kong and Taiwan or from the global centers of contemporary popular culture (United States, Japan, and Europe) was flooding China despite official attempts to limit or stop it. In this arena, as others, there was much greater Chinese activity and participation, but the balance of dependence continued to favor the outside. The only reason why it did not tip even more greatly was the regime's relative success in slowing down the pace of infusion of external influence.

Ideational Influences. In the Maoist era, China exerted much ideological influence on Western and Third World nations. With the Cultural Revolution, such influence ended. Since the post-1978 Deng-led reforms and the turn toward marketization, China began slowly to recover from its ideational isolation, only to suffer a major setback with the death of communism outside of Asia, the Tiananmen incident of 1989, and the resultant Western sanctions. Only in 1992 did Chinese ideational influence again attract attention, this time on the basis of a combination of Confucianism, nationalism, and marketization. Many said this "new" Chinese model could be exported to other Asian nations (even though this combination of ideas was in fact imported from Japan, South Korea, Taiwan, and Singapore). In the mid-1990s, it was still too early to tell whether a resurgence of Chinese ideational influence could be expected. At best, it would be limited to China's Asian neighbors with similar characteristics, not a large group. Beyond that, other ideational influences competed heavily: Islam, Christianity, and democracy. The most, therefore, that could be said was that China had recovered some of its lost influence, that it was holding back (albeit with increasing difficulty) those three external ideas, and that prospects for renewed influence were small. China was not, therefore, interdependent in this arena.

National Security.   Since 1949, when communism came to power in China, Beijing's security depended not only on its own military capability but also on the security policies of the nuclear superpowers, the United States and the Soviet Union. Mao, after all, early on saw the necessity of "learning to one side," and that phrase encapsulated China's own security orientation throughout the Cold War. Even after the end of the Cold War and the demise of the Soviet Union, China remained dependent on the military attitude of the "sole remaining superpower," the United States. Indeed, the post–Cold War period found China even further behind militarily, as evidenced both by the Gulf War and the entire "revolution in military affairs" of which that conflict was an example. China could engage only in a slow climb toward security equality, a process that would take at least three decades and possibly more. Thus, in this area as well, China remained relatively dependent. Of course, with possession of weapons of mass destruction and their means of delivery, with progressive military modernization already under way, and with the relatively benign international security atmosphere prevalent in the 1990s, that dependence was not so great as before, and China could therefore look forward to a time of relative interdependence in the first decades of the twenty-first century, if not security independence.

[In][ter]dependence and Chinese Foreign Relations

It is apparent that in the mid-to-late 1990s, China was not highly interdependent in many arenas that influenced its foreign policy. Indeed, the "balance of dependence" indicated a still-high and perhaps growing degree of Chinese dependence. Certainly Beijing could not base its foreign policy on independence, except in the declaratory sense. China did become highly interactive in regional and global affairs; its degree of participation in international regimes grew greatly; and along several dimensions it promulgated a policy of cooperation. Yet these factors did not add up to a situation of foreign relations interdependence. A large portion of what China did, or wanted to do, abroad depended on the policies of other relevant states or the post–Cold War nature of international relations. This was, in kind if not detail, little different from China's international situation during the four decades of the Cold War, when Beijing was also (at least some of the time) active, participatory, even cooperative—but also relatively dependent. The important difference between the two eras lay in the rise in China's absolute power, the product of its successful modernization drive. But that did not beget a greater degree of foreign relations interdependence, as a comparison of the driving forces of the two eras shows.

The Cold War, 1945–1990, was characterized by American-Soviet superpower bipolarity, with the American-Chinese-Russian strategic triangle at its base and with China as the "swing state"; a rough East-West balance of military power; a nuclear weapons–centered balance of terror; security dominance over economics, other cooperative activity, and North-South relations; international organization subordinate to bipolarity; and intraregional rivalries dependent on bipolarity and therefore attenuated. The post–Cold War period is in many ways the opposite: Bipolarity was extinguished with the Soviet collapse, and the United States became the "sole remaining superpower"; a military balance of power does not exist; international organization experienced a resurgence with construction of many new international regimes; the nuclear threat was much attenuated; intraregional rivalries, freed of the bipolar nuclear overhang, reemerged in religious and ethnic form; economics replaced security as the center of international activity; and cooperative activities, especially as concerned environmental and other global issues, blossomed.

China had to fit itself in as best it could according to these international systemic characteristics. In the post–Cold War period, it could no longer find autonomy through maneuver between the superpowers but had to face the United States with no allies; Chinese military influence declined along with lessened systemic emphasis on security capabilities; Chinese economic influence rose not only because of its rapid economic growth but also because of enhanced international systemic attention to economics; China could maneuver successfully in international organizations and other international regimes but first had to join those from which it had previously been excluded; Beijing participated much more actively in regional affairs but only to the extent that the combination of its power and regional characteristics permitted; China's ideological appeal to, and use for its own purposes of, the global "South" declined, a result of its own ideational semi-isolation and the South's declining intrinsic importance in global affairs; China had to conduct its economic policy according to the "rules" set by the industrial West-North, and Beijing was judged increasingly according to a the amount of divergence between how its leaders ruled the nation internally and international moral standards.

Under these international circumstances, Beijing's foreign policy could only become highly interactive, participatory, and cooperative. But these attributes by themselves did not spell interdependence. Rather, a complex mix of dependence, autonomy (termed independence by the leadership), and interdependence ensued. There was no objective way to arrive at some bottom line as to the balance between the three in China's foreign relations. Indeed, the above analysis indicates many arenas in which

China remained internationally dependent, although the portion of its interdependent behavior–oriented activities may have risen in the 1990s. Subsequent analysis of China's foreign relations interdependence must take account of the very complex nature of the topic, divide it into relevant subcategories, analyze each separately (and quantitatively if possible), find some means (which does not now exist) to reintegrate those results, and only then draw broad conclusions as to interdependence.

Notes

1. For theoretical foundations, see Robert Keohane and Joseph Nye, Jr., *Transnational Relations and World Politics* (Cambridge: Harvard University Press, 1972), and their *Power and Interdependence: World Politics in Transition* (Boston: Little, Brown, 1977). For application to China, see Wendy Frieman and Thomas W. Robinson, "Costs and Benefits of Interdependence: A New Assessment," in *China's Economic Dilemmas in the 1990s: The Problems of Reforms, Modernization, and Interdependence* (Washington, DC: Government Printing Office, 1991, for the Joint Economic Committee, 102nd Congress), pp. 718–740.

2. See, inter alia, Samuel B. Huntington, *The Clash of Civilizations and the Remaking of World Order* (New York: Simon and Schuster, 1996); Michael E. Brown (ed.), *Ethnic Conflict and International Security* (Princeton: Princeton University Press, 1993); Chester A. Crocker and Fen Osler Hampson (eds.), *Managing Global Chaos: Sources of and Responses to International Conflict* (Washington: United States Institute for Peace, 1996); *Foreign Affairs* magazine, *The New Shape of World Affairs: Contending Paradigms in International Affairs* (New York: Council on Foreign Relations, 1997); Kenneth N. Waltz, "The Emerging Structure of International Politics," *International Security*, Spring 1993, pp. 44–79; Charles Hauss, *Beyond Conflict: Transforming the New World Order* (New York: Praeger, 1996); Charles Kegley, Jr., and Gregory Raymond, *A Multipolar Peace? Great Power Politics in the 21st Century* (New York: St. Martin's, 1994); and John Mueller, *Quiet Cataclysm: Reflections on the Recent Transformation of World Politics* (New York: HarperCollins, 1995).

3. Official Chinese pronouncements on formal occasions from 1990 on—Party congresses, Politburo meetings, National People's congresses and their Standing Committee meetings, and New Year's slogans—all contained ritual references to foreign policy independence. But as the 1990s proceeded, the frequency and urgency of such references declined as the complex nature of the post–Cold War world—globalism, multipolarity (or, sometimes, unipolarity), regionalism, and so on—became increasingly apparent. The "classic" era of China's "independent" foreign policy was the 1970s, when if anything China was highly dependent within the strategic triangle, on the Soviet policy of military threat against China, and on the American policy of protecting China from that threat. See James C. Hsiung (ed.), *Beyond China's Independent Foreign Policy* (New York: Praeger, 1985).

4. The classic work is Gottfried Habeler, *The Theory of International Trade* (London: William Hodge, 1956). See also Murray C. Kemp, *The Pure Theory of International Trade* (Englewood Cliffs, NJ: Prentice-Hall, 1964);and Paul A. Samuelson

and William D. Nordhaus, *Economics* (New York: McGraw-Hill, 15th ed., 1996), chapter on international trade.

5. See James A. Caporaso (ed.), "Dependence and Dependency in the Global System," *International Organization*, Winter 1978, and the many sources cited therein, as well as Tony Smith, "The Underdevelopment of Development Literature: The Case of Dependency Theory," *World Politics*, Winter 1979, pp. 247–288.

6. W. W. Rostow, *The Politics of Economic Growth* (New York: Cambridge University Press, 1971); Gabriel A. Almond and G. B. Powell, Jr., *Comparative Politics: A Developmental Approach* (Boston: Little, Brown, 1956); Jason L. Finkle and Richard W. Gable (eds.), *Political Development and Social Change* (New York: Wiley, 1966); Garry D. Brewer and Ronald D. Brunner (eds.), *Political Development and Change* (New York: Free Press, 1975); Lucian W. Pye et al., *Studies in Political Development*, 6 vols. (Princeton: Princeton University Press, 1963–); Uner Kirdar (ed.), *Change: Threat or Opportunity?* 5 vols. (New York: United Nations, 1992); and Mancur Olson, *The Rise and Decline of Nations* (New Haven: Yale University Press, 1982).

7. Helen Hughes (ed.), *Achieving Industrialization in East Asia* (New York: Cambridge University Press, 1988); Roy Hofheinz, Jr., and Kent E. Calder, *The East Asia Edge* (New York: Basic Books, 1982); Frederic C. Deyo (ed.), *The Political Economy of the New Asian Industrialism* (Ithaca: Cornell University Press, 1987); Peter Drysdale, *International Economic Pluralism: Economic Policy in East Asia and the Pacific* (New York: Columbia University Press, 1988); C. Fred Bergsten and Marcus Noland (eds.), *Pacific Dynamism and the International Economic System* (Washington: Institute for International Economics; 1993), and Ezra Vogel, *The Four Little Dragons: The Spread of Industrialization in East Asia* (Cambridge: Harvard University Press, 1991).

8. The foundations of realism are to be found in E. H. Carr, *The Twenty Years' Crisis, 1919–1939: An Introduction to the Study of International Relations* (London: Macmillan, 1939–); Hans J. Morgenthau, *Politics Among Nations* (New York: Knopf, 1948–); and Inis J. Claude, *Power and International Relations* (New York: Random House, 1962). Neorealism was initiated by Kenneth N. Waltz, *Theory of International Politics* (Reading, MA: Addison-Wesley, 1979). See also Hedley Bull, *The Anarchical Society* (New York: Columbia University Press, 1977); and Michael E. Brown et al. (eds.), *The Perils of Anarchy: Contemporary Realism and International Security* (Cambridge: MIT Press, 1995).

9. Barry Buzan et al., *The Logic of Anarchy: Neorealism to Structural Realism* (New York: Columbia University Press, 1993); Robert O. Keohane (ed.), *Neoliberalism and Its Critics* (New York: Columbia University Press, 1986); Charles W. Kegley, Jr., *Controversies in International Relations Theory: Realism and the Neoliberal Challenge* (New York: St. Martin's, 1995); and David A. Baldwin (ed.), *Neorealism and Neoliberalism: The Contemporary Challenge* (New York: Columbia University Press, 1993).

10. Stephen D. Krasner (ed.), *International Regimes* (Ithaca: Cornell University Press, 1983); and Volker Rittberger (ed.), *Regime Theory and International Relations* (New York: Oxford University Press, 1993).

11. See sources on *dependencia* (note 6). The difference between dependence and dependency is the following: Dependence is a given state's external reliance

on other actors in international relations, whereas dependency is the incorporation of a country, or a portion thereof, into the global (capitalist) international system and the domestic distortions that arise as a consequence. Dependency has declined as a topic of interest along with the decline in the appeal of socialism and the apparent triumph of global capitalism. The idea of a spectrum remains.

12. Peter M. Haas (ed.), "Knowledge, Power, and International Policy Coordination," *International Organization*, Winter 1992; Thomas Risse-Kappen (ed.), *Bringing Transnational Relations Back In: Non-State Actors, Domestic Structures, and International Institutions* (New York: Cambridge University Press, 1996); and Edward Kolodziej, "Epistemic Communities Searching for Regional Cooperation," *Mershon International Studies Review*, May 1997, pp. 93–98. It should be noted that the field of epistemic communities is, to some extent, one element of the latter-day emphasis on domestic determinants of foreign policy (interest groups, bureaucratic politics, and so on), which was neglected by classical realist theory and not sufficiently emphasized by neoliberalism. The other element is the idea that democracies do not fight one another and, hence, leads to inquiry into how and when nations convert to democracy (and if they do not, why not), as per note 16.

13. This has become a large field since the end of the Cold War. See Robert Axelrod, *The Evolution of Cooperation* (New York: Basic Books, 1984); Joseph M. Greico, *Cooperation Among Nations* (Ithaca: Cornell University Press, 1990); Andrew Mack and John Ravenhill (eds.), *Pacific Cooperation: Building Economic and Security Regimes in the Asia-Pacific Region* (Boulder: Westview, 1995); Robert O. Keohane, *After Hegemony: Cooperation and Discord in the World Economy* (Princeton: Princeton University Press, 1984); Kenneth A. Oye (ed.), *Cooperation Under Anarchy* (Princeton: Princeton University Press, 1986); Helen Milner, "International Theories of Cooperation Among Nations," *World Politics*, April 1992, pp. 466–496; Martin Feldstein, *International Economic Cooperation* (Chicago: University of Chicago Press, 1988); Michael Taylor, *The Possibility of Cooperation* (Cambridge: Cambridge University Press, 1987); Oran Young, *International Cooperation* (Ithaca: Cornell University Press, 1989); Arthur A. Stein, *Why Nations Cooperate: Circumstance and Choice in International Relations* (Ithaca: Cornell University Press, 1993); and Harry Harding (ed.), "China's Cooperative Relations" (unpublished conference manuscript, 1996 version).

14. The term is an American one, popularized by Clinton administration pronouncements in September 1993. See Anthony Lake, "Speech at Johns Hopkins University, School of Advanced International Studies," September 21, 1993, in *Congressional Record*, 1993, pp. E2293–2298. For engagement and security, see Janne E. Nolan (ed.), *Global Engagement: Cooperation and Security in the Twenty-First Century* (Washington, DC: Brookings, 1994). The term was applied mostly to American policy toward post–Cold War China, being the reverse side of Beijing's policy of opening out. A large American literature has emerged. See, inter alia, James Shinn (ed.), *Weaving the Net: Conditional Engagement with China* (New York: Council on Foreign Relations Press, 1996); Yoichi Funabashi et al., *Emerging China in a World of Interdependence* (New York: Trilateral Commission, 1994); and Audrey and Patrick Cronin, "The Realistic Engagement of China," *Washington Quarterly*, Winter 1996, pp. 141–171. The reverse side of the American policy, in turn, was the idea of containment, about which an equally large literature was being produced, beginning in 1995.

15. "Globalization: The Debate," articles by Dani Rodrik, David Rothkopf, Jacques Attalı, Stephen J. Kobrın, and Claude Moisy in *Foreign Policy*, Summer 1997, pp. 19–77; Hans-Hendrik Holm and Georg Sorensen (eds.), *Whose World Order? Uneven Globalization and the End of the Cold War* (Boulder: Westview, 1995); R. J. Barry Jones, *Globalization and Interdependence in the International Political Economy* (New York: Pinter, 1995); Kwame Anthony Appiah and Henry Louis Gates, Jr., *The Dictionary of Global Culture* (New York: Knopf, 1997); William Grieder, *One World, Ready or Not: The Manic Logic of Global Capitalism* (New York: Simon and Schuster, 1997); Lowell Bruan and Diana Farrell, *Market Unbound: Unleashing Global Capitalism* (New York: Wiley, 1996); Lester C. Thurow, *The Future of Capitalism* (New York: Morrow, 1996); Richard J. Barnett and John Cavanaugh, *Global Dreams: Imperial Corporations and the New World Order* (New York: Simon and Schuster, 1994); George Cho, *Trade, Aid and Global Interdependence* (New York: Routledge, 1995); George C. Lodge, *Managing Globalization in the Age of Interdependence* (San Diego: Pfeiffer, 1995); and Warwick J. McKibbin, *Global Linkages: Macroeconomic Interdependence and Cooperation in the World Economy* (Washington, DC: Brookings, 1991). Most recent literature on economic interdependence falls within the purview of globalization literature.

16. The literature on modernization is divided into purely economic modernization and all other kinds. In the latter case, a further threefold subdivision is based on modernization's influence: on the shape of international relations, on the links between economic modernization and the form of polity (particularly democracy), and on how democracy and international relations are related (especially via the thesis that democracies do not fight one another). For the first, see Charles B. Kindleberger, *Power and Money* (New York: Basic Books, 1970); Klaus Knorr, *Power and Wealth* (Basic Books, 1973); Robert Gilpin, *The Political Economy of International Relations* (Princeton: Princeton University Press, 1987); Joan Edelman Spero, *The Politics of International Economic Relations* (New York: St. Martin's, 1977); and Edward L. Morse, *Modernization and the Transformation of International Relations* (New York: Free Press, 1976). For the second, see Seymour Martin Lipset, "Some Social Requisites of Democracy: Economic Development and Political Legitimacy," *American Political Science Review*, March 1959, pp. 69–105; Gary Marks and Larry Diamond (eds.), *Reexamining Democracy* (Newbury Park, CA: Sage, 1992); Samuel P. Huntington, *The Third Wave: Democratization in the Late Twentieth Century* (Norman: University of Oklahoma Press, 1991); Ronald Inglehart, *Modernization and Postmodernization: Cultural, Economic, and Political Change in Forty Three Societies* (Princeton: Princeton University Press, 1997); Steven Haggard and Robert R. Kaufman, *The Political Economy of Democratic Transitions* (Princeton: Princeton University Press, 1995); Larry Diamond et al. (eds.), *Democracy in Developing Countries: Asia* (Boulder: Lynn Reinner, 1989); and Adam Przeworskii and Fernando Limongi, "Modernization: Theory and Facts," *World Politics*, January 1997, pp. 155–183 (which appears definitive and contains a review of the literature). For the third, see, in an increasingly large field, Michael E. Brown et al., *Debating the Democratic Peace* (Cambridge: MIT Press, 1996); Tony Smith, *America's Democracy: The United States and the Worldwide Struggle for Democracy in the Twentieth Century* (Princeton: Princeton University Press, 1994); Bruce Russett, *Groping for a Democratic Peace: Principles for a Post–Cold War World* (Princeton:

Princeton University Press, 1993); Eugene V. Rostow, *Toward Managed Peace: The National Security Interest of the United States, 1759 to the Present* (New Haven: Yale University Press, 1993); and James Lee Ray, *Democracy and International Conflict* (Columbia: University of South Carolina Press, 1995).

17. Immanuel Hsu, *The Rise of Modern China* (New York: Oxford University Press, 1975), pp. 325–363 and 433–522; and Jonathan Spence, *The Search for Modern China* (New York: Norton, 1990), pp. 194–268.

18. Thomas Gold, "'Just in Time!' China Battles Spiritual Pollution on the Eve of 1984," *Asian Survey*, September 1984, pp. 947–974; and James Tong (ed.), "Party Documents on Anti-Bourgeoise Liberalization and Hu Yaobang's Resignation, 1987," *Chinese Law and Government*, Spring 1988.

19. See, for instance, "Some Questions Concerning the Establishment of a New World Order," and "Partners in Asia-Pacific Economic Cooperation," *Contemporary International Relations*, July 1991 and February 1992, respectively.

20. This is based on a review, for the period September 1989–December 1990, of *Gouji Wenti Yanjiu* (International Studies), *Guoji Zhangwang* (World Outlook), *Foreign Affairs Journal*, *Guoji Zhanlue Yanjiu* (International Strategic Studies), and *Xiandai Guoji Guanxi* (Contemporary International Relations), all organs of various research institutes in Beijing, and *Guoji Wenti* (International Affairs), Shanghai.

21. List based on a review of the journals noted in note 20 for the period January 1991–October 1992, including also *Heping* (Peace).

22. Based on a review of the journals listed in notes 20 and 21.

23. Statistics in the preceding paragraphs, as well as for Tables 9.1, 9.2, and 9.3, were gathered from the following sources: *International Financial Statistics*; *Zhongguo Jinrong* (Chinese Finance); [China] State Statistical Bureau, *Monthly Bulletin of Statistics*; World Bank, *World Tables*; *UNCTAD Trade Figures*; International Monetary Fund, *Direction of Trade Statistical Yearbook*; *China Statistics Yearbook*; *China Statistics Monthly*; *China Economic News*; *Far Eastern Economic Review*; and *China Business Review*. It should be noted that trade statistics are subject to yuan-dollar conversion rates, which varied from year to year, therefore affecting those statistics to the extent the conversion rate fell (as it almost always did). It should also be noted that gross national product figures are those officially supplied by Beijing and not the so-called purchasing power parity figures proposed by the World Bank. Use of the latter significantly increases gross national product, by a factor of two to three.

24. It should be noted that despite efforts to "privatize" most of the state-owned enterprises, beginning with the Fourteenth Party Congress in 1992 and pledges at the Fifteenth Congress in 1997 to continue this work, in fact only 10,000 of the 300,000 such factories had been taken off the state roles by the latter date. Moreover, not only did they continue to be a major drag on the economy, but those that had been "privatized" were in fact merely placed in the hands of provincial and local governments and were not controlled by private stockholders. To many, that meant that an economic crisis—a much lowered growth rate, among other things—would not be long in coming. Were that to occur, exports could be drastically lowered and foreign direct investment could decline substantially, thus making China much more economically dependent.

10

Human Rights in Chinese Foreign Relations

JAMES D. SEYMOUR

Although the problem of human rights has always colored relations between the People's Republic of China and the rest of the world, it did not become a vital issue until the 1989 massacre in Beijing. In this chapter we shall examine this impact of the massacre, and also China's evolving participation in the international human rights regime. That involvement has at times been defensive and at other times assertive and positive. We shall see how foreign governments, despite the limitations on the extent to which the international community can affect a country's internal affairs, have attempted to influence the human rights situation in China and to encourage the country to develop in a more democratic direction.

Historical Background

From the seventeenth until the mid–twentieth century it was generally understood in the West that each state was to enjoy uncompromised sovereignty. This came to mean that a government had absolute authority over the people within its territory, and therefore outsiders could not legitimately interfere in a country's domestic affairs. In the wake of World War II, however, the view became widespread that serious human rights violations in a country were a legitimate subject of transnational concern, both for moral reasons and because an epidemic of human rights violations, even if "domestic," could pose dangers to the international community. In due course, the United Nations adopted four human rights agreements that together constitute the International Bill of Human Rights. First came the thirty-article Universal Declaration of Human Rights, proclaimed in 1948. Though its principles were spelled out only in general terms and did not necessarily have the force of international law, they were "a common standard of achievement for all peoples and all nations," and an implicit limitation on state sovereignty.

The notion of absolute territorial sovereignty came to China relatively late. Historically, there was no clear delineation between the Middle Kingdom *(Zhongguo)* and peripheral nations, so there was no modern concept of territorial sovereignty. An emperor's sway in the outer realms, which were usually inhabited by non-Chinese, was limited by the power and authority of local potentates—unless they were too weak to resist successfully. China, in the nineteenth century, when it became victimized by foreign powers (who took their own sovereignty seriously but ignored the rights of the less-developed countries), embraced the sovereignty concept with a vengeance. Suddenly the old Confucian notions of imperial propriety were swept away, and China was determined to become a centralized empire free of interference by anyone not an ethnic Chinese. This process began with the overthrow of the Manchus in 1911 and was largely completed by the Communists in 1949. That was the year after the adoption of the Universal Declaration of Human Rights by the UN General Assembly, but the Chinese Communists (who were excluded from the UN) had not been consulted about that, and they were disinclined to allow human rights considerations to interfere with their reach for power and social revolution. In their view, each government had virtually unlimited authority to act within its country's boundaries; aggrieved individuals had no recourse to international law.

During the following decades, the international human-rights movement gained popularity and legal standing. In 1966 the United Nations, with the People's Republic of China (PRC) still excluded, rounded out the International Bill of Rights by adopting two detailed human rights covenants. By 1976 both covenants had been accepted by enough countries to be considered "in force," at least with respect to the ratifying countries, though their applicability to nonparticipants is a moot point of international law. One of these treaties, the International Covenant on Civil and Political Rights (ICCPR), deals with rights as they are generally understood in the developed world, including freedom from government interference in the flow of information and ideas, such as imprisoning spokespersons for unwelcome viewpoints. With respect to these matters, China's leaders take a cultural relativist approach: In applying international human rights standards, account must be taken of the diversity of international values, and each government is entitled to make allowances for the nation's historical, social, cultural, and even political realities. Most important, the question of civil liberties should not be artificially politicized or "used as a tool to pursue a certain ideology and political model" (as the West is seen as doing).[1]

The other instrument, the International Covenant on Economic, Social and Cultural Rights (ICESCR), spells out rights much sought after in the developing world, including services and material benefits that governments are supposed to provide their citizens. As we shall see below, the PRC professes to take these rights very seriously.[2]

The Chinese government has long hinted at a willingness to accede to both covenants and finally did sign the ICESCR in 1997. It also accepted the principle of universality of human rights in general—at the same time seeking, along with other countries such as Malaysia, to have some of the provisions of the Universal Declaration reconsidered. It has also accepted certain other human rights agreements, including the conventions respecting the rights of women, children, and refugees; and against genocide, racial discrimination, and torture—altogether seventeen agreements, or so it is claimed.[3] Especially important is the torture convention, which China ratified in 1988. According to Article 2 thereof, authorities have an international obligation to take "effective legislative, administrative, judicial and other measures to prevent acts of torture." Pursuant to its obligations under this convention, China has submitted reports concerning torture in China. This all marked a break with the principle that human rights abuses in a country were none of the international community's business. Unfortunately, these and other reports to United Nations organs tend to be statements of official policy, rather than the result of investigation of local realities.

All the while, the government appears to have had in mind the need to avoid giving Westerners a monopoly over the process of defining human rights. One approach has been to emphasize *group* rights, especially collective economic rights. "Survival rights" are seen as more important than political rights and civil liberties; China's leaders complain that the West focuses on a handful of dissidents while "ignoring the right to subsistence of the majority of the people."[4] Actually, even though vast improvements have been made in the national diet and housing conditions, China turns out to be on rather weak ground when it come to subsistence rights.[5] For example, malnourishment among prisoners has been a serious problem.[6] In addition, 1996 saw the publication of a detailed and searing Human Rights Watch report on the conditions of Chinese orphans and abandoned babies. Still, Beijing has worked to turn the issue of economic and social rights to its advantage. Although the right to development is usually viewed as having both individual and collective components, the latter is seen by Beijing as taking precedence over the former. Indeed, Chinese Communist theorists interpret the right to development as inhering in the state *rather than* the individual, and as such they find it especially suited to their purposes. If there is sufficient eco-

nomic development, they argue, that proves that the country has sufficient democracy.

The World Takes Notice

Although in the 1950s there were complaints from Taiwan and the
United States about repression in China, these were often so politicized
and tied to anti-Communist hysteria that they had little credibility or impact. Unlike the other Communist countries, for a long time Beijing enjoyed largely a free ride when it came to human rights. During the Mao
years, when conditions went from bad to worse, the world was largely
oblivious. But, appreciative of the China's anti-Soviet turn, the United
States (followed by many other countries) began having relations with
China during the later years of the Cultural Revolution, a movement
marked by one of the worst episodes of human rights violations. A few
years later, the crackdown on the Democracy Wall movement followed
immediately upon Deng Xiaoping's upbeat visit to the United States.
Cautious requests from Chinese dissidents for sympathy from President
Jimmy Carter[7] seemed to go unheeded. With China barely "opened," foreign politicians, diplomats, traders, lawyers, church representatives,
travel agents, and academics were reluctant to jeopardize their ability to
pursue their professional interests in China by raising human rights concerns. Then (as is still often the case) even journalists often tended to
write cautiously, at least until near the end of their tour of duty and after
winning a few coveted interviews or a trip to one of the many closed
parts of the country. It was partly because of this absence of any strong
reaction to human rights abuses during the two decades leading up to
1989 that China's leaders were taken by surprise by the strong international reaction to that year's massacre.

Before 1989 it had been largely left to nongovernmental organizations
(NGOs) to blow the whistle on Beijing. Even the NGOs were slow to do
so. Reasons for neglect ranged from lack of information to fear that Western initiatives would be counterproductive. In the mid-1970s this situation began to change. The first organization to pay serious attention to
human rights violations in China was London-based Amnesty International. During the next two decades, other organizations did likewise,
notably Human Rights Watch/Asia, and Human Rights in China. These
organizations' reports have been of high quality, although some others
have issued less-worthy but nonetheless influential propaganda. All told,
the human rights NGOs have constituted a redoubtable international
lobby as well as hundreds of national lobbies (albeit mostly in the West)
pressuring their own governments. In effect, they do much of the journalists' research work for them and thus influence press coverage of

China. All that has obliged Western governments to take cognizance of the PRC's human rights problems. Thus, for the past decade China has been under close international scrutiny.[8] Beijing has had to defend its human rights record to a multidimensional international community, comprising governments, NGOs, and intergovernmental organizations.

Although it is not the purpose of this chapter to evaluate the human rights situation in China, at this point the issues that have raised the greatest concern abroad should be noted. Repression of political dissent receives the most attention. Also of concern are mistreatment of detainees—unfair trials, wrongful imprisonment, poor prison conditions, and torture. The Chinese government now claims that in these respects citizens' rights are protected by laws that are consistent with international standards such as the UN's "Minimal Standards and Regulations for the Treatment of Prisoners." Other important issues are interference with foreign journalists in China, treatment of overseas Chinese students, restrictions on the right of people to emigrate from the PRC,[9] the exporting of prison-made products, and persecution of China's religious groups. The latter issue has been of growing salience. Indeed, members of the U.S. Congress have been so concerned that in 1997 the House Committee on International Relations voted to deny most U.S. visas to Chinese officials responsible for human rights abuses in general and religious persecution in particular (though the measure is unlikely to become law).

China's Response to International Pressure

The PRC's leaders tend to be hypersensitive to attention to its human rights practices. They argue that such concern is an interference in China's internal affairs. Much of China's appeal to Third World governments has been built upon similar sovereignty concerns. The word has been sent out that these countries should support China's rulers today because the next time it might be they who come under international scrutiny for human rights practices. Such warnings as "What is happening to China today is apt to happen to any other developing country tomorrow"[10] often find ready listeners.

Usually China's spokespersons profess to see nothing but avarice underlying foreign concerns about China's human rights situation, and they appear to have persuaded the Chinese people accordingly. There is no appreciation of the modern belief that the public benefits from open, accountable government. On the contrary, in 1996 *People's Daily* found foreign concern all a sinister Western plot.

The essence of U.S. "human rights diplomacy" is the pursuit of power politics with the goal of maintaining its dominant role in the world. This has a

long history . . . , and in this new historical era America still harbors hege-
monist ambitions. Under the cloak of "human rights defender" and the pretext of safeguarding human rights, the United States has run roughshod,
bullying the small and the weak with its strength and suppressing the poor
with its wealth.[11]

But such rhetoric is designed primarily to elicit domestic support for
the Communists and is perhaps not to be taken seriously beyond that.
Since the early 1990s China's leaders, in actually dealing with the outside
world, have taken the more proactive approach to human rights diplomacy. Indeed, since the early 1990s China has been on what might be
termed a human rights offensive. It began with an outpouring of releases
presenting the government's position on human rights. Often stressed is
the West's own flawed human rights record in such places as Los Angeles and Northern Ireland and double standard of attacking China's human rights performance while ignoring that of countries like Israel (the
PRC's "internal affairs" argument to the contrary notwithstanding).
China's human rights record, it is claimed, surpasses that of the United
States with respect to twenty-four areas of concern.[12] Among the various
publications has been a series of white papers on human rights.[13] The
first, which appeared in 1991, was a long, illiberal and somewhat illogical
tract in which past foreign transgressions against China seemed to be
proffered as justifications for the Chinese government's more recent mal-
treatment of its citizens. That white paper met with opposition from Chinese at home and abroad.[14] Actually, though, it did not reject international human rights principles per se; rather, it placed major emphasis on
the progress China had made in advancing economic, social, and cultural
rights. When the record on civil liberties was recounted, it was difficult
for a reader to take it all seriously (for example, the assertion that China
had neither news censorship nor political prisoners[15]). Still, foreign pressures may well have had some impact on official thinking, and the publication of this and subsequent white papers on human rights has been
further implicit acknowledgment that human rights are now the subject
of legitimate (or at any rate inevitable) international concern.

But the Chinese know that more than propaganda is needed to placate
world concern. It is awkward for an American president to do Beijing favors if there has been no demonstrable progress on the human rights
front. Thus, the Chinese government has experimented with the practice
of releasing some of its critics from prison on crucial occasions when foreign support has been urgently sought. When Congress debates Sino-
American trade policy, China sometimes releases either prisoners or at
least upbeat information about them (instead of stonewalling as previously). The most notable example of prisoner diplomacy was the 1993 re-

lease of China's best-known political detainee, Wei Jingsheng, on the eve of the International Olympic Committee's deliberations about whether or not to hold the 2000 Olympics in China. However, China's bid failed, and soon Wei was back in prison.

China's management of the human rights problem is often clumsy. In 1995, when Jiang Zemin and Clinton were about to meet in New York, it happened that the New York Public Library was exhibiting materials relating to the Tiananmen incident. That outraged Jiang, who tried to have the meeting moved out of town. In this instance the added publicity probably swelled crowds at the library. In a similar case, in 1996 Beijing made a major issue of what would otherwise been a routine movie about the Dalai Lama, called *Kundun*. Such crudeness probably costs China's leaders more than is gained, but sometimes they can inflict damage on their adversaries, resulting in a lose-lose situation. In the *Kundun* case, after some hesitation the Walt Disney Company went on to distribute the movie. (Beijing appears not to have realized that backing down would have been devastating to the company's international reputation.) Disney, which is the world's second-largest media and entertainment company, is big enough to survive whatever punishment Beijing dishes out, which may mean lost opportunities to do business in China.

But the main victims of any success Beijing has in manipulating the international media are the would-be audience. Sometimes that audience includes Chinese, as when, in 1994, Beijing persuaded Rupert Murdoch to drop the BBC from his News Corporation satellite television service in northern Asia. That, rather than the Disney scenario, is the usual pattern when international media deal with dictatorships like China's. Although Beijing still tries to jam unwelcome foreign broadcasts[16] and block disapproved Internet sites, the advent of new technologies makes it increasingly difficult to keep the public in the dark.

The IR Costs of Human Rights Abuses

China's human rights shortfall has resulted in costs to the country's international relationships. To compensate for their unpopularity at home, the nation's leaders have long counted on the country's global standing, which requires that they enjoy respect abroad. At one time the idea that China represented the vanguard of socialism carried weight in some international circles, but it no longer does. With the Cold War over, the PRC has lacked the kind of leverage it used to have (casting the swing vote between East and West). When China's human rights abuses began to receive attention from abroad, the international legitimacy of the regime was placed in jeopardy.

Tiananmen mobilized many countries that had hitherto scrupulously avoided the issue of human rights in China, and changed the way foreigners viewed the PRC as an international actor. Until 1989, foreign nations needed to be concerned only with the Chinese *government*. In that sense, dealing with China had been simple. The assumption was that the Chinese "masses" would not generally oppose their government. But polls taken in spring 1989 revealed that the antiestablishment student demonstrators had almost universal support at least among the populace of the capital. Suddenly, everyone from the White House to the Kremlin was confronted with a situation in which there were at least two Chinas: the official one and the one manifested by the millions of demonstrators. China would never be as simple to deal with as it had been.

During the 1990s the conduct of the country's relations with other countries has required the reallocation of a significant portion of China's precious diplomatic capital to dealing with the human rights concerns. In 1991 the United States began to engage China in human rights–related talks, which sometimes resulted in responses, however minimal, on the part of the Chinese side. At first there appeared to be little benefit in all this for China's leaders, and in 1992 Beijing unilaterally suspended these discussions and refused to accept a list of prisoners on whom the lame-duck administration of President George Bush wanted information. The top leadership went as far as to instruct various ministries not to discuss human rights matters with American officials at all. But with the election of Bill Clinton, Beijing must have understood that the issue would not go away.

In another arena, pressure was being applied by international lending agencies. U.S. law already instructed U.S. representatives in such organizations as the World Bank to oppose loans to countries guilty of gross violations of human rights. Thus, immediately after the 1989 massacre, the United States prevented any World Bank loans to China, though later it only abstained from votes concerning such loans rather than blocking them. In the Asian Development Bank (ADB), Washington tried to take a more consistently tough stand. However, by the end of 1992 relations between the ADB and China had been "normalized." Japan (the major voice in the ADB) was proving reluctant to use financial muscle to promote human rights in China. Things did not go so smoothly for the World Bank, which from the mid 1990s on found itself under fire for supposedly funding forced-labor prison camps.[17]

Human Rights and International Business

As for *private* investment in China by foreigners, even as a strictly practical matter, the overwhelming majority of the investors, including those from Asia, usually take human rights into consideration at least to some extent before committing funds. Since the 1989 crackdown it has been more difficult for American companies to invest in China, because the Overseas Private Investment Corporation ceased insuring such investments. Still, many businesses have gone ahead. Once established in China, a growing minority of businesspersons are now willing to actually raise human rights issues with the Chinese. A strong pro-rights stand has been taken by many international companies, including Levi Strauss, Phillips, Van Heusen, Sears Roebuck, and Reebok International. The latter, for example, declared that the company simply would not operate under martial law conditions; it would encourage free association among employees and was determined to keep politics out of the workplace and to resist government attempts to have "problem citizens" dismissed from employment.

Some companies have gone even further and reduced their presence in China. Levi Strauss has done this explicitly because of "pervasive violations of basic human rights."[10] Less explicitly, in 1997 Holiday Inn announced that it would not be renewing its partnership under which it ran the main hotel in Tibet's capital, Lhasa. Holiday Inn's decision to end its decade-long presence at this distinctive location came after much flagrant violation of Tibetans' human rights, and international campaigns calling attention to the company's alleged complicity in the sinification of Tibet at the expense of the Tibetans' cultural rights. The hotel had enabled China to benefit from high-spending tourists, while controlling their movements, local contacts, and communications with the outside world. Although Holiday Inn did not give any reason for leaving Tibet, it hardly needed to. The withdrawal will doubtless restore Holiday Inn's reputation with those concerned with such issues, and cost Beijing some loss of face.

China is not an easy country for foreigners to do business in. McDonald's had to fight for two years to get the local Beijing authorities to compensate it for arbitrarily breaking the twenty-year lease that the company had on its flagship site. Even more serious was the arrest in 1996 of a Shell executive for "obtaining state secrets." When a foreign businessperson is jailed, it complicates and may even poison the relations between his country and China. As one journalist has commented, "Human rights and business rights are just flip sides of the same coin, and the coin is called 'the rule of law.'"[19]

There is a substantial body of international human rights law that is supposed to govern economic transactions and enterprises. For example, the human rights covenants contain many protections for workers. Building on these, various Western countries have enacted laws that try to reach into the foreign workplace. In 1994 the U. S. Congress passed a trade law that cited "internationally recognized worker rights," which included the right of free assembly, collective bargaining, and decent working conditions and living standards, and prohibited forced labor and child labor. Such standards not only presumably limit what international businesses may do but also require importers to avoid indirectly encouraging violations by buying products from noncomplying firms. However, as legal scholars Diane Orentlicher and Timothy Gelatt observed, even though such principles "have a solid foundation in international law, they still have scant support in international practice—at least in the sense of universal compliance with these standards by multinational corporations. Indeed, the globalization of labor markets has, at least in some areas, served to drive down wage levels and to that extent has undermined international assurances of adequate pay."[20]

One particularly knotty (but somewhat overblown) issue involves international commerce in the products of prison labor. Although the Chinese argue that everyone, including a prisoner, has an obligation to work, the conventions of the International Labor Organization prohibit "forced" labor. However, as long as conditions are humane (which in China they often are not), most of the world's prisoners would probably prefer to work than to sit idly in cells. Assuming that the people are legitimately imprisoned in the first place, it can be argued that requiring a prisoner to work does not in itself amount to a human rights violation. A dozen American states have prison labor regimes that operate according to principles analogous to those that are supposed to be in effect in China. It is not against American law to export products made in U.S. prisons, and it is often done. Jeans (marketed as "Prison Blues") made by Oregon prisoners are quite popular in Asia. So the Chinese authorities certainly have a point when they argue that much of the international objection to prison-made exports derives from economic rather than human rights considerations; indeed it was U.S. trade rather than humanitarian concerns that underlay the relevant section of the 1930 Smoot-Hawley Act forbidding prison-made imports. American workers are understandably unhappy at the prospect of having to compete with virtually unpaid Chinese prison labor. Thus, the U.S. Customs service has been turning away such products as diesel engines, machine presses, steel pipe, socket wrenches, and socks. The United States has also sought, with very limited success, to inspect the prisons where exported products are believed to be made. The spirit of Smoot-Hawley notwithstanding, in recent years explicit congressional arguments about "forced labor" have been cast (or at least rationalized) in human rights terms.

As for trade in general, Beijing resents U.S. congressional efforts to make low tariffs contingent on China's passing any human rights test, arguing that this effort masks more sinister intent. Indeed, many Americans, both businesspeople and labor unions, do have an interest in limiting Chinese imports. However, the less self-serving arguments for denying low-tariff treatment have to do with China's poor human rights record. George Bush, who had once been a de facto U.S. ambassador to China, pursued a policy of "constructive engagement" toward China. That meant largely unfettered trade, and Congressional attempts to impose sanctions failed for lack of the two-thirds majority needed to override a presidential veto. Of course, even Bush could not neglect the human rights issue entirely, but his half-hearted attempts to raise the issue with the Chinese were brushed aside. Démarches on behalf of political prisoners were ignored, and promises to stop exporting prison-made products were broken. As one American official ruefully acknowledged, the Chinese seemed determined to "rub our noses in it."[21]

Had the Chinese authorities been more forthcoming, it is possible that human rights would have receded as an issue between the two countries, or at any rate between the Republicans and the Democrats. As it was, the stonewalling of the Chinese only fueled the debate on American policy toward China. During the 1992 presidential campaign, candidate Bill Clinton found himself presented with a rare opportunity, which he fully exploited. He was blisteringly critical of Bush's coddling of the "butchers of Beijing." He said that most-favored-nation treatment for the PRC should be denied on human rights grounds; the remaining problems in U.S.-China relations were to be dealt with by other means. As president, Clinton first seemed to place human rights on an at least equal footing with trade. He quickly appointed as top human rights officer in the State Department a man with a strong human rights background, John Shattuck. The administration began by taking a hard line, and it seemed to get some results. For example, at the Seattle summit in 1993 Clinton made his human rights concerns public, even naming the Chinese prisoners he wanted to see freed; many were. But two years later, when he met Jiang Zemin in New York, it was back to Bush-style "quiet diplomacy"; there was no public naming of prisoners. The U.S. economic relationship with China had been "depoliticized." The Chinese commended Clinton for his nonconfrontational approach; China's human rights situation proceeded to deteriorate.

Although when he extended normal trade privileges (MFN[22]) to China in 1993 Clinton had said that renewal the following year would be conditional on Chinese progress in the human rights area, in fact the policy of linking trade and human rights was short-lived, and it was back to "constructive engagement." Combining free trade with diplomatic pressure was tried for a few years. In 1997, however, it had to be admitted that this combination had failed to promote human rights. China's leaders were winning victory after victory in their bid to stand up to international pressure to improve the rights of Chinese citizens. Linkage had been more effective than "delinkage" in encouraging China's leaders to respect the Chinese people's rights.

The U.S. market is China's largest, so in theory withholding MFN status would be a powerful weapon for promoting human rights in China. But raising tariffs would result in Chinese retaliation, adversely affecting both American businesses that export to China and also Americans doing business inside China. Furthermore, it would be difficult to tailor sanctions so that they impact the state and spare the more pluralistic, marketized sector of the Chinese economy. Both political parties have been in disarray on the issue, Clinton having reversed himself, and the Republicans having difficulty devising sanctions that would not adversely affect their business constituency. Although U.S. public opinion strongly favors putting human rights ahead of trade, and congressional opponents of MFN have been gaining ground (thanks in part to the efforts of the Religious Right), such considerations have never prevailed, because even more powerful interests keep pressing Washington to put trade ahead of human rights.

While the MFN battles have been raging in Washington, other countries, such as France, have been busy making their own little compromises with China. In May 1997 French President Jacques Chirac went on a trade-promoting trip to Beijing and Shanghai. It was in the middle of a French election, and there were many home constituencies to satisfy, including those interested in human rights. Thus, Chirac did "mention" the cases of seventeen imprisoned dissidents, and specifically asked for the release of Wei Jingsheng and Wang Dan.[23] Despite France's long tradition of aiding the victims of human rights abuses in China, however, the priority now was emphatically on trade.

Overall, Europe has actually been quite divided on these issues. Some countries have persisted in emphasizing China's human rights problems. For example, in the mid-1990s, the German and Danish legislatures each held major hearings about human rights in Tibet; the hearings resulted in very strained relations between these countries and China. Denmark, famous for its protection of Jews during World War II, carries more moral weight than its size would otherwise indicate; it has pushed the issue of human rights issue in China at international forums. But the tiny country's vulnerability makes it a lightning rod for Chinese retaliation. As one Danish trader remarked, "What happens is that our Chinese trading partners get orders to stop trading with us, and so refrain from handing in new orders . . . ; no company engaged in China is in any doubt that the political conditions affect trade."[24] Thus, the more most Western countries have tried to "delink" human rights and trade, the more Beijing has insisted on linking them.

Role of the United Nations

Since 1981, PRC representatives have participated in the human rights work of the United Nations. They have been particularly active in efforts concerning the rights of children and migrant workers. China's representatives have also participated in various working groups concerned with such problems as torture. Actually though, the PRC became involved in the international human rights regime rather warily and wanted to do so only to the extent that so doing would expand, rather than diminish, national sovereignty. Thus, in their work in international human rights organs, China's representatives have defended a country's right to impose the death penalty, and worked to limit freedoms in the communications area. They have also tended to resist outside intervention in the world's trouble spots. For example, in international relief efforts, China's leaders give sovereignty considerations priority over the nutritional rights of starving people. In the early 1990s China either opposed or only reluctantly tolerated international efforts to compel local authorities to admit relief missions in such places as Bosnia and Somalia. In 1995 China did support human rights resolutions concerning Bosnia, which seemed to signal some shift in attitude.[25] But in 1997 China's representatives declared that the perpetrators of the Cambodian genocide were beyond the reach of any international tribunal. "The question of Pol Pot is Cambodia's internal affair" and "should be decided by Cambodians themselves without foreign interference."[26]

The United Nations has many commissions and agencies concerned with various aspects of human rights. For example, there is the Subcommission on Prevention of Discrimination and Protection of Minorities, which in 1989 voted to criticize the way various nationalities were treated in China; this marked the first time that a permanent member of the Security Council had been censured on human rights grounds. China is always very sensitive to such initiatives. When, in 1997, imprisoned journalist Gao Yu was awarded the UNESCO/Guillermao Cano World Press Freedom Prize, China's spokesman called it "gross interference" in China's internal affairs (Gao Yu had published analyses of how Communist Party leaders controlled government decisionmaking) and demanded that the action be reversed. Although UNESCO has not had a strong reputation for defending press freedom, the award stood.

There are also special UN events that bear on the subject of human rights. The most important in this decade occurred in 1993, when the organization sponsored a World Conference on Human Rights. Various governments including China's had managed to structure the event in a way that would soften any outcome. First, regional meetings were held, Asia's meeting taking place in Bangkok and heavily influenced by China. Although Japan held out for a more modern construction of human rights principles, the thirty-eight other participants voted to weaken UN efforts in the area of human rights: There should be no interference in any country's internal affairs, and the UN should not condemn individual countries' human rights records. Although development rights were supposed to be given priority, there was hardly any discussion of human rights–related ecological problems like deforestation (which impacts so severely on the lives of many Asians), nor was there serious discussion of issues like child labor or women's rights. Though there were strong dissenting opinions,[27] the prevailing view among the governments represented at Bangkok was that human rights concepts were an alien Western import. The universality of human rights principles seemed to be undermined by the assertion that national cultures must be respected. But all this was just the prevailing *intergovernmental* view; at a parallel conference a large number of Asian NGOs, most of which dissented from the governments' view, made it obvious that the so-called common Asian values was a concept of the powerful, not necessarily of the majority of Asians.

When the final conference was held in Vienna, China's large delegation took an even harder line than it had in Bangkok. The conference might well have collapsed had it not been for the intervention of its secretary-general, Ibrahima Fall. Thus, much to their disappointment, China's representatives could not substantially undermine the international human rights regime. They and their allies were able to delay the creation of the post of UN High Commission for Human Rights, but that was achieved in New York later in the year at a meeting of the General Assembly.

In 1995, in what most Chinese hoped would be a proud moment for the nation, China hosted the Fourth United Nations World Conference on Women. Again, there were really two conferences, the NGOs' and the governments'. Because of a variety of problems, not unrelated to the limited respect that the government had for human rights generally, things went rather sour. To be sure, the governments' conference, held in Beijing, was predictably uneventful. But the NGO conference was another matter. China's leaders had been very wary about that event and worked hard to manipulate it. For example, in violation of its responsibilities on such an occasion, China used the visa process to screen out some unwanted delegates. And those "undesirables" who did manage to slip in were prevented from holding press conferences. Indeed, just before it opened, the NGO conference was moved to the distant and ill-equipped suburb of Huairou, apparently to prevent "unauthorized" (by the government) participation by Chinese, and to insulate the conferees from the nation's realities. Furthermore, the Chinese authorities confiscated handouts, disrupted meetings, and prevented protest demonstrations. All of that was in violation of UN rules for international conferences; it would probably be a long time before organizers of another NGO conference would want to hold their event in China. But the Chinese government seemed generally satisfied with the overall outcome because the governments' conference afforded a good propaganda opportunity. For example, they roundly condemned the "inglorious record" of the United

States regarding women's rights.[28] Scarcely mentioned by the governments' representatives were such Chinese problems as the kidnapping of women and female infanticide. As hosts, the Chinese were also able to manipulate the event by high-profiling preferred leaders (like former president George Bush and his wife, Barbara), while snubbing the less-favored (such as Hillary Clinton, wife of the sitting U.S. president).

The main responsibility for overseeing the world's human rights actually falls to the UN's Geneva-based Human Rights Commission. Until 1996 Europe and the United States were fairly united regarding human rights problems in China, sponsoring resolutions on the subject at the commission each year following the Tiananmen incident. These resolutions did not survive the parliamentary process, and in fact, China's representatives were usually able to prevent any consideration of them. The only exception occurred in 1995, when there was a full-scale debate that stung the Chinese government. Though the motion to criticize the Chinese government was defeated, the PRC was upset that it had been considered at all. During the course of the next year the government invited to China a stream of national leaders from around the world, offering them many inducements in a successful effort to gain their support, or at least neutrality, at Geneva the next year. On the eve of the 1996 meetings, a cocky China was publishing articles in *People's Daily* under such titles as "The Hell with U.S. 'Human Rights Diplomacy.'"[29] At the same time the United States began to waver, and with the commission's having greater representation by nondemocratic countries, China's diplomats (demonstrating considerable parliamentary and political skill) were able to prevent consideration of what was actually an anemic resolution.

By 1997, the deep fissures within the European Union became palpable. After Denmark introduced another mildly worded resolution concerning political imprisonment and lack of freedom of expression in the PRC, China's leaders engaged in the kind of bullying they often accuse others of. "If Denmark insists on doing this, it will end up the biggest loser," warned Foreign Ministry spokesperson Shen Guofang. Copenhagen should "think seriously about the consequences of such action. I can say that relations will be severely damaged in the political and economic areas."[30] After that, the resolution had few supporters. Latin Americans, for example, were afraid that trade ties with China would be adversely affected if they voted in favor of human rights (as most of them actually seemed to prefer). As for Denmark, China made good on its threat about "a rock that will smash down on the Danish government's head,"[31] moving quickly to cancel a high-level exchange that had been previously agreed upon.

The most important result of all this was the disarray and credibility of the Human Rights Commission itself, an organ that had seemed to be gaining stature and influence since the end of the Cold War. For a short time, the Netherlands (which held the rotating presidency of the commission) actually refused to allow consideration of human rights motions pertaining to other countries, as a protest against the China vote. For its part, the PRC is working to "reform" the commission—shrinking its already inadequate budget, diverting the focus away from civil liberties issues, reducing the now-vital role of NGOs, and weakening the commission's research arm, the Human Rights Centre.

The Self-Determination of Peoples

In both international human rights covenants, the very first articles assert: "All peoples have the right to self-determination. By virtue of that right they freely determine their political status and freely pursue their economic, social and cultural development. . . . The States Parties to the present Covenant . . . shall promote the realization of the right of self-determination." Beijing has sometimes been at the forefront of efforts to implement this provision in other parts of the world, but it has always denied its applicability to Hong Kong, Taiwan, or to the non–ethnic Chinese parts of the PRC. For many years, the double standard proved tenable. More recently, however, with China more a world player, awkward situations have arisen. For example, in 1992 Beijing decided that it had to resist UN efforts to protect Iraq's ethnic-minority regions lest a precedent be set whereby one day China might find international forces defending, say, the Tibetans against the Chinese. All UN peacekeeping operations, says Beijing, "must be based on respect for the principle of state sovereignty."[32]

The second white paper (1995) paid considerable attention to the question of PRC ethnic minorities, claiming that their rights were being safeguarded and that of course their territories belonged to China. To be sure, Beijing does have an arguable historical claim to most of China's ethnic-minority territories, but at least in the case of Tibet, the claim is weak. The Chinese now base their territorial claims on the fact that long ago the Mongols and Manchus conquered both China and Tibet. But prior to the Mongol invasions China had recognized Tibetan sovereignty, and during the two most recent periods when China itself was under ethnic Chinese rule (the Ming Dynasty and the Republic), the present "Tibet Autonomous Region" was independent. In fact, in the 1930s the Communists acknowledged the Tibetans' right to be independent. But thereafter the Communists' thinking changed, and in 1951 the Tibetans, losing in the battlefield, were forced agree to Chinese sovereignty over Tibet in a Seventeen-Point Agreement—the ultimate "unequal treaty."

What the international human rights covenants seem to say is that those who form a "people" of a disputed territory with a plausible argument for sovereignty should decide for themselves whether they are to be an independent country or annexed to another country. Although it is not made clear what a "people" is, in 1961 the UN General Assembly declared that the Tibetans met all the requirements for self-determination. Furthermore, Tibetans have suffered egregious violations of their civil liberties. Indeed, vast numbers were killed, and during the Cultural Revolution nearly all Lamaist temples were destroyed. These and subsequent human rights violations exacerbated the already-strong anti-Chinese sentiment. The government's reaction to the territory's political problems has usually been to keep many politically minded Tibetans in prison, though in recent years there has been increasing emphasis on developing the area and integrating Tibet into the Chinese economy.

The issue of human rights violations in Tibet has come before the UN Human Rights Commission in Geneva. European countries have provided strong support for resolutions sharply critical of China's record in the region. One such resolution in 1992 was successfully opposed by the United States, China, and the latter's Third World supporters because it was ambiguous on the self-determination question. The view of the opposition, that the integrity of the state took precedence over the rights of national self-determination, prevailed. In spite of such occasional American support, China complains that Western concern for Tibetans' largely nonexistent human rights problems is a cover for imperialistic designs. This view is perhaps understandable, given Britain's historic meddling in Tibet and CIA assistance to Tibetan guerrillas in the 1950s and 1960s. But Washington's position changed during the Nixon administration, and ever since then the State Department's line has been that Tibet is part of China. Tibetans do have their champions, including some in the U.S. Congress, which has passed resolutions affirming that Tibet is an occupied country. In 1997 Congress successfully pressed the State Department to create the position of "special coordinator" for Tibetan affairs. It was provocative step, bound to cheer Tibetans and outrage the Chinese. Reflecting the sensitivity of the matter, the senior State Department official describing the new position said that the person would only "see that the religious freedom of Tibetans is promoted and that their ethnicity is respected." The new coordinator would have a daunting task. At about the same time as the announcement of the new office, China began insisting that Buddhism, already being discouraged in China proper, was foreign to Tibet; the region's real culture there was declared "socialist"; the policy was reinforced by book bannings and arrests.[33]

The question of self-determination for the PRC's other nationalities has been given even less international consideration. This is true, for example, in the case of the vast territory that some Uygur Turks call Eastern Turkestan, and the Chinese call their "New Territories" (Xinjiang). There is growing sympathy for these and other Muslim nationalities on the part of Middle Eastern countries such as Syria and newly independent Central Asian countries, but there appears to be no substantial support on the part of foreign governments for actual separation. Thus, by the mid-1990s Beijing was taking a rather relaxed, even positive view of international Islam.

There is no longer any question of Chinese sovereignty over the former British colony of Hong Kong. Nonetheless, ever since the 1989 massacre, the rights of the people there have been a serious concern locally and internationally. The colony's British rulers took note and appointed the liberal Chris Patten as the last colonial governor. Patten made important institutional changes, with a view to the permanent establishment of new democratic institutions.[34] Beijing found itself locked in unexpected battles on two fronts: the British and Hong Kong's new democratically elected legislature. The former made a tearful departure on July 1, 1997; members of the latter were summarily dismissed and replaced by Beijing appointees, despite the promise that the new Special Administrative Region would enjoy a high degree of autonomy.

The international community has become committed to monitoring the human rights situation in Hong Kong. The U.S. Congress made it a matter of official concern by passing the 1992 McConnell Act, according to which the United States is to promote Hong Kong's freedom and prosperity. A number of other countries, including Australia and members of the European Union, have committed themselves to observe the situation to see if Beijing keeps promises made in the 1984 Sino-British Declaration to respect basic freedoms there.

The issue of self-determination may yet become relevant to the *Taiwan* situation, but this is not now the case. That is because the government of Taiwan does not deny that the island is part of China.

Conclusion

The fate of human rights in China will be determined largely by the course of political events within the country, with international standards and foreign involvement playing a relatively minor role. But that reality does not prevent the issue from impacting on China's current international relations. China's leaders see human rights as an instrument used selectively by foreigners to pursue other foreign policy objectives. But as China's economic system increasingly comes to resemble that of capitalist countries, the conflict between that country and the democracies is, as much as anything else, a struggle of contending political ideologies. That conflict mirrors a similar struggle going on within China itself. The domestic proponents of democracy are portrayed by the rulers as criminals, the foreigners as anti-China.

The leaders of the PRC say they are determined that the country will become more and more "open." If it does, the government will be increasingly confronted with challenges to its human rights practices. Already, pressures come from many quarters. Some former Soviet satellites are pressing Beijing to respect human rights. Some of those nations whose statehood was restored when the Soviet Union collapsed tend to sympathize with the national aspirations of the PRC's non-Chinese nationalities, and China has had to work hard to neutralize those countries. Right on China's doorstep, South Korea and Taiwan stand as glaring evidence that there is nothing un-Asian or un-Chinese about democracy. Although China's human rights situation has seen much improvement since the 1970s, many other dictatorships went much further and actually transformed themselves into democracies. The ironic result has been that China, whose human rights abuses had been ignored for so long and are now actually diminished, today comes across as one of the world's worst offenders.

International pressures on China to democratize can only increase. One can expect to hear from all sorts of transnational groupings, formal and informal. For example, foreign correspondents, wherever they are from, are apt to insist on the rights of their readers to receive unfettered news (which is impossible if journalists are regularly expelled and their Chinese contacts persecuted), and they will also make appeals on behalf of Chinese journalists. International religious movements will press for the rights of China's Buddhists, Muslims, and Christians.[35] Scholars engaged in research will press for academic freedom for themselves and for their Chinese colleagues. Some foreigners will be arrested (for legitimate reasons or otherwise), which will bring judicial procedures under international scrutiny. International movements (women, labor unionists, environmentalists, gays, and others) are becoming more interested in the problems of their Chinese counterparts. The Internet brings scattered, like-minded activists together in a way that never used to be possible.

And such activities are felt within China, for despite Beijing's best efforts to the contrary, the issue of human rights has become increasingly internationalized. For example, prison wardens are warned that there are international standards that apply to prison conditions and that the world is watching. Political prisoners, especially those who have international reputations, sometimes receive less-harsh treatment than others. Ironically, however, internationalization sometimes has the effect of strengthening the power of the central government. The center's policies regarding the administration of prisons are not as inhumane as the practices of the local officials, who are often out of control. Moreover, "You are embarrassing your country" is apt to be an effective argument in as proud and nationalistic a land as China.

The moral force underpinning human rights diplomacy gives it a legitimacy that even China's leaders have had to recognize. Increasingly, they mouth the principles (however insincerely) and hide their transgressions (though less successfully now than during the Mao era). The game requires considerable investment of bureaucratic and intellectual energy. The government has even organized pseudo-NGOs to interface with NGOs in international forums. One might suppose that the diplomatic capital that has had to be diverted to handle this issue could better be spent in other ways, but that is not the perspective of China's leaders. They must have looked with horror on the trials of two former South Korean rulers in 1996, realizing that "there but for the grace of God . . ." Had Hu Yaobang survived in office, he might have followed in the path of Taiwan's once-brutal ruler Chiang Ching-kuo and pointed the country in the direction of democracy. But China's present rulers have gone too far in the other direction for this to be a likely scenario. Now they are interested primarily in perpetuating their power by any means, and they have succeeded in forging alliances with similarly situated rulers around the world, all of whom fear that a broadened political process would threaten their power. They are all probably right.

Notes

1. Ambassador Li Daoyu, remarks to the UN General Assembly's Human Rights Committee, December 2, 1992. United Press International, December 2, 1992.

2. See Ann Kent, "Waiting for Rights: China's Human Rights and China's Constitutions, 1949–1989," *Human Rights Quarterly* 13:2, May 1991, esp. pp. 193–199.

3. The number seventeen, which cannot be confirmed, is stated in the second white paper on human rights (Foreign Broadcast Information Service, China [hereafter: FBIS-CH], June 10, 1996, p. 39). Only a partial list is supplied (eight conventions and three protocols).

4. Chen Yali, "China Respects Human Rights," *China Daily*, March 14, 1996, p. 4, FBIS-CH, March 15, 1996, p. 4.

5. According to a UN assessment, China's level of development, compared to other countries, actually slipped from 82nd place in 1991 to 108th place in 1996. *Human Development Report* (New York: Oxford University Press, 1991 and 1996), pp. 120 and 136 respectively.

6. See James D. Seymour and Richard Anderson, *New Ghosts, Old Ghosts: Prisons and Labor Reform Camps in China* (White Plains, N.Y.: M. E. Sharpe, 1997), indexed under "health conditions."

7. Gong Min (pseud.), "Letter to President Carter," translated in James D. Seymour, ed., *The Fifth Modernization: China's Human Rights Movement, 1978–1979* (Stanfordville, N.Y: Earl Coleman, 1980), pp. 227–239.

8. Although a few governments did support Beijing in its crackdown on dissidents, the overwhelming majority opposed it, though in widely varying degrees.

For more on the subject, see Seymour, "The International Reaction to the Crackdown in China," in *China Information* (Leiden), April 1990, pp 1–14

9. The right to emigrate is of special concern to Americans. The Jackson-Vanik Amendment to the 1974 U.S. Trade Act states that most-favored-nation (moderate-tariff) trading with nonmarket economies is normally to be conditional on a country's human rights practices, particularly with respect to the right to emigrate. When the law was passed, Congress did not have China in mind. At any rate, the emigration issue is somewhat academic because if Beijing were to honor this right (which it does not), only a small portion of would-be emigrants would be accepted as immigrants in other countries.

10. Chinese delegate Wu Jianmin to the UN Human Rights Commission, *New York Times*, April 24, 1996.

11. Article by Zhong Heshi, *People's Daily*, April 1, 1996, p. 6, FBIS-CH, April 9, 1996, p. 3.

12. New China News Agency [hereafter: NCNA], April 24, 1996, FBIS-CH, April 25, 1996, p. 2.

13. Translated as "Human Rights in China," in both *Beijing Review* 34:44, November 4, 1991, pp. 8–45; and in FBIS-CH, supplement, November 21, 1991, pp. 1–29. Cited hereafter as "White Paper 1," with pagination referring to the FBIS version.

14. Opposition to the white paper was especially pronounced on college campuses. See "Statement on the Human Rights Issue in China," which appeared as a poster at Beijing University. *Ming Bao*, November 16, 1991, p. 6, FBIS-CH, November 18, 1991. Exiled dissidents dismissed it as "all lies."

15. White Paper 1, pp. 6 and 13.

16. In January 1998, Congress passed a bill to more than double the budget for Radio Free Asia's China broadcasting service. Broadcasts were to be in four languages: Mandarin, Cantonese, Tibetan, and Uygur. Beijing had condemned the proposal as an attempt to "impose Western-style human rights and democracy on China." *China News Digest*, October 3, 1997 (via Internet).

17. Harry Wu's charges against the World Bank are detailed in "*Xinjiang laogai ying huu Shi Yin de qian*" [Xinjiang labor reform camps spend World Bank funds], *Shijie ribao* (New York), October 24, 1995. His charges were renewed in 1997, according to Agence France Presse, September 21, 1997 (via Internet). For an evaluation of these charges, see Seymour and Anderson, *New Ghosts, Old Ghosts*, pp. 228–230. For Beijing's reaction, see NCNA, December 22, 1995, FBIS-CH, December 26, 1995, p. 1.

18. Diane F. Orentlicher and Timothy A. Gelatt, "Public Law, Private Actors: The Impact of Human Rights on Business Investors in China," *Northwestern Journal of International Law and Business* 14:1, Fall 1993, p. 107. See also pp. 117–118.

19. Thomas L. Friedman, *New York Times*, December 4, 1996, p. A29.

20. Orentlicher and Gelatt, "Public Law, Private Actors," p. 116.

21. *New York Times*, June 3, 1992, p. A13.

22. In American parlance, the normal minimal tariff regime is known as most-favored-nation treatment, or more commonly MFN.

23. A half year later, Wei Jingsheng was released from prison and expelled from China. However, this seems to have been due more to American than to French pressure. At this writing (February 1998) Wang Dan remains in prison.

24. Palle Steenbol, head of the Chinese sales office of F. L. Smidth. *Politiken,* November 9, 1995 (via Internet).

25. NCNA, December 22, 1995, FBIS-CH, December 22, 1995, p. 11.

26. Chinese Foreign Ministry spokesman Cui Tiankai, quoted in Barbara Crossette, "Beijing Says It Won't Go Along with Creation of Pol Pot Tribunal," *New York Times,* June 24, 1997.

27. Somchai Homlaor, a Thai and head of an NGO called Forum Asia, said of Asia's leaders: "Actually, they are the ones who are importing their development policies from the West: consumerism, capitalism, investment, industrialization. Human rights violations in this country are a by-product of that development: environmental problems, deforestation, the displacement of people, the gap between rich and poor." *New York Times,* March 1, 1996.

28. NCNA, April 11, 1977; BBC *Summary of World Broadcasts,* April 15, 1997, FE/2893, p. G/1.

29. Article by Zhong Heshi, *People's Daily,* April 1, 1996, p. 6, FBIS-CH, April 9, 1996, pp. 3–5.

30. Paul Lewis, "China Warns Denmark on Resolution," *New York Times,* April 8, 1997.

31. Associated Press, April 15, 1997 (via Internet).

32. UN delegate Cheng Jinye, as paraphrased by NCNA, November 13, 1992, FBIS-CH, November 16, 1992, p. 1.

33. Detailed in Tibet Information Network, "Cultural Policy: History Book Banned, Tibetan Culture Declared 'Non-Buddhist,'" August 15, 1997 (via Internet). More information on Tibet is available from the Internet site gopher://gopher.cc.columbia.edu:71/11/clioplus/scholarly/SouthAsia/Tibet.

34. See James D. Seymour, "Hong Kong: The Outlook for Human Rights," *American Asian Review,* Spring 1996, and "Hong Kong's Politics Under Chinese Rule: A Preliminary Assessment," *American Asian Review,* Winter 1997–1998.

35. At this writing, the U.S. Congress appears poised to pass the Wolf-Specter bill, requiring the president to establish a White House Office of Religious Persecution Monitoring, and to make protection of religious rights in all countries a high priority. As presently drafted, the law would mandate certain economic sanctions against countries where religious persecution takes place (forbidding exports of items that facilitate persecution, such as Internet surveillance software). The United States would be required to vote and work against loans from intergovernmental lending agencies to an offending government. Special provision would be made for granting asylum to victims of religious persecution. The main focus is on protecting Christians in such countries as China. Steven A. Holmes, "G.O.P. Leaders Back Bill on Religious Persecution," *New York Times,* September 11, 1997, p. A3; and A. M. Rosenthal, "The Right Message," *New York Times,* September 16. 1997, p. A31.

11

China and the Multilateral Economic Institutions

WILLIAM R. FEENEY

For about two decades, China has pursued a long-term economic development strategy based upon expanded domestic markets; accelerated capital formation; far-reaching monetary, fiscal, and banking reform; and greatly increased reliance on foreign official and private assistance, loans, credits, direct investment, and trade, all within the framework of the global capitalist economic system. Critical components of China's ambitious program to build a prosperous modern economy have been an acceptance of a market economy (euphemistically called "socialism with Chinese characteristics") and participation in the world economy. If domestic reforms have provided economic incentives and institutional foundations for future prosperity, China's open door policy has brought increased access to foreign capital and expertise as well as the longer-range economic benefits of Ricardo's international trade theory of comparative advantage.[1]

Since 1980 China's modernization policies have involved membership and active participation in a number of multilateral economic institutions (MEIs). Although China has received invaluable technical expertise, technology, and capital resources through the MEIs, membership has also entailed an obligation for China to open its economy and institutions to outside scrutiny, study, evaluation, and suggestions regarding its development strategy. The MEIs include the World Bank Group (WBG)—the International Monetary Fund (IMF), the International Bank for Reconstruction and Development (IBRD), or World Bank, and its affiliated agencies, the International Development Association (IDA), the International Finance Corporation (IFC), and the Multilateral Investment Guarantee Agency (MIGA), and the Asian Development Bank (ADB). Though China has been unable thus far to join the General Agreement on Tariffs and Trade (GATT) and its successor, the World Trade Organization (WTO), in September 1996 China's central bank, along with its counterparts in eight of the world's fastest growing economies, was invited to join the prestigious Swiss-based Bank for International Settlements (BIS).[2] This chapter will focus upon China's participation in the MEIs; on the nature and consequences of those relationships for China's economic policies, institutions, and performance; and on a number of current issues and implications for both China and the world community.

China and the United Nations Development Program

China's working relationship with the United Nations Development Program (UNDP) began soon after the adoption of the Four Modernizations program in late 1978, when China unexpectedly requested economic aid. China's relationship with the UNDP led to significant interaction between the UNDP country office in Beijing and all levels of China's bureaucracy, especially in the area of economic planning. The five-year UNDP country programs (CPs) are designed to coincide with China's Five-Year Plans, which are drawn up by the State Planning Commission, based on sectoral submissions by line ministries, and endorsed by China's State Council and National People's Congress. China's initial ad hoc program was in 1979–1981. By 1995, China had completed three five-year country programs, costing nearly U.S.$269 million in UNDP core funding and covering more than 500 development projects.

CP3 (1991–1995) was a more ambitious UNDP commitment to China than its two CP predecessors and funded more than 200 projects as an adjunct to China's Eighth Five-Year Plan.[3] (See Table 11.1.) Attention was focused on rural economic development and production; energy, transport and communications; industrial productivity and profitability; social development and quality of life; and economic and public administration reform and management. CP4, or the First Country Cooperation Framework (CCF1), is the most ambitious of all UNDP China CPs and coincides with China's Ninth Five-Year Plan, for the period 1996–2000. CCF1 will allocate UNDP core resources of around U.S.$100 million, plus about U.S.$121 million in supplementary cost sharing and other anticipated funds, for a total of U.S.$221 million, or more than U.S.$44 million annually.[4] Whereas prior CPs were primarily sources of hard currency, technology transfer, and industrial renovation, CCF1 will integrate its projects with national programs and United Nations global conferences emphasizing poverty elimination, employment promotion, social development (including health and women's issues), and sustainable development, environment, and energy. UNDP projects will seek to attract greater bilateral government and/or bilateral cost sharing to supplement

TABLE 11.1 UNDP Country Program in China, 1979–2000

Country Program (CP)/Country Cooperation Framework (CCF)	No. of Projects	Funding Sources (Million U.S.$)		
		Core UNDP Funding	Supplementary Cost Sharing PRC/Others	Total Funding (Million U.S.$)
Initial Program (1979–1981)	27	15.0	12.5	27.5
UNDP-CP1 (1981–1985)	150+	66.0	15.0	81.0
UNDP-CP2 (1986–1990)	200+[a]	135.9	27.2	163.1
UNDP-CP3 (1991–1995)	200+[a]	152.8	66.4	219.2
Subtotal	500+[a]	268.7	121.1	490.8
UNDP-CCF1 (1996–2000)[b]	<200	100.0	121.0	221.0

[a]These figures are approximations, since many projects overlap from one CP to another.

[b]CP4/CCF1 anticipates fewer but larger projects funded at about the CP3 level, with a decrease in UNDP core funding. These figures are from the UNDP Web homepage dated October 1996 and represent an increase from UNDP core funding of U.S.$76.3 million and U.S.$197.3 million cited in the UNDP CCF1 projection of July 1996.

NOTE: For a complete earlier breakdown of the UNDP projects, see United Nations Development Programme, *The People's Republic of China: Development Cooperation 1994 Report* (Beijing: Office of the UNDP Resident Representative, December 1995), pp. 89–256, passim.

SOURCES: United Nations Development Programme, *UNDP in China* (New York: UNDP, September 1989), pp. 5–6; United Nations Development Programme, *UNDP Advisory Note on the Third Country Programme for the People's Republic of China (1991–1995)* (Beijing: UNDP, January 1990), pp. 2, 4; UN Document, DP/CP/CPR/3, *Third Country Programme for China*, March 22, 1991, pp. 1, 25; UN Document, DP/CCF/CPR/1, *First Country Cooperation Framework for the People's Republic of China (1996–2000)*, July 8, 1996, p. 21.

core resources funding and will fund fewer but larger projects, which will be targeted more heavily to the poorer geographical areas of southern and western China and be linked somewhat to UNDP regional and subregional projects.[5] When CCF1/CP4 concludes in the year 2000, the UNDP-China partnership will have developed and funded more than 700 projects, costing more than U.S.$711 million.

The UNDP has become China's largest multilateral source of grants for technical assistance, and the China country program represents the UNDP's largest such endeavor. Many of these projects have functioned as precursors to more extensive projects undertaken by other MEIs. The UNDP has been able to mobilize and multiply MEI resources through additional funding from the Chinese and other governments, international agencies, and private sources. The UNDP China program has emphasized specialized training for thousands of Chinese national, provincial, and municipal authorities; educational, agricultural, industrial, banking, and technical personnel; preinvestment surveys; technology transfer; research; beneficial small-scale projects in such diverse areas as energy development, agriculture, fishing, forestry, industry, the environment, information processing, and rural development; and more recently Grameen Bank–type rural microloan credit program workshops. In addition to country programs, the UNDP also provides technical assistance to China through so-called intercountry programs (ICPs), which are aimed at fostering regional and subregional cooperation for common development objectives.[6]

From the outset UNDP projects have been developed through a careful process of study, dialogue, option analysis, and consensus building about what is needed to best advance China's own economic objectives. Especially desirable from the Chinese perspective have been the high level of domestic input and the absence of Group of Seven (G-7) contributor predominance based upon a WBG-style weighted voting system. The UNDP-China relationship, in short, has performed a highly important seeding function that has provided China with some of the world's best technology, training, and expertise. These inputs have progressively solidified the Chinese leadership's commitment to basic domestic economic reform and the open door policy, which in turn have contributed fundamentally to China's enviable modernization success.

China and the World Bank Group

A requisite for China's modernization program has been the availability of large-scale capital assistance and broad expertise to maximize the results of such investment and economic reform. As with the UNDP, China's relationship with the WBG has undergone profound changes over time. As part of its modernization strategy China ended its earlier criticism and joined the WBG in 1980. A vital component of effective WBG assistance to China has been extensive and continuing studies of the Chinese economy. Since its landmark 1983 three-volume analysis of the latter, the World Bank and its affiliated institutions have produced a large number of reports and sector studies that have pinpointed problem areas and impediments and have included multiple recommendations and specific projects to overcome developmental barriers. This information in turn has laid the groundwork for China's far-reaching relationship with WBG institutions.

China and the International Monetary Fund

IMF membership has been eminently beneficial to China in implementing its modernization program. The major functions of the 181-member body are overseeing the international monetary system by promoting exchange rate order and stability; facilitating the balanced growth of international trade; addressing temporary balance-of-payments problems through supplemental credits; and offering a full range of technical assistance in central banking, macroeconomic, tax, and budgeting policies, and statistics. The IMF also operates a training facility (the IMF Institute) for the instruction of fiscal, monetary, budgetary, legal, and foreign exchange affairs personnel from developing countries.

Since 1980 IMF resources and expertise have been available to China to cope with trade and budgetary deficits, inflation, the challenges of privatization and foreign investment, and exchange rate and banking difficulties. This relationship has matured into a mutually productive and cooperative working arrangement that includes annual consultations under Article 4 of the Articles of Agreement; publication of IMF materials in Chinese; extensive technical training for Chinese government personnel through the IMF Institute; and a variety of seminars, colloquia, lectures, and informal discussions in statistical data collection, methodology, accounting procedures, macroeconomic, budgetary, and foreign exchange matters; and trade enhancement tools. Perhaps most important has been an increased understanding and acceptance by the Chinese of the vagaries of budget development and projection, the role of the money supply, the variable nature of business and trade cycles, and the verities of the international merchandise and foreign exchange markets.

On two occasions during the 1980s China made monetary drawings from the IMF. In both instances, China's repayment record has been exemplary. China has also sought IMF assistance to cope with recurrent problems of inflation, budget and trade deficits, and their underlying contributory factors, specifically, excessive money supply (credit) expansion, domestic spending levels, and an overvalued renminbi (RMB) (which is denominated in yuan).

The IMF has been especially helpful in reforming China's foreign exchange regime, but this relationship has not always been smooth.[7] Shortly after China joined the IMF, Beijing adopted a RMB internal settlement rate, creating a dual exchange rate system (viz., a higher rate for foreign trade transactions and a lower official rate for nontradable goods) and a de facto RMB devaluation. The system, which required IMF approval, provided export incentives and restricted imports by reducing RMB overvaluation. In 1985 the internal settlement rate was ended in response to foreign exchange scandals, failure to cut imports and significantly boost exports, and IMF complaints that long-term use violated fund standards. China then introduced a more market-oriented foreign exchange swap market system, whereby foreign-funded companies could convert their RMB earnings to foreign exchange at a more favorable rate and more efficiently allocate scarce foreign exchange among domestic users (primarily importers). However, the end result over time was to encourage foreign exchange hoarding, which drove up the RMB swap rate, especially in response to speculative rumors of fuller RMB convertibility, thus taxing exports and indirectly subsidizing imports. Although authorities tried to address the problem with five subsequent RMB devaluations, China ultimately concluded in 1993 with strong IMF backing that in January 1994 the official and swap market exchange rates would be unified at a higher managed floating exchange rate. This reform received strong IMF endorsement, as did China's decision to comply with Article 8 of the IMF Articles of Agreement to make its currency freely convertible on the current account as of December 1, 1996.[8] To a considerable degree the RMB convertibility decision reflects China's growing confidence level after the three-year austerity program (1993–1995), which cut inflation levels from more than 20 percent to a 1996 four-year low of 10 percent, generated trade surpluses in three of the previous four years, more than tripled net foreign direct investment to nearly U.S.$36 billion, quintupled foreign exchange reserves to some U.S.$100 billion (1993–1996), and cut the debt service ratio by more than 20 percent (see Table 11.2).

One of the most serious threats to China's booming economy and its international trade and credit standing is that of a major banking crisis. This threat has received growing IMF attention. China's banks have been the targets of substantial reforms since the early 1980s, but over the past decade bank loans from the four state-owned commercial banks (SOCBs) have increasingly replaced government subsidies to money-losing state-owned enterprises (SOEs). Unlike banks in developed countries, in China *guanxi* (connections)-based and government-mandated lending has been the rule, and loan foreclosure, bankruptcy, and asset liquidation have been the exceptions. Thus, bad loans have ballooned, and even profitable SOEs are often reluctant to repay loans.[9] The difficulty is that China's 102,000 industrial SOEs absorb 60 percent of national investment, receive subsidies equal to one-third the national budget, employ nearly 70 percent of the urban labor force (about 100 million persons); meanwhile up to 70 percent of the industrial SOEs are losing money, and according to the World Bank only about 8 percent are fundamentally viable. Hence, large numbers of bad loans are threatening to offset a very high—40 percent—domestic savings rate.[10] Although recent prosperity has served to paper over the problem, if large numbers of SOEs are unable to pay the interest on their bank debts, the potential liquidity crisis could exceed 20 percent of GDP and four times the country's bank capital.[11] Although the Fifteenth Party Congress in September 1997 endorsed a SOE sell-off in favor of a share-holding system,[12] China could still conceivably become the next Thailand, South Korea, or Indonesia and similarly a candidate for a massive IMF and foreign bank bailout. On balance, however, IMF membership has greatly aided China in achieving and managing its new status as a major trading nation and an emerging superpower in the global economy and continues to provide an invaluable fallback resource in case of future economic hard times.

China and the World Bank and Its Affiliates

China has also enjoyed a highly beneficial and productive relationship with the World Bank (IBRD) and its IDA, IFC, and MIGA affiliates. The primary purpose of the 180-member World Bank and the 159-member IDA has been to promote economic development and structural reform in the less-developed countries (LDCs) by long-term, large-scale financing of projects. World Bank lending capital is raised by member subscriptions, borrowing on the world capital market, retained earnings, and loan repayments. IDA credits derive mostly from member subscriptions, net IBRD earnings transfers, and periodic replenishments from developed member-states.

China has been singularly successful in securing World Bank financial assistance for its modernization program. From 1981 to mid-1996, Beijing received over U.S.$25.5 billion for 173 projects, with U.S.$16.6 billion in IBRD loans to finance 108 projects and U.S.$8.9 billion in IDA credits for 65 projects. This total represents 8.57 percent of all World Bank lending during the same chronological period. Although the Tiananmen Square incident in June 1989 led to a brief World Bank lending freeze, pressure from business interests, changed views by a number of G-7 and World Bank officials (the latter intent on unclogging the administrative

TABLE 11.2   IMF Assistance to China and Key Economic Indicators, 1981–1996

	1981	*1982*	*1983*	*1984*	*1985*	*1986*	*1987*
IMF assistance to China							
IMF credits[a]	450.0	450.0	0.0	0.0	0.0	597.7	597.7
IMF loans balance[a]	309.5	309.5	309.5	309.5	309.5	309.5	278.5
Repurchase/ repayment[a]	0.0	0.0	450.0	0.0	0.0	31.0	61.9
Balance[a]	759.5	759.5	309.5	309.5	309.5	876.2	814.3
Key economic indicators							
Yuan exchange rate (U.S.$)	1.70	1.89	1.98	2.32	2.94	3.45	3.72
Foreign exchange res. (U.S.$ million)	4.78	11.14	14.48	16.71[c]	11.91	10.51	15.24
GDP (trillion Yuan) (1990 prices)	0.787	0.852	0.9411	.077	1.216	1.320	1.466
GNP per cap. (U.S.$)	300	300	300	300	300	300	300
PPP[d] per cap. (U.S.$)	NA	NA	NA	NA	NA	NA	NA
Balance of payments (U.S.$ billion)	NA	6.31	4.14	0.14	(2.44)	(2.05)	4.78
Net FDI[c] (U.S.$ billion)	0.0	0.43	0.64	1.26	1.66	1.88	2.31
Total external debt (U.S.$ billion)	5.80	8.36	9.61	12.08	16.72	23.75	35.50
Debt service ratio[f]	8.2	8.1	10.1	7.4	7.8	8.4	9.6

[a]All of these statistics are denominated in millions of SDRs. SDRs are reserve assets with a currency value determined by summing the values in U.S. dollars, based on market exchange rates, of a basket of five currencies. These figures may not compute precisely due to the effects of rounding.

[b]Prior to January 1994, the official exchange rate was adjusted according to movements in the value of a basket of internationally traded currencies. After that date the interbank foreign exchange market rate was used. Because these currencies floated against the dollar, there are discrepancies from year to year, even though there was no formal devaluation.

[c]Beginning in December 1984 foreign exchange holdings included foreign government securities. Before July 1992 foreign exchange holdings of the Bank of China were listed. Thereafter, only those of the People's Bank of China are listed.

[d]Purchasing power parity is the number of units of a country's currency required to buy the same amounts of goods and services in the domestic market as one dollar would buy in the United States.

[e]Foreign direct investments.

[f]Ratio between total foreign debt and the value of exports.

1988	1989	1990	1991	1992	1993	1994	1995	1996
597.7	597.7	597.7	298.9	0.0	0.0	0.0	0.0	0.0
216.6	154.7	92.8	30.9	0.0	0.0	0.0	0.0	0.0
61.9	61.9	360.8	329.8	0.0	0.0	0.0	0.0	0.0
752.4	690.5	329.8	0.0	0.0	0.0	0.0	0.0	0.0
3.72	3.77	4.78	5.32	5.51	5.76	8.62[b]	8.35[b]	8.31
17.55	17.02	28.59	42.66	19.44[c]	21.20	51.62	73.58	108.68
1.631	1.702	1.855	2.025	2.314	2.626	2.958	3.270	NA
330	350	370	370	470	490	530	620	NA
NA	NA	NA	1,680	1,910	2,330	2,510	2,920	NA
2.37	(0.48)	12.05	14.54	(2.06)	1.77	30.45	22.47	NA
3.19	3.39	3.49	4.37	11.16	27.52	33.79	35.85	NA
42.44	44.93	55.30	60.26	72.43	85.93	100.46	118.09	NA
9.6	11.3	11.7	11.9	10.2	11.1	8.9	9.9	NA

SOURCES: International Monetary Fund, *International Financial Statistics Yearbook 1996* (Washington, D.C.: IMF, 1996), pp. 27, 31, 35, 37, 39, 63, 138, 279, 280; World Bank, *World Debt Tables, 1990–91, External Debt for Developing Countries*, Vol. 2: *Country Tables* (Washington, D.C.: IBRD, 1991), p. 66; World Bank, *Global Development Finance, 1997*, Vol. 2: *Country Tables* (Washington, D.C.: IBRD, 1997), p. 152; International Bank for Reconstruction and Development, *World Tables, 1992* (Baltimore and London: John Hopkins University Press, 1992), pp. 184–187; and World Bank, *The World Bank Atlas* (Washington, D.C.: IBRD, 1982–1997), passim

pipeline), Iraq's military takeover of Kuwait in August 1990, and China's later tacit support for the use of force to expel Iraq from Kuwait effectively ended G-7 objections to unrestricted World Bank loans. From that point on, World Bank lending to China quickly accelerated to record levels, owing to the large number of delayed projects. After 1992–1993, bank loans and credits to China plateaued at about U.S.$3 billion annually, and in 1995–1996, China was the bank's largest borrower for the fifth consecutive year. However, as China's economy has prospered, its percentage of concessional (soft) IDA credits dropped from 32.1 percent in 1992–1993 to 16.2 percent in 1995–1996 (see Table 11.3). It is planned that China's eligibility for soft money will be phased out entirely by year 1998–1999. In 1995–1996 China was cumulatively the third-largest combined IBRD/IDA borrower after India and Mexico and ranked fifth in IBRD loans and second in IDA credits. However, it should be noted that cumulative World Bank lending to China was the lowest of any of the top ten borrowers on a per capita basis (U.S.$21.09) in mid-1996. That compares to U.S.$49.64 for India and a whopping U.S.$274.84 for Mexico (see Table 11.4). The most important cumulative project funding categories for China in the period 1981 to mid-1996 were agriculture (U.S.$6.64 billion), transportation (U.S.$5.91 billion), electric power/energy (U.S.$4.78 billion), education (U.S.$1.61 billion), and industry (U.S.$1.29 billion).[13]

In October 1995 a controversy developed over several bank projects. Allegations were made by Harry Wu, a Chinese-born American human rights activist who had spent nineteen years in Chinese prison camps before emigrating to the United States, that World Bank projects were benefiting forced labor camps *(laogai)* and special farms run by the People's Liberation Army (PLA) in Xinjiang Province in western China. After his 1995 reentry into China and his detention, trial, and expulsion, Wu demanded in a report issued by his Laogai Research Foundation (LRF) in October 1995 that the World Bank appoint an independent commission to investigate the Tarim Basin and other projects in China for their alleged use of forced labor; adopt an official policy against the use of forced labor on all bank projects, with sanctions for violators, and require a sensitizing training program for bank staffers. The World Bank responded by immediately dispatching an investigative team to look into the charges. In December 1995 a bank report concluded that there was no evidence to support Wu's allegations.[14]

China's relationship with the 170-member International Finance Corporation has been less extensive than with the IBRD and the IDA. The IFC is the world's largest multilateral source of financing for private enterprise in emerging economies. It acts as a catalyst to promote productive and profitable private companies by providing loans and equity finance, mobilizing other sources of investment capital, developing capital

TABLE 11.3 World Bank Annual and Cumulative Lending to China, mid-1980 to mid-1996 (Million U.S.$)

	IBRD Loans		IDA Credits		Annual Totals			Cumulative Totals			
	No. of Projects	Total $ Amount	No. of Projects	Total $ Amount	No. of Projects	Total $ Amount	Total % Amount[a]	No. of Projects	Total $ Amount	Total % Amount[b]	Cumulative Numerical Ranking[c]
1980–1981	1	100.0	0[d]	100.0	1[d]	200.0	1.63	1	200.0	1.63	70/125
1981–1982	0	0.0	1	60.0	1	60.0	<0.01	2	260.0	1.03	63/125
1982–1983	5	463.1	1	150.4	6	613.5	4.24	8	873.5	2.20	28/128
1983–1984	5	616.0	5	423.5	10	1,039.5	6.70	18	1,913.0	3.46	18/132
1984–1985	7	659.6	5	442.3	12	1,101.9	7.66	30	3,014.9	4.33	14/136
1985–1986	7	687.0	4	450.0	11	1,137.0	6.97	41	4,151.9	4.83	11/136
1986–1987	8	867.4	3	556.2	11	1,423.6	8.05	52	5,575.5	5.38	8/137
1987–1988	10	1,053.7	4	639.9	14	1,693.6	8.81	66	7,269.1	5.92	6/137
1988–1989	7	833.4	5	515.0	12	1,348.4	6.31	78	8,617.5	5.97	6/137
1989–1990	0	0.0	5	590.0	5	590.0	2.85	83	9,207.5	5.58	6/139
1990–1991	6	601.5	4	977.8	10	1,579.3	6.96	93	10,786.8	5.75	6/142
1991–1992	8	1,577.7	8	948.6	16	2,526.3	11.64	109	13,313.1	6.36	5/160
1992–1993	10	2,155.0	8	1,017.0	18	3,172.0	13.39	127	16,485.1	7.07	5/176
1993–1994	8	2,145.0	6	925.0	14	3,070.0	14.73	141	19,555.1	7.70	5/177
1994–1995	13	2,359.5	3	630.0	16	2,989.5	13.32	157	22,554.6	8.16	4/178
1995–1996	13	2,490.0	3	480.0	16	2,970.0	13.91	173	25,524.6	8.57	3/180
Total	108	16,618.9	65	8,905.7	173	25,524.6					

[a]Percentage of total annual World Bank lending.

[b]Percentage of cumulative World Bank lending beginning in 1981.

[c]China's annual ranking as a cumulative borrower compared to total Word Bank membership.

[d]This project, though jointly funded by the IBRD and the IDA, was considered an IBRD project. The same practice was utilized in a number of subsequent jointly funded projects.

SOURCES: World Bank, Annual Report [hereafter cited as IBRD, AR] 1981 (Washington, D.C.: IBRD, 1981), pp. 120, 121, 188; IBRD, AR, 1982 (Washington, D.C.: IBRD, 1982), pp. 118, 119, 184; IBRD, AR, 1983 (Washington, D.C.: IBRD, 1983), pp. 126, 127, 218; IBRD, AR, 1984 (Washington, D.C.: IBRD, 1984), pp. 139, 142, 210; IBRD, AR, 1985 (Washington, D.C.: IBRD, 1985), pp. 145, 146, 166; IBRD, AR, 1986 (Washington, D.C.: IBRD, 1986), pp. 137, 138, 158; IBRD, AR, 1987 (Washington, D.C.: IBRD, 1987), pp. 139, 140, 160; IBRD, AR, 1988 (Washington, D.C.: IBRD, 1988), pp. 131, 132, 152; IBRD, AR, 1989 (Washington, D.C.: IBRD, 1989), pp. 158, 159, 178; IBRD, AR, 1990 (Washington, D.C.: IBRD, 1990), pp. 156, 157, 178; IBRD, AR, 1991 (Washington, D.C.: IBRD, 1991), pp. 161, 162, 182; IBRD, AR, 1992 (Washington, D.C.: IBRD, 1992), pp. 176, 177; IBRD, AR, 1993 (Washington, D.C.: IBRD, 1993), pp. 155, 167, 185; IBRD, AR, 1994 (Washington, D.C.: IBRD, 1994), pp. 144, 146, 230, 233; IBRD, AR, 1995 (Washington, D.C.: IBRD, 1995), pp. 70, 104–123, passim, and IBRD, AR, 1996 (Washington, D.C.: IBRD, 1996), pp. 244, 247–249.

TABLE 11.4 Summary of Total Cumulative IBRD Loans and IDA Credits to Ten Largest Borrowers, as of June 30, 1996 (Million U.S.$)

	IBRD Loans			IDA Credits			Combined Lending			
Country	No.	$ Amount	% of Total	Country	No.	$ Amount	% of Total	Country	No.	$ Amount	% of Total	$ Amount Per Capita[a]
1. Mexico	155	26,332.5	9.38	1. India	213	23,529.9	24.27	1. India	373	47,263.5	12.51	49.64
2. India	160	23,733.6	8.45	2. China	65	8,905.7	9.19	2. Mexico	155	26,332.5	6.97	274.84
3. Brazil	214	23,116.7	8.23	3. Bangladesh	147	7,152.5	7.38	3. China	173	25,524.6	6.76	21.09
4. Indonesia	211	22,820.4	8.13	4. Pakistan	101	4,735.5	4.88	4. Indonesia	257	23,752.2	6.29	114.96
5. China	108	16,618.9	5.92	5. Ghana	84	3,069.9	3.17	5. Brazil	214	23,116.7	6.12	142.10
6. Turkey	116	12,619.9	4.50	6. Tanzania	84	2,819.9	2.91	6. Turkey	126	12,798.4	3.39	204.80
7. Argentina	74	11,676.2	4.16	7. Kenya	68	2,581.4	2.66	7. Argentina	74	11,676.2	3.09	336.60
8. Philippines	137	9,525.9	3.39	8. Uganda	59	2,240.9	2.31	8. Pakistan	183	10,749.7	2.85	83.14
9. Rep. of Korea	110	8,599.0	3.06	9. Ethiopia	56	2,158.5	2.23	9. Philippines	142	9,820.1	2.60	131.81
10. Colombia	143	8,588.9	3.06	10. Sri Lanka	65	2,057.1	2.12	10. Rep. of Korea	116	8,709.8	2.31	191.43
Total[b]	3,923	280,739.0	100.0		2,680	96,941.8	100.0		6,603	377,680.8	100.0	

[a]Based on population as of July 1996. Central Intelligence Agency, *The World Factbook 1996* <http://www.odci.gov/cia/publications/nsolo/wfb-all.htm>.

[b]Cumulative totals for all borrowing states.

SOURCE: World Bank, *Annual Report, 1996* (Washington, D.C.: IBRD, 1996), pp. 244–247.

markets, and offering a broad range of advisory services and technical assistance to businesses and governments. From 1985 until the Tiananmen Square incident, China sought and received minimal IFC support. Thereafter, no additional IFC loans were made to China until 1992 because of a U.S.-backed freeze, a significant erosion of private investor confidence in the future of economic reforms, and contention within the Chinese Communist Party over further economic liberalization and the role of private venture capital in that process. At the conclusion of the Fourteenth CCP Congress in October 1992, Vice Premier Zhu Rongji met with an IFC delegation and agreed to a U.S.$600 million investment program in China. An IFC resident mission was quickly opened in Beijing, and IFC staff thereafter conducted seminars throughout the country to introduce Chinese enterprises to IFC investment options.

Between 1992 and 1996 the IFC arranged twenty-three loans to Chinese enterprises, totaling U.S.$382.4 million (see Table 11.5). In some instances multiyear loans were made to the same enterprise, and beginning in 1995 the IFC promoted international syndication of its loans to private-sector borrowers. Although most of the projects to date have involved foreign joint ventures, increasingly the IFC has directed its attention to both the private sector and the so-called TVEs, or town and village enterprises. The IFC has also indicated a willingness to work with SOEs that seek to become less than 50 percent state owned and assist in rehabilitating and restructuring them for privatization through public stock listing. In 1993 the IFC became a major promoter of foreign portfolio investment through "country funds" by launching a China "global index" containing eighty-one stocks capitalized at U.S.$17 billion and a narrower "investable index" of sixteen stocks with a market value of U.S.$1.7 billion. Finally, IFC advisory services have provided China with project assistance and foreign investment advice (jointly operated with the IBRD) through the FIAS, or Foreign Investment Advisory Service, while the TATF, or Technical Assistance Trust Funds Program, has utilized consultants to help Chinese entrepreneurs prepare high-quality business proposals and to provide legal and financial expertise to assist China in developing capital markets and in promoting small- and medium-sized enterprises.

China's expanded utilization of IFC funding has also led to a commensurate rise in MIGA contracts since 1992. MIGA, or the Multilateral Investment Guarantee Agency, is a 134-member World Bank affiliate created in 1988 to support foreign direct investment in developing countries through investment insurance against noncommercial risks such as currency transfer restrictions, expropriation, war and civil disturbance, and breach of contract by the host government. From 1992 to the end of 1996,

TABLE 11.5 IFC Commitments to China, mid-1986 to mid-1996 (Million U.S.$)

	1986	1987	1988	1989	1990	1991	1992	1993	1994	1995	1996	Total
Total IFC loans	15.0	0.0	8.0	18.0	0.0	0.0	16.4	35.7	28.5	102.5	171.2	395.3[a]
Total syndications[b]	0.0	0.0	0.0	0.0	0.0	0.0	0.0	0.0	0.0	77.0	256.4	333.4
Other financing	0.0	0.0	0.0	0.0	0.0	0.0	0.0	0.0	0.0	10.0	4.0	14.0

[a]The IFC investment portfolio for China in 1996 in the form of outstanding loans and equity (at cost) was equal to $172.4 million.

[b]Typically, a loan agreement between the IFC and a borrower consists of an amount financed for the IFC's own account and the remainder placed with international commercial lenders. The IFC has promoted the syndication of its loans as a means of enabling private-sector borrowers to gain access to long-term project finance from international market lenders. The IFC stake in a project is limited to 25 percent of its value.

SOURCES: International Finance Corporation, *Annual Report* [hereafter cited as IFC, *AR*], 1987 (Washington, D.C.: IFC, 1987), p. 65; IFC, *AR, 1988* (Washington, D.C.: IFC, 1988), p. 73; IFC, *AR, 1989* (Washington, D.C.: IFC, 1989), p. 70; IFC, *AR, 1992* (Washington, D.C.: IFC, 1992), p. 104; IFC, *AR, 1993* (Washington, D.C.: IFC, 1993), p. 123; IFC, *AR, 1994* (Washington, D.C.: IFC, 1994), pp. 51, 134, 135; IFC, *AR, 1995* (Washington, D.C.: IFC, 1995), pp. 40, 131; IFC, *AR, 1996* (Washington, D.C.: IFC, 1996), p. 55; and International Finance Corporation, *IFC Investment Portfolio 1996* (Washington, D.C.: IFC, 1996), p. 10.

MIGA negotiated eighteen guarantee contracts with China valued at nearly U.S.$140 million, equal to 5.7 percent of the four-year cumulative total contract value and fourth highest of thirty-nine countries with guarantee contracts (see Table 11.6).

In sum, China has derived a broad range of benefits from WBG membership. These include (1) the preparation and dissemination of numerous detailed and highly professional studies on virtually every aspect of the Chinese economy by skilled IMF and World Bank analysts; (2) short-term balance-of-payments and budgetary deficit assistance through the IMF; (3) access to a large pool of lending capital at either market or zero interest rates to finance costly infrastructural projects and finished products for domestic consumption and export; (4) a rapidly growing portfolio of private investments and insurance guarantees through the IFC and MIGA; (5) extensive training and educational opportunities in the form of fellowships and scholarships, specialized courses, seminars, colloquia, workshops, conferences, study tours, and published materials and statistical data on the global economy for mid- and top-level·Chinese career functionaries at IMF and IBRD headquarters, country missions in Beijing, and through the IMF Institute and the World Bank Economic Development Institute (EDI); and (6) strong external support and legitimation on a global scale for China's economic modernization program.

China's WBG membership has been an important factor not only in the economic policy decisions of the Chinese political leadership but also in the creation of an extended government bureaucratic structure to manage the relationship. WBG research findings and recommendations have played major roles in the formulation and implementation of China's five-year plans, and IBRD- and IDA-funded projects have become an integral part of that planning cycle. Since its WBG entry, China has become a determined self-serving advocate for its own modernization. If China's pre-1989 WBG relationship was an important hallmark of its political maturity and acceptance by the existing global economic order, the brief, eighteen-month Tiananmen relationship hiatus succumbed to China's skill in playing its UN veto card threat prior to the Gulf War and to G-7 fears of hard-line permanency that could freeze their businesses out of the world's largest marketplace. The October 1992 CCP reform policy confirmation allowed China to reassert its claim to even more than its traditional share of the WBG pie, with the added benefit of accelerating IFC-MIGA private enterprise commitments. Although Third World countries may at times resent China's success at their expense in gaining access to capital from the WBG, donor governments, and the foreign private sector, Beijing's example certainly should serve as a role model for others committed to rapid economic modernization.

TABLE 11.6 MIGA Guarantee Contracts with China, mid-1992–1996

	1992–1993	1993–1994	1994–1995	1995–1996	1996[a]	Cumulative 1992–1996[a]
No. of contracts with China	1	3	7	3	4	18
Total no. of contracts	27	38	54	68	21	208
Value of contracts with China (U.S.$ million)	0.54	11.60	67.93	33.30	25.93	139.30
Total value of contracts (U.S.$ million)	374.00	372.60	672.60	862.00	169.60	2,450.80
China's percentage of total contract value	0.14	3.11	10.10	3.86	15.29	5.68
China's ranking by percent contract value	17/17[b]	17/24[b]	6/34[b]	4/39[b]	NA	NA

[a]First two quarters of FY 1996 to December 31, 1996.
[b]The second figure is the number of countries with guarantee contracts.
SOURCES: Multilateral Investment Guarantee Agency, *Annual Report, 1993* [hereafter cited as *AR*] (Washington, D.C.: MIGA, 1993), pp. 19, 28, 44; MIGA, *AR, 1994* (Washington, D.C.: MIGA, 1994), pp. 14, 23, 50; MIGA, *AR, 1995* (Washington, D.C.: MIGA, 1995), pp. 12, 18–20, 50; MIGA, *AR, 1996* (Washington, D.C.: MIGA, 1996), pp. 14, 23–25, 62; and *MIGA News* 5 (Spring 1997): 1, 3.

China and the Asian Development Bank

In March 1986 China became the forty-seventh member of the Asian Development Bank (ADB) after a three-year contest with Taiwan over the issue of Taipei's expulsion from the bank along earlier WBG lines. In the end a face-saving formula was devised whereby Beijing was awarded the Chinese seat, and Taiwan remained a bank member with the designation of "Taipei, China." Accordingly, China conceded ADB membership status to Taiwan comparable to that of Hong Kong.

The ADB is a fifty-six-member regional development bank that is committed to the economic development of its thirty-three so-called developing member countries (DMCs) by utilizing many of the same approaches as the World Bank, IDA, and IFC on a regional scale. As with the World Bank and its affiliates, China has experienced a generally expanding relationship with the ADB except for a much-curtailed two-year period following the Tiananmen Square incident. Once U.S. and G-7 policy changed, however, a large backlog of ADB loans and technical assistance projects was unblocked, and since 1993 ADB lending to China has soared to an annual average of U.S.$1.1 billion. By the end of 1996, China had gleaned more than U.S.$6.4 billion in loans and nearly U.S.$40 million for technical assistance projects and preparatory, advisory, and operational grants from the bank, another U.S.$52 million for technical assistance from other sources, and more than U.S.$900 million in project co-financing, for a grand ADB total of more than U.S.$6.4 billion (see Table 11.7).

As the largest and most populous bank member, China has established itself as the fifth-largest cumulative borrower and ranked as the leading loan recipient after 1995. China has been able to use the bank to accelerate its developmental pace and boost its regional visibility, prestige, and reputation for fast-track success. Even more important, China's ADB participation has set a significant political precedent by legitimizing a formal organizational relationship with Taiwan for burgeoning mainland-Taiwan trade, for massive Taiwanese investment on the mainland, and for the concept of "one country, two systems," based upon Beijing's July 1997 Hong Kong takeover.

China and the GATT/WTO

A logical outgrowth of China's modernization program and growing involvement in the world economic and trade system has been Beijing's long-term effort to join the GATT and its WTO successor. The GATT was an international regime to facilitate trade among its members by developing rules on reciprocity, nondiscrimination, and transparency and by sponsoring periodic multilateral trade negotiations. Even after its 1971

TABLE 11.7 ADB Annual and Cumulative Lending to China, 1986–1996 (Million U.S.$)

	No. Loans Approved	ADB $ Loan Amount[a]	% Annual Loan Amount[a]	No. Technical Assistance Projects	ADB T.A. Project $ Amount[b]	JSF T.A. Financing[c]	T.A. Financing from Other Sources[d]	No. Co-Financed Projects	Co-Fin. Project $ Amount	Total ADB Annual $ Amount[e]	Total ADB Cumulative $ Amount[e]
1986	0	0.0	0.0	1	0.075	0.000	0.000	0	0.0	0.075	0.075
1987	2	133.3	1.0	5	0.652	0.000	0.750	0	0.0	133.952	134.027
1988	4	282.9	13.7	10	1.110	1.831	0.418	1	3.0	284.010	418.037
1989	1	39.7	1.8	6	0.285	3.300	0.000	0	0.0	39.985	458.022
1990	1	50.0	2.0	4	1.777	0.000	0.000	0	0.0	51.777	509.799
1991	6	496.3	13.6	30	10.217	3.609	0.600	2	63.0	506.217	1,016.160
1992	9	903.0	22.8	33	9.632	4.135	0.000	3	307.0	912.632	1,192.648
1993	8	1,050.0	26.4	38	7.159	9.139	0.000	0	0.0	1,057.159	2,985.807
1994	8	1,167.0	46.5	41	3.646	13.076	0.715	3	133.0	1,170.646	4,156.453
1995	10	1,201.0	29.7	45	4.903	12.469	1.037	2	307.0	1,205.903	5,362.356
1996	11	1,102.0	28.4	25	4.417	8.677	0.000	1	100.0	1,106.417	6,468.773
Total	60	6,425.2		238	43.873	56.236	3.520	12	913.0	6,468.773	6,468.773

[a]This amount does not include any funding from the soft money Asian Development Fund (ADF).

[b]That portion of Technical Assistance project cost contributed by the ADB.

[c]That portion of Technical Assistance project cost contributed by the Japan Special Fund (JSF).

[d]These sources include the UNDP and the government of France. The ADB acts as an administrator of the grant for the financing source.

[e]These totals include only the ADB loan and technical assistance amounts and exclude JSF and other funding sources. These figures do not include five private-sector loans and investments in the amount of $87.3 million financed by the AFIC.

SOURCES: Asian Development Bank, Loan, Technical Assistance and Private Sector Approvals, no. 921 (January 1992), pp. 1, 22–23, 60; Asian Development Bank, Annual Report [hereafter cited as AR] 1987 (Manila: ADB, 1988), p. 154; ADB AR, 1990 (Manila: ADB, 1991), pp. 195, 196, 198, 222, 223; ADB, AR, 1992 (Manila: ADB, 1993), pp. 177, 180, 196, 197, 206, 207; ADB, AR, 1993 (Manila: ADB, 1994), pp. 170, 177, 196, 197, 204, 205; ADB, AR, 1994 (Manila: ADB, 1995), pp. 188, 195, 198, 214, 224, 225; ADB, AR, 1995 (Manila: ADB, 1996), pp. 212, 219, 222, 224, 238, 239, 248, 249; ADB, AR, 1996 (Manila: ADB, 1997), pp. 260, 267, 270, 272, 286, 287, 296, 297.

UN seating, China regarded the GATT as a rich man's club and chose not to participate, though it closely monitored GATT activities. When China applied to join the GATT in July 1986, its foreign trade regime, despite some limited reforms, was very far removed from GATT-qualifying criteria. Impediments included broad official administrative controls (in the form of extensive central planning, quasi-monopolistic state trading companies, a preferential import-export licensing system known as trading rights, export subsidies/dumping, and strict foreign exchange regulation and artificial nonmarket rates); high tariffs; various nontariff barriers and discriminatory rules against foreign firms, including quotas and statutory inspection requirements; the lack of unified national treatment through differential bureaucratic and regional procedures and arrangements (including special economic zones); the overall lack of transparency in the form of arbitrary and secret internal rules *(neibu)*, and finally the absence of a system of consistent and enforceable business law.

China's GATT application process involved a lengthy outline of its laws, regulations, and procedures on all aspects of trade and investment; the establishment of a GATT China Working Group (CWG) to examine the document and to receive and consider answers to a large number of questions on reforms either implemented or under way; intensive negotiations beginning in Fall 1992 between China and the GATT CWG on a protocol of accession to bring China's laws, regulations, and procedures into line with GATT rules; the establishment of parallel bilateral working groups between China and its major trading partners (the United States, the European Union, and Japan) to negotiate specific terms of China's accession protocol; and finally the achievement of consensus among GATT members on the acceptability of the final document. However, the various working groups were unable to reach consensus on an acceptable accession protocol prior to the formal establishment of the World Trade Organization (WTO) in January 1995. Thus, China failed to qualify as a WTO founding member, which left Beijing deeply resentful, especially toward the United States.

The GATT negotiating process was hindered by several general issues. First was the complication introduced in January 1990 when Taiwan applied to join the GATT under Article 33 as "The Customs Territory of Taiwan, Penghu, Kinmen, and Matsu." In September 1992 the contracting parties and the Beijing and Taipei authorities were able to agree on the establishment of a GATT Taiwan Working Group (TWG) to examine Taiwan's application. But China adamantly insisted that Taipei not join the organization before Beijing was admitted. Thus, Taiwan also failed to qualify as a WTO founding member. Second was the question of China's joining the GATT as a developing rather than a developed country, which would confer enhanced benefits. Third was the problem posed by the Jackson-Vanik Amendment to the 1974 U.S. Trade Act, which requires that as a nonmarket country, China must be certified annually by the U.S. president as allowing free emigration, a condition applied to China since 1980 but more stringently so since Tiananmen Square, in order to retain its most-favored-nation, or MFN, status. However, this requirement would contravene unconditional and permanent MFN trade status conferred by GATT membership. Finally and most important was the need for an acceptable trade regime reform package involving market access; tariff and nontariff barriers; national uniform treatment for foreign firms and products in China; temporary safeguards against Chinese export surges; unrestricted trading rights for foreign businesses operating in China; elimination of discriminatory restrictions and conditions on foreign investment in China and monopolistic state trading companies; export subsidies; an industrial policy that protects infant industries and mandates local material content and minimum production-export levels; substantial foreign exchange controls and renminbi inconvertibility; and lastly an assurance of transparency in economic and commercial policy making. Although serious hard bargaining really began in March 1993, most of these issues remained essentially unresolved by the various working groups when the WTO replaced the GATT in 1995.

U.S. insistence on "commercially viable terms" for Chinese reforms has been the major road block to China's entry into the WTO. Though a draft protocol was developed by December 1994, only limited Chinese concessions were forthcoming over the next year.[15] In November 1995 the United States expressed a willingness to phase in implementation provisions and presented a secret thirteen-page detailed "road map" to Chinese negotiators that spelled out what China was expected to do to win U.S. approval.[16] Although the Chinese noted that the U.S. "road map" was a "positive step," they complained that the demands were more stringent than those applied to other WTO applicants, and they made no immediate response. Though some later forward movement occurred and a revised draft protocol was completed in March 1997, no breakthroughs were achieved.[17] The principal stumbling blocks remain market-access provisions and the specific wording of nine annexes, which spell out exactly how China will meet its protocol obligations.[18]

The WTO China entry issue has been seriously affected by domestic political factors in both China and the United States. Because WTO-based reforms would exert a pronounced domestic socioeconomic and political impact, the post-Deng leadership wants to ensure that a final agreement would not jeopardize Party controls, its own legitimacy, and national bureaucratic support. Ideally, any deal should facilitate the recentralization of national government power, authority, and controls and positively address such pressing national problems as those connected with the SOEs.

Finally, China's new leadership views the entire WTO accession process in political as well as economic terms and as a way to advance China's emerging global economic superpower status while preserving the long cultural legacy of Confucian-Communist political authoritarianism and its own political legitimacy.

But it is domestic U.S. politics that has emerged as the newest and potentially most difficult hurdle blocking China's WTO entry. It was clear prior to the 1996 U.S. presidential election that in China's view a Clinton win would bolster chances for a fast-track deal sometime in 1997. However, Clinton, despite his victory, was forced to respond to the concerns of a broad array of interest groups by insisting on commercially viable terms. Important divisions emerged over the issue. Although the U.S.-China Business Council generally supported early WTO entry, an emergent bipartisan and ideologically diverse coalition has expressed concerns over a host of issues. The latter include the Hong Kong reversion process, intellectual property rights and piracy, a burgeoning bilateral trade imbalance that increased from U.S.$39.5 billion in 1996 to an estimated U.S.$45 billion in 1997, human rights, forced abortion, religious persecution of Christians and Muslims, Tibet, Taiwan, arms sales to Pakistan and Iran, and U.S. agricultural exports. As an aspiring contender for the Democratic presidential nomination in 2000, House Minority Leader Richard Gephardt (D-Mo.) sponsored a measure supported by many of his congressional colleagues as well as the AFL-CIO to require a congressional vote on China's WTO entry. By far the most damaging development, however, was what has been termed Donorgate, or apparent attempts to buy political influence prior to the 1996 U.S. elections through large-scale illegal campaign contributions to the Democratic National Committee and to the Clintons' legal defense fund from Asian businesspersons with interests in China, an attempt possibly orchestrated by the Chinese Embassy in Washington. Though many campaign donations were ultimately returned, the charges triggered two broad congressional investigations as well as a preemptive self-protective move away from the issue by the Clinton administration. Regardless of whether the charges are true, the speculation regarding China's role in the affair will likely delay any near-term WTO accession and permanent MFN status for China, simply because the Clinton administration will not want to appear to be making what could be viewed as a payoff for political contributions or because of fear of charges of possible espionage.[19]

Conclusions and Prognosis

China's MEI affiliations have proved enormously beneficial in its drive for modernization and economic superpower status. Membership has enabled Beijing to utilize valuable foreign professional expertise to analyze the strengths and weaknesses of its economy, jointly draft a long-range development blueprint, and provide broad and sophisticated training for large numbers of Chinese technical experts and officials. China has tapped a huge pool of lending capital to garner billions of dollars in grants, loans, and concessionary credits to cope with temporary monetary and trade imbalances and to finance an ambitious array of essential but costly infrastructural, developmental, and production projects. MEIs have provided a vital structural framework within which brainstorming, dialogue, interaction, bargaining, and decisionmaking can take place and have facilitated close personal and professional contact between China's bureaucratic, technical, managerial, and emerging entrepreneurial elites and numerous foreign development experts and investors. Such interaction has sensitized Chinese policymakers to the psychological, methodological, and policy requisites for successful economic development and has advanced the national as well as the policymakers' own vested career interests. MEIs have been a major factor in tilting Chinese economic policy in the direction of continuing reform while acculturating and socializing an entire younger generation of Chinese technocrats in the techniques of economic growth. They have served to enhance the confidence levels of international business, bankers, and investors who make decisions on foreign direct investment, commercial lending, and trade arrangements. Finally, MEIs have enmeshed China more firmly into the international community and theoretically have raised the stakes against precipitous and ill-advised adventurism, especially in regard to Taiwan and the contested Spratly Islands in the South China Sea.

It is clear that China will continue to be a major beneficiary of MEI participation. But continued economic success may depend on the commitment of China's new leadership to a regime and policies that at a minimum avoid future Tiananmen excesses, especially regarding Hong Kong, and at best embrace gradual political liberalization and accountability. China's decision to reject the orthodox Maoist statist and autarkic development model in favor of the classical Smith-Ricardian global economic approach was a calculated gamble to jump-start a moribund economy. For Deng Xiaoping and his successors, that choice and its attendant MEI participation were an integral hedge in China's shift to a market economy (with due deference to socialist characteristics) and a major and increasingly successful gamble. By relying on capitalist-style competition to unleash traditional Chinese entrepreneurial dynamism, supplemented by MEI and other official and private foreign capital resources and technical assistance, China's leaders have presided over a period of unprecedented economic growth. From the perspective of the developed West, globalization and interdependence should lead not only to a more prosperous China but also to one that will increasingly embrace such principles as tolerance of differences, periodic political accountability, a rule of law, and a respect for human rights. But from a Chinese leadership perspective, such innovations portend chaos and weakness in a world of assertive nationalism, fierce economic competition, and power politics.[20] As China's emergence as an economic superpower becomes a reality in the twenty-first century, the ultimate outcome may well be a Greater China predicated on Confucian Singaporean rather than Lockean and Jeffersonian principles. The Chinese leadership strongly believes that it has succeeded in raising prosperity levels because of, rather than in spite of, a continuing authoritarian political framework. As China's power expands, the West as well as the MEIs are likely to have less, not more, leverage over this process.

By joining the WTO, China hopes to parlay its bet on global economic multilateralism by maximizing the rewards of greater foreign direct investment, export earnings, and domestic prosperity levels and minimizing the costs of reforming its socialist command economy and import regime. China has proved to be a stubborn and tenacious negotiator. The United States thus far has resisted the temptation to cut a political rather than a commercially viable deal. Successive U.S. administrations have recognized that far greater leverage for meaningful and equitable reform can be exerted prior to rather than after China's WTO accession. However, it can be argued that China has done very well without WTO membership to date, and should Donorgate and other political considerations further prolong the negotiation period, the losers may well be China's G-7 trading partners, since the clocks for the various WTO dispute settlement mechanisms and transitional issue periods will start ticking only upon accession. In the meantime the MEIs will still be available to China to offset possible future adverse economic developments and instability and enable China to operate as a self-serving Group of One committed to recapturing the modern-day power and prestige of the Middle Kingdom.

Notes

1. The basis of Ricardo's theory is that any two nations will benefit if each one specializes in producing and exporting those goods that it makes comparatively cheaply and acquires as imports goods that it could produce only at higher cost.

2. "Central Bankers' Group Adding to Ranks," *New York Times* (hereafter cited as *NYT*), September 10, 1996, p. D10. Other central bank invitees included those from Brazil, Hong Kong, India, Mexico, Russia, Saudi Arabia, Singapore, and South Korea. For earlier works on China's participation in the multilateral economic institutions, see my chapters in the 1984, 1989, and 1994 editions of Samuel S. Kim, ed., *China and the World* and especially Harold K. Jacobson and Michel

Oksenberg, *China's Participation in the IMF, the World Bank, and GATT: Toward a Global Economic Order* (Ann Arbor: University of Michigan Press, 1990).

3. For details, see UN Document DP/CP/CPR/3, *Programme Planning: Country and Intercountry Programmes and Projects: Third Country Programme for China*, March 22, 1991, and *UNDP Advisory Note on the Third Country Programme for the People's Republic of China (1991–1995)* (Beijing: UNDP, January 1990), pp. 9–19.

4. See UN Document DP/CCF/CPR/1, *UNDP: Country Cooperation Frameworks and Related Matters: First Country Cooperation Framework for the People's Republic of China (1996–2000)*, July 8, 1996, p. 1.

5. Ibid., pp. 7–9.

6. Examples include the Tumen River Development Program, the Northeast Asia Agricultural Cooperation and Support Program, and the Upper Mekong River Basin Program. See UNDP (1996). Asia Regional and Northeast Asia Subregional Programmes: <http://www.edu.cn/undp/regional/regional.htm> (October 1996).

7. See Cecil R. Dipchand, Zhang Yichun, and Ma Mingja, *The Chinese Financial System* (Westport, CT: Greenwood Press, 1994), chap. 6; and Gao Xiao Hang and On Kit Tam, "China's Foreign Exchange System," in On Kit Tam, ed., *Financial Reform in China* (New York: Routledge, 1995), chap. 7.

8. The current account measures the flow of money into and out of the country and is trade related, covering payments for goods and services and repatriation of profits from Chinese operations by foreign countries. The renminbi would not be convertible for capital account transactions, including direct and equity investments, which still require government approval. See Kirsten Sylvester, "On the Road to RMB Convertibility," *China Business Review* [hereafter cited as *CBR*] 24 (January-February 1997): 20–21.

9. See Craig S. Smith, "China Scrambles to Avert Banking Crisis," *Wall Street Journal* [hereafter cited as *WSJ*], August 6, 1996, p. A10. Even though the People's Bank of China, the central bank, requires banks to maintain a risk-adjusted capital-adequacy ratio of no less than 8 percent, none of the SOCBs meets this requirement.

10. See Raymond L. Blanchard, Jr., "The Heart of Economic Reform," *CBR* 24 (January-February 1997): 17, 20, 24; and Klaus Schmidt-Hebbert and Luis Servén, *Saving Across the World: Puzzles and Policies*. World Bank Discussion Paper No. 354 (Washington, D.C.: IBRD, 1997), p. 139. In January 1997 China shut down the China Agribusiness Development Trust and Investment Corporation (CATIC), which was set up in 1988 to channel loans and aid from the World Bank, the ADB, and other development agencies to China's agricultural sector. CATIC's takeover was prompted by excessive real estate speculation, a collapse in property values, China's extended austerity program, and possible corruption. See Kathy Chen, "China's Closing of Big Financial Firm Is Another Sign of the Sector's Weakness," *WSJ*, January 9, 1997, p. A6; and Elaine Kurtenbach, "Big Losses Hit Banks in China," *Washington Post*, February 18, 1997, p. A18.

11. Blanchard, "The Heart of Economic Reform," p. 24.

12. Seth Faison, "China's Leader Announces Sell-Off of State Enterprises," *NYT*, September 1997, p. 5.

13. World Bank, *Annual Report* (Washington, D.C., IBRD, 1981–1996), passim.

14. This conclusion was confirmed by a leading World Bank official in an interview in March 1997. For the October 1995 LRF report entitled "The World Bank and Chinese Forced Labor: Mistake or Moral Bankruptcy?" and a follow-up April 1996 report entitled "The World Bank and the Chinese Military—Incompetence or Cover Up?" see the *LRF Newsletter* <http://www.christusrex.org/www1/sdc/sep96c.htm> and <http://www.christusrex.org/www1/sdc/Dec95a.htm>.

15. For the December 1994 draft protocol, see "Draft Protocol and Working Party Report," *Inside U.S. Trade* [hereafter cited as *IUST*] 13 (January 27, 1995): S2–S12.

16. Although the specific details are classified, the "road map" provided the basis for detailed negotiations over each of the specific areas of disagreement. See "U.S. Softens Demands on China Accession into World Trade Body," *IUST* 13 (December 1, 1995): 1, 20–21.

17. See "New Draft Protocol on China WTO Accession," *IUST* 15 (March 14, 1997): 23–29.

18. The annexes include products subject to state trading for imports and exports, designated trading, phased elimination of nontariff measures, products and services subject to price controls, products subject to export duties, subsidies, and statutory inspection requirements.

19. In June 1997 President Clinton reauthorized China's MFN status for another year, and the Congress failed to overturn his action. There have been serious questions raised about the role of Mochtar Riady, head of the powerful Indonesia-based Lippo Group, which had major economic interests in Arkansas and China, and his protégé, John Huang, who was a friend of President Clinton, the top Lippo USA executive, and later, from July 1994 to December 1995, the principal deputy assistant secretary for international trade in the Clinton Commerce Department. Well before his Commerce appointment, not only was Huang granted a top-secret security clearance without the standard investigation, but also he retained that clearance for more than a year after he left Commerce to become a top fund-raiser for the Democratic National Committee. Huang eventually became a target of investigations by the FBI and the U.S. Congress regarding possible connections to Chinese intelligence organizations through a Hong Kong Lippo affiliate. One commentator has speculated that given Huang's access to the Oval Office and his Commerce position, he would have had access to U.S. trade secrets and negotiating positions of great value to China. William Safire, "Sleaze at the Top," *NYT*, October 17, 1996, p. A27, and William Safire, "Lippo Suction," *NYT*, October 28, 1996, p. A13. See also David E. Sanger, "U.S. Officials Say China Is Not Ready for Trade Organization," *NYT*, August 4, 1997, pp. A1, A7.

20. Wang Jisi, "Pragmatic Nationalism: China Seeks a New Role in World Affairs," *Oxford International Review* 5 (Winter 1994): 29.

12

China's Environmental Diplomacy

ELIZABETH C. ECONOMY

The evolution of Chinese environmental foreign relations over the past two decades has been characterized by both the enduring values of post-1949 Maoist foreign policy and the emergence of new ideals of global interdependence. In formal global environmental negotiations, China combines traditional foreign policy rhetoric with recalcitrant policy stances. This approach is designed to further three important objectives: protecting Chinese sovereignty; gaining access to foreign technology, funds, and training; and sustaining China's rapid economic growth. In taking such an approach, China perpetuates the themes that predominate in the realm of high politics—traditional Chinese values of sovereignty, Third World/First World dichotomies, and image. Thus, once again the rhetoric of the past remains the voice of the present.

China's current position on environmental issues is to minimize its responsibility to take action and to decouple responsibility from its contribution to the problem at hand. Chinese negotiators put forward a threefold rationale: First, China is a developing state and as such must place priority on economic development; second, if the PRC is to address environmental degradation, domestic problems take priority over transnational or global concerns; and third, it is incumbent upon the advanced industrialized states that polluted and degraded the earth as they developed economically to pay for the lesser-developed states to respond to these global environmental problems.

In recent years, China has not confined this rhetoric to justify its own policy. It has also utilized such rhetoric as a platform to gain support within the community of developing nations. Along with India, China frequently occupies a leadership role among the developing states in international environmental negotiations.

Bolstering China's confident stance in these global environmental negotiations is the fact that PRC participation is integral to the success of
any significant global environmental accord. China is among the world's
largest contributors to three of the most critical global environmental
problems: biodiversity loss, climate change, and ozone depletion. The international community has acknowledged that any global environmental
accord must meet China's interests and needs in each of these areas. The
Chinese policymakers responsible for shaping China's negotiation strategies have effectively translated China's dual status as a key contributor
to these problems and as a developing country into substantial leverage
in international environmental negotiations.

China's combative negotiating position notwithstanding, international
actors have had a significant influence in shaping Chinese domestic environmental politics and foreign relations. The demands of participating in
global environmental regimes have forced Chinese leaders to establish
new domestic institutions and processes for managing their participation
in those regimes. Most important, these new institutions and processes
favor the interests of the environmentally proactive actors within China
by radically reconfiguring the very nature of PRC environmental politics.
As Peter Gourevitch has demonstrated through his work on the "second
image reversed," domestic linkages to foreign policy are important not
only for the impact that domestic politics have on a state's foreign policy
but also for the impact of international actors on a state's domestic politics.

Throughout the period immediately preceding and following the 1992
United Nations Conference on Environment and Development
(UNCED), for example, the Chinese government established a host of
new institutions, bureaucratic processes, and policy initiatives to address
both domestic and global environmental problems. In addition, it permitted the formation of environmental nongovernmental organizations, began to use the media as an investigative tool for environmental corruption, and empowered the court system to punish polluting enterprises.
Indeed, an entirely new vocabulary surrounding environmental protection emerged within China because of its interaction with the international community. In short, the infrastructure to enable the link between
international and domestic policy appeared to be in place.

However, what has emerged instead has been a bifurcated process:
The actors, institutions, and beliefs promulgated at international negotiations have remained consistent, but a second set of actors and institutions
advancing a different set of interests and operating at a relatively distinct
level of diplomacy has emerged. China has thus far defied conventional
policy linkage by maintaining two distinct evolutionary paths with respect to environmental foreign relations.

Emboldened by the attention and interest paid to China's environmental protection efforts by the international community, Chinese leaders such as Qu Geping, head of the National People's Congress Committee on Protection of Natural Resources and the Environment, and Song Jian, chairman of the State Science and Technology Commission (SSTC), have assumed prominent roles in conducting Chinese environmental foreign relations. They are the key participants in the scientific discussions that typically precede political negotiations on the environment. More important, they have established a second level of diplomacy, one that engages the international community in assisting Chinese environmental protection efforts through financial and technology transfers and training opportunities. These actors offer greater environmental expertise and a more environmentally proactive stance than their more powerful counterparts in agencies such as the Ministry of Foreign Affairs and the State Planning Commission. They pursue a higher level of integration with the international community and evidence a stronger commitment to address international environmental issues. On the domestic front, these actors advocate more stringent environmental protection laws and improved enforcement efforts. All the while, however, more conservative agencies continue to rebuff any attempts by the international community to make them more accountable for China's environmental damage.

Not surprisingly, the international community has responded to the Chinese expert community with an outpouring of financial and technical assistance. It is anxious that China address the environmental havoc wreaked by its economic successes and, in the process, that China play a constructive role in responding to the global environmental problems to which it has become a major contributor.

What has emerged over the course of the past decade in Chinese environmental foreign relations, therefore, has been a highly successful two-pronged negotiation strategy, which involves both formal political negotiations and informal, but increasingly structured, negotiations involving international lending institutions, foreign foundations and governments, and communities of international experts. Certainly, the interests and objectives of the Chinese actors at both levels of diplomacy overlap in some critical ways: for example, gaining access to technology transfer and sources of funds, developing training opportunities, and promoting a positive image within the international community. Yet they differ in their ultimate goals and visions for both China's domestic environmental future and its response to global environmental problems.

This chapter concludes that the implicit strategy of divide and conquer is not sustainable in the long run and that convergence between the two levels of diplomacy is inevitable. As China becomes integrated into the international system of environmental agreements and organizations and as its economy continues to grow, the international community will place increasing expectations and pressure on China to adhere to international norms and to assume the responsibilities, not merely the rights, that are accorded a significant power.

The Early Years of Environmental Diplomacy

Throughout Chinese history, economic development, war, and societal indifference have taken a devastating toll on the environment. Without protection by the state or an effective legal system, land was squandered, water resources degraded, forests denuded, and natural wonders despoiled. Such practices intensified with the economic and social turmoil of the Great Leap Forward and Cultural Revolution during the 1950s and 1960s.

In 1972, however, in keeping with China's decision to reestablish political and economic relations with the rest of the world, Premier Zhou Enlai arranged for a Chinese delegation to participate in the United Nations Conference on the Human Environment (UNCHE). From the perspective of the West, China's participation at the conference was relatively unconstructive, if not disruptive. The PRC couched its statements in grandiose political rhetoric, without much consideration of the environmental issues at hand. For example, Chinese delegate Chang Hsien-Wu stated, "One of the main reasons why pollution of the atmosphere is becoming a serious problem in some areas, is the willful discharge of harmful substances by monopoly capitalistic groups in disregard of the safety of the local people. Another reason, is the policy of plunder, aggression and war wantonly pursued by the super-Powers." He continued:

> The Chinese delegation is opposed to certain major powers practicing control and plunder under the name of the human environment, and the shifting by these Powers of the cost of environment protection onto the shoulders of the developing countries under the guise of international trade. ... The urgent task before the developing countries is to shake off the plunder undertaken by imperialism, colonialism and neo-colonialism of various descriptions, and to develop their national economies independently.[1]

Despite this seemingly inauspicious beginning, the PRC delegation's report, along with a series of environmental disasters, prompted the Chinese leaders to look more closely at their environmental protection practices and to organize in June 1973 the First National Conference on Environmental Protection. In addition, a leading group composed of representatives from the Ministries of Planning, Agriculture, Communications, Water Conservancy, Public Health, and Industry was established to review China's environmental situation and practices and to consider what steps China should take to address its environmental problems.[2]

Throughout the 1970s and early 1980s, a series of important meetings were held, and a number of regulations were passed to control industrial and marine pollution.[3] In addition, several structural reorganizations were enacted to strengthen the environmental protection bureaucracy. For example, in January 1984, the Chinese leadership convened the Second National Conference on Environmental Protection; in May, it established the Environmental Protection Commission, attached to the State Council. This commission, composed of participants from more than thirty government ministries and bureaus, reviewed environmental policies, initiated new plans, and organized environmental activities.[4]

As the PRC entered the 1990s, guarded optimism concerning the future of environmental protection prevailed. Although officials at the Third National Conference on Environmental Protection, in May 1989, acknowledged that there were serious failings in the implementation of environmental regulations, others remained hopeful. For example, Qu Geping, who had become chief administrator of the National Environmental Protection Agency (NEPA), commented that the government now realized that environmental problems could exert a significant impact on development, on the strength of the country, and on the stability of the society.[5]

This nascent domestic environmentalism was matched by a cautious, but fairly proactive, approach on the international front. Despite China's actions at the UNCHE, throughout the 1970s and early 1980s there was a strong interest in participating in international environmental activities on the part of the Chinese. China's interest, however, was very selective. In a number of cases, for example, marine dumping, the Chinese were not significant contributors to the problem. Their motives, therefore, were primarily political: to rejoin the international community across the full spectrum of affairs, to keep Taiwan from asserting itself as the representative of China in international bodies,[6] and to develop a coterie of trained environmental and scientific experts who could transmit relevant knowledge to China to help with domestic environmental problems.

In general, during this period China acceded to treaties several years after their inception. In the case of the London Dumping Convention, for example, the Chinese signed on to the convention over a decade after it had been established internationally. The Chinese were careful to ensure that their domestic laws and capabilities were reasonably in keeping with the demands of the international treaty prior to their joining the treaty. Before the PRC acceded to the London Dumping Convention in 1985, it had passed its own Marine Environmental Protection Law, which was modeled on the convention. The long lead time also permitted the relevant Chinese ministries to study the domestic ramifications of the issue, jockey among themselves for the lead Chinese position in the international negotiations, and balance their competing interests to arrive at the formal Chinese negotiating position. During the course of the negotiations, the Chinese representatives maintained a low profile, studying the technical points of the proposed treaty, and developing expertise by participating as often as possible in training seminars and technical development efforts.[7]

It should be stressed that the early global environmental issues did not impose significant changes in Chinese environmental practices. Even so, the international community did not always count on the PRC to support international measures. Although various international actors encouraged the PRC to accede to international environmental conventions, since the PRC was not a significant contributor to the problem,[8] it was again as much an issue of image as one of environmental protection. That may have contributed to the relatively low profile that the Chinese maintained during the 1970s and early 1980s.

Whatever were the advances that took place on the domestic or international political fronts, China's concern for economic growth was always its highest priority. As a result, implementation of environmental regulations was haphazard and enforcement remained lax. Chinese leaders were reluctant to back up their laws with an adequate environmental protection apparatus for fear that economic development would be hampered. They set fees for polluting enterprises too low to act as an incentive for action; and their investment in environmental protection remained well below the level necessary merely to prevent the environmental situation from declining further. Furthermore, promoting environmental protection became an even more difficult task as the financial costs of addressing the problems of the global environment increased.

Establishing the Guiding Principles of
China's Formal Environmental Diplomacy

During the late 1980s and early 1990s, two global environmental issues—ozone depletion and global climate change—placed Chinese environment and development policies under intense international scrutiny. These issues were important because, unlike previous global environmental problems, the ramifications were potentially devastating—including, in the case of global climate change, the complete submergence of some small island states because of sea level rise—and the environmental, health, and economic costs associated with them were exorbitant. In addition, these global environmental phenomena differed substantially in nature from previous environmental problems, because the treaties designed to respond to them would entail substantial financial and human resource commitments.

China's contribution to these problems, when viewed from a historical perspective, was inconsequential. Both global climate change and ozone depletion result primarily from industrial processes related to development rather than from natural phenomena. China's relatively late industrial development, therefore, meant that compared to Europe and the United States, it bore little responsibility for the current global environmental state. However, owing to its sheer size and the magnitude of its industrial development throughout the 1980s, at the time of the negotiations it had become one of the chief contributors. In terms of ozone depletion, China's consumption of the ozone-depleting substances was roughly 3 percent of the world total in 1986 prior to the negotiations. By 1994, its consumption had soared to 18 percent. Similarly, during the late 1980s, China ranked third in total contribution to global climate change (by the mid-1990s, China ranked second after the United States; and conservative estimates indicate that China will surpass the United States as the chief contributor of CO_2 by the year 2020).

The emergence of ozone depletion and global climate change on the international political agenda resulted in a confluence of three important issues for China: China's importance as a contributor to these environmental problems, the potentially exorbitant costs to the Chinese economy of responding to the problems, and the attention that China was receiving from the international community regarding its contribution. This combination of issues prompted Chinese leaders to reevaluate their relatively ad hoc approach to global environmental negotiations. In response, they established a more formal set of principles and guidelines for negotiating global environmental issues.

In spring 1990, in the midst of negotiating both the London Amendments to the Montreal Protocol and the scientific aspects of the climate change negotiations, the Ministry of Foreign Affairs (MOFA), NEPA, the State Planning Commission (SPC), and the SSTC convened a meeting to establish the guiding principles of environmental protection for international negotiation. Prior to the meeting, three perspectives appeared to dominate within the specialist and policymaking communities: the traditional, the developmental, and the international. They encompassed a broad spectrum of views, ranging from those who encouraged China to play a cooperative role to those who claimed that responsibility for global environmental protection rested entirely with the advanced industrialized countries.

The traditional perspective was well articulated by officials from the Ministry of Foreign Affairs, whose representatives dominated China's delegations to formal environmental negotiating sessions. Those officials couched China's responsibility to respond to global environmental problems in terms of the advanced industrialized countries' debt to the developing nations for destroying the environment.[9] In other words, primary responsibility for addressing climate change and ozone depletion rested with the developed states. In addition, the MOFA called for a new international economic order that would eliminate those factors not favorable to developing China's economy.

The most common perspective, however, was the developmental. Supporters of this view espoused the view that China ought to make some contribution to the international effort to respond to climate change and ozone depletion in part because it was a member of the international community but primarily because the PRC, too, would be affected. At the same time, caveats were attached: Environmental protection had to be premised on sufficient economic development; in the current situation, economic growth in the PRC was more important than environmental problems; and when the PRC reached the appropriate stage of development, it could begin to introduce environmental protection measures in exchange for economic development assistance.[10]

The international perspective, which emphasized China's responsibility to the international community to participate in international environmental accords, was voiced with less frequency. Some officials argued that as a member of the international community, China had a responsibility to participate in a positive fashion. At the same time, such arguments were cognizant of the potential payoffs for cooperative behavior: an improved image for the PRC in the international arena, access to technology and funds, and stronger environmental management techniques. As one environmental lawyer articulated in support of such a view, "Good intentions in environmental protection internally will gain us backing internationally and promote international understanding."[11] Such practical considerations of the costs and benefits for cooperation were evidenced during the PRC domestic debate over the Montreal Protocol, when NEPA officials argued that the failure to sign an agreement to decrease and eventually eliminate ozone-depleting substances would harm imports and exports, and that China would benefit from financial support from international sources.[12]

What emerged from these domestic debates and the spring 1990 meeting were five principles that closely resembled the traditional perspective:

1. Environment and development should be integrated, but environmental protection should not be achieved at the expense of the economy. Environmental protection can only be effective when development has been attained.

2. From a historical perspective, the developed countries are responsible for global environmental degradation and the current problems with greenhouse gas emissions. China should not talk about responsibility.
3. Developed countries should provide resources for implementation of agreements or declarations signed. This financial resource should not be considered assistance but compensation from the developed countries.
4. Developed countries should find suitable mechanisms to develop sustainable programs. In order to accommodate national intellectual property rights, the governments of the developed countries should buy the technology from companies and sell it to developing nations at below-market prices.
5. The sovereignty of natural resource rights must be respected. No country can interfere with the decisions of another with regard to the use of its natural resources.[13]

Chinese officials first employed these arguments in an international forum during the negotiations of the London Amendments to the Montreal Protocol in 1990. The PRC, cooperating closely with India, argued that since the developed countries were responsible for most of the damage, they should bear the brunt of the cost of solving the problem of ozone depletion. In addition, China claimed that the developing countries had to consider their immediate economic needs before they worried about global environmental problems for which they were not responsible. The pressure exerted by the PRC and India resulted in the establishment of a multilateral fund to support the development and implementation of chlorofluorocarbon (CFC) substitutes, with China and India receiving special allotments.[14]

The success of these negotiations, as well as the potentially even more costly impending negotiations on climate change, likely prompted the PRC to move decisively to forestall any international movement to place pressure on China to take action to respond to climate change. In June 1991, with their principles in hand, the Chinese moved to the fore of the international negotiation process on climate change. They invited forty-one developing countries to attend the Ministerial Conference of Developing Countries on Environment and Development in Beijing to discuss global environmental and development issues.

The purpose of the meeting was to develop a united bargaining position in preparation for the UNCED political negotiations the following year. Despite resistance from a few of the other states, at the conclusion of the conference, all the participants signed the conference document, the "Beijing Ministerial Declaration on Environment and Development."

China's five principles set the tenor for the document and appeared directly in several places. The developing states assumed virtually no responsibility for environmental degradation or climate change. The document stated, "Ever since the Industrial Revolution, the developed countries have over-exploited the world's natural resources. . . . In view of their main responsibility for environmental degradation and their great financial and technological capabilities, they must take the lead in eliminating the damage to the environment as well as in assisting the developed countries to deal with the problems facing them."[15] The declaration also argued that environmental considerations should not be used as an excuse for interference in the internal affairs of the developing countries, to introduce any forms of conditionality in internal affairs of the developing countries, or to impose trade barriers affecting the development efforts of the developing countries. Finally, it stated that the developed countries were responsible for past and present excessive emissions of greenhouse gases and therefore would have to be the ones to take immediate action. The developing countries could not be expected to accept any obligations in the near future.[16]

During the treaty negotiations on climate change, China played a key role in limiting the mandate of the convention and protecting state sovereignty. China gained a reputation for advocating a "skeleton of a convention . . . a toothless jaw bone."[17] For example, China pushed hard for voluntary reporting of greenhouse gas emissions and opposed all efforts to require publication of regular reviews of the progress of individual states on the implementation of greenhouse gas control measures.[18] NGO observers further commented that the Chinese were difficult to get along with and had a bad attitude. According to one of these same observers, India, Brazil, and China together were often referred to as the "Gang of Three."[19]

Although China and India were allied on the issue of global climate change and ozone depletion, Western observers to the negotiations on the London Amendments to the Montreal Protocol noted that the Chinese demonstrated a far more practical side to their negotiations. China appeared much more willing to sacrifice its stated principles for financial and technical assistance. In the words of one U.S. observer to the ozone negotiations, "The Chinese were willing to cut a deal."[20] Thus, as soon as the multilateral fund was established, China conceded all other points of principle.

The Rise of Techno-Diplomacy

Tough bargaining, recalcitrance, and polemics typically have been the hallmarks of Chinese environmental diplomacy in formal international negotiations. At the same time, a second form of diplomacy has emerged, one that reflects a markedly different style and agenda. This diplomatic approach—which might be termed *techno-diplomacy*—is rooted in a cooperative rather than confrontational stance. It advocates China's working together with the international community to address global environmental problems and committing real domestic resources to resolve global environmental problems.

The agenda, although encompassing the MOFA's appeal for funds and technology transfer, is pursued primarily by scientific and environmental elites and emphasizes the need to elevate the status of environmental protection relative to economic development; recognizes the threat of global environmental problems to the PRC; and manifests a commitment to strengthen China's capacity to respond to domestic and international environmental problems. In addition, techno-diplomacy attempts to use the international community to bring pressure to bear on the less environmentally proactive elements within the Chinese bureaucracy.

Prior to the late 1980s, the Chinese scientific and environmental community concentrated exclusively on gaining access to training opportunities and foreign technology. The various United Nations secretariats that oversaw the international environmental agreements typically offered extensive educational programs and some technology transfer for the expert communities in developing states. As party to the London Dumping Convention, China's State Oceanographic Administration took advantage of the training courses on monitoring ocean dumping and developing an adequate legal system that were offered by the United Nations Environment Programme and the International Marine Organization. And China, after joining the World Heritage Convention in 1985, began to take advantage of management-training seminars and international assistance to restore such national treasures as the Mogao Grottoes.[21]

It was not until the Montreal Protocol and the Framework Convention on Climate Change were under negotiation, however, that the Chinese scientific community began to take a much more active role in the process of PRC environmental diplomacy. The concept of epistemic communities captures well the political process by which the international scientific and environmental experts and Chinese specialists worked together on these issues to try to set the environmental agenda and shape the policy options for the Chinese leadership.[22] Because of the extensive scientific component inherent in both treaties, the formal negotiations were preceded by lengthy scientific discussions that required the participation of the Chinese scientific community. This process of scientific negotiation engendered an unprecedented degree of consultation between the domestic and the international expert communities. In addition, these conventions demanded a substantial amount of research and data gathering by experts from each country. In China, this effort prompted the establishment of an extensive coordinating bureaucracy, whose job it was to collect the necessary data for the scientific discussions. This activity—both within the domestic Chinese expert community itself and between the Chinese and the international expert communities—generated a newly unified and aggressive environmental community within the PRC.

In October 1990, the environmental and scientific communities launched their first diplomatic offensive. Then-head of NEPA Qu Geping, SSTC chairman Song Jian, and president of the Development Research Center of the State Council Ma Hong convened a three-day, high-profile international meeting, the International Conference on the Integration of Economic Development and Environment in China. The conference brought together Chinese leaders and international experts to discuss issues pertaining to the program's directive, "China and the World in the Nineties." This was the first of the international conferences hosted by Beijing to focus on environmental concerns, and the participants from outside China included representatives from the World Bank and UNDP; business executives from Shell and Sumitomo, and the heads of nongovernmental organizations such as the Rockefeller Foundation and the World Wide Fund for Nature. The Chinese were represented by diverse ministers and vice ministers from industry, environmental and economic agencies, and the provinces.

The conference had several goals: first, to increase the understanding of China's environmental problems within the international community; second, to encourage China's less proactive actors to become more proactive, and third to advance the cause of technology and funds transfer to China from the advanced industrialized states, UN organizations, foundations, and corporations.

Qu Geping used his position as conference chairman to bring international pressure to bear on the somewhat less environmentally inclined ministry representatives, who also were attending, such as the Minister of Energy Huang Yicheng, State Planning Commission Vice Chairman Chen Guangjian, and head of the MOFA's Department of International Organizations Chen Jian. Each of these officials' presentations stressed either the economic imperatives of advancing development at the expense of the environment or the primary responsibility of the developed countries to address pollution issues, since they had consumed global resources and degraded the environment in their drive to industrialize.[23] In contrast, representatives from the Ministry of Agriculture, the Ministry of Water Conservancy, and the Development Research Center of the State Council claimed that China's pollution stemmed primarily from China's inappropriate pricing system of natural resources, the traditional view that resources are inexhaustible, and poor management techniques at local levels.[24] In his summation, Qu Geping carefully delineated each industrial and environmental arena in which he believed that China should take stronger action to improve environmental protection measures.[25]

Soon after this meeting, Song Jian set out publicly an alternative formula to the one presented at formal diplomatic negotiations. He stated: "As we develop the economy, we must guarantee a balanced ecological environment and maintain in good order our natural resources so that future generations will have their rightful heritage. To this end, we should be ready to pay more or, if necessary, slow down the economic development."[26]

This more environmentally proactive effort was given a dramatic boost by the advent of the 1992 United Nations Conference on Environment and Development (UNCED). Whereas the 1972 United Nations Conference on the Human Environment had sparked an initial interest in environmental protection in China, preparation for the 1992 UNCED paved the way for an important shift in the consciousness and politics of the environment in the PRC. Although the Chinese delegation to the UNCED, led by Li Peng, not surprisingly reflected traditional values and rhetoric, the UNCED had a profound effect on environmental policies, institutions, and thinking in the PRC.

In terms of actual policy change in the PRC, the most important result of the UNCED was the formation of a Chinese action plan to implement a policy of sustainable development. The UNCED produced a consensus document, *Agenda 21*, which was a global call to action on issues of sustainable development and encompassed every environmental issue from local air pollution to biodiversity. Within one year, China became the first country to develop its own national Agenda 21 based on the global action plan. China's Agenda 21 involved input from over 300 Chinese ministries, commissions and local governments. It was composed of 78 projects in four areas: sustained development strategies, rational utilization of national resources, economic sustained development, and social sustained development. The priority program for China's Agenda 21, however, was issued in 1996 and included 128 projects.[27] These projects were scheduled to be incorporated into the Ninth Five-Year Plan; however, in the end, the plan referred to environmental protection only in much broader terms.

During summer 1994, the techno-diplomats initiated their second effort to engage the international community. The State Science and Technology Commission vice president, Deng Nan, stated:

> The development of the economy and technology has made it possible for us to increase investment to deal with environmental problems, but economic development in China at present is basically resource oriented. It is possible that development will bring about destruction of the ecology and

worsening of the environment. If environmental problems are ignored in the process of development economic development will be severely hampered. We should extensively launch international cooperation.[28]

In July 1994, shortly after Deng Nan's statement, China held a second high-level meeting to garner international financial support for the national Agenda 21 projects. Representatives from twenty countries, international institutions, and enterprises agreed to support approximately forty of the sixty-two high-priority projects that the Chinese outlined. These included: sustainable agricultural development, pollution control and clean energy, and the development of communications. In order for the national Agenda 21, estimated to cost $4 billion overall, to succeed, the international community, according to Song Jian, would have to supply 30 to 40 percent of the funds for these projects.[29] Officially, in 1996, the Chinese claimed that about one-third of the $4 billion had been raised (one-third from foreign sources, with U.S. institutions the largest donor). However, according to one SSTC official, these figures are likely inflated.[30]

Chinese participation in the UNCED also engendered institutional change. Because of the emphasis placed on nongovernmental actor participation in the UNCED, genuine environmental nongovernmental organizations emerged in China, although they have yet to demonstrate their ability to play a significant role in environmental protection affairs, especially global environmental affairs. In 1993, Liang Congjie, a prominent Chinese historian, established the first registered environmental NGO, Friends of Nature. Friends of Nature focuses on environmental education, which has been sanctioned and supported by the government, and is a critical, relatively inexpensive, and fairly innocuous means of improving the environmental situation in China. Since that time, a number of other environmental NGOs have emerged, including the China Forum of Environmental Journalists, Women and the Environment, and the Global Village Environmental Culture Institute. At the same time, the Chinese have been quick to perceive the international desire to support NGOs in China; in one case, a village in Inner Mongolia established itself as an NGO and received funding from the Conference of Parties on Desertification.

Moreover, in order to implement China's Agenda 21, the State Science and Technology Commission and the State Planning Commission (the lead organizations overseeing China's Agenda 21), have established an Agenda 21 center, which is housed within the SSTC compound in Beijing. The NEPA, SETC, MOFA and MOFTEC occupy second- and third-tier positions. In addition there are more than fifty ministries and government agencies referred to as stakeholders in the Agenda 21 process. Local governments are also developing their own Agenda 21 bureaus to ensure that sustainable development principles are incorporated in urban planning.[31]

Other institutional innovations are less directly linked to the UNCED but are in keeping with Western principles of environmental protection. For example, NEPA began supporting *Huanjing Bao* (Environmental News), a monthly publication that explores environmental issues and exposes environmental wrongdoing, even though in many instances the latter involves local environmental protection bureau officials. In addition, a national news program sponsored by NEPA covers local pollution issues and periodically offers exposés on polluting enterprises. China has even developed radio call-in shows that encourage Chinese citizens to ask questions about environmental issues such as endangered species.

China has also looked directly to the United States and multilateral institutions for assistance in revising their environmental laws. One of the most significant innovations in national environmental protection law has been the right of the environmental protection bureaus (EPBs) to take polluting enterprises to court. The court system is the strongest lever that NEPA and the local EPBs possess in cases where enterprises or other local bureaus balk at paying the fees. Although there have not been many cases brought to trial at this point, there have been some in which polluting firms have paid their fines or been shut down because of a court order.

The Efficacy of Dual Diplomacy

Overall, Chinese environmental diplomacy has evidenced remarkable success both in the formal political negotiations and in the diplomatic efforts of the environmental and scientific elites. In formal political negotiations for both the Montreal Protocol and the Framework Convention on Climate Change, China successfully protected its sovereignty by preventing the linkage of aid or implementation of sanctions to any formal agreement to change China's environmental practices. Moreover, the advanced industrialized states, responding to the strong lobbying of China and India, established a funding mechanism to help implement the Montreal Protocol. At the same time, the most significant successes have involved techno-diplomacy and the increasing integration of China into the international environmental community.

According to one estimate, fully 80 percent of China's environmental protection budget is derived from abroad.[32] Overall, China is the largest recipient of total environmental aid from the World Bank and has received extensive support from the Global Environmental Facility, the Asian Development Bank, the United Nations Development Program, and bilateral sources. According to one study, "International institutions have more than $4 billion earmarked for environment-related projects in China."[33] During 1990–1995, the Asian Development Bank set aside

U.S.$2.07 billion for 15 projects in the PRC. And its plans for 1996–1999 include an additional $2 billion for environment-related projects.[34] China is also launching 173 projects on ozone depletion with the help of U.S.$105.6 million from the Multilateral Fund of the Montreal Protocol.

In addition, bilateral assistance has been flowing to the PRC for environmental protection. Japan is the largest donor of environmental aid and has made such assistance to China a priority within its Overseas Development Aid budget. For the 1996–1998 period, Japan pledged a total of U.S.$5.8 billion in loans and grants; over one-third of the projects are related to the environment. Japan also funded a $100 million Japan-China Friendship Environmental Protection Center in Beijing and has granted an additional $182 million to support demonstration projects in China. Here, too, in the negotiations with the Japanese, the Chinese have been relatively successfully in delinking "sovereign" political concerns from aid. The Japanese Overseas Development Aid Charter states explicitly that countries that "cause concern" in human rights, the environment, arms exports, and the development of weapons of mass destruction" would have their aid reviewed. (Although the Chinese managed to avoid such a review for human rights purposes, their grant-in-aid was in fact temporarily suspended in 1996 because of Chinese nuclear testing.)

Even when the international scientific and environmental community has failed to support Chinese environmental policy, if other sectors of the international community become engaged, China has still proved highly effective in capturing foreign assistance and support. The best example of this is the Three Gorges Dam project. In this case, international experts condemned the project; the Chinese scientific community was divided on the merits of the dam; and there was serious debate over the project within the National People's Congress during 1992. Those opposed to the dam—both within and outside China—argued that the project was unsound on several grounds: It would require the relocation of over one million Chinese citizens; precious arable land would be flooded; ancient cultural relics would be destroyed; and the reservoir created by the dam would become filled with sediment and prevent the passage of some ships; among others. Despite these criticisms, the Chinese government elected to proceed with the dam.

Initially, the PRC faced a dearth of international financial support for the dam: The World Bank indicated that it would not assist the PRC; and Chinese plans to issue bonds on the international financial market were dashed by the lack of interest. Nonetheless, as the Chinese advertised the scope of the foreign business opportunities, governments set aside their environmental and human rights concerns and embraced the opportunity to help their domestic firms win bids on various aspects of the project by providing financial assistance and insurance through their export credit agencies.[35] Only the United States, led by the U.S. State Department, withheld support through its Export-Import Bank.

Future Prospects for China's Environmental Foreign Relations

The evolution of two relatively distinct levels of Chinese environmental diplomacy has brought the PRC significant rewards in funding, technology, and training opportunities from the international community. At the same time, the PRC has needed to undertake only a highly circumscribed set of commitments to respond to the interests of this same international community.

Four clear challenges that threaten the sustainability of the PRC's dual diplomacy, however, have emerged. How China resolves these challenges will determine the viability of each path of diplomacy.

The first challenge is posed by the very process of integration with the international community. Whereas this integration has clearly strengthened the hand of environmental authorities in China, it has also brought greater international scrutiny. The scientific and environmental elites who are conducting the second level of diplomacy, Song Jian, Qu Geping, and Xie Zhenhua, among others, consider China's increasing integration into the system of international environmental agreements and organizations critical to their ability to improve and enforce domestic environmental laws, including those designed to fulfill international obligations. With higher levels of international assistance, both financial and technical, however, come growing expectations that China will meet its international obligations.

Yet, it is far from certain that China can meet these growing expectations. There is widespread resistance among local authorities, who are eager to maximize economic growth, to the implementation of environmental laws. Song Jian has decried this pattern of behavior, commenting, "The conduct that sacrifices the environment to seek high economic profits is as harmful as smuggling narcotics and marketing fake medicines and must be severely punished."[36] During an inspection tour of local and provincial environmental protection efforts in 1993–1995 by the National People's Congress and the State Environmental Protection Commission, the inspection teams uncovered more than 3,000 violations of state environmental protection laws and regulations.[37] Song Jian has called for local governments to improve their efforts, but thus far there is little evidence that changes are in the offing. Continued poor implementation of international treaty obligations undoubtedly will strain the goodwill of sympathetic international actors, possibly causing funds and other opportunities to diminish significantly. How this first tension is resolved will in good measure determine the future of China's environmental foreign relations.

A second, related, challenge is posed by the very success of the interaction between Chinese institutions and the international community. While the environment has been rising in priority on the leaders' agenda, in good measure due to international attention to the issue, various agencies have been attempting to co-opt the issue to serve their own bureaucratic interests. The low standing of NEPA—which does not hold ministerial rank—has made this process of co-optation much easier. NEPA also is excluded from lead positions in environmental efforts and has been forced to develop separate initiatives. Thus, even as the SSTC and the SPC pursue Agenda 21 initiatives, the National Environmental Protection Agency has established its own Transcentury Green Project Plan (1995–2010), which competes directly with the Agenda 21 in terms of focus and need for international funding. This type of bureaucratic maneuvering poses a serious challenge to the eventual success of the techno-diplomats' efforts.

The third challenge to the continued viability of this dual diplomacy is the increasing politicization of the environment as an issue in Chinese foreign relations more generally. During the period of relatively tense political relations between the United States and China in 1995–1997, for example, the concept of sustainable development began to take on new meaning in China. Although the Western concept, which was introduced most notably at the UNCED, had always had a rather confused semantic pedigree, it was adopted quickly by both Chinese specialists and generalists as a goal for Chinese development and environment practices. Leaders used the term *sustainable development* in many different ways: to mean sustained development (the alleviation of poverty requires sustained growth); to mean first economic development, then environmental protection; and to mean the incorporation of environmental considerations in economic development through the use of environmental economics and other appropriate incentives and regulations or laws. However, in 1995–1997, there was increasing discussion in the Chinese media suggesting that sustainable development was part of a master plan by the advanced industrialized countries (and especially the United States) to contain China by forcing it to slow the pace of economic growth in order to protect the environment. This suggests that the techno-diplomats, who themselves have advocated such a cooling in economic development, may lose their battle to advance environmental protection as a domestic and foreign policy priority because of this linkage with broader political considerations. Indeed, future Chinese commitments to global environmental protection may well be held hostage to the state of the Sino-American relationship.

Whereas the first three challenges suggest that China may be inclined to turn inward in order to protect other (higher-priority) interests and risk the loss of international funds and other perquisites, the final challenge indicates otherwise. The range of political reforms—among them the emergence of genuine NGOs, an activist media, an enlivened and empowered National People's Congress—offers opportunities for the evolution of a broader popular consensus in support of the efforts of the techno-diplomats. Although such a transformation is unlikely to take place within the next three to five years, there is ample evidence to suggest that especially in wealthier regions, long-term environmental considerations are rising on the agenda of local authorities and the populace.[38] Thus, over the coming decade, a growing commitment to environmental protection and to the values and goals espoused by the techno-diplomats may well emerge from the ground up. These four challenges currently remain unanswered and the tensions within China's dual diplomacy unresolved. Overall, however, the deepest challenge is posed by the fourth one: the transformation of China's political system. Whether such a transformation will occur in time to prevent continued irreversible damage to China's own, as well as the global, environment is unlikely. But if the current political trends continue, the prognosis is better than good that in the case of the environment, change will prevail over continuity and sustained development may in fact become sustainable development.

Notes

1. "Report of the United Nations Conference on the Human Environment," UN Document A/conf.48/14/Rev.1.

2. Geping Qu, "A Synopsis on the Course of Development on China's Environmental Protection," *Environmental Management in China* (Beijing: China Environmental Press, 1991), 213–220.

3. Ibid., 220.

4. Ibid., 222.

5. Geping Qu, "Opening up Environmental Protection with Chinese Characteristics," Geping Qu, *Environmental Management in China*, 114.

6. Michel Oksenberg and Elizabeth Economy, "China: Implementation Under Economic Growth and Market Reform," in Harold Jacobson and Edith Brown Weiss, *Strengthening Compliance with International Environmental Accords* (MIT Press, forthcoming).

7. Ibid.

8. One important exception to this was the Convention on Trade in Endangered Species.

9. NEPA official, interview by author, Beijing, June 1992.

10. Ibid.

11. "Taolun Woguo de Huanjing Waijiao Zhengce" (A discussion of China's foreign environmental policy), *Zhongguo Huanjing Guanli* 1 (1992): 7–9.

12. NEPA official, interview by author and Michel Oksenberg, Beijing, October 1994.

13. SSTC official, interview by author, Beijing, April 1992. See Elizabeth Economy, "Negotiating the Terrain of Global Climate Change Policy in the Soviet Union and China: Linking International and Domestic Decisionmaking Pathways" (Dissertation, University of Michigan, 1994).

14. Larry Stammer, "Chinese Delegates to Seek Beijing's Approval for Pact to Protect Ozone," *Los Angeles Times*, June 29, 1990, A8.

15. "Beijing Ministerial Declaration on Environment and Development," Beijing SSTC, 1991, 1–3.

16. Ibid.

17. "ECO," no. 6 (December 16, 1991): 3.

18. "ECO," no. 9 (December 19, 1991): 1.

19. "ECO," no. 5 (December 13, 1991): 2.

20. Interview with U.S. Environmental Protection Agency official, Washington, D.C., July 1992.

21. Oksenberg and Economy, "China: Implementation."

22. For a fuller discussion of the concept of epistemic communities, see the special issue on this topic in *International Organization* 46, no. 1 (Winter 1992).

23. Martin Lees, "China and the World in the Nineties," Conference Summary Report, Beijing, January 25, 1991, 30–31.

24. Ibid., 9–19.

25. Ibid., 22.

26. Foreign Broadcast Information Service [hereafter FBIS], *Daily Report, China,* December 27, 1990, 31.

27. *Priority Programme for China's Agenda 21* (Beijing: Administrative Center for China's Agenda 21, 1996).

28. FBIS, *Daily Report, China,* June 29, 1994, 22.

29. FBIS, *Daily Report, China,* July 11, 1994, 31.

30. SSTC official, interview by author, Beijing, November 1996.

31. Ibid.

32. Miranda Schreurs's talk at the Woodrow Wilson Center, Washington, D.C., June 4, 1997.

33. Daniel C. Esty and Seth S. Dunn, "Greening U.S. Aid to China," *China Business Review,* January-February 1997, 44–45.

34. Ibid.

35. Nancy Dunne and Tony Walker, "Power Hungry on the Gorges," *Financial Times,* February 17, 1997.

36. FBIS, *Daily Report, China,* January 9, 1995, 14.

37. *China Daily,* January 9, 1995, p. 2.

38. See for example, Elizabeth Economy, *Reforms and Resources: The Implications for State Capacity in the PRC,* American Academy of Arts and Sciences Occasional Paper, 1997.

PART FOUR

Prospects

13

Chinese Foreign Policy: Retrospect and Prospect

ALLEN S. WHITING

Looking Back from Abroad

Before predicting the course of Chinese foreign policy in the twenty-first century it is sobering to recall the failures at such efforts since 1949.[1] In 1950 U.S. policymakers did not anticipate China's entry into the Korean War. It did not seem logical for a country that had just achieved national unity after more than a decade of Japanese invasion and civil war to take on the world's strongest military power. But the cost-benefit calculus of Beijing did not accord with that projected by Washington. Chinese defensive concerns prompted offensive action, which inflicted on U.S. forces the most humiliating reversal they had ever experienced.[2]

Confronted with the Sino-Soviet alliance, U.S. policymakers hoped eventually to divide Beijing from Moscow. But few, inside or outside the government, thought this division would occur in the near future. Yet in 1959–1960 Mao Zedong's attack on Nikita Khrushchev's leadership of international communism and Mao's behavior as an ally destroyed that relationship. As a result, China lost its only major source of military weapons and industrial assistance. Once again political goals outweighed practical losses. Then in the mid-1960s came Mao's Great Proletarian Cultural Revolution, with the most extreme manifestation of revolutionary fervor and xenophobia since establishment of the People's Republic. Few observers anticipated any likelihood of improved relations between Beijing and Washington before Mao's death. More immediately, such a development seemed impossible while China was helping Vietnam to resist American bombing, with mounting casualties on both sides.[3] Yet eight months after President Lyndon Johnson began negotiations with Hanoi in March 1968, Beijing signaled interest in détente and entered serious negotiations one year later. Because China perceived a threat from the Soviet Union, it placed national security interests over ideology and explored the possible gain from the strategic triangle.

These surprises in China's relations with the two superpowers came in part from the idiosyncratic role of Mao. His rationality did not correspond to the logic of cost-benefit calculus attributed to Beijing by foreign observers.[4] Of course, relations are bilateral, and some explanatory power lies with the behavior of Khrushchev and his successors as well as with President Richard Nixon. Basically, however, the initiative in these instances lay with Mao, who exercised supreme authority in Chinese foreign policy until his death in 1976.

Less dramatic surprises caught the attention of foreign observers under Deng Xiaoping's rule. In 1978 Deng established diplomatic relations with the United States without resolving the question of arms sales to Taiwan. His short-lived invasion of Vietnam in 1979 and his establishment of Special Economic Zones in 1980 with generous concessions to foreign investment were less-extreme initiatives than those of Mao. Nonetheless, their implications were equally unexpected and far-reaching for the broad framework of Chinese foreign policy. In his final years Deng shocked Washington with military exercises, including missile firings, in the Taiwan Strait, in reaction to the Clinton administration's giving a visa to the Taiwan president, Lee Teng-hui, for an address at Cornell University.[5]

These reflections on past forecasting caution against undue confidence in projecting Beijing's present foreign policy into the twenty-first century. We do not know how the regime will evolve. No alternative is in sight, but one must keep in mind that the sudden collapse of Communist rule in the Soviet Union was not foreseen far in advance. Nor do we know how the dynamic interplay of central, regional, and provincial interests will impact on foreign policy decisions that cut across them.[6] For example, should the regime seriously threaten the use of force against Taiwan, bad relations with Japan and the United States would reduce foreign investment and trade, in turn affecting local interests. Bureaucratic, factional, and military-civilian conflicts cannot be foreseen, much less the personal risk-taking proclivities of Jiang Zemin and his successors with respect to both national and personal interests.

In creative scenarios one can hypothesize a wide range of alternative futures with different contexts and varying time frames. But to consider everything that is conceivably possible over the next decade or two is an exercise in contingency planning beyond our need. A more prudent approach is to outline reasonable probabilities projected seven to ten years ahead. Within these specified limits, basic issues determining the general thrust of Chinese foreign policy will be considered; the basic assumption will be that China will remain united under Communist rule, with the guidelines for foreign policy as laid down by Deng and reaffirmed by

Jiang.[7] These guidelines posit economic development as the first priority, followed closely by territorial integrity, with special emphasis on the recovery of Taiwan.

These two policy goals can be contradictory, and their implications will vary for the three alternative frameworks for foreign policy: conflict, cooperation, and competition. We will examine how each of these frameworks may impact specific relationships, bilateral and multilateral, recognizing that foreign policy can be proactive, reactive, and interactive. This variation places responsibility on other capitals for influencing, if not determining, future Chinese foreign policy. Thus forecasting is contingent on how others relate to China as well as vice-versa. This caveat should be kept in mind, even though it will not be reiterated at each point.

High Conflict Potential: Taiwan

With collapse of the Soviet Union, U.S. foreign policy specialists turned to the prospects for China's becoming a major threat to peace and security in East Asia. Concern arose from various quarters.[8] Historians and political scientists argued that rising powers tended to challenge the existing international system, seeking to replace the dominant power or powers. They pointed to Germany in the nineteenth century and again in the twentieth, as well as Japan after World War I. From the inception of the People's Republic in 1949, its public stance against imperialism and demand for a New Economic Order gave credence to such analysis.

Specialists on China emphasized self-images of the Middle Kingdom and a cultural tradition of assertive domination over neighboring peoples.[9] Beijing's 1950 intervention in Korea, 1962 border war with India, clashes with Soviet border troops in 1969, limited invasion of Vietnam in 1979, and seizure of South China Sea islands between 1974 and 1995 add strength to this view. It is reinforced by China's extensive territorial claims at sea that clash with Korea, Japan, Vietnam, the Philippines, Malaysia, and Brunei. In fact, were Beijing to extend its alleged claims to an Exclusive Economic Zone (EEZ) in each case, it would control the Yellow Sea, the East China Sea, and most of the South China Sea. Last but not least is its avowal to use force if necessary to prevent Taiwan's becoming independent.

These offshore claims have additional motivation beside the standard nationalistic insistence on sovereignty and territorial integrity. First and foremost, all of these waters are believed to contain sizable reserves of oil and natural gas.[10] Exploration and feasibility studies have not been carried out, because foreign firms have stayed away in light of the international disputes. But with China's economy expanding at a higher rate than available power, the country's energy needs are acute. Although coal reserves are vast, the pollution impact of their exploitation at home and abroad is serious. Oil and natural gas reserves on land are remote from major points of consumption. Nuclear power is expensive and possibly hazardous. Hydroelectric power will become more important when the Three Gorges Dam comes on line in the next century, but it will still fall short of demand. Under these circumstances, the promise of offshore hydrocarbons is an valuable component for an economy serving 1.3 billion people. Unfortunately the promise of offshore hydrocarbons also beckons Japan, which must import 90 percent of its energy supply.

Second, strategic considerations place a premium on control of Taiwan and the adjacent waters. The acquisition of this area by Japan after it defeated China in 1894–1895 provided Tokyo with a base for invading China in 1937 and seizing Southeast Asia in 1941. Denial of Taiwan to a potential enemy safeguards east China, traditionally a major industrial and agricultural sector. Offensively, Taiwan dominates the trade routes to Japan. It also could advance Chinese air and sea power two hundred miles from mainland bases for projection in the West Pacific. Control of the South China Sea likewise poses a potential threat of interruption to Sea Lanes of Communication (SLOC) vital for Japan as well as for the maritime states of Southeast Asia.

Critics of "China threat" scenarios counter by pointing to Beijing's use of force in defensive reaction to perceived threats in 1950 and 1962, whereas border disputes with Burma, Nepal, and Pakistan were settled by compromise.[11] Mongolia's independence and the delimitation and demarcation of the extensive border were formally recognized, steps never taken by the Republic of China. In 1962 the PLA withdrew from virtually all the territory seized during its border war with India and the status quo ante has held ever since. After the collapse of the Soviet Union, Beijing arrived at previously disputed border agreements with Russia, Kazakhstan, and Kyrgystan and reached a partial settlement of the frontier dispute with Vietnam. As for present disputes at sea, compromise may eventuate from economic interdependence, given China's trade and investment ties to Japan, the United States, and, to a lesser extent, the Association of Southeast Asian (ASEAN) states. The threat of economic sanctions could be a deterrent against using military force.

Meanwhile China increasingly interacts with its East Asian neighbors through the ASEAN Regional Forum (ARF), the Asia Pacific Economic Cooperation forum (APEC), and recurring bilateral exchanges, from summitry to ministerial and lesser levels. This interaction may gradually reduce concern over potential threats and induce acceptance of the idea of gain through compromise and cooperation. None of this can be expected to come quickly or easily. China's "century of shame and humiliation," from the Opium War to its establishment of "New China," is central to the regime's image of historical wrongs to be redressed.[12] Indeed critics of the "China threat" approach warn that it could become a self fulfilling prophecy: Preoccupation with defense and perception of threats could cause Beijing to interpret this term as a covert effort to "keep China down," requiring a more assertive posture in response.

These two approaches produce markedly different future scenarios and might be simplistically categorized as pessimistic and optimistic. But serious proponents of each view do not make their projections predetermined or inevitable. Instead they call for different policies toward China, which might lessen or increase the likelihood of one or the other forecast. This uncertainty places emphasis on contingency and context and introduces reactive and interactive elements for a more complex and varied forecast. Within such a format, a better calculation of the conflict potential in Chinese foreign policy can be attempted, but one should recognize that subjective factors can obscure objective ones for both the analyst abroad and the policymakers in Beijing.

Of all the territorial disputes on Beijing's agenda, Taiwan presents the greatest conflict potential should the two sides not work out a mutually satisfactory settlement of their respective claims to sovereignty and authority. This positive outcome is not inconceivable. Both sides are acutely aware of the costs of war, especially to Taiwan. The observation that "Chinese should not fight Chinese" has been made on both sides. Communication between Beijing and Taipei occurs repeatedly through multiple channels. Face-saving formulas can be advanced privately to avoid public embarrassment. But the limitations on compromise remain severe for the mainland as well as for Taiwan. For nearly fifty years Chinese officials have insisted that the island had to be united with the People's Republic. If any leader were to abandon this stance and favor Taiwanese independence, he would risk his political life. At the top he would be opposed by the most nationalistic group in China, the PLA.[13] The goal of military modernization reportedly is to have by 2010 sufficient capability to take Taiwan and deter U.S.-Japan involvement if necessary.[14] In the meantime the professional military are not ready to jump the gun, civilian rhetoric notwithstanding. As David Shambaugh has shown, the PLA leadership emergent under Jiang has fought on various fronts since 1950.[15] It knows its limitations in the high-technology type of weaponry utilized during the Gulf War. Exercises in the Taiwan Strait revealed weaknesses as well as strengths in potential combat with Taiwan's newly upgraded air and naval forces.[16] Nonetheless, acquiescence in a permanently separated Taiwan would invite PLA opposition, based on basic patriotism as well as on the strategic calculations outlined above.

At the level of mass public opinion, visitors to China report that recovery of Taiwan has recently become a conscious goal more than at any time since nationwide "liberate Taiwan" demonstrations in the 1950s. Television portrayal of the 1995 and 1996 military exercises dramatically defined the island's importance and the possibility of conflict, inspiring a wave of nationalism supportive of the regime, a secondary objective of the exercises.[17] The dispatch of two American aircraft carrier task forces in implicit protection of the island added drama to the situation, but the PLA missile firings seemed to defy them. This image of international confrontation over "an internal affair of China" has been furthered by media accusations that Tokyo and Washington have secretly conspired to frustrate unification and encourage Taiwanese independence.

Beijing appears to be ready to wait out the next seven to ten years in hope that benign management of Hong Kong will persuade Taiwan to accept the PRC definition of full autonomy under the "one country, two systems" formula. In 1996 Jiang was reported to have privately cautioned his colleagues against "impetuosity" and named 2010 as the year for a final reckoning. In 1997 he publicly reassured his national audience that Taiwan's recovery would be realized "eventually." Meanwhile the economic status quo is mutually advantageous to both sides in terms of trade, travel, and investment. The waiting time is also commensurate with the time needed for military modernization and accords with the usual wish of a leader to pass a difficult problem on to his successor. Finally, waiting provides the opportunity to pressure Japan diplomatically so as to dissuade or deter it from supporting possible U.S. intervention. The U.S.-Japan alliance has a two-edged impact on Taiwan policy. As a suspected supporter of the island's permanent separation, the alliance provokes militant rhetoric. Because it wields superior military force, it inhibits military action.

Under these circumstances the critical catalyst for a PLA attack appears to be Beijing's sense of Taipei's intentions. If mainland policymakers see independence under one guise or another as an inexorable trend in Taiwan's domestic politics and foreign policy, then in due course Beijing is likely to use force to stop it. Blandishments and threats having failed to bring about a successful reunification, military action will follow. However the attack may be mounted, it will be designed so as to preempt foreign intervention and minimize casualties, but miscalculation can occur on both counts. In sum, the conflict potential for Chinese policy toward Taiwan is low in the near future but high in the long run.

Low Conflict Potential: Disputes at Sea

China's offshore claims are of two kinds. For the Yellow and East China Seas, Beijing's ownership claims are based on the existence of a continental shelf that extends from the mainland less than 250 meters below the surface. For the South China Sea, ownership claims over the vast array of islands, reefs, and shoals are based on prior presence, affirmed by the Republic of China and reaffirmed by the People's Republic of China.[18] As already indicated, the nationalistic motivation to establish territorial integrity is furthered in all three cases by expected—although not yet proven—reserves of natural gas and oil that might relieve China's long-standing energy deficit. Unfortunately, this speculative treasure trove of hydrocarbons impels neighboring states to press rival claims, albeit belatedly in the case of the South China Sea. Finally, the long-standing Chinese antipathy toward Japan adds another dimension of assertiveness, symbolized by repeated political confrontation over the unpopulated rocky outposts known in Japanese as the Senkaku Islands and in Chinese as Diaoyutai.

Despite the attraction of potential oil and gas together with the sensitive issue of national sovereignty, the conflict potential of these disputed claims at sea is low. The high paraffin content of the oil found in the mainland reserves of northeast China and Shandong Province requires special refining facilities existing only in Japan. This presumably foreshadows what lies further afield in the Yellow Sea. Neither in quantity nor in quality are these conjectured reserves worth using force at the risk of relations with either North or South Korea, let alone the political repercussions elsewhere in East Asia. In 1974 Beijing formally protested when Seoul and Tokyo concluded a joint exploration agreement for adjacent waters, pointing out that nothing could be undertaken without Chinese concurrence. However circumstances prevented the Korean-Japanese venture from being fully implemented and the protest was not pressed further.

The East China Sea presented a far more promising field of hydrocarbon reserves, according to early preliminary studies, but nearly thirty years have elapsed without further systematic exploration. One small U.S. firm, in defiance of a Department of State warning against activity in disputed waters, signed a contract with the Chinese, but nothing followed. Uncertainty as to the size of the reserves and the economic feasibility of exploitation leaves the reportedly vast reserves of unknown value. This uncertainty in turn must be weighed against the costs of conflict with Japan, which has an arguable basis for access to whatever may lie on the shelf, since it extends almost to the main islands.

The costs of conflict with Japan are multiple. Most immediately is the question of U.S. response to an attack on its ally even should fighting be limited to action at sea in a disputable area. This hypothetical contingency has already risen in connection with the Senkaku (Diaoyutai) Islands, northeast of Taiwan, at the edge of the continental shelf. The islands were transferred to Japanese administrative authority together with the U.S. return of Okinawa. However, Washington did not recognize full Japanese ownership of these islands, as it did with Okinawa, and subsequently carefully avoided taking sides in the dispute.

In recent years Beijing has steadfastly protested Japanese right-wing groups that position a shipping light or a Japanese flag or pose for photographs on the Senkakus. On each occasion Chinese demonstrations in Taipei and Hong Kong have voiced public anger, with small numbers attempting to land on the islands. Usually they were peacefully prevented by Japanese coast guard ships, although in one instance a Hong Kong demonstrator drowned in the process. Curiously, Beijing refused permission for parallel protests requested by university students despite media criticism of the Japanese intrusions. Nevertheless, in 1995 Chinese jet fighters reportedly overflew the area, triggering a response by Japanese fighters without any contact. In 1995 and 1996 Chinese ocean survey ships sailed along the islands and further up the Ryukyu island chain, whereupon Tokyo formally protested that they had entered Japanese waters without permission.

Beijing's refusal to allow public protests over the Senkakus illustrates the contradictory priorities of economic development and territorial integrity. Trade with Japan is valued for the importation of technology and investment and for the exportation of textiles and other low-cost consumer goods. The complementarity of the two economies at this stage of their respective development makes Japan a particularly advantageous partner. This advantage is strengthened by the absence of political threats of embargo such as exist with Sino-American trade on the basis of human rights and other matters. Japan is the most important trading partner of China, and China ranks second for Japan. But at the same time, the issue of territorial integrity is especially sensitive at both elite and mass levels because of Japan's recurring aggression against China in 1894, 1931, and 1937. The last instance evokes special anger because of the Nanjing Massacre, when tens of thousands were raped and hundreds of thousands slaughtered by Japanese troops in five weeks of mayhem. In 1985 university student demonstrations against Japan inspired by this and other issues alerted the regime that the volatile sentiment over the Senkakus might get out of control and have negative consequences for the overall relationship.[19]

Thus, although the potential economic gain of control over the entire East China Sea is great, so are the potential military and economic costs of fighting Japan. Objectively the optimum solution would be agreement by both sides on dividing control along the median line approximating equidistance from the two coasts, a traditional principle for countries adjoining a continental shelf. Subjectively, however, the political obstacle for Chinese policymakers arises from the heritage of hatred for Japan, focused publicly by the Senkaku Islands dispute. Within the leadership, fortunately, avoidance of combat can be defended because of the economic as well as the military consequences.

By comparison, the military and economic consequences of China's using force to secure its claims in the South China Sea are far less serious, but so are the likely gains with respect to oil and gas.[20] As elsewhere, the conflicting claims have deterred foreign firms from investing in the necessary surveys and test drilling to assess the extent and economic feasibility of exploiting suspected reserves. Beijing has proposed joint exploration, bilateral and multilateral, without conceding sovereignty, but none of the rival claimants have agreed. Because four of the ASEAN states have overlapping jurisdictional lines with one another as well as with China, there is no simple median line solution. Moreover, the conflicting ownership claims are further complicated by EEZ calculations. Simultaneous multilateral concessions on sovereignty, as in Antarctica and the North Sea, appear to be the only alternative. So far, however, domestic politics in all the countries, wholly apart from the potential returns of ownership over underwater resources, has prevented compromise on this highly nationalistic issue.

The political impasse has not stopped China from unilateral action. In 1974 it took the Paracel Islands by force when they were held by South Vietnam, probably to preempt their falling under Hanoi's control after the Vietnam War. In 1988 the Chinese seized another pair of much smaller islands while defeating a few Vietnamese ships and troops. In 1995 the PLA occupied Mischief Reef, claimed by Manila, and refused to vacate it despite a vocal Philippine protest and private ASEAN pressure. Lesser probes by Chinese naval ships and territorial marker expeditions in 1996–1997 expanded points of control in the Spratlys without combat. These tactics are suggestive of a larger strategy drawn from *weiji* or *go*, an Asian board game. Unlike in chess or checkers, where capturing pieces is important, in *weiji* or *go* players seek to occupy space so as gradually to surround and deny their opponent any movement. In the South China Sea this strategy has the political advantage of avoiding direct attack and of appearing aggressive.

Meanwhile the ASEAN agreement on the nonuse of force notwithstanding, all the contesting parties quietly continue to strengthen positions already held. Yet despite the continued military buildup in each of the countries, the likelihood of conflict remains low as far as Chinese policy is concerned. Until modernization of the PLA permits full and continuous power projection over the South China Sea, local combat is not necessarily to Chinese advantage, because of the distances from PLA bases and the upgrading of indigenous capabilities.[21] Equally important are political considerations. Neither ASEAN nor its affiliated organization,

ARF, is a collective military security system. But ASEAN is the strongest regional grouping in East Asia and as such poses a political problem. Openly confronting ASEAN members, singly or collectively, could push the organization to anti-China alignment with the United States or tilt it toward Japan, a rival for leadership in East Asia.

The political-military linkages from ASEAN outward are sufficient to justify Chinese concern over this prospect. In the late 1960s Britain, Australia, New Zealand, Singapore, and Malaysia concluded the Five-Power Defense Agreement (FPDA) in response to London's decision to pull back all forces east of Suez by 1971. In the 1990s Indonesia became an informal observer-participant in annual FPDA joint exercises. Then in 1995, Indonesia became apprehensive over Beijing's refusal to forswear any overlapping claims in the seabed approaching Natuna Island, one of the largest potential oil and gas reserves in East Asia and just below ambiguous lines on Chinese maps that virtually surround the South China Sea. Jakarta finally broke its long-standing opposition to defense pacts. It signed a military agreement with Canberra pledging "to consult each other in the case of adverse challenges to either party or to their common security interests, and, if appropriate, consider measures which might be taken either individually or jointly and in accordance with the processes of each party."[22] Both sides denied that this agreement constituted a military alliance or that it was directed against any specific threat. But these politically diplomatic disavowals notwithstanding, interviews in ASEAN showed unanimity in seeing the agreements as a military-political response to China's posture. Beijing's failure to report the agreement in its principal media suggested it shared this ASEAN view.

Meanwhile the United States enjoys access to various facilities to support its air and naval contingents passing through or exercising in the region. Although no formal bases replace those lost in the Philippines, agreements with Indonesia, Singapore, Malaysia, and the Philippines quietly encourage an American military presence without provoking any public Chinese response. In 1996 Britain, for its part, concluded a military agreement with the Philippines on joint exercises, and the deputy commander in chief of the British navy pledged to continue naval visits in the region after returning Hong Kong to China, because of anticipated tensions, such as a China-Taiwan confrontation. In 1996–1997 Manila also activated military cooperation agreements with Thailand, Singapore, Malaysia, Australia, South Korea, and France.

The prospect of provoking a greater military alignment constrains Chinese behavior but has not compelled Chinese compromise. China's claims extend across all three adjoining bodies of water, and any concession in one could prejudice its position in the other two. The domestic political obstacles to compromise with ASEAN members are small compared the obstacles to compromise with Japan, as is the presumed amount of potential energy resources that might be given up. But abandoning the historical basis of alleged sovereignty in the South China Sea weakens China's claim to the Senkaku Islands. Thus whereas the likelihood of conflict is low, so are the chances for Chinese compromise unless it were to come as part of an overall policy of cooperation in East Asia.

Cooperation Prospects

The data on China's membership in universal international organizations and treaties show an impressive increase on both counts since Mao's death. Iain Johnston's research puts China's participation in the former at 90 percent of comparable U.S. memberships, with its treaty accessions representing a similar proportion of the maximum potential.[23] In itself this membership says nothing about Chinese behavior in organizations or its implementation of agreed-upon treaties. All states seek to advance their own national interests, giving as little as possible in order to gain as much as possible. In this regard cooperation is a limited concept that most commonly is self-serving and induced by a host of cost-benefit calculations rather than simply going along with whatever others desire or demand.[24]

Within this limited framework, however, there is a potential basis for increased cooperation emerging from association with a group where values, norms, and institutionalized behavior provide intangible rewards of status or punishment of censure. The assumption that private, prolonged discourse can reduce tension and lessen conflict underlies what is loosely called "the ASEAN way."[25] When the five founding members gathered initially in 1967, the Philippines laid claim to Sabah, in Malaysia, and Indonesia had recently tried to subvert Malaysia with guerrilla war. Boundaries left by the European colonial powers did not accord with natural demographic, geographic, or economic groupings, leaving a heritage rife with disputes. Moreover, considerations of internal security against Chinese-supported Communist insurgencies combined with external uncertainties, as U.S. involvement in the Vietnam War seemed doomed to defeat, which would leave Hanoi the most powerful capital in the region, backed by the Soviet Union. Under the circumstances, softening the immediate international disputes was necessary if internal security were to be addressed as prior to external security.

Thirty years later the Philippine claim to Sabah has been neither withdrawn nor settled. But it has not erupted into conflict. Other boundary disputes remain on the table between Malaysia and Indonesia as well as between Malaysia and Singapore. However, in the meantime, various forms of bilateral and multilateral political, economic, and military cooperation short of formal security alliance have realized the original ASEAN goals. These in turn have spawned ARF, an explicit security-oriented grouping that includes virtually all the East Asian countries except North Korea plus Russia, Canada, the United States, Australia, New Zealand, and the European Union. Like ASEAN, ARF is not a collective military security organization. It has minimal structure and places exclusive emphasis on the exchange of views, with no action and or implementing capability. Meetings may include heads of state, ministers, and defense officials, but whatever the level, three ASEAN rules apply: (1)exchanges remain private; (2)agreement is by consensus; and (3)internal affairs are excluded.[26]

Over the past decade, China has gradually progressed from skeptic to observer to participant as a dialogue partner with ASEAN and full member of ARF. However, this change in posture has not been accompanied by substantive change in policy. For example, China initially refused to allow multilateral discussion of its South China Sea claims. By the time of the fourth annual ARF meeting in 1997, Beijing agreed that the issue could be addressed, but no new Chinese position emerged. That same year for the first time Beijing cohosted with Manila an intercession meeting on confidence-building measures (CBMs). But shortly thereafter, the Chinese navy escorted an oceanographic survey ship in the vicinity of islands occupied by Philippine troops. Manila's protest prompted the PRC embassy spokesman to declare that such action was justified because all the islands, reefs, and shoals within the Spratly Island complex belonged to China.[27] Just prior to this incident, another Chinese ship drilled in waters claimed by Vietnam. Hanoi protested and mobilized ASEAN ambassadors who backed its position. In both cases the ships withdrew, declaring their mission had been completed.

Earlier the 1995–1996 PLA exercises in the Taiwan Strait had prompted ASEAN members to communicate their concern privately to Beijing while expressing support privately to Washington for its dispatch of aircraft carriers as a deterrent. But at no time have ASEAN members collectively spoken in public about specific Chinese provocations, although it ritualistically reiterates the call for peaceful resolution of disputes, formalized in the 1976 ASEAN Treaty of Amity and Cooperation. In 1992 Beijing expressed support for the treaty but did not sign it. These circumstances leave unclear to what extent ASEAN can influence Chinese behavior.[28] On the one hand, the organization, soon to include all ten Southeast Asian nations, constitutes a prestigious grouping. On the other hand, it offers only private admonitions to counter Beijing's assertive actions. Meanwhile its members are seen by some in Beijing as exploiting any opportunity to take what should be China's rightful energy resources. As one writer alleged: "An area of more than 800,000 square kilometers within China's traditional maritime boundaries has been illegally delineated into the domain of other countries, with 410,000 square kilometers taken by the Philippines, 270,000 by Malaysia, 70,000 by Vietnam, 50,000 by Indonesia, and the remainder by Brunei. These countries, which border the Spratly islands, have drilled 120 oil wells within China's boundaries."[29]

To counter this trend, vast PLA expenditures and years of work for a naval base are "aimed at meeting the requirements of future sea battles."[30] An extraordinary effort is needed to transform tiny islands that may be barely above the water in high tide or typhoons into viable bases for armed forces. Concrete caissons towed hundreds of miles by barge from Hainan are sunk onto coral reefs. All food and water must be shipped. Ironically the largest island in the Spratlys is held by Taipei, not Beijing. PRC media recount heroic tales of human endurance under incredible adversity "protecting China's strategic frontier."

Yet some Chinese commentators question the consequences of an assertive nationalistic posture. One acknowledged, "It is inevitable for some nearby small ASEAN nations to feel apprehensive about China."[31] He explained how the weak defense capabilities of ASEAN members "forced" them into "allowing the United States to exercise military functions, to a certain extent." He also claimed that their "maintaining a balanced relationship with various larger countries . . . is not negative and passive but active and positive." This had "turned ASEAN into a major factor affecting the balance among larger nations."

In a wider context, other writers have suggested that compromise and cooperation might serve China's interests better than confrontation. Using the Middle East peace process as an example, one asserted: "The result of noncompromise toward other countries can only be, internally, excessive propaganda of nationalism and national superiority, leading normal nationalist sentiment to the dead end of national bias. The external result would be a lack of friends and isolation."[32] Somewhat surprisingly, the director the PRC Naval Military Research Institute acknowledged: "Within the three million square kilometers of maritime space under Chinese jurisdiction, there are demarcation differences between China and its neighbors. . . . All three seas must be divided fairly with neighboring nations in accordance with international law."[33] In a separate line of inquiry, Yong Deng, a U.S. professor of political science and international relations, has reviewed recent Chinese academic writings on international relations.[34] He found a nascent neoliberal school of analysis based on emerging interdependence and globalization contending with the traditional mainstream realist paradigm in Chinese publications.

It is too soon to leap from these scattered references to forecast the evolution of a dramatic increase in cooperation and compromise in Chinese foreign policy. However, a salient, albeit single, change in this direction is Beijing's signing the Comprehensive Ban on Nuclear Testing (CBNT).[35] China lags behind Russia and the United States in the development of nuclear weapons. Continued testing can serve safe maintenance of existing stocks as well as the development of new capabilities. Bureaucratic opposition must have been strong, judging from the slow and successive changes in the Chinese position during the prolonged negotiation of the CBNT. Beijing continued tests up to the final moment, in contrast with Russia and the United States, which had announced test suspensions. But in the final analysis, the Chinese calculation of political gain in joining the international community apparently outweighed the calculation of loss in relative military capability.

In April 1997 a much lower level of compromise and cooperation in the military sphere emerged when a five-power agreement was signed in Moscow, pledging China, Russia, Kazakhstan, Kyrgystan, and Tajikistan to reduce troop concentrations and withdraw them one hundred kilometers on both sides of the border. No details were available on timing and precise location, but border guards were exempt, a loophole of potential importance, since China's limited war with India in 1962 was publicly described as fought by "border troops."[36] On the surface, at least, Chinese agreement to troop reduction and withdrawal would seem to have necessitated considerable bureaucratic debate. In recent years dissidence among Moslems, particularly the Uyghurs, in the autonomous region of Xinjiang, which is adjacent to the territory of the other four signatories, resulted in bombings, grenade attacks, assassinations, arson, and riots.[37] After a particularly large demonstration in February 1997, arrests and executions were followed by lengthy official attacks on "separatists" allegedly plotting an "Islamic Republic in East Turkestan." The struggle was described as "life and death" and "long-lasting." Accusations of "foreign plotters" attempting to stir up "religious war" prompted an official Pakistani denial that any such activity came from that country. But in the Kazakhstan capital, Almaty, spokespersons for various dissident groups held press conferences to publicize disturbances in Xinjiang they claimed to sponsor. In addition, the security head of Kazakhstan acknowledged that unrest was an internal affair but held that "the violent suppression being carried out by Chinese authorities" was also to blame.

In this context the five-power agreement seems paradoxical for Chinese security interests, since it could weaken security in a vulnerable area that has seen repeated Moslem revolts for more than a century.[38] Media treatment of the disturbances portrays the threat of "separatist activity" as coming from "a handful" of armed dissidents but nonetheless as requiring attention in the long run. Some Chinese commentary links the activity with allegations of separatist movements in Tibet and Taiwan, suggesting a larger context for concern, perhaps based on the occasional co-operation of these groups in lobbying the U.S. Congress on human rights in China. Nevertheless Beijing's extensive publicizing of the five-power agreement as its taking leadership in confidence-building measures may signal interest in similar cooperation elsewhere.

In this regard the official *People's Daily* editorial on the thirtieth an-niversary of the formation of ASEAN sounded parallel themes. Under the heading "Persist in Dialogue and Cooperation," it praised the organi-zation as "an important force of peace and development on the world stage." Its rise "has proven from one angle that a multi-polar world has taken shape conducive to resisting hegemonism and power politics." ARF represents "a unique form of dialogue on the Asia-Pacific security issues."

Interviews with ASEAN officials in 1995–1996 showed reluctance to speak of a "China threat" but frank acknowledgment of a "challenge" posed by China's past record, its present claims, and its future power. Im-plicit in the officials' formulation of strategy for the near term was seek-ing a balance of politics whereby the various differences between Beijing and ASEAN countries could be aired in multilateral discussions. That might thwart any Chinese effort to divide and prevail. No one argued against the importance of a continued U.S. presence in East Asia or its Japanese alliance. But this balance of power was not seen as critical to de-terring or containing Chinese military force in the immediate future. Be-cause Chinese postures remain essentially political and verbal rather than militarily assertive, a balance of politics might induce Beijing to compromise and cooperation and thereby mitigate the likelihood of con-flict at a later date. The *People's Daily* editorial encourages hope of this eventuality, but the test will be China's ultimate stance on claims of sov-ereignty over the East Asian seas. As a first step, Beijing must spell out exactly what is meant by the broken lines surrounding the South China Sea on Chinese maps. Four years of informal unofficial workshops in Jakarta failed to elicit any explanation.

In contrast with these territorial disputes, Beijing has been cooperative on the crucial issue of stopping North Korean nuclear proliferation and inducing Pyongyang to enter four-party talks to end the state of war on the peninsula. This helped to lessen tension in northeast Asia during the uncertain leadership transition from Kim Ilsong to his son, complicated further by incipient famine in the north. Less threatening in the short run but equally important over time are environmental issues—particularly pollution—and drug control. In these two areas Chinese participation in bilateral and multilateral efforts manifests cooperation despite serious problems of domestic management. These developments serve Chinese interests, whether by improving national security in Korea or by improving the health of the Chinese people. The more such calculations can be made in Beijing, the greater is the prospect for cooperation.

Competition Prospects: The United States and Japan

The People's Republic has challenged the U.S. leadership in one way or another since its inception in 1949. For the first two decades the challenge was defensively motivated by the American effort to destabilize Communist rule on the mainland and offensively driven by the ideological imperative to fight U.S. imperialism. Then in 1969 Mao's sense of a greater threat from the Soviet Union prompted him to strike a balance by improving relations with Washington. Ten years of this triangular strategy prompted Moscow to ease relations with Beijing. However, it took another decade for this relaxation to take effect, culminating in Mikhail Gorbachev's visit to Beijing in 1989, and in the interim a Sino-American alignment was prolonged. Two years later, the collapse of the Soviet Union removed the "Russian threat" completely and with it any need to side with Washington against Moscow.

Since then, Chinese policy toward the United States has mixed cooperation with competition for defining the East Asian balance of power. Until 1996 the U.S. military presence, although attacked rhetorically in Chinese media, was tacitly accepted in private as a safeguard against Japan's developing its own military defenses. This situation made the Tokyo-Washington alliance preferable to a wholly independent Japan. However the deployment of U.S. aircraft carriers to the waters off Taiwan when PLA missile firings bracketed off the island's shipping lanes was followed by a Clinton-Hashimoto summit for rewriting the guidelines on U.S.-Japanese military cooperation. One of the two carriers, the *Independence*, served as the platform for Clinton's main appearance. Although the meeting had been planned long before the Taiwan Strait standoff, the coincidence of the timing and the subsequent Japanese statements heightened Chinese suspicion that the new guidelines envisioned U.S.-Japanese intervention in a future Taiwan Strait crisis.

In its public expression this concern focused more on Tokyo than on Washington. That focus was tactically necessary because Jiang Zemin's visit to the White House in 1997 realized a long-held goal, both national and personal. Sino-American relations had reached their nadir after Tiananmen, recovered somewhat in successive years, and plummeted again in 1995–1996. Summitry in multilateral settings such as APEC and the UN is secondary to the formal exchange of bilateral visits. The visit of Jiang, as head of party and government, elevated China's status to the highest level of diplomacy, unprecedented in Sino-American relations. In addition, as nominal successor to Deng Xiaoping but still lacking equivalent political clout, Jiang needed all the elevation in status possible. In this context it would have been unseemly to belabor Clinton unduly for the Hashimoto summit.

Strategically the Japanese focus was also justified in its own regard. Over the long run Chinese analysts see Japan as a greater threat than the United States.[39] Short of war, Japanese hegemony in East Asia is projected as a goal of Tokyo. History testifies to rivalry between China and Japan for influence as inherent in their relationship to each other and the region. As the Middle Kingdom, China was ascendant. But as the nineteenth century ended, Tokyo exploited the collapsing Qing vulnerability to extend Japanese power to Korea and northeast China. In the 1930s Japanese aggression moved from China to all of East Asia. Defeat in World War II eliminated Japan from the power balance except as part of the U.S. alliance system. In 1950 "new China" restored its sense of power in the Korean War as an ally of the Soviet Union. But self-inflicted economic catastrophe resulted from the Great Leap Forward and the split with Moscow, followed by political anarchy and xenophobia in the Cultural Revolution. At Mao's death, China remained isolated and stagnant while Japan was bursting forth as the fastest-rising economic power in the world.

Sino-Japanese relations are economically sound but politically fragile. Chinese media miss few opportunities to belabor Tokyo for nationalistic expressions by right-wing groups and conservative cabinet members. Any attempt in textbooks or private publications to tone down or deny Japanese war crimes, especially the Nanjing Massacre, is excoriated as evidence of incipient militarism. "Remember the past as a guide to the future" ritualistically reminds Chinese audiences of the potential danger of future Japanese power. It also serves to pressure Tokyo to comply with Beijing's demands by exploiting whatever feeling of guilt may remain there. As occasion permits, Chinese media relay similar sentiments from other East Asian nations, in particular South Korea and the Philippines, with a sense of grievance over Japanese atrocities. This implicitly places Beijing in the position of speaking for a larger constituency against Tokyo.

Competition and power rivalry is universal in international relations and may be peacefully contained. History need not be repeated. Franco-German relations show that competition can coexist with cooperation and replace conflict. But whether that example serves to forecast the evolution of Sino-Japanese relations in the next decade is most doubtful. The North Atlantic Treaty Organization under U.S. leadership provided a defining institutional context within which postwar Germany gradually recovered full status in accordance with French sensibilities. Planning for a joint Franco-German military force signaled final reconciliation between the two traditional enemies. But no such institution exists in East Asia within which to reorder the historical heritage of past conflict, much less to redefine the Middle Kingdom sense of superiority over neighboring peoples, first and foremost over Japan. China's reluctance to support Japan's permanent membership in the UN Security Council reflects this historical memory.

Yet possibly ameliorating these negative factors are practical problems that require cooperation for solution. This cooperation may take the edge off competition, as interaction produces mutual gain. Korea could be one such instance. The peninsula has traditionally been a point of competition between China and Japan. However, controlling nuclear proliferation in the north and the simultaneous threat of famine there brought Beijing, Tokyo, Seoul, and Washington into continuous close consultation with one another as well as with Pyongyang. The process took years and has had an uncertain outcome. Nevertheless it created unprecedented interaction among these competitive states.

In 1997 the commemoration of the twenty-fifth anniversary of diplomatic relations prompted summitry in Beijing and Tokyo, preceded by the announcement of a new bilateral fisheries treaty described by Japan as "virtually shelving the territorial dispute over the Senkaku Islands."[40] Prime Minister Hashimoto and Premier Li Peng agreed on environmental cooperation whereby Japanese antipollution equipment will be installed in two model cities with another hundred cities linked for monitoring air and water pollution. Environmental pollution is particularly threatening for both China and Japan and provides a strong impetus for cooperation to prevail over competition. In addition, dialogue in multilateral forums such as ARF and APEC, together with small-group interaction in intercession meetings, can familiarize Chinese and Japanese with one another at different generational levels in noncompetitive contexts. Stereotypes and preconceptions take time to modify, but the process is possible if repetitive experience contradicts them. For the next decade, however, the competitive factors will outweigh the cooperative as far as Sino-Japanese relations are concerned.

In Conclusion

As the People's Republic approaches its fiftieth anniversary, external relations are more stable than they were at the fortieth. The explosion of public dissidence and regime repression at Tiananmen triggered a chain of critical foreign reactions. Among the industrialized states China became a virtual pariah. There is no guarantee that another outburst of domestic unrest will not evoke further repression and similar responses abroad. In 1997 discontented workers demonstrated in various cities, and on occasion serious riots resulted. Economic problems abound, including the disposition of massive bankrupt state industries with thousands of employees, a floating population of perhaps 100 million that moves from city to city in search of jobs, and demands from less-advantaged areas for sharing the wealth and rising standards of living enjoyed in the regions privileged as points for foreign trade and investment. Meanwhile increasing crime and corruption plagues the regime and demoralizes its citizens.

Should the leadership feel besieged at home, its sense of threat from abroad may increase, recalling the classic Chinese admonition, "Trouble within, trouble without." This could evoke more-assertive postures on such sensitive matters as Taiwan and offshore territorial claims. The linkage between domestic politics and foreign policy would be reinforced if other governments were to react as in 1989. Yet even under these circumstances, the foregoing assessment of the likelihood of conflict remains. Cooperation might decrease and competition increase. But the use of force at Chinese initiative would probably be constrained by the calculation of military and economic costs weighed against the possible gains. As in past decades, assertive Chinese postures in rhetoric and military deployment do not necessarily translate into aggression.

Against this cautiously negative scenario, a modestly positive one is also possible. The regime might muddle through economic crises as it has in recent years, neither wholly resolving them nor allowing them to break up the country. Fear of Cultural Revolution chaos or at least of another Tiananmen repression may inhibit dissidence. Tempered nationalism may suffice as a substitute for discredited Marxism–Leninism–Mao Zedong Thought to provide a patina of legitimacy for CCP rule. The recovery of Hong Kong and to a lesser extent Macao can mark a high point in redressing "a century of shame and humiliation" and redound to the regime's credibility. In this context there is no need to fear that external threat will exploit internal disarray. The regime will resist external pressure that could increase such disarray, whether the pressure be directed at human rights in general or more specific pressures on behalf of Tibetans, Uyghurs, and intellectuals. But in the absence of a general deterioration of social order, this resistance will be contained within the framework of larger issues in bilateral and multilateral negotiations, as occurred in the post-Tiananmen decade.

Clouding this prospect of a benign internal and external context for Chinese foreign policy is one central challenge: Taiwan. Beijing, until it is confident that the island will not seek formal and permanent independence, will remain prepared to exercise force and perhaps use it if that eventuality appears imminent. Until Beijing can trust Washington and Tokyo not to encourage this development, it will view those capitals with suspicion. This potentially volatile situation places considerable responsibility on all parties, including Taiwan, to so act as to preserve peace in the Taiwan Strait. How such actions will accord with the domestic imperatives of each party must be determined at the time. Americans will feel impelled to protect Taiwan as a democratic state with which the United States has had a special relationship since 1950. Japanese will feel constrained from confronting China over Taiwan as an internal affair of China, with which Japan had a painful relationship from 1894 to 1945. Ultimately, of course, the final decision for conflict or compromise lies in Beijing, although the catalyst for that decision may be the interaction of domestic politics and foreign policy on Taiwan.

Seen from this perspective, the forecast of a stronger China necessarily threatening peace in East Asia overlooks two factors. First, that forecast is basically unidirectional insofar as the sole determinant is Chinese intentions. But Chinese policy is a function of external behavior as well as Chinese intentions. A critical question will be how Beijing perceives and anticipates the actions of Tokyo, Washington, Taipei, and the ASEAN members with respect to the key issues of territorial integrity and national unity. Misperception and miscalculation can plague policymaking, as it has in the past, but that is a separate problem from the problem of intention. Second, over the next five to ten years, the Chinese military capability to project force will remain nearly one generation behind that of the United States, Japan, and even some Southeast Asian neighbors. Major limitations in the human, financial, and material resources for acquiring and utilizing weapons with cutting-edge technology will delay catching up with, much less surpassing, U.S. and Japanese capabilities.

The incorporation of China in regional political and economic regimes has no certain influence on intentions and behavior. However the possibility of positive influence cannot be ruled out in advance. The positive changes in Chinese foreign policy during the twenty years of Deng Xiaoping's rule were as radical as his domestic reforms. Yet their success required reciprocal changes by other powers. All the relationships in East Asia are developing uncertainly in a new post–Cold War context. The outcome may well determine the shape of China's role in global affairs in the twenty-first century. The weight of China, with the world's largest population and eventually the largest economy, will be felt far beyond East Asia. This potential power places a premium on understanding Chinese foreign policy and helping to shape it constructively through international interaction on the basis of mutual interest in peace and stability.

Notes

1. For a review of my own record of hits and misses see Allen S. Whiting, "Forecasting Chinese Foreign Policy: International Relations Theory v. the Fortune Cookie," in Thomas W. Robinson and David Shambaugh, eds., *Chinese Foreign Policy: Theory and Practice* (Oxford: Oxford University Press, 1994), pp. 506–23.

2. Chen Jian, *China's Road to the Korean War: The Making of the Sino-American Confrontation* (New York: Columbia University Press, 1994)

3. Chen Jian, "China's Involvement in the Vietnam War, 1964–69," *China Quarterly*, no. 142, June 1995, pp. 356–87.

4. John W. Garver, *Foreign Relations of the People's Republic of China* (Englewood Cliffs, N.J.: Prentice-Hall, 1993), presents an excellent recapitulation of these developments, based on Chinese sources not available before.

5. John W. Garver, *Face Off: China, The United States, and Taiwan's Democratization* (Seattle: University of Washington Press, 1997).

6. Michael D. Swaine, *China: Domestic Change and Foreign Policy* (Santa Monica, Calif.: Rand Corporation, 1995).

7. Michael Yahuda, "Deng Xiaoping: The Statesman," *China Quarterly*, no. 135, September 1993, pp. 551–72.

8. Richard Bernstein and Ross H. Munro, *The Coming Conflict with China* (New York: Knopf, 1997), won widespread attention as the most complete statement of "China threat."

9. Alastair Iain Johnston, *Cultural Realism: Strategic Culture and Grand Strategy in Chinese History* (Princeton: Princeton University Press, 1995), presents a closely researched account of China's past strategic writings and behavior that conforms with but does not support the "China threat" school.

10. Ji Guoxing, *Maritime Jurisdiction in the Three China Seas* (San Diego: Institute on Global Conflict and Cooperation, University of California, 1995), presents an overview of claims and resources with maps.

11. Allen S. Whiting, "The Use of Force by the People's Republic of China," *Annals of The American Academy of Political and Social Science* 402, July 1972, pp. 55–66.

12. Andrew J. Nathan and Robert S. Ross, *The Great Wall and the Empty Fortress: China's Search for Security* (New York: Norton, 1997), examines the historic and contemporary contexts for China's preoccupation with defense.

13. Allen S. Whiting, "Chinese Nationalism and Foreign Policy After Deng," *China Quarterly*, no. 142, June 1995, pp. 295–316; and Whiting, "The PLA and China's Threat Perceptions," ibid., *China Quarterly*, no. 146, June 1996, pp. 596–615.

14. Alfred D. Wilhelm, Jr., "Future Trends in the Growth and Role of the Chinese Military," *Washington Journal of Modern China*, Winter-Spring 1996, pp. 28–50. Wilhelm served in Beijing as the U.S. military attaché and lectured at the PRC National Defense University.

15. David Shambaugh, "China's Post-Deng Military Leadership," unpublished paper made available by the author.

16. Paul B. Godwin, "Uncertainty, Insecurity, and China's Military Power," *Current History*, September 1997, pp. 252–57, compares weapons systems on both sides.

17. You Ji, "Making Sense of War Games in the Taiwan Strait," *Journal of Contemporary China* 6, no. 15, pp. 287–305.

18. Ibid., pp. 8–16. The analysis of Ji, a professor in the Shanghai Institute for International Studies, favors the PRC position.

19. Allen S. Whiting, *China Eyes Japan* (Berkeley: University of California Press, 1989), draws on interviews with students and officials.

20. Eric Hyer, "'Dangerous Shoals': An Introduction to the South China Sea Disputes," *American Asian Review* 12, no.4, Winter 1994, pp. 1001–16.

21. William J. Dobson and M. Taylor Fravel, "Red Herring Hegemon: China in the South China Sea," *Current History*, September 1997, pp. 258–63.

22. Allen S. Whiting, "ASEAN Eyes China: The Security Dimension," *Asian Survey* 37, no. 4, April 1997, pp. 299–322. This article draws on interviews with security officials in Jakarta.

23. Data provided by the author in roundtable discussion, American Political Science Association, August 30, 1997.

24. For a critical assessment of China's role and behavior, see Samuel S. Kim, "China as a Great Power," *Current History*, September 1997, pp. 246–51.

25. Michael Antolik, *ASEAN and the Diplomacy of Accommodation* (Armonk, N.Y.: M. E. Sharpe, 1990).

26. Alastair Iain Johnston, "The Myth of the ASEAN Way? Explaining the Evolution of the ASEAN Regional Forum," paper presented at Joint Conference on Security Institutions: Effects and Dynamics, March 17–19, 1997, Free University of Berlin and Center for International Affairs, Harvard University. Draft paper made available by the author.

27. I was given this same sweeping claim in 1981 at a private briefing by officials in the Ministry of Foreign Affairs.

28. For thoughtful suggestions, see Lee Lai To, "ASEAN and the South China Sea Conflicts," *Pacific Review*, 8, no. 3, 1995, pp. 521–45.

29. Lin Mu, "The Aviation Dream of the Chinese People," *Shidian*, no. 7, July 1994, in Foreign Language Broadcast Information [hereafter cited as FBIS]-China, August 24, 1994.

30. *Jiefangjunbao*, March 17, 1995, in FBIS-China, April 23, 1997.

31. Shi Yongming, "The Elevated Status and Influence of the ASEAN After the Cold War," *Guoji Wenti Yanjiu* (International Studies), January 13, 1997, in FBIS-China, April 23, 1997.

32. Tang Guanghui, "An Analysis of Post–Cold War Security," *Shijie Zhishi* (World Affairs), October 1, 1996, in FBIS-China, February 14, 1996. For virtually identical language more explicitly addressed to Chinese foreign relations, see Zhang Yiping, "A New View of Post–Cold War World Security," *Xiandai Guoji Guanxi* (Contemporary International Relations), February 20, 1997, in FBIS-China, May 13, 1997. Zhang bases his lengthy analysis explicitly on Robert Keohane and Joseph Nye, *Power and Interdependence*, published in Chinese in 1992.

33. Liu Zhenhuan, "Commentary on 'UN Law of the Sea' Part Two," *Guofang* (National Defense), November 15, 1996, in FBIS-China, February 14, 1997.

34. Draft paper provided by the author.

35. Alastair Iain Johnston, "Learning Versus Adaption: Explaining Change in Chinese Arms Control Policy in the 1980s and 1990s," *China Journal*, no. 35, January 1996, pp. 27–61.

36. Allen S. Whiting, *The Chinese Calculus of Deterrence: India and Vietnam* (Ann Arbor: University of Michigan Press, 1975).

37. Dru C. Gladney, "Rumblings from the Uyghur," *Current History*, September 1997, pp. 287–90, and Xinjiang media.

38. Lillian Craig Harris, "Xinjiang, Central Asia and the Implications for China's Policy in the Islamic World," *China Quarterly*, no. 133, March 1993, pp. 111–29.

39. Whiting, "The PLA and China's Threat Perceptions."

40. "Hashimoto Seeks to Allay China Concern on Defense," Kyodo in English, FBIS-East Asia, September 5, 1997.

Bibliography

This bibliography has grown out of our teaching and research experience in the field of Chinese foreign policy studies. Our basic aim is to familiarize students with the range and type of materials currently available for exploring in greater depth the various issues of Chinese foreign relations covered in this volume, with emphasis on the post–Cold War developments. Journal articles are included only where published books and monographs are spotty. With a few notable exceptions, the selection favors the more recent publications.

The PRC publications listed below are available in major research libraries in the United States and Europe. Subscriptions to such periodicals as *Beijing Review, Guoji wenti yanjiu, Liaowang,* and *Qiushi* can be obtained through China Books and Periodicals in San Francisco. Foreign Broadcast Information Service, *Daily Report—China* (FBIS-China), is the most useful and widely consulted reference in English; it is now available on line (http://wnc.fedworld.gov) on a subscription-fee basis and includes English translations of important PRC newspaper and journal articles and monitored radio broadcasts on both domestic and international issues.

Non-PRC English-language sources are arranged topically, approximating somewhat the organization of the book. Major newspapers and journals of particular value for the study of Chinese foreign policy include *American Asian Review, Asian Affairs, Asian Wall Street Journal* (Hong Kong), *China Journal* (Canberra), *Far Eastern Economic Review* (Hong Kong), *Foreign Affairs, Foreign Policy, International Affairs* (London), *International Journal* (Toronto), *International Organization, International Security, International Studies Quarterly, Issues and Studies* (Taipei), *Journal of Contemporary China, Journal of Northeast Asian Studies, New York Times, Orbis, Pacific Affairs* (Vancouver), *Pacific Review* (Oxford), *Political Science Quarterly, Washington Post, World Policy Journal,* and *World Politics.*

PRC Publications

Beijing Review (Weekly, English; March 4, 1958–; *Peking Review* before January 1, 1979).

Cai Jianwei, ed., *Zhongguo da zhanlue* [China's grand strategy]. Haikou: Hainan chubanshe, 1996.

Cai Tuo, *Dangdai quanqiu wenti* [Contemporary global problems]. Tianjin: Tianjin renmin chubanshe, 1994.

Changes and Development in China (1949–1989). Beijing: Beijing Review Press, 1989.

Chen Luzhi and Li Tiecheng, eds. *Lienheguo yu shijie zhixu* [The United Nations and world order]. Beijing: Beijing yuyan xueyuan chubanshe, 1993.

Chen Shicai. *Guoji fayuan toushi* [A perspective on the International Court of Justice]. Beijing: Zhongguo youyi chuban gongsi, 1984.

Chen Zhongling. *Problems in International Strategy.* Hong Kong: Man Hai Language Publications, 1989.

China Daily (English, 1982–).

China's Foreign Economic Legislation. Vol. 1. Beijing: Foreign Languages Press, 1982.

China's Foreign Economic Legislation. Vol. 2. Beijing: Foreign Languages Press, 1986.

China's Foreign Relations: A Chronology of Events (1949–1988). Beijing: Foreign Languages Press, 1989.

Dai Qing. *Yangtze! Yangtze!* Trans. Nancy Liu, Wu Mei, Sun Yougeng, and Zhang Xiaogang. London: Earthscan, 1994.

Deng Xiaoping, *Deng Xiaoping wenxuan, 1975–1982* [The selected works of Deng Xiaoping, 1975–1982]. Beijing: Renmin chubanshe, 1983.

_____. *Jianshe you zhongguo tse de shehui zhuyi* [Building socialism with Chinese characteristics]. Beijing: Renmin chubanshe, 1987.

_____. *Fundamental Issues in Present-Day China.* Beijing: Foreign Languages Press, 1985.

Deng Zhenglai, ed. *Wang Tieya wenxuan* [Selected works of Wang Tieya]. Beijing: Zhongguo zhengfa daxue chubanshe, 1993.

Du Gong, ed. *Zhuanhuan zhong de shijie geju* [World patterns in the midst of transformation]. Beijing: Shijie zhishi chubanshe, 1992.

Du Xichuan and Zhang Lingyuan. *China's Legal System: A General Survey.* Beijing: New World Press, 1990.

Fang, Percy Jucheng, and Lucy Guinong Fang. *Zhou Enlai—A Profile.* Beijing: Foreign Languages Press, 1987.

Faxue yanjiu [Legal research]. (Bimonthly, April 1979–; edited by the Institute of Law, Chinese Academy of Social Sciences, Beijing).

Feng Tejun and Song Xinning, eds. *Guoji zhengzhi gailun* [An introduction to International Politics]. Beijing: Zhongguo renmin daxue chubanshe, 1992.

Gao Jingdian, ed. *Deng Xiaoping guoji zhanlue sixiang yanjiu* [A study of Deng Xiaoping's thought on International strategy]. Beijing: Guofang daxue chubanshe, 1992.

_____. *Guoji zhanlue xue gailun* [An introduction to the study of international strategy]. Beijing: Guofang daxue chubanshe, 1995.

Guan Jixian. *Gao jishu jubu zhangzheng zhanyi* [Campaigns in high-tech limited wars]. Beijing: Guofang daxue chubanshe, 1993.

Guo Longlong et al. *Lienheguo xinlun* [New theories of the United Nations]. Shanghai: Shanghai jiaoyu chubanshe, 1995.

Guofang xiandaihua [National defense modernization]. Beijing: Kexue puji chubanshe, 1983.

Guoji heping nian: Xueshu taolunhui ziliao huibian [The international year of peace: An anthology of materials from an academic symposium]. Beijing: Shehui kexue wenxian chubanshe, 1986.

Guoji wenti yanjiu [Journal of International Studies]. (Quarterly, July 1981–; edited by the Institute of International Relations, Beijing).

Guoji xingshi nianjian [Yearbook of International Affairs]. Shanghai: Zhongguo dabaikequanshu chubanshe. (Annual, 1982–; edited by the Shanghai Institute of International Studies).

Han Nianlong, ed. *Dangdai Zhonguo waijiao* [Contemporary Chinese foreign relations]. Beijing: Zhongguo shehui kexue chubanshe, 1987. (An official history of Chinese foreign relations covering the period 1949–1986 prepared by the PRC Foreign Ministry.)

He Xin. *Zhonghua fuxing yu shijie weilai* [China's revival and the world's future]. Vols. 1–2. Sichuan: Sichuan renmin chubanshe, 1996.

Hongqi [Red Flag]. (Semi-monthly; June 1958-June 1988; the official organ of the Central Committee of the Chinese Communist Party).

Hu Yaobang. *For Friendship and Cooperation*. Beijing: Foreign Languages Press, 1985.

Huan Xiang, ed. *Dangdai shijie zhengzhi jingji jiben wenti* [Basic problems of contemporary world political economy]. Beijing: Shijie zhishi chubanshe, 1989.

Huang Shuofeng. *Zonghe guoli lun* [On comprehensive national strength]. Beijing: Zhongguo shehui kexue chubanshe, 1992.

Information Office of the State Council. "Human Rights in China." *Beijing Review* 34:44 (November 4, 1991): 8–45; also in FBIS-China, supplement, November 31, 1991, pp. 1–29.

Information Office of the State Council. "Tibet—Its Ownership and Human Rights Situation," in FBIS-China, supplement, October 9, 1992, pp. 1–23.

Jiang Jiliang, ed. *Guoji guanxi xue gailun* [Introduction to International Relations]. Beijing: Shijie zhishi chubanshe, 1989.

Jin Yinzhong and Ni Shixiong. *Guoji guanxi lilun bijiao yanjiu* [A comparative study of international relations theory]. Beijing: Zhongguo shehui kexue chubanshe, 1992.

Lan Mingliang. *Guoji zuzhi gaikuang* [A survey of international organizations]. Beijing: Falu chubanshe, 1983.

Legislative Affairs Commission of the Standing Committee of the National People's Congress of the People's Republic of China, comp. *The Laws of the People's Republic of China, 1979–1982*. Vol. 1. Beijing: Foreign Languages Press, 1987.

_____. *The Laws of the People's Republic of China, 1983–1986*. Vol. 2. Beijing: Foreign Languages Press, 1987.

Li Tiecheng, ed. *Lienheguo de licheng* [United Nations Chronicle]. Beijing: Beijing yuyan xueyuan chubanshe, 1993.

Liang Shoude, ed. *Guoji zhengzhi lunji* [Anthology of International Politics theories]. Beijing: Beijing chubanshe, 1992.

_____ *Guoji zhengzhi xinlun* [New theories of International Politics]. Beijing: Beijing daxue chubanshe, 1996.

Liang Shoude and Hong Yinxian. *Guoji zhengzhi xue gailun* [An introduction to International Politics]. Beijing: Zhongyang bianyi chubanshe, 1994.

Liu Ding, ed. *Guoji jingjifa* [International economic law]. Beijing: Zhongguo ren min daxue chubanshe, 1984.

Liu Jinzhi and Yang Huaisheng, eds. *Zhongguo dui Chaoxian he Hanguo zhengci wenjian huibian 1 (1949–1952)* [A collection of documents on China's policy toward North and South Korea, 1949–1952, vol. 1]. Beijing: Zhongguo shehui kexue chubanshe, 1994.

_____. *Zhongguo dui Chaoxian he Hanguo zhengci wenjian huibian 2 (1953–1957)* [A collection of documents on China's policy toward North and South Korea, 1953–1957, vol. 2]. Beijing: Zhongguo shehui kexue chubanshe, 1994.

_____. *Zhongguo dui Chaoxian he Hanguo zhengci wenjian huibian 3 (1958–1962)* [A collection of documents on China's policy toward North and South Korea, 1958–1962, vol. 3]. Beijing: Zhongguo shehui kexue chubanshe, 1994.

_____. *Zhongguo dui Chaoxian he Hanguo zhengci wenjian huibian 4 (1963–1973)* [A collection of documents on China's policy toward North and South Korea, 1963–1973, vol. 4]. Beijing: Zhongguo shehui kexue chubanshe, 1994.

_____. *Zhongguo dui Chaoxian he Hanguo zhengci wenjian huibian 5 (1974–1994)* [A collection of documents on China's policy toward North and South Korea, 1974–1994, vol. 5]. Beijing: Zhongguo shehui kexue chubanshe, 1994.

Liu Haishan and Li Mei. *Caijun yu guojifa* [Disarmament and international law]. Chengdu: Sichuan renmin chubanshe, 1990.

Ma Hong, ed. *Modern China's Economy and Management.* Beijing: Foreign Languages Press, 1990.

Ma Shaolei et al, *Guoji guanxi xinlun* [New theories of international relations] (Shanghai: Shehui kexue chubanshe, 1994.

Mao Zedong, *Mao Zedong sixiang wansui* [Long Live Mao Zedong's thought]. N.p.: 1967.

_____. *Mao Zedong sixiang wansui* [Long Live Mao Zedong's thought]. N.p.: August 1969.

_____. *Selected Works of Mao Tse-tung,* 4 vols. Peking: Foreign Languages Press, 1961, 1965.

_____. *Selected Works of Mao Tse-tung.* Vol. 5. Peking: Foreign Languages Press, 1977.

_____. *Mao Zedong xuanji* [Selected works of Mao Zedong]. Beijing: Renmin chubanshe, 1969. (The first four volumes in Chinese published as one volume).

_____. *Mao Zedong waijiao wenxuan* [Selected documents on Mao Zedong's diplomacy]. Beijing: Zhongyang wenxian chubanshe and Shijie zhishi chubanshe, 1994.

Nie Rongzhen. *Nie Rongzhen huiyilu* [Memoirs of Nie Rongzhen]. Beijing: Jiefangjun chubanshe, 1984.

Pan Guang, ed. *Dangdai guoji weiji yanjiu* [Research on contemporary international crises]. Beijing: Zhongguo shehui kexue chubanshe, 1989.

Pei Jianzhang, ed. *Xin Zhongguo waijiao fengyun* [The storms of New China's foreign relations]. 3 vols. Beijing: Shijie zhishi chubanshe, 1990, 1991, and 1994.

Pei Jianzhang, ed. *Zhonghua renmin gongheguo waijiao shi* [Diplomatic history of the PRC, 1949–1956]. Beijing: Shijie zhishi chubanshe, 1994.

Peng Dehuai. *Memoirs of a Chinese Marshall.* Beijing: Foreign Languages Press, 1984.

Peng Guangqian and Yao Youzhi, eds. *Deng Xiaoping zhanlue sixiang lun* [On Deng Xiaoping's thought on strategy]. Beijing: Jiefangjun kexue chubanshe, 1994.

Peng Qian, Yang Mingjie and Xu Deren. *Zhongguo weishenme shuo bu?* [Why can't China say no?] Beijing: Xinshijie chubanshe, 1996.

PRC Ministry of Foreign Affairs. *Mao Zedong waijiao wenxuan* [Selected works of Mao Zedong diplomacy]. Beijing: Shijie zhishi chubanshe, 1994.

Priority Programme for China's Agenda 21. Beijing: The Administrative Center for China's Agenda 21, 1996.

Qin Xuanren, ed. *Guoji jingji maoyi guanxi—lilun he shijian* [International economic trade relations—theory and practice]. Beijing: Zhongguo duiwai fanyi chuban gongsi, 1985.

Qiushi [Seeking truth]. (July 1, 1988–; the successor to *Hongqi;* the official journal of the Central Committee Party School.)

Qu Geping. *Zhongguo huanjing wenti ji duice* [China's environmental problems and policies]. Beijing: Zhongguo huanjing kexue chubanshe, 1989.

_____. *Zhongguo de huanjing guanli* [China's management of the environment]. Beijing: Zhongguo huanjing kexue chubanshe, 1989.

_____. *Environmental Management in China.* Beijing: China Environmental Press, 1991.

Renmin ribao [People's Daily] (June 15, 1948–; the official organ of the Central Committee of the Chinese Communist Party).

Renmin ribao suoyin [Index to People's Daily]. (Monthly; 1951–).

Shen Jueren, ed. *Dangdai Zhongguo duiwai maoyi* [Foreign trade of Contemporary China]. 2 Vols. Beijing: Dangdai Zhongguo chubanshe, 1992.

Shijie zhishi [World knowledge]. (Semimonthly; September 1934–).

Shijie zhishi nianjian [World Knowledge Yearbook]. (Annual, 1952–1966, 1982–).

Social Sciences in China. (Quarterly in English; 1980–; edited by the Chinese Academy of Social Sciences).

Song Qiang et al. *Zhongguo keyi shuo bu* [China can say no]. Beijing: Zhonghua gongshang lianhe chubanshe, 1996.

Song Yiming. *China's Concept of Security.* Geneva: United Nations Institute for Disarmament Research, 1986. (United Nations Publication Sales No. GV.E.86.0.1)

State Council. *China's Agenda 21: White Paper on China's Population, Environment, and Development in the Twenty-First Century.* Beijing: China Environmental Science Press, 1994.

_____. *Wo guo guangyu quanqiu huanjing wenti de yuanze lizhang* [The principled position of our country on global environmental problems]. Beijing: Zhongguo huanjing kexue chubanshe, 1992.

State Statistical Bureau. *Statistical Yearbook of China, 1995.* Beijing: China Statistical Publishing House, 1995. (Annual)

Sun Haichen, comp. and trans. *The Wiles of War: Thirty-Six Military Strategems from Ancient China.* Beijing: Foreign Languages Press, 1991.

Tian Zengpei, ed. *Gaige kaifang yilai de Zhongguo waijiao* [Chinese diplomacy after reform and opening]. Beijing: Shijie zhishi chubanshe, 1993.

Wang Huijiang and Li Boxi. *China Toward the Year 2000.* Beijing: New World Press, 1989.

Wang Jie, ed. *Lienheguo zaofeng tiaozhan* [The United Nations encounters challenges]. Beijing: Zhongyang bianyi chubanshe, 1994.

Wang Jisi. "Guoji guanxi lilun yu Zhongguo waijiao yanjiu" [International relations theory and Chinese foreign policy studies], *Zhongguo shehui kexue jikan* [Chinese Social Science Quarterly] (Winter 1993): 83–93.

Wang Jisi, ed. *Wenming yu guoji zhengzhi: Zhongguo xuezhe ping Hengtingdun de wenming chongtu lun* [Civilization and international politics: Chinese Scholars on Huntington's Clash Theory]. Shanghai: Shanghai renmin chubanshe, 1995.

Wang Shengzhu, ed. *Guoji guanxi shi* [The history of international relations]. Vol. 1. Wuhan: Wuhan daxue chubanshe, 1983.

_____. *Guoji guanxi shi* [The history of international relations]. Vol. 2. Wuhan: Wuhan daxue chubanshe, 1983.

Wang Taiping, ed. *Deng Xiaoping waijiao sixiang yanjiu lunwen ji* [A collection of research papers on Deng Xiaoping's thought on foreign relations]. Beijing: Shijie zhishi chubanshe, 1996.

Wang Tieya, ed. *Guojifa* [International law]. Shijiazhuang: Falu chubanshe, 1981.

Wang Yizhou. *Dangdai guoji zhengzhi xilun* [Analysis of contemporary international politics]. Shanghai: Shanghai renmin chubanshe, 1995.

Wei Ganen and Chen Tianxiang, eds. *Shijie zhengshi jingji yu guoji guanxi* [World political economy and international relations]. Guangzhou: Zhongshan daxue chubanshe, 1994.

Wei Min et al., eds. *Guojifa gailun* [An introduction to international law]. Beijing: Guangming ribao chubanshe, 1986.

Wu Xiuquan. *Eight Years in the Ministry of Foreign Affairs*. Beijing: New World Press, 1985.

Xiandai quoji guanxi [Contemporary International Relations]. (Irregular, October 1981–; edited by the Institute of Contemporary International Relations, Beijing)

Xiao Guangwu and Zong Yue, eds. *Dangdai shijie zhengzhi jingji yu guoji guanxi* [Contemporary world political economy and international relations]. Beijing: Zhongguo zhanwang chubanshe, 1990.

Xia Xudong and Wang Shuzhong, eds., *Zouxiang 21 shijl de ZhongMei guanxi* [Towards the Sino-American relations of the twenty-first century]. Beijing: Dongfang chubanshe, 1996.

Xie Yixian. *Waijiao zhihui yu moulue: Xin Zhongguo waijiao lilun he yuanze* [Diplomatic wisdom and strategy: Theory and principles of new China's foreign relations]. Zhengzhou: Henan renmin chubanshe, 1993.

Xu Jiatun. *Xu Jiatun Xiang Gang huiyilu* [Xu Jiatun's Hong Kong memoirs]. Hong Kong: Lianhebao yeshu, 1992.

Yan Xuetong. *Zhongguo guojia liyi fengxi* [Analysis of Chinese national interests]. Tianjin: Tianjin renmin chubanshe, 1996.

Yang Gongsu. *Waijiao lilun yu shijian* [Diplomatic theory and practice]. Chengdu: Sichuan daxue chubanshe, 1992.

Yuan Ming, ed. *Kua shiji de tiaozhan: Zhongguo guoji guanxi xueke de fazhan* [Facing the challenges of the twenty-first century: The development of China's international relations discipline]. Chongqing: Chongqing chubanshe, 1993.

_____. *Guoji guanxi shi* [History of international relations]. Beijing: Beijing daxue chubanshe, 1994.

Zhang Jiliang. *Guoji guanxi gailun* [An introduction to international relations]. Beijing: shijie zhishi chubanshe, 1990.

Zhao Lihai. *Lianheguo xianzhang de xiugai wenti* [The problems of the United Nations charter review]. Beijing: Beijing daxue chubanshe, 1981.

_____. *Haiyangfa de xin fazhan* [The new development of the law of the sea]. Beijing: Beijing daxue chubanshe, 1981.

Zheng Duanmu, ed. *Guojifa* [International law]. Beijing: Beijing daxue chubanshe, 1989.

Zhong Wenxian, comp. *Mao Zedong: Biography, Assessment, Reminiscences.* Beijing: Foreign Languages Press, 1986.

Zhongguo baike nianjian [Chinese encyclopedic yearbook]. Beijing: Zhongguo dabaikequanshu. (Annual, 1980–; edited by the Chinese Encyclopedia Publisher).

Zhongguo fazhi bao [China legal journal] (three times a week August 1980–July 1986; daily since then).

Zhongguo guojifa niankan [Chinese yearbook of international law]. Beijing: Zhongguo duiwai fanyi chuban gongsi. (Annual, 1982–; edited by the China International Law Society).

Zhongguo waijiao [Chinese foreign relations]. Beijing: Zhongguo Renmin Daexue shubao ziliao zhongxin. (Monthly, 1988–; edited by the Center of Books and Newspapers Materials, Chinese People's University, Beijing).

Zhongguo waijiao gailan [Survey of Chinese foreign relations]. Beijing: Shijie zhishi chubanshe. (Annual, 1987–; edited by the editorial office of diplomatic history, the PRC Ministry of Foreign Affairs).

Zhou Zhonghai. *Guoji haiyang fa* [International law of the sea]. Beijing: Zhongguo zhengfa daxue chubanshe, 1987.

Non-PRC Publications in English

The Study of Chinese Foreign Policy and International Relations

Alker, Hayward R. *Rediscoveries and Reformulations: Humanistic Methodologies for International Studies.* New York: Cambridge University Press, 1996.

Breslauer, George W., and Philip E. Tetlock, eds. *Learning in U.S. and Soviet Foreign Policy.* Boulder, Colo.: Westview Press, 1991.

Buzan, Barry, Charles Jones, and Richard Little. *The Logic of Anarchy: Neorealism to Structural Realism.* New York: Columbia University Press, 1993.

George, Alexander L. *Bridging the Gap: Theory and Practice in Foreign Policy.* Washington, D.C.: United States Institute of Peace Press, 1993.

Goldstein, Judith, and Robert O. Keohane, eds. *Ideas and Foreign Policy: Beliefs, Institutions, and Political Change.* Ithaca, N.Y.: Cornell University Press, 1993.

Harding, Harry. "The Study of Chinese Politics: Toward a Third Generation of Scholarship." *World Politics* 36, 2 (January 1984): 284–307.

——. "International Studies in China." *China Exchange News* 20, 3–4 (Fall/Winter 1992): 2–6.

Hermann, Charles F., Charles W. Kegley, Jr., and James N. Rosenau, eds. *New Directions in the Study of Foreign Policy.* Boston: Allen & Unwin, 1987.

Hughes, Barry B., Steven Chan, and Charles W. Kegley, Jr., "Observations on the Study of International Relations in China." *International Studies Notes* 19:3 (Fall 1994): 17–22.

Kapur, Harish, ed. *As China Sees the World: Perceptions of Chinese Scholars.* London: Frances Pinter, 1987.

Katzenstein, Peter J., ed. *The Culture of National Security: Norms and Identity in World Politics.* New York: Columbia University Press, 1996.

Keohane, Robert O., and Helen V. Milner, eds. *Internationalization and Domestic Politics*. New York: Cambridge University Press, 1996.

Kim, Samuel S. "Advancing the American Study of Chinese Foreign Policy." *China Exchange News* 20, 3–4 (Fall/Winter, 1992): 18–23.

Kubalkova, Vendulka, and Albert Cruickshank. *Marxism and International Relations*. New York: Oxford University Press, 1989.

McGowan, Pat, and Charles W. Kegley, Jr., eds. *Foreign Policy and the Modern World-System*. Beverly Hills, Calif.: Sage Publications, 1983.

Murray, Douglas P. *International Relations Research and Training in the People's Republic of China*. A special report of the Northeast Asia–United States Forum on International Policy. Stanford: Stanford University, 1982.

Ng-Quinn, Michael. "The Analytic Study of Chinese Foreign Policy." *International Studies Quarterly* 27 (June 1983): 203–224.

Robinson, Thomas, and David Shambaugh, eds. *Chinese Foreign Policy: Theory and Practice*. New York: Oxford University Press, 1994.

Rosenau, James N. *Turbulence in World Politics: A Theory of Change and Continuity*. Princeton: Princeton University Press, 1990.

_____. "China in a Bifurcated World: Competing Theoretical Perspectives." In *Chinese Foreign Policy: Theory and Practice*, ed. Thomas W. Robinson and David Shambaugh. New York: Oxford University Press, 1994, 524–551.

Rozman, Gilbert. "China's Soviet Watchers in the 1980s: A New Era in Scholarship." *World Politics* 37, 3 (July 1985): 435–474.

Ruggie, John Gerald, ed. *Multilateralism Matters: The Theory and Praxis of an Institutional Form*. New York: Columbia University Press, 1993.

Shambaugh, David. "China's National Security Research Bureaucracy." *China Quarterly*, no. 110 (June 1987): 276–304.

_____. "New Sources and Research Opportunities in the Study of China's Foreign Relations and National Security." *China Exchange News* 20, 3–4 (Fall/Winter 1992): 24–27.

Shambaugh, David, and Wang Jisi. "Research on International Studies in the People's Republic of China." *PS* 17, 4 (Fall 1984): 758–764.

Shih, Chih-yu. *The Spirit of Chinese Foreign Policy: A Psychological View*. London: Macmillan, 1990.

_____. *China's Just World: The Morality of Chinese Foreign Policy*. Boulder, Colo.: Westview Press, 1993.

Snyder, Jack. "Richness, Rigor, and Relevance in the Study of Soviet Foreign Policy." *International Security* 9:3 (Winter 1984/85): 89–108.

_____. *Myths of Empire: Domestic Politics and International Ambition*. Ithaca, N.Y.: Cornell University Press, 1991.

Swaine, Michael D. *China: Domestic Change and Foreign Policy*. Santa Monica, Calif.: Rand Corporation, 1995.

Walker, Stephen, ed. *Role Theory and Foreign Policy Analysis*. Durham, N.C.: Duke University Press, 1987.

Waltz, Kenneth N. *Theory of International Politics*. Reading, Mass.: Addison-Wesley, 1979.

Wang, Jianwei. *Sino-US Mutual Images in the Post–Cold War Era*. Hong Kong: Oxford University Press, forthcoming.

Wang Jisi. "International Relations Theory and the Study of Chinese Foreign Policy: A Chinese Perspective." In Thomas W. Robinson and David Shambaugh, eds., *Chinese Foreign Policy: Theory and Practice*. Oxford: Clarendon Press, 1994, pp. 481–505.

Whiting, Allen S. "Chinese Foreign Policy: A Workshop Report." *SSRC Items* 31 (March–June 1977): 1–3.

Yahuda, Michael, ed. *New Directions in the Social Sciences and Humanities in China*. New York: St. Martin's Press, 1986.

Yuan Ming and Wang Jisi. "A Chinese View of International Relations Studies in China." *China Exchange News* 20:3–4 (Fall-Winter 1992): 9–11.

Zelikow, Philip. "Foreign Policy Engineering: From Theory to Practice and Back Again." *International Security* 18:4 (Spring 1994): 143–171.

Zhao Quansheng. *Interpreting Chinese Foreign Policy: The Micro-Macro Linkage Approach*. Hong Kong: Oxford University Press, 1996.

The Weight of the Past

Banno, Masataka. *China and the West 1858–1861: The Origins of the Tsungli Yamen*. Cambridge: Harvard University Press, 1964.

Fairbank, John K. "China's Foreign Policy in Historical Perspective." *Foreign Affairs* 47, 3 (April 1969): 449–63.

Fairbank, John K., ed. *The Chinese World Order: Traditional China's Foreign Relations*. Cambridge: Harvard University Press, 1968.

Fitzgerald, C. P. *The Chinese View of Their Place in the World*. London: Oxford University Press, 1965.

Franke, Wolfgang. *China and the West*, trans. R. A. Wilson. New York: Harper Torch Books, 1967.

Gittings, John. *The World and China, 1922–1972*. New York: Harper & Row, 1974.

Hsü, Immanuel C. Y. *China's Entrance into the Family of Nations: The Diplomatic Phase, 1858–1880*. Cambridge: Harvard University Press, 1960.

Hunt, Michael. *The Genesis of Chinese Communist Foreign Policy*. New York: Columbia University Press, 1996.

Hunt, Michael H., and Niu Jun, eds. *Toward a History of Chinese Communist Foreign Relations, 1920s–1960s*. Washington, D.C.: Woodrow Wilson International Center for Scholars, n.d.

Jenner, W. J. F. *The Tyranny of History: The Roots of China's Crisis*. New York: Penguin Books, 1992.

Johnston, Alastair Iain. *Cultural Realism: Strategic Culture and Grand Strategy in Chinese History*. Princeton: Princeton University Press, 1995.

Kirby, William C. "Traditions of Centrality, Authority, and Management in Modern China's Foreign Relations." In Thomas W. Robinson and David Shambaugh, eds., *Chinese Foreign Policy: Theory and Practice*. New York: Oxford University Press, 1994, pp. 13–29.

Mancall, Mark. *China at the Center: 300 Years of Foreign Policy*. New York: Free Press, 1984.

Reardon-Anderson, James. *Yenan and the Great Powers: The Origins of Chinese Communist Foreign Policy, 1944–1946*. New York: Columbia University Press, 1980.

Rossabi, Morris, ed. *China Among Equals: The Middle Kingdom and Its Neighbors.* Berkeley: University of California Press, 1983.

Shih, Chih-yu. *The Spirit of Chinese Foreign Policy: A Psychological View.* London: Macmillan, 1990.

Spence, Jonathan D. *To Change China: Western Advisers in China, 1620–1960.* New York: Penguin Books, 1980.

Teng, Ssu-yu, and Fairbank, John K. *China's Response to the West: A Documentary Survey, 1839–1923.* Cambridge: Harvard University Press, 1954.

Waldron, Arthur. *The Great Wall of China: From History to Myth.* Cambridge: Cambridge University Press, 1990.

Wright, Arthur. "Struggle v. Harmony: Symbols of Competing Values in Modern China." *World Politics* 6, 1 (October 1953): 31–44.

Zhang Yongjin. *China in the International System, 1918–20: The Middle Kingdom at the Periphery.* New York: St. Martin's Press, 1991.

General Works: Contemporary Developments

Bernstein, Richard, and Ross H. Munro. *The Coming Conflict with China.* New York: Knopf, 1997.

Christensen, Thomas J. "Chinese Realpolitik." *Foreign Affairs* 75:5 (September/October 1996): 37–52.

Dobson, William J., and M. Taylor Fravel. "Red Herring Hegemon: China in the South China Sea." *Current History* 96:611 (September 1997): 258–263.

Dreyer, June T., ed. *Chinese Defense and Foreign Policy.* New York: Paragon House, 1989.

Faust, John R., and Judith F. Kornberg. *China in World Politics.* Boulder, Colo.: Lynne Rienner Pub., 1995.

Gallagher, Michael C. "China's Illusory Threat to the South China Sea." *International Security* 19:1 (Summer 1994): 169–194.

Garver, John W. *Foreign Relations of the People's Republic of China.* Englewood Cliffs, N.J.: Prentice-Hall, 1993.

Hao, Yufan, and Huan, Guocang, eds. *The Chinese View of the World.* New York: Pantheon Books, 1989.

Harding, Harry, ed. *China's Foreign Relations in the 1980s.* New Haven: Yale University Press, 1984.

Harris, Stuart, and Gary Klintworth, eds. *China as a Great Power: Myths, Realities and Challenges in the Asia-Pacific Region.* New York: St. Martin's Press, 1995.

Hsiung, James C., and Kim, Samuel S., eds. *China in the Global Community.* New York: Praeger, 1980.

Kim, Samuel S. "China's Pacific Policy: Reconciling the Irreconcilable." *International Journal* 50:3 (Summer 1995): 461–487.

_____. "China as a Great Power." *Current History* 96:611 (September 1997): 246–251.

Lin, Bih-jaw, and James T. Myers, eds. *Contemporary China in the Post–Cold War Era.* Columbia: University of South Carolina Press, 1996.

Nathan, Andrew J., and Robert S. Ross. *The Great Wall and the Empty Fortress: China's Search for Security.* New York: W. W. Norton, 1997.

Robinson, Thomas W. "Chinese Foreign Policy from the 1940s to the 1990s." In Thomas W. Robinson and David Shambaugh, eds., *Chinese Foreign Policy: Theory and Practice*. Oxford: Clarendon Press, 1994, pp. 555–602.

Roy, Denny. "Hegemon on the Horizon? China's Threat to East Asian Security." *International Security* 19:1 (Summer 1994): 149–168.

Segal, Gerald. "East Asia and the 'Constrainment' of China." *International Security* 20:4 (Spring 1996): 107–135.

Shambaugh, David. "Containment or Engagement of China? Calculating Beijing's Responses." *International Security* 21:2 (Fall 1996): 180–209.

Shinn, James, ed. *Weaving the Net: Conditional Engagement with China*. New York: Council on Foreign Relations Press, 1996.

Sutter, Robert G. *Chinese Foreign Policy: Developments After Mao*. New York: Praeger, 1986.

Wang, Jianwei, and Zhimin Lin. "Chinese Perceptions in the Post–Cold War Era." *Asian Survey* 32:10 (October 1992): 902–917.

Whiting, Allen S., ed. Special Issue on Chinese Foreign Relations, *The Annals of the American Academy of Political and Social Science* 519 (January 1992).

Yahuda, Michael. *China's Role in World Affairs*. New York: St. Martin's Press, 1978.

_____. *Towards the End of Isolationism: China's Foreign Policy After Mao*. New York: St. Martin's Press, 1983.

Zhao Quansheng. *Interpreting Chinese Foreign Policy: The Micro-Macro Linkage Approach*. Hong Kong: Oxford University Press, 1996.

Competing Determinants and Explanations

Armstrong, J. D. *Revolutionary Diplomacy: Chinese Foreign Policy and the United Front Doctrine*. Berkeley: University of California Press, 1977.

Bialer, Seweryn, ed. *The Domestic Context of Soviet Foreign Policy*. Boulder, Colo.: Westview Press, 1981.

Dittmer, Lowell. *Sino-Soviet Normalization and Its International Implications, 1945–1990*. Seattle: University of Washington Press, 1992.

East, Maurice A., Stephen A. Salmore, and Charles F. Hermann, eds. *Why Nations Act: Theoretical Perspectives for Comparative Foreign Policy Studies*. Beverly Hills, Calif.: Sage Publications, 1978.

Gottlieb, Thomas M. *Chinese Foreign Policy Factionalism and the Origins of the Strategic Triangle*. Santa Monica, Calif.: Rand Corporation, 1977, R-1902-NA.

Kim, Samuel S. *The Maoist Image of World Order*. Princeton, N.J.: Center of International Studies, Princeton University, 1977.

Liao, Kuang-sheng. "Linkage Politics in China: Internal Mobilization and Articulated External Hostility in the Cultural Revolution, 1967–1969." *World Politics* 28 (July 1976): 590–610.

Lieberthal, Kenneth. *The Foreign Policy Debate in Peking As Seen Through Allegorical Articles*. Santa Monica, Calif.: Rand Corporation, 1977, P-5768.

Ng-Quinn, Michael. "Effects of Bipolarity on Chinese Foreign Policy." *Survey* 26 (Spring 1982): 102–130.

_____. "The Analytic Study of Chinese Foreign Policy." *International Studies Quarterly* 27 (June 1983): 203–224.

Pollack, Jonathan D. *China's Potential as a World Power*. Santa Monica: Rand Corporation, 1980, P–6524.

Schram, Stuart, ed. *Chairman Mao Talks to the People*. New York: Pantheon, 1974.

Yu, Bin. "The Study of Chinese Foreign Policy: Problems and Prospect." *World Politics* 46 (January 1994): 235–261.

Zhao Quansheng. "Domestic Factors of Chinese Foreign Policy: From Vertical to Horizontal Authoritarianism." *Annals of the American Academy of Political and Social Science* 519 (January 1992): 158–178.

The Decisionmaking Process

Axelrod, Robert, ed. *Structure of Decision: The Cognitive Maps of Political Elites*. Princeton: Princeton University Press, 1976.

Barnett, A. Doak. *The Making of Foreign Policy in China*. Boulder, Colo.: Westview Press, 1985.

Bobrow, Davis B, Steve Chan, and John A. Kringen. *Understanding Foreign Policy Decisions: The Chinese Case*. New York: Free Press, 1979.

Chan, Steve. "Chinese Conflict Calculus and Behavior: Assessment from a Perspective of Conflict Management." *World Politics* 30 (April 1978): 391–410.

Goncharov, Sergei, John W. Lewis, and Xue Litai. *Uncertain Partners: Stalin, Mao, and the Korean War*. Stanford: Stanford University Press, 1993.

Gurtov, Melvin, and Byong-Moo Hwang. *China Under Threat: The Politics of Strategy and Diplomacy*. Baltimore, Md.: Johns Hopkins University Press, 1980.

Hamrin, Carol Lee. "Elite Politics and the Development of China's Foreign Relations." In Thomas Robinson and David Shambaugh, eds., *Chinese Foreign Policy: Theory and Practice*. Oxford: Clarendon Press, 1994, pp. 70–109.

Hamrin, Carol Lee, and Suisheng Zhao, eds. *Decisionmaking in Deng's China*. Armonk, N.Y.: M. E. Sharpe, 1995.

Jacobson, Harold K., and Michel Oksenberg. *China's Participation in the IMF, the World Bank, and GATT*. Ann Arbor: University of Michigan Press, 1990.

Li Fan. "The Question of Interests in the Chinese Policy-Making Process." *China Quarterly*, no. 109 (March 1987): 64–71.

Lieberthal, Kenneth, and Michel Oksenberg. *Policy Making in China: Leaders, Structures, and Processes*. Princeton: Princeton University Press, 1988.

Lu Ning. *The Dynamics of Foreign-Policy Decisionmaking in China*. Boulder, Colo.: Westview Press, 1997.

Oksenberg, Michel. "Economic Policy-Making in China: Summer 1981." *China Quarterly*, no. 90 (June 1982): 165–194.

Shambaugh, David. "China's National Security Research Bureaucracy." *China Quarterly*, no. 119 (June 1987): 276–304.

Swaine, Michael D. *The Role of the Chinese Military in National Security Policymaking*. Santa Monica, Calif.: Rand Corporation, 1996.

Sylvan, Donald A., and Steve Chan, eds. *Foreign Policy Decision Making: Perception, Cognition and Artificial Intelligence*. New York: Praeger, 1984.

Tretiak, Daniel. "Who Makes Chinese Foreign Policy Today (Late 1980)." *Australian Journal of Chinese Affairs*, no. 5 (1981): 137–157.

Whiting, Allen S. *China Crosses the Yalu: The Decision to Enter the Korean War.* New York: Macmillan, 1960.

_____. "New Light on Mao: Quemoy 1958: Mao's Miscalculations." *China Quarterly*, no. 62 (June 1975): 263–270.

Diplomatic and Negotiating Style

Chang, Jaw-ling Joanne. "Negotiation of the 17 August 1982 U.S.-PRC Arms Communique: Beijing's Negotiating Tactics." *China Quarterly*, no. 125 (March 1991): 33–54.

Cohen, Raymond. *Negotiating Across Cultures.* Washington, D.C.: United States Institute of Peace Press, 1991.

Hsu, Kai-yu. *Chou En-lai: China's Gray Eminence.* Garden City, N.Y.: Doubleday, 1968.

Kapp, Robert A., ed., *Communicating with China.* Chicago: Intercultural Press, 1983.

Keith, Ronald C. *The Diplomacy of Zhou Enlai.* London: Macmillan, 1989.

Kreisberg, Paul H. "China's Negotiating Behavior." In Thomas W. Robinson and David Shambaugh, eds., *Chinese Foreign Policy: Theory and Practice.* Oxford: Clarendon Press, 1994, pp. 453–77.

Lall, Arthur. *How Communist China Negotiates.* New York: Columbia University Press, 1968.

Pye, Lucian. *Chinese Commercial Negotiating Style.* Cambridge, Mass.: Oelgeschlager, Gunn & Hain, 1982.

Ross, Robert S. *Negotiating Cooperation: The United States and China, 1969–1989.* Stanford: Stanford University Press, 1995.

Solomon, Richard H. *Chinese Negotiating Behavior: A Briefing Analysis.* Santa Monica: Rand Corporation, 1985.

Tung, Shih-Chung. *The Policy of China in the Third United Nations Conference on the Law of the Sea.* Geneva: Graduate Institute of International Studies, 1981.

Wilhelm, Alfred D., Jr. *The Chinese at the Negotiating Table: Style and Characteristics.* Washington, D.C.: National Defense University Press, 1994.

Young, Kenneth T. *Negotiating with the Chinese Communists: The U.S. Experience.* New York: McGraw-Hill, 1966.

Zhai Qiang. "China and the Geneva Conference of 1954." *China Quarterly*, no. 129 (March 1992): 103–122.

China and the Soviet Union/Russia

Boris, Oleg B. *Sino-Soviet Relations, 1945–1973: A Brief History.* Moscow: Progress Publishers, 1975.

Borisov, O. B., and B. T. Koloskov. *Soviet-Chinese Relations, 1945–1980.* Moscow: Mysl Publishers, third supplemental ed., 1980.

Chang, Gordon H. *Friends and Enemies: The United States, China, and the Soviet Union, 1948–1972.* Stanford: Stanford University Press, 1990.

Dittmer, Lowell. *Sino-Soviet Normalization and Its International Implications, 1945–1990.* Seattle: University of Washington Press, 1992.

Garver, John W. *Chinese-Soviet Relations, 1937–1945: The Diplomacy of Chinese Nationalism*. New York: Oxford University Press, 1988.

Goldstein, Joshua S., and John R. Freeman. *Three-Way Street: Strategic Reciprocity in World Politics*. Chicago: University of Chicago Press, 1990.

Goldstein, Steven M. "Nationalism and Internationalism: Sino-Soviet Relations," in Thomas W. Robinson and David Shambaugh, eds., *Chinese Foreign Policy: Theory and Practice*. New York: Oxford University Press, 1994, pp. 224–65.

Kim, Ilpyong, ed. *The Strategic Triangle: China, the United States, and the Soviet Union*. New York: Paragon House, 1987.

Medvedez, Roy A. *China and the Superpowers*. Trans. Harold Shukman. Oxford: Basil Blackwell, 1986.

Menon, Rajau. "The Strategic Convergence Between Russia and China." *Survival* 39:2 (Summer 1997): 101–125.

Ross, Robert S., ed. *China, the United States, and the Soviet Union: Tripolarity and Policy Making in the Cold War*. Armonk, N.Y.: M. E. Sharpe, 1993.

Rozman, Gilbert. "Moscow's China-Watchers in the Post-Mao Era: The Response to a Changing China." *China Quarterly*, no. 94 (June 1983): 231–236.

_____. *The Chinese Debate About Soviet Socialism, 1978–1985*. Princeton: Princeton University Press, 1987.

_____. *A Mirror for Socialism: Soviet Criticisms of China*. Princeton: Princeton University Press, 1985.

Wich, Richard. *Sino-Soviet Crisis Politics: A Study of Political Change and Communication*. Cambridge: Harvard University Press, 1980.

Zagoria, Donald S. *The Sino-Soviet Conflict 1956–1961*. Princeton: Princeton University Press, 1962.

China and the United States

Atlantic Council of the United States and National Committee on United States–China Relations. *United States and China Relations at a Crossroads*. Washington, D.C.: Atlantic Council of the United States, 1993.

Brzezinski, Zbigniew. *Power and Principle*. New York: Farrar, Strauss, Giroux, 1983.

Carter, Jimmy. *Keeping Faith: Memoirs of a President*. New York: Bantam Books 1982.

Chang, Gordon H. *Friends and Enemies: The United States, China, and the Soviet Union, 1948–1972*. Stanford: Stanford University Press, 1990.

Chen Jian. *China's Road to the Korean War: The Making of the Sino-American Confrontation*. New York: Columbia University Press, 1994.

Christensen, Thomas J. *Useful Adversaries: Grand Strategy, Domestic Mobilization, and Sino-American Conflict, 1947–58*. Princeton: Princeton University Press, 1996.

Fairbank, John K. *The United States and China*. 4th ed. Cambridge: Harvard University Press, 1979.

Foot, Rosemary. *The Practice of Power: U.S. Relations with China Since 1949*. Oxford: Clarendon Press, 1995.

Garver, John W. *Face Off: China, the United States, and Taiwan's Democratization.* Seattle: University of Washington Press, 1997.

_____. *The Sino-American Alliance: Nationalist China and the U.S. Cold War Strategy in Asia.* Armonk, N.Y.: M. E. Sharpe 1997.

Goldstein, Joshua S., and John R. Freeman. *Three-Way Street: Strategic Reciprocity in World Politics.* Chicago: University of Chicago Press, 1990.

Harding, Harry. *A Fragile Relationship: The United States and China Since 1972.* Washington, D.C.: Brookings Institution, 1992.

Harding, Harry, and Yuan Ming, eds. *Sino-American Relations, 1945–1955: A Joint Reassessment of a Critical Decade.* Wilmington, Del.: Scholarly Resources, 1989.

Hunt, Michael H. *The Making of a Special Relationship: The United States and China to 1914.* New York: Columbia University Press, 1983.

Hunt, Michael, et al., *Mutual Images in U.S.-China Relations.* Occasional Paper no. 32. Washington, D.C.: Wilson Center, June 1988.

Kissinger, Henry A. *White House Years.* Boston: Little, Brown and Co., 1979.

_____. *Years of Upheaval.* Boston: Little, Brown and Co., 1982.

Lampton, David M., and Alfred D. Wilhelm, eds. *United States and China: Relations at a Crossroads.* Lanham, Md.: University Press of America, 1995.

Metzger, Thomas A., and Ramon H. Myers, eds. *Greater China and U.S. Foreign Policy.* Stanford: Hoover Institution, 1996.

Oksenberg, Michel, and Elizabeth Economy. *Shaping U.S.-China Relations: A Long-Term Strategy.* A Council on Foreign Relations Study Group Report. New York: Council on Foreign Relations, 1997.

Ross, Robert S. *Negotiating Cooperation: The United States and China, 1969–1989.* Stanford: Stanford University Press, 1995.

Ross, Robert S., ed. *China, the United States, and the Soviet Union: Tripolarity and Policy Making in the Cold War.* Armonk, N.Y.: M. E. Sharpe, 1993.

Schaller, Michael. *The United States and China in the Twentieth Century.* New York: Oxford University Press, 2nd ed., 1990.

Shambaugh, David. *Beautiful Imperialist: China Perceives America, 1972–1990.* Princeton: Princeton University Press, 1991.

Vogel, Ezra F., ed. *Living with China: U.S.-China Relations in the Twenty-First Century.* New York: Norton, 1997.

Wang, Jianwei. *Sino-U.S. Mutual Images in the Post–Cold War Era.* Hong Kong: Oxford University Press, forthcoming.

China and Japan

Garrett, Banning, and Bonnie Glaser. "Chinese Apprehensions About Revitalization of the U.S.-Japan Alliance." *Asian Survey* 37:4 (April 1997): 383–402.

Hellman, Donald C., ed., *China and Japan: A New Balance of Power.* Lexington, Mass.: Lexington Books, 1976.

Howe, Christopher, and Brian Hook, eds. *China and Japan: History, Trends, and Prospects.* Oxford: Oxford University Press, 1994.

Hsiung, James C., and Steven I. Levine, eds. *China's Bitter Victory: The War with Japan, 1937–1945.* Armonk, N.Y.: M. E. Sharpe, 1992.

Iriye, Akira. *China and Japan in the Global Setting*. Cambridge: Harvard University Press, 1994.

Lee, Chae-Jin. *Japan Faces China: Political Economic Relations in the Postwar Era*. Baltimore, Md.: Johns Hopkins University Press, 1976.

_____. *China and Japan: New Economic Diplomacy*. Stanford: Hoover Institution Press, 1984.

Ono, Shuichi. *Sino-Japanese Economic Relationships: Trade, Direct Investment, and Future Strategy*. Washington, D.C.: World Bank, 1992.

Radke, Kurt Werner. *China's Relations with Japan, 1945–83: The Role of Liao Chengzhi*. Manchester: Manchester University Press, 1990.

Shih, Chih-yu. "Defining Japan: The Nationalist Assumption in China's Foreign Policy." *International Journal* 50:3 (Summer 1995): 539–63.

Taylor, Robert. *The Sino-Japanese Axis: A New Force in Asia?* London: Athlone Press, 1985.

_____. *China, Japan, and the European Community*. London: Athlone Press, 1990.

Wang, Qingxin Ken. "Recent Japanese Economic Diplomacy in China." *Asian Survey* 33:6 (June 1993): 625–641.

Whiting, Allen S. *China Eyes Japan*. Berkeley: University of California Press, 1989.

_____. "China and Japan: Politics Versus Economics." *Annals of the American Academy of Political and Social Science* 519 (January 1992): 39–51.

China and Europe

Bailes, Alyson J. "China and Eastern Europe: A Judgment on the Socialist Community." *Pacific Review* 3:3 (1990): 222–242.

Biberaj, Elez. *Albania and China: A Study of an Unequal Alliance*. Boulder, Colo.: Westview Press, 1986.

Boardman, Robert. *Britain and the People's Republic of China 1949–1974*. New York: Macmillan, 1976.

Jain, Jagdish P. *China in World Politics: A Study of Sino-British Relations, 1949–1975*. New Delhi: Radiant Press, 1976.

Kapur, Harish. *China and the European Economic Community: The New Connection*. Boston: Martinus Nijhoff, 1986.

_____. *Distant Neighbours: China and Europe*. London: Pinter 1990.

Shambaugh, David. "China and Europe." *Annals of the American Academy of Political and Social Science* 519 (January 1992): 101–114.

_____. *China and Europe: 1949–1995*. London: Contemporary China Institute, School of Oriental and African Studies, University of London, 1996.

Shaw, Yu-ming, ed. *China and Europe in the Twentieth Century*. Taipei: Institute of International Relations, 1986.

Tang, James Tuck-Hong. *Britain's Encounter with Revolutionary China, 1949–54*. New York: St. Martin's Press, 1992.

Taylor, Robert. *China, Japan, and the European Community*. London: Athlone Press, 1990.

Yahuda, Michael B. "China and Europe: The Significance of a Secondary Relationship." In Thomas W. Robinson and David Shambaugh, eds., *Chinese Foreign Policy: Theory and Practice*. New York: Oxford University Press, 1994, pp. 266–282.

China and the Third World

Abidi, A. H. H. *China, Iran, and the Persian Gulf.* Atlantic Highlands, N.J.: Humanities Press, 1982.

Bitzinger, Richard A. "Arms to Go: Chinese Arms Sales to the Third World." *International Security* 17:2 (Fall 1992): 84–111.

Calabrese, John. *China's Changing Relations with the Middle East.* London and New York: Garland Publishing, 1991.

_____. "Peaceful or Dangerous Collaborators? China's Relations with the Gulf Countries." *Pacific Affairs* 65:4 (Winter 1992–93): 471–485.

The Challenge to the South. The Report of the South Commission. New York: Oxford University Press, 1990.

Chang, Pao-min. *Kampuchea Between China and Vietnam.* Singapore: Singapore University Press, 1985.

_____. *The Sino-Vietnamese Territorial Dispute.* New York: Praeger, 1986.

Gable, Vincent. *China and India: Economic Reform and Global Interaction.* London: Royal Institute of International Affairs, 1995.

Garver, John W. "China and South Asia." *Annals of the American Academy of Political and Social Science* 519 (January 1992): 67–85.

Harris, Lillian. *China Considers the Middle East.* London: Tauris, 1993.

Harris, Lillian, and Robert Worden, eds. *China and the Third World: Champion or Challenger?* Dover, Mass.: Auburn House, 1986.

Harris, Nigel. *The End of the Third World: Newly Industrializing Countries and the Decline of an Ideology.* London: Tauris, 1986.

Jackson, Robert H. *Quasi States: Sovereignty, International Relations and the Third World.* New York: Cambridge University Press, 1990.

Jackson, Steven F. "China's Third World Foreign Policy: The Case of Angola and Mozambique, 1961–93." *China Quarterly*, no. 142 (June 1995): 388–422.

Johnson, Cecil. *Communist China and Latin America.* New York: Columbia University Press, 1970.

Kim, Samuel S. *The Third World in Chinese World Policy.* Princeton: Center of International Studies, Princeton University, 1989.

Klintworth, Gary. "China's Evolving Relationship with APEC." *International Journal* 50:3 (Summer 1995): 488–515.

Krasner, Stephen D. *Structural Conflict: The Third World Against Global Liberalism.* Berkeley: University of California Press, 1985.

Lee, Chae Jin. *China and Korea: Dynamic Relations.* Stanford: Hoover Institution, 1996.

Lee Lai To. "ASEAN and the South China Sea Conflicts." *Pacific Review* 8:3 (1995): 521–545.

Malik, J. Mohan. "China-India Relations in the Post-Soviet Era: The Continuing Rivalry." *China Quarterly*, no. 142 (June 1995): 317–355.

Martin, Edwin W. *Southeast Asia and China: The End of Containment.* Boulder, Colo.: Westview Press, 1977.

Mortimer, Robert A. *The Third World Coalition in International Politics.* 2nd ed. Boulder, Colo.: Westview Press, 1984.

Ogunsanwo, Alaba. *China's Policy in Africa, 1958–1971.* New York: Cambridge University Press, 1979.

Ross, Robert S. *The Indochina Tangle: China's Vietnam Policy, 1975–1979.* New York: Columbia University Press, 1988.

_____. "China and Post-Cambodia Southeast Asia: Coping with Success." *Annals of the American Academy of Political and Social Science* 519 (January 1992): 52–66.

Schichor, Yitzhak. *The Middle East in China's Foreign Policy, 1949–1977.* New York: Cambridge University Press, 1979.

_____. "China and the Middle East Since Tiananmen." *Annals of the American Academy of Political and Social Science* 519 (January 1992): 86–100.

Segal, Gerald. "China and Africa." *Annals of the American Academy of Political and Social Science* 519 (January 1992): 115–126.

Snow, Philip. *The Star Raft: China's Encounter with Africa.* Ithaca, N.Y.: Cornell University Press, 1988.

South Commission. *The Challenge to the South.* New York: Oxford University Press, 1990.

Van Ness, Peter. *Revolution and Chinese Foreign Policy: Peking's Support for Wars of National Liberation.* Berkeley: University of California Press, 1971.

Vertzberger, Yacov. *China's Southwestern Strategy: Encirclement and Counterencirclement.* Westport, Conn.: Greenwood, 1985.

Wang, Chien-hsun. "Peking's Latin American Policy in the 1980s." *Issues and Studies* 27:5 (May 1991): 103–118.

Whiting, Allen S. "ASEAN Eyes China: The Security Dimension." *Asian Survey* 37:4 (April 1997): 299–322.

Military and Strategic Policy

Adelman, Jonathan R., and Chih-yu Shih. *Symbolic War: The Chinese Use of Force, 1840–1980.* Taipei: Institute of International Relations, 1993.

Allen, Kenneth W., Glenn Krumel, and Jonathan D. Pollack. *China's Air Force Enters the Twenty-First Century.* Santa Monica, Calif.: Rand Corporation, 1995.

Bitzinger, Richard A. "Arms to Go: Chinese Arms Sales to the Third World." *International Security* 17:2 (Fall 1992): 84–111.

Chen Jian. "China's Involvement in the Vietnam War, 1964–69." *China Quarterly,* no. 142 (June 1995): 356–87.

Chen, Min. *The Strategic Triangle and Regional Conflicts: Lessons from the Indochina Wars.* Boulder, Colo.: Lynne Rienner Pub., 1992.

Dellios, Rosita. *Modern Chinese Defense Strategy: Present Developments, Future Directions.* New York: St. Martin's Press, 1990.

Dittmer, Lowell. "The Strategic Triangle: An Elementary Game Theoretical Analysis." *World Politics* 33:4 (July 1981): 485–515.

Dreyer, June Teufel. "Regional Security Issues," *Journal of International Affairs* 49:2 (Winter 1996): 391–411.

Folta, Paul Humes. *From Swords to Plowshares? Defense Industry Reform in the PRC.* Boulder, Colo.: Westview Press, 1992.

Garrett, Banning, and Bonnie Glaser. "Chinese Perspectives on Nuclear Arms Control." *International Security* 20:3 (Winter 1995/96): 43–78.

_____. "Multilateral Security in the Asia-Pacific Region and Its Impact on Chinese Interests: Views from Beijing." *Contemporary Southeast Asia* 16:1 (June 1994): 14–34.

Garver, John W. "China's Push Through the South China Sea: The Interaction of Bureaucratic and National Interests." *China Quarterly,* no. 132 (December 1992): 999–1028.

Gill, Bates, and Taeho Kim. *China's Arms Acquisitions from Abroad: A Quest for "Superb and Secret Weapons."* SIPRI Research Report No. 11. Oxford: Oxford University Press, 1995.

Godwin, Paul H. B. "From Continent to Periphery: PLA Doctrine, Strategy and Capabilities Toward 2000." *China Quarterly,* no. 146 (June 1996): 443–487.

Grimmett, Richard F. *Conventional Arms Transfers to the Third World, 1986–1993.* Washington, D.C.: Congressional Research Service, Library of Congress, 94-612 F, July 29, 1994.

Hood, Steven J. *Dragons Entangled: Indochina and the China-Vietnam War.* Armonk, N.Y.: M. E. Sharpe, 1992.

Johnston, Alastair Iain. *China and Arms Control.* Ottawa: Canadian Centre for Arms Control and Disarmament, 1986.

_____. "China's New 'Old' Thinking." *International Security* 20:3 (Winter 1995/96): 5–42.

_____. "Learning Versus Adaptation: Explaining Change in Chinese Arms Control Policy in the 1980s and 1990s." *China Journal,* no. 35 (January 1996), pp. 36–43.

_____. "Prospects for Chinese Nuclear Force Modernization: Limited Deterrence Versus Multilateral Arms Control." *China Quarterly,* no. 146 (June 1996): 548–576.

_____. "Cultural Realism and Strategy in Maoist China." In Peter J. Katzenstein, ed., *The Culture of National Security: Norms and Identity in World Politics* (New York: Columbia University Press, 1996), pp. 216–269.

Lewis, John Wilson, and Xue Litai. *China Builds the Bomb.* Stanford: Stanford University Press, 1988.

Lewis, John W., Hua Di, and Xue Litai. "Beijing's Defense Establishment: Solving the Arms-Export Enigma." *International Security* 15:4 (Spring 1991): 87–109.

Lewis, John W., and Xue Litai. *China's Strategic Seapower: The Politics of Force Modernization in the Nuclear Age.* Stanford: Stanford University Press, 1994.

Lin, Chong-pin. *China's Nuclear Weapons Strategy.* Lexington, Mass.: Lexington Books, 1988.

The Military Balance 1997–98. London: The International Institute for Strategic Studies, 1997.

Nelsen, Harvey W. *Power and Insecurity: Beijing, Moscow, and Washington, 1949–1988.* Boulder, Colo.: Lynne Rienner Pub., 1989.

Pillsbury, Michael, ed. *Chinese Views of Future Warfare.* Washington, D.C.: National Defense University Press, 1996.

Ryan, Mark A. *Chinese Attitudes Towards Nuclear Weapons: China and the United States During the Korean War.* Armonk, N.Y.: M. E. Sharpe, 1989.

Sawyer, Ralph D., trans. *The Seven Military Classics of Ancient China.* Boulder, Colo.: Westview Press, 1993.

Schichor, Yitzhak. *East Wind over Arabia.* Berkeley: University of California Institute of East Asian Studies, 1989.

Segal, Gerald. *Defending China.* New York: Oxford University Press, 1985.

Tien, Chen-Ya. *Chinese Military Theory: Ancient and Modern.* London: Mosaic Press, 1992.

Whiting, Allen S. *The Chinese Calculus of Deterrence*. Ann Arbor: University of Michigan Press, 1975.

Zhang, Shu Guang. *Deterrence and Strategic Culture: Chinese-American Confrontations, 1949–1958*. Ithaca, N.Y.: Cornell University Press, 1992.

China and the Global Political Economy

Brahm, Laurence J. *Foreign Exchange Controls and Strategies for the People's Republic of China*. Hong Kong: Longman Group, 1990.

Crane, George T. *The Political Economy of China's Special Economic Zones*. Armonk, N.Y.: M. E. Sharpe, 1990.

Jones, R. J. Barry. *Globalization and Interdependence in the International Political Economy*. New York: Pinter, 1995.

Khan, Zafar Shah. *Patterns of Direct Foreign Investment in China*. Washington, D.C.: World Bank, 1991.

Kleinberg, Robert. *China's "Opening" to the Outside World: The Experiment with Foreign Capitalism*. Boulder, Colo.: Westview Press, 1990.

Lardy, Nicholas. *Foreign Trade and Economic Reform in China, 1978–1990*. Cambridge: Cambridge University Press, 1992.

_____. *China in the World Economy*. Washington, D.C.: Institute for International Economics, 1994.

Lin The-chang. "Foreign Aid: A Theoretical Framework for Analyzing Communist China's Foreign Policy." *Issues and Studies* 27:5 (May 1991): 78–102.

Moore, Thomas G. "China as a Latecomer: Toward a Global Logic of the Open Policy." *Journal of Contemporary China* 5:12 (July 1996): 187–208.

Oksenberg, M., P. Potter, and W. Abnet. *Advancing Intellectual Property Rights: Information Technologies and the Course of Economic Development in China*. Seattle: National Bureau of Asian Research, 1996.

Pearson, Margaret M. *Joint Ventures in the People's Republic of China*. Princeton: Princeton University Press, 1991.

Reardon, Lawrence C. "The Rise and Decline of China's Export Processing Zones." *Journal of Contemporary China* 5:13 (November 1996): 281–303.

Ren Ruoen and Chou Kai. "China's GDP in U.S. Dollars Based on Purchasing Power Parity." World Bank Working Paper No. 1415. Washington, D.C.: World Bank, 1995.

Shirk, Susan. *How China Opened Its Door: The Political Success of the PRC's Foreign Trade and Investment Reforms*. Washington, D.C.: Brookings Institution, 1994.

Wang, Hong. *China's Exports Since 1979*. New York: St. Martin's Press, 1993.

Wang, Hongying. *Law, Diplomacy and Transnational Networks: The Dynamics of Foreign Direct Investment in China*. Hong Kong: Oxford University Press, forthcoming.

World Bank. *China Between Plan and Market*. Washington, D.C.: World Bank, 1991.

_____. *China: Reform and the Role of the Plan in the 1990s*. Washington, D.C.: World Bank, 1992.

_____. *World Development Report 1997*. New York: Oxford University Press, 1997.

_____. *China 2020: Development Challenges in the New Century*. Washington, D.C.: World Bank, 1997.

———. *China Engaged: Integration with the Global Economy.* Washington, D.C.: World Bank, 1997.

Yeats, Alexander J. *China's Foreign Trade and Comparative Advantage: Prospects, Problems, and Policy Implications.* Washington, D.C.: World Bank, 1991.

Chinese and Global Human Rights

Aird, John S. *Slaughter of the Innocents: Coercive Birth Control in China.* Washington, D.C.: American Enterprise Institute Press, 1990.

Amnesty International. *China: The Massacre of June 1989 and Its Aftermath.* New York: Amnesty International, April 1990.

———. *China: Punishment Without Crime.* New York: Amnesty International, September 1991.

———. *Torture in China.* New York: Amnesty International, December 1992.

Asia Watch. *Continuing Religious Repression in China.* New York: Asia Watch, a Division of Human Rights Watch, June 1993.

Chiu, Hungdah. "Chinese Attitudes Toward International Law of Human Rights." In Victor Falkenheim, ed., *Chinese Politics from Mao to Deng.* New York: Paragon House, 1989, pp. 237–270.

Cohen, Roberta. "People's Republic of China: The Human Rights Exception." *Human Rights Quarterly* 9:4 (November 1987): 447–549.

Davis, Michael C., ed. *Human Rights and Chinese Values: Legal, Philosophical, and Political Perspectives.* Hong Kong: Oxford University Press, 1995.

De Bary, Theodore, and Tu Weiming, eds. *Confucianism and Human Rights.* New York: Columbia University Press, 1997.

Donnelly, Jack. *Universal Human Rights in Theory and Practice.* Ithaca, N.Y.: Cornell University Press, 1989.

Dreyer, June Teufel. *China's Forty Millions: Minority Nationalities and National Integration in the People's Republic of China.* Cambridge: Harvard University Press, 1976.

Drinan, Robert F., and Teresa T. Kuo. "The 1991 Battle for Human Rights in China." *Human Rights Quarterly* 14:1 (February 1992): 21–42.

Edwards, R. Randle, Louis Henkin, and Andrew J. Nathan. *Human Rights in Contemporary China.* New York: Columbia University Press, 1986.

Forsythe, David P. *The Internationalization of Human Rights.* Lexington, Mass.: Lexington Books, 1991.

Forsythe, David P., ed. *Human Rights and Development: International Views.* New York: St. Martin's Press, 1989.

Han Minzhu, ed. *Cries for Democracy: Writings and Speeches from the 1989 Chinese Democracy Movement.* Princeton: Princeton University Press, 1990.

Hsiung, James C., ed. *Human Rights in East Asia: A Cultural Perspective.* New York: Paragon House, 1985.

Human Rights Watch. *The Human Rights Watch Global Report on Prisons.* New York: Human Rights Watch, 1993.

———. *Detained in China and Tibet: A Directory of Political and Religious Prisoners.* New York: Human Rights Watch, 1994.

Human Rights Watch/Asia. *Death by Default: A Policy of Fatal Neglect in China's State Orphanages*. New York: Human Rights Watch, 1996.

Kent, Ann. *Human Rights in the People's Republic of China*. Canberra: Peace Research Center, Australian National University, 1990.

_____. *Between Freedom and Subsistence: China and Human Rights*. New York: Oxford University Press, 1993.

_____. "China and the International Human Rights Regime: A Case Study of Multilateral Monitoring, 1989–1994." *Human Rights Quarterly* 17:1 (February 1995): 1–47.

_____. *China, the United Nations and Human Rights: Compliance, Learning, and Effectiveness*. Philadelphia: University of Pennsylvania Press, forthcoming.

Liu Binyan. *China's Crisis, China's Hope*. Cambridge: Harvard University Press, 1990.

"Manifesto of the Alliance for Human Rights in China." *Index on Censorship* 8 (September–October 1979): 3–6.

Nathan, Andrew J. *Chinese Democracy*. New York: Columbia University Press, 1985.

_____. *China's Crisis: Dilemmas of Reform and Prospects for Democracy*. New York: Columbia University Press, 1991.

_____. "Human Rights in Chinese Foreign Policy." *China Quarterly*, no. 139 (September 1994): 622–43.

_____. "China: Getting Human Rights Right." *Washington Quarterly* 20:2 (Spring 1997): 135–151.

_____. "China and the International Human Rights Regime." In Michel Oksenberg and Elizabeth Economy, eds., *China Joins the World: Progress and Prospects* (New York: Council on Foreign Relations Press, forthcoming).

Onuma, Yasuaki. "In Quest of Intercivilizational Human Rights: 'Universal' vs. Relative Human Rights Viewed from an Asian Perspective." Occasional Paper No. 2. San Francisco: Center for Asian Pacific Affairs, Asia Foundation, March 1996.

Rummel, R. J. *China's Bloody Century: Genocide and Mass Murder Since 1990*. New Brunswick, N.J.: Transaction Publishers, 1991.

Seymour, James D. "Human Rights and the Law in the People's Republic of China." In Victor Falkenheim, ed., *Chinese Politics from Mao to Deng*. New York: Paragon House, 1989, pp. 271–297.

_____. "The Rights of Ethnic Minorities in China: Lessons of the Soviet Demise." *American Asian Review* 11:2 (Summer 1993): 44–56.

Tibet Information Network and Human Rights Watch/Asia. *Cutting Off the Serpent's Head: Tightening Control in Tibet, 1994–1995*. New York: Human Rights Watch, 1996.

Tibet Under Communist Chinese Rule: A Compilation of Refugee Statements, 1958–1975. Gangchen Kyoshong, Dharamsala, India: Information and Publication Office of His Holiness the Dalai Lama, 1976.

United Nations Development Programme. *Human Development Report, 1997*. New York: Oxford University Press, 1997. (annual)

United States Department of State. *Country Reports on Human Rights Practices for 1996*. Washington, D.C.: U.S. Government Printing Office, 1997. (Annual)

Van Ness, Peter. "Human Rights and International Relations in East Asia." *Ethics and International Politics*, July 1992, 43–52.

_____ "Addressing the Human Rights Issue in Sino-American Relations." *Journal of International Affairs* 49:2 (Winter 1996): 309–331.

Vincent, R. J. *Human Rights and International Relations.* New York: Cambridge University Press, 1986.

Wei, Jingsheng. *The Courage to Stand Alone: Letters from Prison and Other Writings,* trans. Kristina M. Torgeson. New York: Viking, 1997.

Wu, Hongda Harry. *Laogai: The Chinese Gulag.* Boulder, Colo.: Westview Press, 1992.

Wu, Yuan-li, et al. *Human Rights in the People's Republic of China.* Boulder, Colo.: Westview Press, 1988.

Science and Technology

Bauer, E. E. *China Takes Off: Technology Transfer and Modernization.* Seattle: University of Washington Press, 1986.

De Sola Pool, Ithiel. *Technologies Without Boundaries: On Telecommunications in a Global Age.* Cambridge: Harvard University Press, 1990.

Ding, Jingping. "Technical Transformation and Renovation in PRC Industry." In Denis Fred Simon, ed., *The Emerging Technological Trajectory of the Pacific Rim.* Armonk, N.Y.: M. E. Sharpe, 1995, pp. 239–255.

Frieman, Wendy. "International Science and Technology and Chinese Foreign Policy." In Thomas W. Robinson and David Shambaugh, eds., *Chinese Foreign Policy: Theory and Practice.* New York: Oxford University Press, 1994, pp. 158–196.

Haas, Ernst B., Mary Pat Williams, and Don Babai. *Scientists and World Order: The Uses of Technical Knowledge in International Organizations.* Berkeley: University of California Press, 1977.

"Knowledge, Power, and International Policy Coordination," special issue, *International Organization* 46:1 (Winter 1992).

Leibo, Steven A. *Transferring Technology to China.* Berkeley: University of California Institute of East Asian Studies, 1985.

Liu Jing-tong. *On Introducing Technology to China.* New York: China-International Business Series, Columbia University, 1983.

Orleans, Leo. *Science in Contemporary China.* Stanford: Stanford University Press, 1981.

Ridley, Charles P. *China's Scientific Policies: Implications for International Cooperation.* Washington, D.C.: American Enterprise Institute for Public Policy Research, 1976.

Saich, Tony. *China's Science Policy in the 80s.* Manchester: University of Manchester Press, 1989.

Simon, Denis Fred. *China's Evolving Computer Industry: The Role of Foreign Technology Transfers.* Washington, D.C.: Office of Technology Assessment, 1986.

Simon, Denis Fred, ed. *The Emerging Technological Trajectory of the Pacific Rim.* Armonk, N.Y.: M. E. Sharpe, 1995.

_____. *Techno-Security in an Age of Globalization: Perspectives from the Pacific Rim.* Armonk, N.Y.: M. E. Sharpe, 1997.

Simon, Denis Fred, and Detlef Rehn. *Technological Innovation in China: The Case of Shanghai Semiconductor Industry.* Cambridge: Ballinger, 1988.

Simon, Denis Fred, and William Fischer. *Technology Transfer to China.* Cambridge: Ballinger, 1989.

Simon, Denis Fred, and Merle Goldman, eds. *Science and Technology in Post-Mao China.* Cambridge: Harvard University Press, 1989.

Suttmeier, Richard P. *Science, Technology, and China's Drive for Modernization.* Stanford: Hoover Institution Press, 1980.

U.S. Congress, Office of Technology Assessment. *Technology Transfer to China.* Washington, D.C.: Office of Technology Assessment, 1987.

Wang, Yeu-Farn. "China's Science and Technology Policy, 1949–1989." Department of Political Science, University of Stockholm, Stockholm, Sweden, 1993.

Zhou Yuan. "Reform and Restructuring of China's Science and Technology System." In Denis Fred Simon, ed., *The Emerging Technological Trajectory of the Pacific Rim.* Armonk, N.Y.: M. E. Sharpe, 1995, pp. 213–38.

Environmental Diplomacy

Barber, Margaret, and Grainne Ryder, eds. *Damming the Three Gorges: What Dam Builders Don't Want You to Know.* London: Earthscan, 1990.

Brown, Lester R. *Who Will Feed China? Wake-up Call for a Small Planet.* New York: Norton, 1995.

Brown, Lester R., et al. *State of the World, 1998.* Washington, D.C.: Worldwatch Institute, 1997 (Annual).

Conly, Shanti R., and Sharon L. Camp. *China's Family Planning Program: Challenging the Myths.* Country Study Series No. 1. Washington, D.C.: Population Crisis Committee, 1992.

Economy, Elizabeth. *Reforms and Resources: The Implications for State Capacity in the PRC.* Cambridge: American Academy of Arts and Sciences, 1997.

Hao, Yufan. "Environmental Protection in Chinese Foreign Policy." *Journal of Northeast Asian Studies* 11:3 (Fall 1992): 25–46.

He Bochuan. *China on the Edge: The Crisis of Ecology and Development.* San Francisco: China Books and Periodicals, 1991.

Hulme, M., et al. *Climate Change Due to the Greenhouse Effect and Its Implications for China.* Gland, Switzerland: World Wide Fund for Nature, 1992.

Glaser, Bernhard, ed. *Learning from China?* London: Allen & Unwin, 1987.

Goldstone, Jack A. "Imminent Political Conflict Arising from China's Environmental Crises." Occasional Paper Series of the Project on Environmental Change and Acute Conflict No. 2 (December 1992): 41–58.

Jhaveri, Nayna. "The Three Gorges Debacle." *Ecologist* 18:2 (1988): 56–63.

Johnson, T., Li Junfeng, Jiang Zhongxiao, and R. Taylor, eds. *China: Issues and Options in Greenhouse Gas Emissions Control.* Washington, D.C.: World Bank, 1996.

"Knowledge, Power, and International Policy Coordination," special issue, *International Organization* 46:1 (Winter 1992).

Liftin, Karen T. *Ozone Discourses: Science and Politics in Global Environmental Cooperation.* New York: Columbia University Press, 1994.

Lu Yingzhong. *Fueling One Billion: An Insider's Story of Chinese Energy Policy Development.* Washington, D.C.: Washington Institute Press, 1993.

Luk, Shiu-hung, and Joseph Whitney, eds. *Megaproject: A Case Study of China's Three Gorges Project.* Armonk, N.Y.: M. E. Sharpe, 1992.

Ostrom, Elinor. *Governing the Commons: The Evolution of Institutions for Collective Action.* New York: Cambridge University Press, 1990.

Ostron, Benjamin C. *Conquering Resources: The Growth and Development of the PLA's Science and Technology Commission for National Defense.* Armonk, N.Y.: M. E. Sharpe, 1991.

Qu Geping and Li Jinchang. *Population and the Environment in China.* Boulder, Colo.: Lynne Rienner Pub., 1994.

Robinson, Thomas W., ed. *The Foreign Relations of China's Environmental Policy.* Washington, D.C.: American Enterprise Institute, August 1992.

Ross, Lester. *Environmental Policy in China.* Bloomington: Indiana University Press, 1988.

Ryle, Martin. *Ecology and Socialism.* London: Radius, 1988.

Sims, Holly. "The Unsheltering Sky: China, India, and the Montreal Protocol." *Policy Studies Journal* 24:2 (1996): 201–214.

Smil, Vaclav. "Environmental Change as a Source of Conflict and Economic Losses in China." *Occasional Paper Series of the Project on Environmental Change and Acute Conflict* No. 2 (December 1992): 5–39.

_____. *China's Environmental Crisis: An Inquiry into the Limits of National Development.* Armonk, N.Y.: M. E. Sharpe, 1993.

_____. "Who will Feed China?" *China Quarterly,* no. 143 (September 1995): 801–13

_____. *Environmental Problems in China: Estimates of Economic Costs,* East-West Center Special Reports, No. 5. Honolulu: East-West Center, April 1996.

Wapner, Paul. *Environmental Activism and World Civic Politics.* Albany: State University of New York Press, 1996.

Weiss, Edith Brown. *In Fairness to Future Generations: International Law, Common Patrimony, and Intergenerational Equity.* Dobbs Ferry, N.Y.: Transnational Publishers, 1989.

Woodard, Kim. *The International Energy Relations of China.* Stanford: Stanford University Press, 1980.

World Bank. *Environment and Development.* Washington, D.C.: World Bank, 1984.

_____. *The World Bank and the Environment: First Annual Report, Fiscal 1990.* Washington, D.C.: World Bank, 1990.

_____. *World Development Report, 1992: Development and the Environment.* New York: Oxford University Press, 1992.

_____. *Clear Water, Blue Skies: China's Environment in the New Century.* Washington, D.C.: World Bank, 1997.

World Commission on Environment and Development. *Our Common Future.* New York: Oxford University Press, 1987.

World Resources Institute. *World Resources 1996 97.* New York: Oxford University Press, 1997. (Annual)

Young, Oran R. *International Cooperation: Building Regimes for Natural Resources and the Environment.* Ithaca, N.Y.: Cornell University Press, 1989.

Young, Oran R., and Gail Osherenko, eds. *Polar Politics: Creating International Environmental Regimes.* Ithaca, N.Y.: Cornell University Press, 1993.

National Identity and "Greater China"

Bloom, William. *Personal Identity, National Identity, and International Relations.* New York: Cambridge University Press, 1990.

Brown, Michael E., et al., eds. *Nationalism and Ethnic Conflict.* Cambridge: MIT Press, 1997.

Bueno de Mesquita, Bruce, David Newman, and Alvin Rabushka. *Red Flag over Hong Kong.* Chatham, N.J.: Chatham House, 1996.

Chang, Parris H., and Martin H. Lasaster. *If PRC Crosses the Taiwan Strait: The International Response.* Lanham, Md.: University Press of America, 1992.

Cheng, Tun-jen, and Stephan Haggard, eds. *Political Change in Taiwan.* Boulder, Colo.: Lynne Rienner Pub., 1992.

Chien, Frederick F. "A View from Taipei." *Foreign Affairs* 70:5 (Winter 1991–1992): 93–103.

Clough, Ralph N. *Reaching Across the Taiwan Strait.* Boulder, Colo.: Westview Press, 1993.

Cushman, Jennifer, and Wang Gungwu, eds. *Changing Identities of the Southeast Asian Chinese Since World War II.* Hong Kong: Hong Kong University Press, 1988.

Dittmer, Lowell, and Kim, Samuel, eds. *China's Quest for National Identity.* Ithaca, N.Y.: Cornell University Press, 1993.

Dreyer, June Teufel. *China's Forty Millions: Minority Nationalities and National Integration in the People's Republic of China.* Cambridge: Harvard University Press, 1976.

Duara, Prasenjit. "De-Constructing the Chinese Nations." *Australian Journal of Chinese Affairs* 30 (July 1993): 1–26.

Friedman, Edward. *National Identity and Democratic Prospects in Socialist China.* Armonk, N.Y.: M. E. Sharpe, 1995.

Gellner, Ernst. *Nations and Nationalism.* Ithaca, N.Y.: Cornell University Press, 1983.

Gladney, Dru C. *Ethnic Nationalism in the People's Republic.* Cambridge, Mass.: Council on East Asian Studies, Harvard East Asian Monograph no. 149, 1991.

_____. "Rumblings from the Uyghur." *Current History* 96:611 (September 1997): 287–90.

Goldstein, Mylvyn C. *Tibet, China, and the United States: Reflections on the Tibet Question.* Washington, D.C.: Atlantic Council, 1995.

"Greater China," special issue, *China Quarterly*, no. 136 (December 1993).

Hartland-Thunberg, Penelope. *China, Hong Kong, Taiwan and the World Trading System.* New York: St. Martin's Press, 1991.

Heberer, Thomas. *China and Its National Minorities: Autonomy or Assimilation.* Armonk, N.Y.: M. E. Sharpe, 1989.

Lilley, James R., and Chuck Downs, eds. *Crisis in the Taiwan Strait.* Washington, D.C.: National Defense University Press, 1997.

Lin, Zhiling, and Thomas W. Robinson, eds. *The Chinese and Their Future: Beijing, Taipei, and Hong Kong.* Washington, D.C.: American Enterprise Institute Press, 1992.

Long, Simon. *Taiwan: China's Last Frontier.* New York: St. Martin's Press, 1991.

Myers, Raymond H., ed. *The Republic of China and the People's Republic of China: Two Societies in Opposition.* Stanford: Hoover Institution Press, 1991.

Pye, Lucian W. "How China's Nationalism Was Shanghaied." *Australian Journal of Chinese Affairs* 29 (January 1993): 107–133.

Segal, Gerald. *The Fate of Hong Kong.* London: St. Martin's Press, 1993.

Simon, Denis Fred, and Michael Y. M. Kau, eds. *Taiwan: Beyond the Economic Miracle.* Armonk, N.Y.: M. E. Sharpe, 1992.

Su, Xiaokang, and Wang Luxiang. *Deathsong of the River: A Reader's Guide to the Chinese TV Series "Heshang."* Introduced, translated and annotated by Richard W. Bodman and Pin P. Wan. Ithaca, N.Y.: East Asia Program, Cornell University, 1991.

Sung, Yun-Wing. *The China-Hong Kong Connection: The Key to China's Open-Door Policy.* New York: Cambridge University Press, 1991.

Sutter, Robert, and William R. Johnson, eds. *Taiwan's Role in World Affairs.* Boulder, Colo.: Westview Press, 1994.

Tu Wei-ming, ed. *The Living Tree: The Changing Meaning of Being Chinese Today.* Stanford: Stanford University Press, 1994.

Unger, Jonathan, ed. *Chinese Nationalism.* Armonk, N.Y.: M. E. Sharpe, 1996.

Van Kemenade, Willem. *China, Hong Kong, Taiwan, Inc,.* trans. Diane Webb. New York: Knopf, 1997.

Vogel, Ezra F. *The Four Little Dragons: The Spread of Industrialization in East Asia.* Cambridge: Harvard University Press, 1991.

Wachman, Alan M. *Taiwan: National Identity and Democratization.* Armonk, N.Y.: M. E. Sharpe, 1994.

Wang, Enbao. *Hong Kong, 1997: The Politics of Transition.* Boulder, Colo.: Lynne Rienner Pub., 1995.

Wang Gungwu. *China and the Chinese Overseas.* Singapore. Times Academic Press, 1991.

_____. *The Chineseness of China: Selected Essays.* Oxford: Oxford University Press, 1992.

Whiting, Allen S. "Chinese Nationalism and Foreign Policy After Deng." *China Quarterly,* no. 142 (June 1995): 295–316.

Yahuda, Michael. "The Foreign Relations of Greater China." *China Quarterly,* no. 136 (December 1993): 687–710.

_____. *Hong Kong: China's Challenge.* New York: Routledge, 1996.

International Law and International Organizations

Bartke, Wolfgang. *The Agreements of the People's Republic of China with Foreign Countries, 1949–1990.* Munich: Institute of Asian Affairs, 2nd and enl. ed., 1992.

Chai, Trong R. "Chinese Policy Toward the Third World and the Superpowers in the UN General Assembly, 1971–1977: A Voting Analysis." *International Organization* 33 (Summer 1979): 391–403.

Chan, Gerald. *China and International Organizations: Participation in Non-Governmental Organizations Since 1971.* New York: Oxford University Press, 1989.

Chang, Luke T. *China's Boundary Treaties and Frontier Disputes.* Dobbs Ferry, N.Y.: Oceana, 1982.

Chayes, Abram, and Antonia Handler Chayes. *The New Sovereignty: Compliance with International Regulatory Agreements.* Cambridge: Harvard University Press, 1995.

Chiu, Hungdah. *Agreements of the People's Republic of China: A Calendar of Events 1966–1980.* New York: Praeger, 1981.

_____. "Chinese Attitudes Towards International Law in the Post-Mao Era, 1978–1987." *International Lawyer* 21:4 (Fall 1987): 1127–1166.

_____. "Chinese Attitudes Toward International Law of Human Rights." In Victor Falkenheim, ed., *Chinese Politics from Mao to Deng.* New York: Paragon House, 1989, pp. 237–270.

Chu, Yun-han, ed. *The Role of Taiwan in International Economic Organizations.* Taipei: Institute for National Policy Research, 1990.

Cohen, Jerome Alan, and Hungdah Chiu. *People's China and International Law: A Documentary Study,* 2 vols. Princeton: Princeton University Press, 1974.

Davis, James, and Andrew Cortell. "How Do International Institutions Matter? The Domestic Impact of International Rules and Norms." *International Studies Quarterly* 40:4 (December 1996):

Falk, Richard A., Samuel S. Kim and Saul H. Mendlovitz, eds. *The United Nations and a Just World Order.* Boulder, Colo.: Westview Press, 1991.

Feinerman, James V. "The Quest for GATT Membership." *China Business Review* 19 (May-June 1992): 24–27.

_____. "Chinese Participation in the International Legal Order: Rogue Elephant or Team Player?" *China Quarterly,* no. 141 (March 1995): 186–210.

Franck, Thomas M. *The Power of Legitimacy Among Nations.* New York: Oxford University Press, 1990.

Greenfield, Jeanette. *China and the Law of the Sea, Air, and Environment.* Germantown, Md.: Sijthoff & Noordhoff, 1979.

_____. *China's Practice in the Law of the Sea.* Oxford: Clarendon Press, 1992.

Hsiung, James C. *Law and Policy in China's Foreign Relations: A Study of Attitudes and Practice.* New York: Columbia University Press, 1972.

Jacobson, Harold K., and Michel Oksenberg. *China's Participation in the IMF, the World Bank, and GATT.* Ann Arbor: University of Michigan Press, 1990.

Kenworthy, James L. *Guide to the Laws, Regulations, and Policies of the People's Republic of China on Foreign Trade and Investments.* New York: William S. Hein, 1990.

Kim, Samuel S. "The People's Republic of China and the Charter-Based International Legal Order." *American Journal of International Law* 62 (April 1978): 317–349.

_____. *China, the United Nations, and World Order.* Princeton: Princeton University Press, 1979.

_____. "Whither Post-Mao Chinese Global Policy?" *International Organization* 35 (Summer 1981): 433–465.

_____. "The Development of International Law in Post-Mao China: Change and Continuity." *Journal of Chinese Law* 1, no. 2 (Fall 1987): 117–160.

_____. "Reviving International Law in China's Foreign Relations." in June T. Dreyer, ed., *Chinese Defense and Foreign Policy.* New York: Paragon House, 1989, pp. 87–131.

_____. "International Organizations in Chinese Foreign Policy." *Annals of the American Academy of Political and Social Science* 519 (January 1992): 140–157.

_____. "China's International Organizational Behaviour." In Thomas W. Robinson and David Shambaugh, eds., *Chinese Foreign Policy: Theory and Practice*. New York: Oxford University Press, 1994, pp. 401–434.

_____. "China and the United Nations." In Elizabeth Economy and Michel Oksenberg, eds., *Involving China in World Affairs*. New York: Council on Foreign Relations Press, forthcoming.

McDonnell, J. E. D. "China's Move to Rejoin the GATT System: An Epic Transition." *World Economy* 10 (September 1987): 331–350.

McKenzie, Paul D. "China's Application to GATT: State Trading and the Problem of Market Access." *Journal of World Trade* 24 (October 1990): 133–150.

Mendlovitz, Saul H., and Burns H. Weston, eds. *Preferred Futures for the United Nations*. Irvington-on-Hudson, N.Y.: Transnational Publishers, 1995.

Morici, Peter. "Barring Entry? China and the WTO." *Current History* 96:611 (September 1997): 274–277.

Moser, Michael, ed. *Foreign Trade, Investment, and the Law in the People's Republic of China*. New York: Oxford University Press, 1987.

Oldham, John R., ed. *China's Legal Development*. Armonk, N.Y.: M. E. Sharpe, 1986.

Rajan, M. S., V. S. Mani, and C. S. R. Murthy, eds. *The Nonaligned and the United Nations*. New York: Oceana, 1987.

Shinobu, Takashi. "China's Bilateral Treaties, 1973–82: A Quantitative Study." *International Studies Quarterly* 31:4 (December 1987): 439–456.

St. John MacDonald, Ronald, ed. *Essays in Honour of Wang Tieya*. London: Martinus Nijhoff Publishers, 1994.

Tzou, Byron N. *China and International Law: The Boundary Disputes*. New York: Praeger, 1990.

Van Walt van Praag, Michael C. *The Status of Tibet: History, Rights, and Prospects in International Law*. Boulder, Colo.: Westview Press, 1987.

The Future of China and World Order

Bachman, David. "Succession Politics and China's Future." *Journal of International Affairs* 49:2 (Winter 1996): 370–389.

Baum, Richard. "China After Deng: Ten Scenarios in Search of Reality." *China Quarterly*, no. 145 (March 1996): 153–175.

Biersteker, Thomas J., and Cynthia Weber, eds. *State Sovereignty and Social Construct*. New York: Cambridge University Press, 1996.

Camilleri, Joseph, and Jim Falk. *The End of Sovereignty? The Politics of a Shrinking and Fragmenting World*. Aldershot, England: Edward Elgar, 1992.

Choucri, Nazli, and Thomas W. Robinson, eds. *Forecasting in International Relations: Theory, Methods, Problems, Prospects*. San Francisco: W. H. Freeman, 1978.

Cox, Robert W., ed., *The New Realism: Perspectives on Multilateralism and World Order*. Tokyo: United Nations University Press, 1997.

Funabashi, Y., Michel Oksenberg, and H. Weiss, eds. *An Emerging China in a World of Interdependence*. New York: Trilateral Commission, 1994.

Hamrin, Carol Lee. *China and the Challenge of the Future: Changing Political Patterns*. Boulder, Colo.: Westview Press, 1990.

Huntington, Samuel P. *The Clash of Civilizations and the Remaking of World Order.* New York: Simon & Schuster, 1996.

Jervis, Robert. "The Future of World Politics: Will It Resemble the Past?" *International Security* 16:3 (Winter 1991–1992): 39–45.

Kennedy, Paul. *Preparing for the Twenty-First Century.* New York: Random House, 1993.

Kim, Samuel S. *China In and Out of the Changing World Order.* Princeton: Center of International Studies, Princeton University, 1991.

Oksenberg, Michel, and Kenneth Lieberthal. "Forecasting China's Future." *National Interest,* no. 5 (Fall 1986): 18–27.

Our Global Neighborhood. Report of the Commission on Global Governance. New York: Oxford University Press, 1995.

Sakamoto, Yoshikazu, ed. *Global Transformation: Challenges to the State System.* Tokyo: United Nations University Press, 1994.

Sutter, Robert. "China's View of the 'New World Order': Possible Implications for Sino-U.S. Relations." *CRS Report for Congress* (September 11, 1991).

_____. *Shaping China's Future in World Affairs: The Role of the United States.* Boulder, Colo.: Westview Press, 1996.

Whiting, Allen S. "Forecasting Chinese Foreign Policy: IR Theory vs. The Fortune Cookie." In Thomas W. Robinson and David Shambaugh, eds., *Chinese Foreign Policy: Theory and Practice.* New York: Oxford University Press, 1994, pp. 506–523.

About the Editor
and Contributors

Samuel S. Kim (Ph.D., Columbia) is adjunct professor of political science and senior research associate at the East Asian Institute of Columbia University. He is the author or editor of over a dozen books on Chinese foreign policy and world order studies. His articles have appeared in leading professional journals on China and international relations, including *American Journal of International Law, China Quarterly, International Interactions, International Journal, International Organization, Journal of Chinese Law, Journal of Peace Research, World Politics,* and *World Policy Journal.*

David Bachman (Ph.D., Stanford) is an associate professor at the Henry M. Jackson School of International Studies, University of Washington. He is the author of *Chen Yun and the Chinese Political System; Bureaucracy, Economy, and Leadership in China: The Institutional Origins of the Great Leap Forward;* and *Yan Jiaqi and China's Struggle for Democracy* (coeditor and cotranslator with Yang Dali). His articles have appeared in *Asian Survey, Current History, Fletcher Forum of World Affairs, Issues and Studies, Pacific Affairs,* and *World Politics.*

Elizabeth C. Economy (Ph.D., Michigan) is fellow for China at the Council on Foreign Relations and cochair of the Woodrow Wilson Center's working group on China and the Environment. She is coeditor of *The Internationalization of Environmental Protection* and author of the American Academy of Arts and Sciences report *Reforms and Resources: The Implications for State Capacity in the PRC.* She also has contributed chapters to several edited volumes. She is currently writing a book on Chinese environmental politics.

William R. Feeney (Ph.D., SAIS, Johns Hopkins) is a professor of political science at Southern Illinois University at Edwardsville. He is coeditor, with William T. Tow, of *U.S. Foreign Policy and Asian-Pacific Security* and is a contributor to anthologies. He has published articles in *Asian Affairs, Current History, Korea and World Affairs, Asian Thought and Society, Asian Survey,* and *Current Scene.*

John W. Garver (Ph.D., University of Colorado) is professor in the School of International Affairs at the Georgia Institute of Technology. He is a member of the editorial board of *China Quarterly* and the *Journal of American-East Asian Relations* and a member of the National Committee on U.S.-China Relations. He is the author of more than fifty articles dealing with China's foreign relations and six books, including *The Foreign Relations of the People's Republic of China* (Prentice-Hall, 1993), *Face Off: China, the United States, and Taiwan's Democratization;* and *The Sino-American Alliance: Nationalist China and the U.S. Cold War Strategy in Asia.*

Paul H. B. Godwin (Ph.D., Minnesota) is professor of international affairs at the National War College. He is coauthor of *The Making of a Model Citizen in Communist China*, editor of and contributor to *The Chinese Defense Establishment: Continuity and Change in the 1980s*, and a contributor to numerous anthologies. His articles have appeared in learned journals, including *Annals of the American Academy of Political and Social Science, Comparative Politics, Comparative Communism, Contemporary China, Current History*, and *China Quarterly*. He was a visiting professor in the fall of 1987 at the Chinese People's Liberation Army National Defense University in Beijing.

Alastair Iain Johnston (Ph.D., Michigan) is a John L. Loeb Associate Professor of the Social Sciences in the Government Department at Harvard University. He is the author of *Cultural Realism: Strategic Culture and Grand Strategy in Chinese History*. He has published articles and book chapters on ancient Chinese military thought, nuclear doctrine, arms control and environmental diplomacy, learning theory, strategic culture, and East Asian international relations.

Donald W. Klein (Ph.D., Columbia) is professor of political science at Tufts University. He is coauthor of *Biographic Dictionary of Chinese Communism, 1921–1965*, and *Rebels and Bureaucrats: China's December 9ers* and is a frequent contributor to anthologies and learned journals. He is an editorial board member of *China Quarterly, Asian Survey*, and *Pacific Affairs*.

Steven I. Levine (Ph.D., Harvard) is senior research associate at Boulder Run Research in Hillsborough, North Carolina. He coedited, with Philip West and Jacqueline Hiltz, *American Wars in Asia: A Cultural Approach to History and Memory*, has written extensively on various aspects of Chinese foreign policy, and has taught at Columbia University, Duke, and the University of North Carolina at Chapel Hill. He is currently involved in promoting international education at the grade-school level.

Thomas W. Robinson (Ph.D., Columbia) is president of American Asian Research Enterprises, Arlington, Va., adjunct professor of national security at Georgetown University, and course chairperson (China) at the Foreign Service Institute, Department of State. Formerly director of the Asian Studies Program at the American Enterprise Institute, Washington, D.C., he is the author, editor, or coeditor of *Chinese Foreign Policy: Theory and Practice; The Chinese and Their Future: Beijing, Hong Kong, and Taipei; Democracy and Development in East Asia: South Korea, Taiwan, and the Philippines; Forecasting in International Relations*; and *The Cultural Revolution in China*. His articles and chapters on Chinese politics and foreign relations have appeared in more than fifty other books and journals.

James D. Seymour (Ph.D., Columbia) is senior research scholar at Columbia University's East Asian Institute. His books include *China: The Politics of Revolutionary Reintegration; The Fifth Modernization: China's Human Rights Movement, 1978–1979*; and *China's Satellite Parties*. He recently coauthored *New Ghosts, Old Ghosts: Prisons and Labor Reform Camps in China*, and coedited *End of Empire? Chinese Dissidents Rethink Tibet*.

Peter Van Ness (Ph.D., University of California, Berkeley) is associate professor in the Graduate School of International Studies at the University of Denver and research associate in the Contemporary China Centre at Australian National University in Canberra. His published work includes: *Revolution and Chinese For-*

eign Policy; Market Reforms in Socialist Societies: Comparing China and Hungary (editor); and *Australia's Human Rights Diplomacy* (coauthor). He is currently editing a book on the human rights debate and writing a monograph "How to Avoid a Cold War with China."

Allen S. Whiting (Ph.D., Columbia) was director of the Office of Research and Analysis, Far East, in the U.S. Department of State (1962–1966) and deputy consul general, Hong Kong (1966–1968), and is currently Regents Professor of Political Science at the University of Arizona. He has produced many books, including *China Crosses the Yalu, The Chinese Calculus of Deterrence, Siberian Development and East Asia, China Eyes Japan,* and *China's Foreign Relations* (ed.), and has contributed numerous articles to leading professional journals on China and international relations.

Index

Abortion, 259
ACD. *See* Arms control and disarmament
Accountability, 261
ADB. *See* Asian Development Bank
Afghanistan, 43, 65
Africa, 151
Agenda 21, 25, 276, 277, 281
Agriculture, 248, 259
Aid, 6, 13, 135, 140, 146, 147, 164, 240, 271
   environmental, 278–279, 280
  official development assistance (ODA),
    134, 139, 174
AIDS, 165(n7)
Aircraft, 120, 121, 137, 173, 181, 182, 185,
   186, 294
Akihito (Emperor), 174
Albright, Madeleine, 91
Algeria, 103
Alliances, 18, 34, 55–56, 62–63, 67, 69, 92,
   100, 117, 118–119, 129, 130, 143, 144,
   155, 163, 173, 176, 187, 188, 189, 196,
   236
Amnesty International, 220
Anarchy, 17, 18, 21, 57, 58, 59, 70, 73, 197
Annan, Kofi, 161
Anwar, Dewi Fortuna, 163
APEC. *See* Asia-Pacific Economic
   Cooperation
ARF. *See* Association of Southeast Asian
   Nations, ASEAN Regional Forum
Arms control and disarmament (ACD), 5,
   24, 25, 26, 69, 73, 96, 145
Arms sales, 63, 91, 97, 99, 101, 103, 120–121,
   134, 137, 143, 145, 173, 181–182, 259,
   288
Art of War (Sun Zi), 13
Ascendant-China thesis, 1, 28, 50, 80(n2),
   94. *See also* Great power status

ASEAN. *See* Association of Southeast Asian
   Nations
Asia-European Conference (1996), 137
Asian Development Bank (ADB), 6, 139,
   224, 239, 255, 256(table), 278–279
Asia-Pacific Economic Cooperation
   (APEC), 146, 162, 290, 304
Association of Southeast Asian Nations
   (ASEAN), 6, 26, 137, 146, 147,
   161–163, 177, 290, 295–296, 297, 298
  ASEAN Regional Forum (ARF), 6, 26, 74,
   75, 86(n58), 99, 146, 150(n44), 163,
   168(n48), 177, 290, 298, 301, 304
  Treaty of Amity and Cooperation (1976),
   298
Australia, 133, 158, 160, 175, 176, 177, 178,
   234, 296, 298
Authoritarianism, 196, 197, 259, 261
Autonomy, 59–60, 66, 67, 74, 110, 189, 211,
   234, 292

Balance of power, 17, 19, 55, 56, 59, 60–61,
   65, 82(n28), 83(n30), 121, 197, 301
  balancing behavior, 60, 62, 65, 66, 68, 70,
   131, 163, 299, 302
Bangladesh, 165(n13)
Bank for International Settlements (BIS),
   240
Banks, 128, 244–245, 261(n2), 280
  central banks, 240, 261(n2), 262(n9)
Barnett, A. Doak, 15, 16
"Beijing Ministerial Declaration on
   Environment and Development"
   (document), 272–273
Beijing Review, 141
Belarus, 159
Belief systems, 85(n51)
Bernstein, Richard, 6, 92
Bessyrtnich, Alexander, 123

Biodiversity, 265
Biological/chemical weapons, 5, 99, 174
BIS. *See* Bank for International Settlements
Borders, 43, 64, 83(n35), 122–123, 124(fig.),
    129, 130, 174, 175, 290
    troop reductions at, 122, 300
Bosnia, 229
Bo Yibo, 43
Brazil, 273
Brezhnev doctrine, 67
Britain, 135, 136, 177, 233, 234, 296
Brunei, 162, 289, 298
Buddhism/Buddhists, 233, 235
Burma, 43, 165(n13), 290
Bush, Barbara, 231
Bush, George, 96–97, 106, 111(n17), 224, 227,
    231

Cambodia, 99, 103, 229
Canada, 11, 12, 85(n55), 133, 160, 298
Capitalism, 71, 95, 148, 157, 164, 196, 260
Carbon dioxide (CO$_2$), 270
Carter, Jimmy, 220
CATIC. *See* China Agribusiness
    Development Trust and Investment
    Corporation
CBMs. *See* Confidence-building measures
CBNT. *See* Comprehensive Ban on Nuclear
    Testing
CCF1. *See* First Country Cooperation
    Framework
CCP. *See* Chinese Communist Party
Censorship, 207, 222
Central Military Commission (CMC), 38,
    39, 40, 41, 179
Change/continuity, 12
Chang Hsien-Wu, 267
Chechnya, 117
Chengdu Aviation Industrial Corporation,
    182
Chen Guangjian, 275
Chen Jian, 275
Chen Yi, 38, 43, 44
Chen Yun, 45, 46
Chiang Ching-kuo, 236
Chi Haotian, 122–123
Child labor, 230
China Agribusiness Development Trust
    and Investment Corporation (CATIC),
    262(n10)
China: Arms Control and Disarmament (State
    Council), 187

China as status quo power, 176
China Can Say No (Song Qiang et al.), 94
China Institute for International Strategic
    Studies (CISS) journal, 178
China threat theory, 5, 86(n58), 100, 145,
    157, 160–161, 186–187, 289, 290, 291,
    301
Chinese Communist Party (CCP), 37, 48,
    251, 253, 305
    Central Committee, Central Foreign
        Affairs Office, 38–39
    Fifteenth Party Congress, 6, 22, 29(n3),
        107, 245
    Secretariat, 39
    vertical vs. horizontal organization,
        37–38
Chirac, Jacques, 228
Christianity/Christians, 209, 235, 238(n35),
    259
Christopher, Warren, 97, 106
CIA. *See* United States, Central Intelligence
    Agency
CISS. *See* China Institute for International
    Strategic Studies journal
Class struggle, 43
Climate change, 265, 269–273
Clinton, Bill, 3, 64, 93, 97, 106, 144, 174, 223,
    227, 259, 263(n19), 302
Clinton, Hillary, 231
CMC. *See* Central Military Commission
Coalitions. *See* Alliances
Cold War, 18, 60, 97–98, 116, 142, 193, 194,
    210, 211. *See also* Post–Cold War
    period
Colonialism, 70, 71, 196, 267. *See also*
    Imperialism
Coming Conflict with China (Bernstein and
    Munro), 6, 92
Commonwealth of Independent States, 115
Communication/transportation, 207–208,
    229, 248
Communism, 148, 259. *See also* Chinese
    Communist Party
Comparative advantage, 239
Competition, 302–304
Compliance behavior, 27
Comprehensive Ban on Nuclear Testing
    (CBNT), 300
Comprehensive Test Ban Treaty (CTBT), 5,
    26, 46–48, 73, 75, 77, 99, 103
Computers, 47, 105, 207
Conference on Disarmament, 24, 77

Confidence-building measures (CBMs), 103, 122–123, 175, 187, 188, 298, 301
Confucianism, 209, 218, 259, 261
Consensus, 17, 43, 50, 97, 242, 282, 298
Constructivism, 56, 57, 58, 69–70
Containment strategy, 178, 188
Cooperation, 198, 202, 211, 242, 271, 274, 290, 297–302, 304
Coordination mechanisms, 38, 49
Corruption, 305
Council on Foreign Relations, 112(n29)
Country programs (CPs), 240, 241(table), 242
CPs. *See* Country programs
Crime, 305
CTBT. *See* Comprehensive Test Ban Treaty
Cui Jian, 110
Cultural Realism (Johnston), 12–13
Cultural Revolution, 38, 40, 41, 45, 147, 155, 208, 209, 220, 233, 267, 287, 303
Cultural theory, 12
Culture, 209. *See also* Sino-American relations, and U.S. popular culture
Currency, 244
Current account, 244, 262(n8)
CWG. *See* General Agreement on Tariffs and Trade, China Working Group
Czechoslovakia, 67

Dalai Lama, 107, 223
Death penalty, 229
Deaths, 7, 43, 233
Debt, 7, 204, 244, 245
Decentralization, 49
Decisionmaking, 16, 20, 22, 23, 34–35, 37, 42–43, 48, 49, 50, 58–59, 71, 74, 229
Democracy, 95–96, 101, 109, 110, 157, 193, 197, 199, 209, 220, 234, 235
  democratic peace theory, 14, 198
Democracy Movements, 103, 220. *See also* Tiananmen massacre
Demonstrations, 294, 300
Deng Nan, 276–277
Deng Xiaoping, 15, 34, 37, 39, 40, 43, 44, 45, 46, 47, 52(n12), 95, 101, 114, 122, 125, 141, 143, 151, 156, 164, 201, 220, 260, 287
Denmark, 228, 231
Dependence/dependency, 198, 211–212, 212(n3), 213(n11)
  balance of dependence, 208, 209, 210
  Dependencia, 196, 199, 201

Desert Storm, 181. *See also* Gulf War
Dessler, David, 57, 69
Determinism, 58
Deterrence, 46, 67, 83(n35), 177, 188, 290
  limited, 5, 180
Devaluation, 244
Development, 196, 202, 219–220, 229, 236(n5), 237(n27), 239, 245, 255, 260, 264, 269, 270, 271, 275, 276–277, 294
  sustainable, 281, 282
  See also Economy, growth; United Nations, Development Program
Diaoyutai/Senkaku Islands, 40, 143, 145, 293–294, 295, 297, 304
Diplomacy, 35, 66, 69, 77, 78, 101, 157, 158, 161, 236
  environmental/techno-diplomacy, 266, 267–269, 273–278, 280–282
  full diplomatic relations, 173
  military-to-military, 174, 186–187
  See also Leaders, official visits of
Disney Corporation, 107, 109, 223
Dittmer, Lowell, 115
Donorgate, 259, 261
Drugs, 301

EAEC. *See* East Asian Economic Caucus
Earth Summit (1992), 78
East Asian Economic Caucus (EAEC), 162
East China Sea, 289, 292, 293
Economics, 197
Economy, 5, 6–8, 17, 41, 43, 45, 50, 95, 99, 121, 138, 157, 164, 171, 211, 233, 239, 304
  China as potential market, 164
  depressions, 66
  economic interdependence, 204–206
  economic theory, 195–196
  growth, 6–7, 26, 63, 73, 260, 264, 269, 271, 280, 281, 289. *See also* Development
  key economic indicators, 246–247(table)
  reforms, 22, 48, 95, 157, 193, 206, 242, 244, 245, 251, 253, 260
  socialist market economy, 206, 260
  threat to, 244
  See also Trade; World economy
EDI. *See* World Bank, Economic Development Institute
Education, 208–209, 248, 253. *See also* Students
EEC/EU. *See* Europe, European Economic Community/European Union

EEZ. *See* Exclusive Economic Zone
Egypt, 159
Electric power, 248, 290
Elites, 12, 71, 93, 130, 144, 189, 274, 278
Emigration. *See* Immigration
Energy issues, 289–290, 298–299. *See also*
    Electric power; Oil
Environmental issues, 5, 24, 25, 26, 71, 73,
    145, 203, 230, 264–282, 290, 301, 304
  challenges to dual diplomacy, 280–282
  costs, 7, 270, 277, 278–279
  court system for, 278
  Montreal Protocol concerning, 270, 271,
    272, 273, 278, 279
  National Conferences on Environmental
    Protection, 267, 268
  negotiation strategy, 266
Environmental Protection Commission, 268
Epistemic communities, 23–24, 71, 198, 200,
    214(n12), 274
Ethiopia, 159
Europe, 133–137, 146, 148, 228, 233
  European Economic Community/
    European Union (EEC/EU), 135–137,
    136(table), 138, 147, 231, 234, 298
Exchange rates, 243, 244
Exclusive Economic Zone (EEZ), 289, 295
Export-led growth, 196–197, 199, 202

Fall, Ibrahima, 230
FALSG. *See* Foreign Affairs Leading Small
    Group
Farber, Henry, 14
Fast-food industry, 105
FDI. *See* Investments, foreign direct
    investments
FIAS. *See* Foreign Investment Advisory
    Service
Films, 209, 223
First Country Cooperation Framework
    (CCF1), 240, 241(table), 242
Five-Power Agreement, 123, 300, 301
Five-Power Defense Arrangement (FPDA),
    175, 176–177, 296
Five-Year Plans, 240, 253, 276
Flying Fish military exercise, 176–177
Forced labor, 224, 248
Foreign Affairs Leading Small Group
    (FALSG), 38–39, 49, 116
Foreign exchange reserves, 6. *See also*
    Exchange rates

Foreign Investment Advisory Service
    (FIAS), 251
Foreign policy
  behavior-centered approach, 11
  causes/consequences concerning, 22, 23
  changes in post-Mao, 24–27
  dimensions of, 35–37
  domestic determinants, 11–16, 17, 50,
    214(n12), 265, 305
  domestic/external linkage determinants,
    22–27
  external/systemic determinants, 17–22,
    58
  failures predicting, 287–289
  fragmentation of U.S., 96
  future of, 27–28, 48–50, 291–306
  independence of, 65, 83(n31), 194,
    212(n3)
  and interdependence, 210–212. *See also*
    Interdependence
  key issues, 9–11
  lessons concerning, 147
  and normative structures, 72–78. *See also*
    International norms; Normative
    structures
  organizations determining, 38–39
  Third World line in, 155
  variables concerning, 10
  See also Diplomacy; International
    relations theory
FPDA. *See* Five-Power Defense
    Arrangement
Framework Convention on Climate
    Change, 278
France, 46, 47, 135, 137, 160, 186, 228, 296,
    303
Franck, Thomas, 20
Friends of Nature, 277

Gang of Four, 45, 67, 147
Gang of Three, 273
Gao Yu, 229
GATT. *See* General Agreement on Tariffs
    and Trade
GDP. *See* Gross domestic product
Gelatt, Timothy, 226
General Agreement on Tariffs and Trade
    (GATT), 117, 139–140, 255, 257–259
  China Working Group (CWG), 257
  trade regime reform package for, 258
  See also World Trade Organization
General Staff Department, 39–40, 44

Gephardt, Richard, 259
Germany, 5, 6, 28, 74, 127, 135, 136, 160, 204,
    205, 228, 303
Gingrich, Newt, 102
Gleditsch, Nils Petter, 14
Global citizenship, 29(n3)
Global Environmental Facility, 278
Globalization, 6, 8, 15, 22, 23, 29(n3), 49,
    164, 194, 200, 203, 261, 299
    as universalization of interdependence,
    198, 199
Gorbachev, Mikhail, 65, 114, 115, 122, 134,
    302
Gourevitch, Peter, 23, 265
Gowa, Joanne, 14
Grachev, Pavel, 123, 182
Grain, 36
Great Leap Forward, 19, 36, 43, 66, 267, 303
Great legal leap outward, 20, 25
Great power status, 6, 8–9, 28, 66, 67, 74, 79,
    85(n51), 99, 129–130, 151, 171, 172,
    178, 245, 259, 261
Greece, 160
Gross domestic product (GDP), 6–7, 204
Group of Seven (G-7), 117, 157, 164, 165(n4),
    242, 245, 248, 253
G-7. See Group of Seven
Gulf War, 61, 115, 173, 181, 193, 194, 248,
    290

Harding, Harry, 109
Hashimoto Ryutaro, 141, 144, 149(n24),
    168(n50), 176, 302, 304
Hegemonism, 159. See also United States, as
    hegemon
History, 12, 13, 74, 201, 217–220, 290–291,
    294, 303
Holiday Inn (Lhasa), 225
Hong Kong, 102, 134, 136, 137, 140, 197,
    204, 232, 234, 259, 260, 292, 305
Hua Guofeng, 37, 40, 41, 135, 141
Huang, John, 263(n19)
Huang Yicheng, 275
Huanjing Bao (Environmental News), 278
Hughes, Patrick, 188
Human development index, 165(n10)
Human rights, 5, 24, 71, 73, 74, 77, 87(n66),
    91, 92, 93, 94, 96, 105, 107–110, 139,
    145, 154, 157, 158–160, 167(nn 31, 32),
    217–236, 259, 261, 279
    historical background, 217–220
    and international business, 224–228

laws concerning, 25
    and MFN, 106, 174, 227–228
    NGOs for, 167(n31), 220, 230, 236
    and subsistence rights, 219
    universality of, 219, 230
    white papers on, 25, 222, 232
Human Rights Watch, 219, 220
Hu Yaobang, 39, 141, 236

IBRD. See World Bank
ICCPR. See International Covenant on Civil
    and Political Rights
ICESCR. See International Covenant on
    Economic, Social and Cultural Rights
IDA. See International Development
    Association
Ideology, 148, 155, 157, 209–210, 234
IFC. See International Finance Corporation
IGOs. See Intergovernmental organizations
IMF. See International Monetary Fund
Immigration 125–126, 237(n9), 258
Imperialism, 14, 28, 153, 156, 171, 172, 196,
    267, 289. See also Colonialism
Income, 7
India, 6, 36, 43, 47, 63, 77, 99, 103, 116, 159,
    175, 248, 264, 272, 273, 278, 290, 300
Indonesia, 68, 161, 162, 175, 177, 263(n19),
    296, 297, 298
Industry, 248, 270, 304. See also State-owned
    enterprises
Infanticide, 231
Inflation, 244
Intellectual property rights, 104, 259
Intellectuals, 110
Intentions, 57, 67, 79
Interdependence, 21–22, 193–212, 261, 264,
    290, 299
    Chinese views of, 201–203
    economic, 204–206
    See also under Modernization
Intergovernmental organizations (IGOs),
    20, 297
International Bill of Human Rights, 217
International Conference on the Integration
    of Economic Development and
    Environment, 275
International Covenant on Civil and
    Political Rights (ICCPR), 218
International Covenant on Economic, Social
    and Cultural Rights (ICESCR), 219
International Development Association
    (IDA), 239, 245, 248, 249–250(tables)

International Finance Corporation (IFC), 239, 245. 248, 251, 252(table), 253
International Labor Organization, 226
International law, 20, 25, 69, 73, 218, 226, 299
International Marine Organization, 274
International Monetary Fund (IMF), 156, 162, 243–245, 246–247(table), 253
   IMF Institute, 253
International movements, 235
International norms, 19–21, 27, 57, 59. *See also* Normative structures
International Olympic Committee, 223
International regimes, 197–198, 200, 211
International relations theory, 11, 12, 14, 56, 59, 77, 78, 197
Internet, 207, 223, 235
Investments, 6, 105, 136, 137, 146, 156, 162, 201, 202, 208, 251, 253, 288, 290
   foreign direct investments (FDI), 134, 140, 148(n2), 216(n24), 244, 251, 261
   and human rights, 224–225
IR. *See* International relations theory
Iran, 63, 103, 174, 259
Iraq, 63, 115, 116, 232
Islam, 63, 115, 209, 234, 235. *See also* Muslims
Israel, 173, 182, 222
Italy, 135, 160

James, Harold, 28
Japan, 5, 6, 7, 28, 40, 50, 74, 99, 127, 130, 133–134, 137–146, 147, 160, 174, 209, 224, 229, 289, 290, 293, 294–295, 303, 304, 306
   economy, 196, 204
   occupation of China, 141, 294
   Overseas Development Aid Budget, 279
   prime ministers' visits to China, 140–141
   Self-Defense Forces (SDF), 185
   See also Tawain, and Japan/Europe; *under* United States
Japan-China Friendship Environmental Protection Center, 279
Japan-China Science, Technology, and Cultural Centre, 140
Jarvis, Robert, 27
Jiang Qing, 45
Jiang Zemin, 6, 15, 19, 22, 29(n3), 37, 38, 47, 49, 52(nn 11, 12), 63, 91, 93, 97, 126, 135, 141, 152, 161, 163, 288, 292
   and Clinton, 174, 223, 227, 302–303

and Yeltsin, 115–117, 175
Johnson, Lyndon, 287
Johnston, Alastair Iain., 12–13, 297
Journalists, 220, 235
Judiciaries, 142, 278

Kaifu Toshiki, 140
Kajiyama Seiroku, 145
Kant, Immanuel, 14
Kazakhstan/Kyrgyzstan, 123, 175, 187, 290, 300
Khrushchev, Nikita, 287, 288
Kim Young Sam, 142
Korea, 99, 100, 289. *See also* Korean War; North Korea; South Korea
Korean War, 34, 36, 42–43, 48, 287, 303
Kundun (film), 223

Labor costs, 138, 154
Land mines, 75, 77
Laos, 36
Laroche, Béatrice, 165(n8)
Latin America, 151, 231
Leaders, 15, 16, 34, 37, 38, 39, 41, 42, 48, 50, 52(n11), 71, 76, 77, 79, 93, 94, 95, 161, 221, 222, 224, 236, 238(n27), 258, 259, 260, 261, 269, 270, 295, 301
   official visits of, 135, 140–141, 152, 157–158, 174, 187, 302
   See also Summits
Learning, 21, 24, 26
Lee, Martin, 102
Lee Teng-hui, 101–102, 103, 160, 174, 288
Legitimacy, 19, 20, 21, 67, 76, 133, 223, 258, 259, 305
Lei Feng, 110
Lenin, V. I., 14
Levi Strauss company, 225
Levy, Jack, 14
Liang Congjie, 277
Li Baodong, 159
Liberalism, 129. *See also* Neoliberalism
Lieberthal, Kenneth, 16
Lin Biao, 41, 67, 155
Li Peng, 37, 38, 52(n12), 116, 118, 122, 135, 137, 141, 145, 146, 152, 162, 276, 304
Lippo Group, 263(n19)
Liu Huaqing, 120, 181
Liu Huaqiu, 158
Li Xiannian, 38
Loans, 224, 244–245, 248, 249–250(tables), 251, 255, 256(table), 279

London Dumping Convention, 268, 274
Luo Ruiqing, 40

Macao, 305
McDonald's, 225
Machinery, 127, 138
Magao Grottoes, 274
Mahathir, Mohamad, 162
Ma Hong, 275
Mak Joon Nam, 163
Malawi, 165(n7)
Malaysia, 77, 161, 162, 173, 175, 177, 187,
    219, 289, 296, 297, 299
Mali, 159
Managerial model, 27
Mansfield, Edward, 14
Mao in command model, 15, 16
Maoz, Zeev, 12
Mao Zedong, 15, 16, 19, 21, 34, 36, 37, 41,
    42, 43, 44–45, 46, 66–67, 83(n30), 94,
    151, 155, 156, 164, 201, 220, 287, 288,
    302, 303
Marine dumping, 268
Marine Environmental Protection Law, 268
Material power structures, 56, 59–68, 70, 78,
    79, 80(n12), 83(n30)
Media, 74, 93, 94, 96, 107, 125, 207, 223,
    237(n16), 278, 281, 282, 292, 294, 299,
    300, 302
MEIs. *See* Multinational economic
    institutions
Mexico, 248
MFN. *See* Most Favored Nation status
Middle East, 103
Middle Kingdom, 218, 261, 289, 303, 304
MIGA. *See* Multilateral Investment
    Guarantee Agency
Military issues, 3, 5, 38, 39–40, 41, 50, 60,
    117, 127, 144, 171
    civil-military relations, 41
    expenditures, 4, 60–61, 61(fig.), 62, 64–65,
        81(nn 16, 17), 103, 143, 172, 185
    military-to-military relations, 174
    naval power, 4, 40, 100, 102, 120, 121,
        144, 160, 176–177, 179–180, 182–183,
        185–186, 290, 292, 295, 296, 299, 302
    use of force, 13, 14, 35–36, 72, 102, 147,
        160, 161, 162, 163, 248, 288, 289, 290,
        292, 305, 306
    See also Arms sales; Missiles; Nuclear
        weapons; People's Liberation Army

Ministerial Conference of Developing
    Countries on Environment and
    Development, 272–273
Ministry of Foreign Affairs (MOFA), 15, 35,
    39, 74, 270, 271, 277
Ministry of Foreign Trade, 41, 75
Minorities, 232
Mischief Reef, 295
Missiles, 64, 103, 120, 137, 174, 181, 183, 184,
    186
    missile defenses, 180
    See also Nuclear weapons; Taiwan,
        missile exercises near
Missile Technology Control Regime
    (MTCR), 5–6, 174
Modelski, George, 81(nn 16, 17)
Modernization, 36, 45, 95, 164, 203, 205, 242,
    243, 245, 253, 259
    Four Modernizations, 147, 156, 240
    and interdependence, 198–199, 200, 204,
        207, 209
    literature on, 215(n16)
    See also under People's Liberation Army
MOFA. *See* Ministry of Foreign Affairs
Mongolia, 43, 290
Montreal Protocol. *See under* Environmental
    issues
Morgenthau, Hans, 17
Most Favored Nation (MFN) status,
    106–107, 174, 227–228, 237(n9), 258,
    259, 263(n19)
MTCR. *See* Missile Technology Control
    Regime
Multilateral Investment Guarantee Agency
    (MIGA), 239, 245, 251, 253, 254(table)
Multilateralism, 74–75, 86(n58), 261
Multinational corporations, 226
Multinational economic institutions (MEIs),
    26, 238(n35), 239–261, 270
    list of, 239
Munro, Ross, 6, 92
Murdoch, Rupert, 223
Music, 110
Muslims, 234, 235, 259, 300. *See also* Islam

Nakasone Yasuhiro, 141
Nanjing Massacre, 294, 303
National Environmental Protection Agency
    (NEPA), 268, 270, 277, 278
    Transcentury Green Project Plan, 281
National identity, 3, 13–14, 16, 18, 28, 154

Nationalism, 28, 66, 77, 145, 147, 148, 161, 189, 200, 209, 291, 292, 293, 299, 305
National liberation struggles, 155
National People's Congress, 279, 280, 282
NATO. *See* North Atlantic Treaty Organization
Natuna Island, 296
Natural resources, 272, 273, 275
Naval power. *See under* Military issues
Neoliberalism, 197–198, 202
Neorealism, 56, 57, 58, 59–60, 61–62, 68, 69, 70, 72, 77, 78, 81(n17), 82(n29), 84(n46), 197, 201, 214(12). *See also* Structural realism
NEPA. *See* National Environmental Protection Agency
Nepal, 43, 159, 290
New International Economic Order (NIEO), 18, 202, 271, 289
New Territories, 233–234
New World Order, 133. *See also* New International Economic Order
New Zealand, 175, 296, 298
NGOs. *See* Nongovernmental organizations
Ng Quinn, Michael, 65, 84(n38)
NIEO. *See* New International Economic Order
Nixon, Richard, 94, 134, 156, 288
Non-Aligned Movement, 165(n4)
Nongovernmental organizations (NGOs), 20, 87(n66), 167(n31), 220, 230, 275
  environmental, 265, 273, 277, 282
  pseudo-NGOs, 236
Non-Proliferation Treaty (NPT), 5, 99, 103
Normative structures, 56, 58, 68–78, 79
  ways of affecting behavior, 71–72, 84(n41)
  See also International norms
North Atlantic Treaty Organization (NATO), 18, 117, 134, 157, 303
North Korea, 63, 103, 104, 142, 293, 301, 304. *See also* Korea
North-South relations, 202–203, 206, 211. *See also* Third World
NPT. *See* Non-Proliferation Treaty
Nuclear exports, 4
Nuclear weapons, 5, 36, 46–48, 66, 98, 116, 140, 154, 156, 163, 180, 183–184, 188, 279, 300, 301, 304. *See also* Proliferation
Nye, Joseph, 187

ODA. *See* Aid, official development assistance
Oil, 63, 138, 143, 147, 289, 290, 293, 295, 296, 299
Okinawa, 294
Oksenberg, Michel, 16
"One country, two systems" formula, 292
Orentlicher, Diane, 226
Overseas Chinese, 134, 162, 164
Overseas Private Investment Corporation, 225
Ozone depletion, 265, 269–273, 279

Pakistan, 43, 63, 98, 103, 159, 259, 290, 300
Paracel Islands, 295
Patten, Chris, 234
People's Bank of China (central bank), 240, 262(n9)
People's Daily, 159, 221–222, 231, 301
People's Liberation Army (PLA), 4, 38, 39, 46–47, 49, 75, 97, 103, 154, 248, 290
  modernization of, 4, 46, 61, 104, 119–122, 130, 142, 172, 178–180, 182–184, 185, 188, 291, 292. *See also* Sino-Russian relations, arms sales to China
  PLA Air Force (PLAAF), 185
  PLA Navy (PLAN), 179–180. *See also* Military issues, naval power
  rapid-reaction units, 180
  See also Military issues
Philippines, 159, 161, 162, 175, 177, 187, 289, 295, 296, 297, 298, 299, 303
PLA. *See* People's Liberation Army
PLAAF. *See* People's Liberation Army, PLA Air Force
PLAN. *See* People's Liberation Army, PLA Navy
Polarity, 56–57, 60, 65, 68, 70, 78, 81(nn 16, 17), 83(n30), 84(n38), 98, 161, 177–178
Political prisoners, 222–223, 224, 227, 228, 235
Post–Cold War period, 3–9, 18, 21, 28, 49, 61, 67, 94, 95, 97–104, 157, 172–173, 177–184, 188, 199, 211
Postmaterialism, 71, 74
Poverty line, 7
Power distribution, 17, 59–60, 61, 67, 68, 70, 72, 80(n12), 82(n30)
Primakov, Yevgeny, 121
Prison labor, 226, 227
Privatization, 216(n24), 251

Proliferation, 71, 73, 74, 75, 77, 145, 301, 304.
  See also Non-Proliferation Treaty
Public relations, 75–76

Qian Qichen, 11, 91, 123
Qu Geping, 266, 268, 275–276, 280

Radio Free Asia, 237(n16)
Rational actor model, 16, 17, 59, 93
Reagan, Ronald, 97
Realism, 17, 57, 203, 214(n12). *See also*
  Neorealism; Structural realism
Realpolitik, 13, 26, 63, 74, 79, 95
Reebok International, 225
Reforms, 26, 29(n3), 46, 49, 109, 125, 171,
  185, 201, 209, 261, 282
  WTO-based, 258
  See also under Economy
Regional issues, 28, 50, 74, 99–100, 103, 145,
  146, 150(n44), 160, 161–162, 176–177,
  178, 186, 187, 188, 202, 211, 229, 242,
  255
Religious persecution, 221, 238(n35), 259
Renminbi (RMB) devaluation, 244
Repression, 92, 221, 304. *See also* Tiananmen
  massacre
Reputation, 76, 77–78
Revolutions, 155, 164
RFE. *See* Russia, Russian Far East
Riady, Mochtar, 263(n19)
RMB. *See* Renminbi devaluation
Rockefeller Foundation, 275
Rodionov (Russian defense minister), 182
Rosenau, James, 11
Rule of law, 261
Russia, 4, 8, 19, 61(fig.), 100, 131, 157, 164,
  194, 300
  Russian Far East (RFE), 123, 124(fig),
  125, 129
  See also Sino-Russian relations; *under*
  United States
Ryukyu island chain, 294

Sabah, 297
Satisficing behavior, 15–16
Saudi Arabia, 138
Savings, 7
Scholarship, 5, 24
Schweller, Randall, 57, 58
Science, 9–10, 201, 208
SDF. *See* Japan, Self-Defense Forces

Second-image explanation, 14
  second image reversed thesis, 23, 265
Secrecy, 103
Security issues, 4–5, 13, 16, 22, 36, 39, 44, 49,
  50, 59, 62, 66, 68, 71, 75, 99, 103,
  112(n29), 150(n44), 155, 163, 171–172,
  174–184, 186, 187, 197, 200, 210
  East Asian bilateral/multilateral ties, 175
  internal threats, 19, 297
  origins of post–Cold War strategy,
  172–173
  post–Cold War policy, 177–184, 188
Self-determination, 232–234
Self-identification, 76, 77
Self-sufficiency, 36, 45, 134, 201, 202
Senkaku Islands. *See* Diaoyutai/Senkaku
  Islands
Shambaugh, David, 291
Shattuck, John, 227
Shen Guofang, 231
Siberia, 64
Singapore, 77, 162, 173, 175, 177, 197, 209,
  261, 296, 297
Sino-American relations, 3–4, 11, 13, 17, 50,
  91–110, 155, 220, 227, 298
  constructive engagement, 227
  as cooperative/conflictual, 62, 62(fig.),
  65, 66, 67, 81(n21), 83(n31), 93, 95,
  96–97, 103, 109, 110, 117, 173, 174, 287,
  302–303
  economic relations, 104–107
  in post–Cold War period, 97–104
  and Soviet threat, 94, 95
  trade, 64, 104, 106, 138
  and U.S. elections, 94, 107, 259
  and U.S. popular culture, 105, 107,
  109–110
  weight each country attaches to, 93
Sino-Russian relations, 63–64, 99, 114–131,
  172, 187, 290, 298
  arms sales to China, 99, 120–121, 181–182
  as strategic cooperative partnership, 117,
  118–119, 120, 129–131, 157, 161, 175,
  181
  trade, 125, 126–129, 128(table), 142
Sino-Soviet relations, 18, 34, 36, 42, 43, 55,
  65, 66, 67, 83(nn 31, 35), 95, 133, 155,
  156, 181, 287–288, 303
Snyder, Jack, 10, 14
SOCBs. *See* State-owned commercial banks
Socialization, 26, 58, 69, 74, 86(n58)

SOEs. *See* State-owned enterprises
Soft drink market, 105
Somalia, 229
Somchai Homlaor, 238(n27)
Song Jian, 266, 275, 276, 277, 280
Soros, George, 162
South Africa, 167(n32)
South China Sea, 143, 144, 145, 162, 175,
    176, 177, 179, 180, 184, 189, 260, 289,
    290, 293, 295, 296, 297, 298, 301
South Korea, 6, 8, 63, 126, 137, 142, 163, 173,
    175, 176, 197, 204, 209, 235, 236, 293,
    296, 303, 304. *See also* Korea
Sovereignty, 21, 22, 23, 25, 49, 71, 79,
    85(n55), 98, 159, 164, 171, 175, 189,
    234, 291, 295, 297, 301
    and environmental issues, 264, 272, 273,
        278, 279
    and human rights, 217, 218, 221, 229
    as normative structure, 72–74
    Westphalian model of, 73, 74
Soviet Union, 4, 8, 11, 60, 81(n16), 82(n30),
    94, 193. *See also* Sino-Soviet relations
Spain, 160
Special Economic Zones, 36, 288
Spratly Islands, 143, 176, 260, 295, 298, 299
Stalin, Joseph, 42
State Council, 187, 268
State Environmental Protection
    Commission, 280
State Oceanographic Administration, 274
State-owned commercial banks (SOCBs),
    244, 262(n9)
State-owned enterprises (SOEs), 6, 22,
    29(n3), 48, 107, 216(24), 244–245, 251,
    258, 304
State Planning Commission, 41, 240, 270,
    277
States, 57–58, 59–60, 70, 72, 73, 76, 84(n46),
    197, 219
    rogue, 98, 103
    weak/declining, 19, 22, 69, 71
    See also Sovereignty
State Science and Technology Commission,
    277
Status, 68. *See also* Great power status
Strange, Susan, 8
Strategic culture, 12–13, 171–172, 188, 189
Structural realism, 12, 13, 17–21, 63–64. *See
    also* Neorealism
Students, 134, 140, 156, 208, 294
Submarines, 120, 177, 182, 183, 185

Subsidies, 244, 245
Summits, 115–117, 163, 174, 175, 227, 302
Sun Zi, 13
Swaine, Michael, 15
Switzerland, 158
Syria, 234

Taiwan, 3, 47, 55, 63, 67–68, 73, 91, 92, 93,
    95, 96, 97, 99, 100–102, 115–116, 117,
    126, 127, 130, 133, 136, 143, 155, 173,
    175, 176, 184, 189, 197, 204, 232, 235,
    236, 255, 257, 260, 268, 289, 291–292,
    305–306
    air and naval forces, 186
    and Japan/Europe, 134, 136, 137, 140,
        143–145, 306
    missile exercises near, 36, 102, 147, 157,
        160, 163, 174, 288, 292, 298, 302
Tajikistan, 123, 175, 187, 300
Tanaka Kakuei, 140
Tariffs, 226–227
TATF. *See* Technical Assistance Trust Funds
    Program
Technical Assistance Trust Funds (TATF)
    Program, 251
Technology, 136, 140, 180–184, 201, 208, 272,
    291, 294. *See also* Diplomacy,
    environmental/techno-diplomacy;
    People's Liberation Army,
    modernization
Textbooks, 141, 303
Thailand, 161, 162, 165(n13), 175, 177,
    185–186, 187, 296
Theories, 9–10, 20, 195–197. *See also*
    International relations theory
Theory of International Politics (Waltz), 17,
    31(n37)
Third Front, 44–45
Third World, 151–164, 201, 206, 221, 253
    criteria concerning, 152, 153, 165(n4)
Threat assessments, 56, 66, 67, 79, 80(n12)
Three Gorges Dam project, 279, 290
Three-worlds theory, 151, 152, 156
Tiananmen massacre (4 June 1989), 19, 96,
    139, 147
    consequences of, 62, 67, 107, 134, 146,
        156, 158, 172, 173, 181, 193, 203, 223,
        224, 245, 258, 304
Tibet, 93, 94, 96, 107, 225, 228, 232, 233, 300
Torture, 219, 229
Tourism, 134, 140, 156, 162
Town and village enterprises, 251

TRA. *See* United States, Taiwan Relations Act

Track I/II dialogues, 74, 75

Trade, 41–42, 45–46, 91, 114, 133–134, 135–136, 162, 136(table), 137, 142, 147, 194, 201, 227, 228, 231, 255, 288, 290
  growth, 204
  imbalance in, 259
  imports/exports, 36, 42, 45, 63, 64, 104, 126, 129, 138, 204, 205, 207(table), 216(n24), 226, 244, 261, 271. *See also* Export-led growth
  with Japan, 138, 139(table), 294
  laws concerning, 225–226
  statistics, 216(n23)
  surpluses, 244
  tariffs, 226–227. *See also* Most Favored Nation status
  terms of trade, 195, 196
  trade dependence, 7, 64–65, 204, 205–206, 205–206(tables)
  traditional trade theory, 195–196, 199, 239
  See also under Sino-American relations; Sino-Russian relations

Transportation. *See* Communication/transportation

Treaties, 5–6, 27, 43, 67, 69, 75, 77, 129, 142, 187, 218, 232, 269, 270, 274, 280, 297, 298

Tung Chee Hwa, 102

Two China policy, 142, 143, 144

Ukraine, 159

UNCED. *See* United Nations, Conference on Environment and Development

UNCHE. *See* United Nations, Conference on the Human Environment

UNCLOS. *See* United Nations, Convention on the Law of the Sea

UNDP. *See* United Nations, Development Program

United Nations, 21, 23, 24, 26–27, 116, 133, 155, 228–232, 274
  Conference on Environment and Development (UNCED), 25, 265, 276, 277, 278, 281
  Conference on the Human Environment (UNCHE), 267, 276
  Convention on the Law of the Sea (UNCLOS), 25

Development Program (UNDP), 153, 165(nn 7, 10), 240–242, 275, 278
  Environment Programme, 274
  General Assembly, 233
  Human Development Report 1996, 153, 165(n4)
  Human Rights Commission, 108, 154, 158, 159, 230, 231–232, 233
  peacekeeping operations, 232
  Security Council, 4, 115, 154, 173, 229, 304
  Universal Declaration of Human Rights, 158, 162, 217–218
  World Conference on Human Rights (1993), 158, 229
  World Conference on Women (1995), 230–231

United States, 6, 7, 35, 82(n30), 127, 175, 204, 205, 292, 296, 306
  business interests in, 96, 99, 106, 107, 228
  Central Intelligence Agency (CIA), 203
  Congress, 96, 101, 106, 174, 221, 225, 226, 228, 233, 234, 237(n16), 238(n35), 263(n19)
  Export-Import Bank, 280
  Freedom from Religious Persecution Act, 107
  as hegemon, 18, 19, 60, 61, 62, 98, 118, 152, 157, 161, 173, 174, 176, 177, 222
  Jackson-Vanik Amendment, 237(n9), 258
  and Japan, 19, 63, 92, 100, 117, 131, 142, 143, 144, 145, 146, 148, 157, 163, 168(n50), 175, 176, 178, 188, 292, 302
  McConnell Act (1992), 234
  military spending, 61(fig.), 81(n16)
  and Russia, 116, 127
  Smoot-Hawley Act (1930), 226
  Taiwan Relations Act (TRA), 101, 102
  Trade Act of 1974. *See* United States, Jackson-Vanik Amendment
  Wolf-Specter bill, 238(n35)
  See also Sino-American relations

U.S.-China Business Council, 259

Use of force. *See under* Military issues

Uyghurs, 300

Values, 107

Vietnam, 36, 65, 99, 100, 116, 135, 173, 177, 288, 289, 290, 298, 299

Vietnam War, 147, 287, 295, 297

Wages, 226

Wa Li, 115
Walt, Steve, 80(n12)
Waltz, Kenneth, 17, 18, 31(n37)
Wanandi, Jusuf, 163
Wang Dan, 107, 228, 237(n23)
Wang Jiaxiang, 15, 43, 44
Wars, 5, 13, 36, 43, 61, 83(n35), 121, 153, 172,
    178–179, 181, 188, 297, 300
  causes of, 14, 28
WBG. See World Bank Group
Wei Jingsheng, 107, 109, 223, 228, 237(n23)
Wendt, Alexander, 57, 58
Whiting, Allen, 162
Will, George, 111(n18)
Wilson, Woodrow, 14
Women, 230–231, 235
Workers' rights, 225–226
World Bank (IBRD), 6, 18, 156, 216(n23),
    224, 237(n17), 248, 249–250(tables),
    251, 253, 275, 278, 279
  Economic Development Institute (EDI),
    253
World Bank Group (WBG), 239, 242–243,
    253
World economy, 16, 36, 153–154, 156, 157,
    202, 239, 253, 260

World Heritage Convention, 274
World Trade Organization (WTO), 105, 117,
    157, 240, 255, 257, 258–259, 261
World War II, 217
World Wide Fund for Nature, 275
WTO. See World Trade Organization
Wu, Harry, 237(n17), 248
Wu Jianmin, 154

Xie Zhenhua, 280
Xinjiang, 300

Yang Shangkun, 115
Yang Yong, 40
Yellow Sea, 289, 292, 293
Yeltsin, Boris, 19, 63, 64, 114, 115–117, 157,
    175, 182
Yomiuri Shimbun, 145
Yong Deng, 299

Zhang Aiping, 40
Zhao Ziyang, 15, 37, 38, 52(n12), 135, 141
Zhou Enlai, 37, 39, 43, 44, 45, 46, 267
Zhu Muzhi, 166(n25)
Zhu Rongji, 251
Zimbabwe, 159